SCORSESE

A Journey Through
The American Psyche

D1361491

Plexus, London

All rights reserved including the right of
reproduction in whole or in part in any form
Copyright © 2005 by Plexus Publishing Limited
Published by Plexus Publishing Limited
25 Mallinson Road
London SW11 1BW
www.plexusbooks.com
First Printing

British Library Cataloguing in Publication Data

Scorsese : a journey through the American psyche. - (Ultra screen series)
    1.Scorsese, Martin, 1942 - - Criticism and interpretation
    I. Woods, Paul A.
    791.4'3'0233'092

    ISBN 0 85965 355 2

Printed in Great Britain by Bell & Bain Ltd
Cover design by Brian Flynn
Book design by Rebecca Martin

Contents

AMERICANA

1980s INTERLUDE

THE SACRED & THE PROFANE

Introduction

By Paul A. Woods

The last bastion of the cinema as we once knew it was born in Queens, NY, on 17 November 1942. Though he spent his early years in this New York City suburb, the young Martin Scorsese's parents, Charles and Catherine, met with reduced circumstances by the time he was seven or eight years old, and opted to return to their old neighbourhood of Little Italy. It was here, on the Lower East Side of Manhattan, that little Marty soaked up the urban culture that would permeate his adolescence and young adulthood. On the predominantly Sicilian-American Elizabeth Street, he was first exposed to the influences that would make his best films such a compelling hybrid of the sacred and the profane.

For religiosity and urban rage sat side by side. The iconography of Roman Catholicism would be visually imprinted on a mind that, to paraphrase his old friend and filmmaking influence Michael Powell, feasts on images. As Scorsese himself describes it, the only sanctuary from the daily brutal grind for a slight young asthmatic boy was in 'a movie theatre or a church'. So the icons of the silver screen took on a similar significance to holy idolatry – and became a similar passion.

An altar boy at Old St. Patrick's Cathedral, where his parents married in the 1930s, young Marty was devout enough to enter a Catholic seminary in 1956, while still in his early teens. But the movies won out. Scorsese said goodbye to his ecclesiastic studies when he enrolled at New York University in the early 1960s, where he would study filmmaking under Haig Manoogian, his original mentor, and make his first short films: *What's a Nice Girl Like You Doing in a Place Like This?* (1963), *It's Not Just You, Murray!* (1964), and later, while working at NYU as a teacher himself, *The Big Shave* (1967).

Still, the church and the movie theatre would remain inextricably linked. Like many people indoctrinated with Catholicism at an early age, Scorsese was both spiritually elevated and haunted by its doctrines and its iconography. From Charlie's St. Francis complex in *Mean Streets* (1973) through to the agonised Frank Pierce's search for redemption in *Bringing Out the Dead* (1999), via the nonconformist Christian angst of *The Last Temptation of Christ* (1988), he remained the most inherently spiritual of major Western filmmakers – albeit one who knew that engaging with life entails a compromise between the world, the flesh and the devil.

Seen from the contemporary end of Scorsese's career, his independent feature debut, *Who's That Knocking at My Door?* (1967), seems underwhelming. Main character J.R.'s emotional turmoil and religious baggage is a youthful rite of passage, something he'll learn to live with – rather than a black dog that stalks his tracks, as with the filmmaker's more obsessively destructive characters. On the other side of the coin, his exploitation assignment for Roger Corman, *Boxcar Bertha* (1972), showed

The most dynamic symbiotic relationship in the cinema: Martin Scorsese is cinematically reunited with Robert De Niro after seven years, for GoodFellas *(1990).*

his flair for handling physical violence, but without the psychological intimacy that makes his later violent scenes such a personal assault.

Under the tutorship of Professor Manoogian, Scorsese might have become an underground exponent of neo-*vérité*, in the tradition of his late friend and secondary mentor John Cassavetes. But, fortunately, any tendency toward this kind of worthy purity was corrupted by the influence of popular cinema. By the time the filmmaker developed his own personal style, with *Mean Streets*, it was an energised hybrid of classic old Hollywood, Italian neo-realism, the French New Wave and the richly coloured artifice of the Archers (Brit filmmaking partnership Powell and Pressburger).

Mean Streets almost immediately earned a critical reputation as the anti-*Godfather* – these were the footsoldiers of the Mafia, we were told, not the power-playing upper echelons. But that's actually much truer of the later *GoodFellas* (1990). *Mean Streets* is not so much a gangster film as a character study of friends who live on the verges of criminality.

It also exhibited an early version of the 'film geek' sensibility – but without the emphasis on action or exploitation elements of the later Tarantino school. For the 'action' in Scorsese is strictly human interaction. The violence in his films, from *Mean Streets* onward, is less about Peckinpah-style ballets of blood (with the notable exception of *Taxi Driver*'s climax) than sudden emotional explosions. This hustling new Hollywood *arriviste* was seamlessly weaving the stuff of life into a cinematic fabric. As he later confirmed, with breathless fervour, 'If it's not personal, I can't be there in the morning.'

(To gauge how the pop-cinema that Scorsese begot has now cannibalised itself, the reader only has to compare the real-life anecdote about reviving a girl from a heroin OD, by his roguish buddy Steve Prince, in Scorsese's documentary *American Boy* [1978] – 'I had a medical dictionary. You know how you give an adrenaline shot? . . . you have to put it in a stabbing motion.' – with the fictional version in *Pulp Fiction*.)

Mean Streets tailored the speech and the jukebox sound of New York into a naturalistic whole. It also set the template for a move away from original soundtrack music. Seen from our vantage point, it's commonplace. But back then, Charlie's head hitting the pillow to 'Be My Baby' or Johnny Boy's peacock strut to 'Jumpin' Jack Flash' was a pretty audacious innovation. (In terms of his personal musical taste, Scorsese's penchant for the rootsier side of Americana has endured through documentaries on The Band, the blues, and now a biodoc of Bob Dylan for BBC TV.)

Mean Streets also marked the point at which the quietly intense Harvey Keitel was supplanted by the more physically demonstrative Robert De Niro, in his role as the Scorsese-surrogate figure. If it seems incongruous that such a slight, physically unimposing man should identify with his explosive male leads, it's because they're acting as emotional beasts of burden for us all – but not least for the brittle, hypersensitive director.

The films of Scorsese have often externalised the human psyche. Travis Bickle's escalating psychosis, Jake La Motta's inner struggle and outer brutality, Jesus' doubt and self-division, all envelop the viewer in their protagonist's predicament. What might seem, in everyday life, to be the personal crisis of an initially insignificant individual is magnified to an epic level. It's cinematic expressionism at its purest. For

Scorsese quickly transcended the confines of his Italian-American microculture, to become the cinematic chronicler of subterranean America.

Taxi Driver (1976) is perhaps the most daring work of mainstream American cinema, and the greatest film to come of the 1970s 'New Hollywood' – owing an equal amount to the depth-plumbing original screenplay by Paul Schrader, the epoch-defining performance by De Niro, and Scorsese's sense of pseudo-documentary realism.

Almost more of a phenomenon than a film, *Taxi Driver* delineates that part of modern American history when the gun-toting misfit, loner and madman made his presence felt, becoming heroic in his own eyes. The character of outsider icon Travis was inspired by Arthur Bremer, an introverted janitor who tried to impress a girl by shooting a would-be presidential candidate. The huge irony of *Taxi Driver*, that a psychotic killer becomes a hero by switching to the abusers of a child prostitute as his targets, is matched only by the film's fallout. That the deranged John Hinckley shot the President to get the attention of Jodie Foster, child star of *Taxi Driver*, is in part a testament to the film's power – though more so to the fact that America was living through the age of psycho-as-celebrity.

Raging Bull (1980), while not equal to the infernal catharsis that is *Taxi Driver*, has a pugnacious compulsiveness all of its own. A semi-fictionalised account of fallen middleweight champ Jake La Motta's turbulent life, *Raging Bull* deserves its near universal reverence as Scorsese's most inherently, masochistically religious work. For the brutish La Motta is the macho inferiority complex personified. Seeking redemption via his shot at the title, he can only lash out at his opponents, his wife, his brother, at everyone close to him, angry that his rage hasn't elevated him to the place where he believes he has a right to be. More adept at soaking up punishment than at the fine art of pugilism, his greatest wrath is reserved for himself, a bloody self-crucifixion where he still refuses to hit the canvas. ("You couldn't put me down, Ray!")

The King of Comedy (1983), while seen as a less successful film (both artistically and commercially, though its original box-office performance was hardly much worse than that of *Raging Bull*), is a chilling masterpiece. It clinically dissects a culture in which now, more than ever, we are conditioned to believe that media celebrities are somehow more 'real' than Joe Shmoe and his private, personal concerns.

The Last Temptation of Christ (1988), far from being the sacrilegious sexfest described by religious zealots (most of whom hadn't seen it), is a moving existential drama about the torment of a flesh-and-blood being destined (and doomed) to be both god and man – only resolving his crisis with a personal blood sacrifice. To those of us who see religion in purely metaphorical terms, and don't share Scorsese's faith (a faith sometimes denied and oft tested throughout his life and career), it remains a paradoxically gritty supernatural story about the Passion that lies at the heart of Christianity. With hindsight, it's amusing to look back and see the fundamentalists scream 'blasphemy!' at something so faithful to the spirit of the Gospels, where Christ rejects his humanity and his sexuality to return to the agonies of the cross, taking the sins of the world on his shoulders.

GoodFellas was a milestone, both in signifying a return to critical acclaim for an artist written off far too prematurely, and in being Scorsese's first *real* gangster movie. For the association of his name with the underworld is less a case of 'authenticity' than temperament – Scorsese observed men like these in the old neighbourhood with an astutely keen eye, but he wasn't one of their own.

Violently self-serving men tend to live their lives at a feverish pitch, even the quietest of them displaying a cultivated lack of control when it suits them. Such operatic displays of emotion suit Scorsese – whose characters' emotions often rapidly escalate into histrionics – down to the ground.

GoodFellas reinvented the gangster movie for the 1990s. Look again at its pseudo-*vérité* style, its *nouvelle vague* influences, narrative sleight of hand, eclectic soundtrack and casual ultraviolence, and see how often the crime films of subsequent years have aspired to be *GoodFellas*, but fallen short of it. For Scorsese's film, in celebrating the seductiveness of total amorality, is most terrifying in its closely observed behavioural tics rather than its overt violence. (De Niro's attempt to set up his best friend's wife Lorraine Bracco to be killed, with a smile and a point of the finger, is a chillingly realistic reminder that there's very little honour amongst thieves.)

Since *GoodFellas* resurrected his reputation, Scorsese has been canonised by many as a latter-day Saint of Cinema. But his less iconic films can only be assessed as a matter of subjective taste. Speaking purely personally, *New York, New York* (1977) holds a fascination in its strictly movie-style recreation of an era; *The Color of Money* (1986) is an adequate annex – though not equal – to *The Hustler*; *Kundun* (1997) is a curiosity, albeit an interesting one, reaching toward a spiritual universality in a world of violence.

But everyone who thinks Scorsese's first (and only) remake, *Cape Fear* (1991), was a step down the creative ladder should replay its sex-crime psychodrama against the more smouldering, less hysterical 1962 b/w original by J. Lee Thompson. The contrast is educative, and (like playing Don Siegel's *The Killers* against Robert Siodmak's, or the Nic Cage remake of *Kiss of Death* against the Victor Mature original) works surprisingly in favour of the remake.

And *Casino* (1995), however much it's been criticised as a carbon copy of *GoodFellas*, is an epic elaboration of its theme of vicious avarice (crime reporter and *GoodFellas* screenwriter Nicholas Pileggi proving himself as integral a Scorsese collaborator as Paul Schrader, or even his uniquely empathic editor Thelma Schoonmaker).

Now in his sixties, Martin Scorsese has confounded his own expectations by achieving a personal, as well as artistic, longevity. This former husband of the perennially beautiful Isabella Rossellini and lover of the endearingly wacky Liza Minnelli has apparently found domestic serenity with his fifth wife, Helen Morris. According to critic Roger Ebert's assessment (see page 19) of a younger, more angst-ridden Scorsese, any such contentment would seem to carry the threat of creative sterility.

But then, consider the darkly *agitato Bringing Out the Dead*, possibly his most underrated film. A harrowing circular odyssey in an ambulance around a ghostly, forsaken early 1990s nighttime Manhattan, it hardly indicates complacency. Similarly, *Gangs of New York* (2002), while it disappointed some in not providing another reunion with De Niro (though a malevolent Daniel Day-Lewis amply fills his boots), and offended some with its matter-of-fact depiction of the mayhem and racist violence of the Civil War draft riots, is as exciting a Western (or 'Eastern') as Sergio Leone never made.

What rankles with others is how the millennial Scorsese has swapped Robert De

Niro, his virtual alter ego onscreen, for Leo DiCaprio. And it's true that, as capable an actor as DiCaprio is (he came to Scorsese as recommended by De Niro), the good looks that brought him to prominence can work in inverse proportion to his impact in character. His second role for Scorsese, as Howard Hughes in *The Aviator* (2004), is a creditable performance, but this old-fashioned tale of Old Hollywood would have been a disappointing swansong if it marked the end of the director's career.

But Scorsese is still not resting on his laurels. Once again on the far side of critical deification – and still not honoured by the Academy, who refused Best Film Oscars to *Taxi Driver, Raging Bull* and *GoodFellas* – he remains as productive as ever. With his next feature, *The Departed* (2006), he's followed the current Hollywood vogue for remaking hit Far Eastern movies (in his case the Korean *Infernal Affairs,* relocated to Boston) – but, as a drama about gangsters and law enforcement infiltrating each other, it seems to offer up a classic Scorsese scenario of guilt and redemption (while marking a welcome return to the crime genre for the first time since *Casino*).

However many personal film projects remain unmade, there seems to be no let-up in his productivity at an age when many filmmakers have embraced retirement, or given in to it out of a sense of despair. Whether *Dino*, his collaboration with Pileggi on the life of quintessential Italian-American entertainer Dean Martin, or his planned documentary on the history of British film (yet another influence to pay homage to) come to fruition or not, Scorsese gives no indication he will ever stop devouring celluloid (*not* digital video) by the mile.

Ultimately, as he said at his Acceptance Speech for the 1996 John Huston Award for Artists' Rights, 'Look, let's face it, the cinema – the classical cinema – is gone. It's over. The cinema as we know it, up to now, is disappearing.' He remains one of the last of the generation to be influenced by the *auteurs*-for-hire (if that's not too contradictory a term) of the old Hollywood studio system, by his early heroes Ford, Hawks, Vidor and Kazan.

But in Martin Scorsese, the classical cinema still finds a focus – albeit one filtered through the sensibilities of Manhattan, or even Old Europe, rather than modern Hollywood.

Who's That Knocking at The Door?

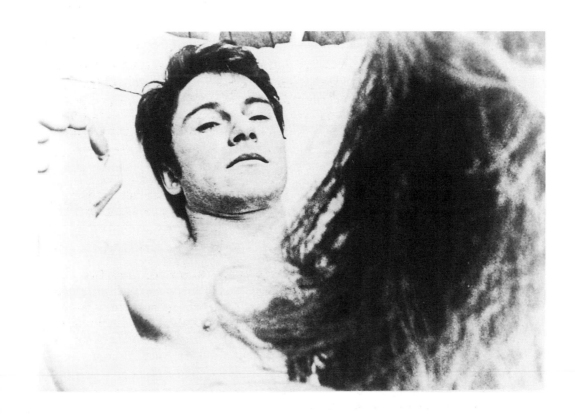

MARTIN SCORSESE
Interviewed by James Truman

Was it always your impulse to lose your innocence, to discover low-life?
I simply had no choice. As much as I wanted to fantasise and run away from it, I couldn't. There's no doubt that that's why I went to so many movie theatres when I was growing up. But as soon as I walked out I was thrown back into a pretty harsh reality. There was no twilight world between the two. Absolutely nothing. The only place to get a respite was a movie theatre or a church.

What was Little Italy like then?
It was fairly similar to the form it took in *Mean Streets*. It was an area that was extremely depressing at times and yet very much full of life. I grew up on Elizabeth Street, which was a block away from Mott Street, and two blocks from Mulberry Street. Elizabeth was more populated by Sicilians, whereas Mulberry was more populated by Neapolitans. So the Sicilians stuck together and the Neapolitans stuck together. From the twenties through the fifties it was packed with life. Each block was an incredible microcosm of life. There's only a sense of it left now, like the Alleva cheese store, where Francis Coppola still buys his cheese.

Were there a lot of street fights?
There were even fights in the movie theatres, especially in the mid-fifties when the gangs started. But there weren't really teenage gangs *a la High School Confidential* in my area, because they were all Italians and it was kind of *déclassé* to be a gang member, I think. If you were going to be involved in any criminal activity, it was more likely to be something that was feeding into a much bigger organisation, if you understand. It was all much more discreet, and actually much, much more classy. [*laughs*]

Were you ever recruited by the Mafia?
No, I don't think so. You're not recruited. It's part of a certain way of life. Some people are just born into it. There's no question of ever becoming anything else. My family was not that way.

Did it appear glamorous to you?
Oh, extremely glamorous. The reason I had Cesare Danova play the Uncle Giovanni character in *Mean Streets* was because of a glamorised image I had of one man when I was growing up. He was a very big man in one of the crime families, and he was *the* man in the neighbourhood. I was close friends with his nephew, he was very sweet with me, let me play on his roof, in fact he let me shoot *Who's That Knocking?* on his

In Who's That Knocking?, *J.R. (Keitel) displays a madonna/whore complex that dooms his relationship with a young woman. It would be echoed by Charlie in* Mean Streets.

roof. He was terrific with us. He was later written about in books. It turned out he was an incredible killer. To me, growing up, he looked like Cary Grant. He wore silk suits like Cary Grant wore in *Houseboat.* When I see a picture of him today, in a book or magazine, he certainly doesn't look like Cary Grant. He looks pretty ugly. Then, I thought he was absolutely gorgeous. So when I cast Cesare I made a mistake. The fantasy took over a little too strongly! It didn't come off great.

When did you begin your religious schooling?
When I was eight years old. My parents weren't very religious, but when I was eight we moved in with my grandparents, and I was taken out of public school, where I had no religious training, and sent to St Patrick's School, which was part of the local cathedral. It had Irish nuns, which was really interesting. The church, the archdiocese, didn't seem to realise this was an Italian neighbourhood – they kept sending Irish nuns from Dublin. That, of course, didn't go down well with the Italians, especially when the nuns hit the kids. The parents would then come round and beat up the nuns. You really had to learn to survive by your wits.

Were these nuns apocalyptic?
Absolutely. Within a year I wanted to be a missionary. I wanted to get leprosy. You know, send me to the worst place on earth.

What were your nightmares about?
They came from the nuns giving us air raid drills. This was the early fifties, at the beginning of the Cold War. We'd be sitting in class and suddenly the principal would say over the loudspeaker: 'Attention! Take cover!' Then we had to get under our desks and hide. I remember the nuns saying, 'Whenever you hear a low-flying plane, it could be it.' Of course, there were no jets at that time, all planes were low-flying, so every day was terrifying. Then sometimes they'd do an epic air raid drill. They'd take us all out of the classroom and lead us to the catacombs under the church. And we'd have to pray with the rosary under the church, echoing among the graves. That was very grim. We were told that this was what the fire of Hell would be like.

Do you feel grateful for this now?
It's difficult to say. You wonder how much of it stayed with you, and a part of you wishes there hadn't been that painful period between twelve and twenty. I think a lot of it could just be me, how seriously I take things. Evidently I was extremely impressionable because I've not been able to get past a lot of that stuff. Images from then are always coming back to me. The camera movement in a lot of my films certainly comes from creeping around those catacombs, with those sound effects of the echoing rosary. But there were other boys there who have grown up much better adjusted about it all.

Did you know Robert De Niro then?
Not really. We knew each other from afar when we were about sixteen. He came

from a different neighbourhood. We occasionally ventured forth to have drinks at each other's social clubs on Friday nights. He wasn't always that friendly. Then I met him again in 1970 at a Christmas dinner. He said, 'Sometime we've really got to make a film about that neighbourhood,' and I told him I already had, which was *Who's That Knocking?* He saw it a few months later and liked it, so I told him about this script I'd written called *Mean Streets.* Within the next year, miraculously, the film got made.

What kind of girls did you go out with when you were a teenager?
It's complicated because there were different types of girls. There were the tough, chewing-gum girls, like the Shangri-Las, who were from Queens. They were extremely attractive to us. They were really healthy girls, much less screwed up than us. I was always mortified, extremely shy, about the idea of talking to them, or asking them to dance. Most of my friends were much faster with women than I was. I remember switching allegiances to a different group of guys who were going to college. Their girls were a little easier to break into . . . that is, talk to. I was at a seminary at the time, preparing for the priesthood. I became fascinated with girls. It kind of broke the work I was doing at the seminary, and after a year they asked me to leave. My intention was always to go back, until I went to New York University in 1960 and started taking film classes.

What choices had you made in your life by that time?
I knew that I was going to live by my wits, rather than by my arm, by muscle, like many of the young boys I grew up with. I never really believed in that. I just saw too much muscle being used. I not only saw it on the streets, but on the news, in movies, on TV, the same thing. I didn't respect those people. I was afraid of them, I often got beaten up by them, but I didn't respect them.

WHAT'S A NICE GIRL LIKE YOU DOING IN A PLACE LIKE THIS?
Reviewed by Jonathan Romney

Aspiring writer Algernon, a.k.a. Harry, arrives in New York and moves into a studio, but finds himself unable to write, meanwhile becoming obsessed with a picture of a man in a boat. At a party he throws, he meets a girl; they fall in love and marry, spending their honeymoon at the uncompleted site of the World Fair. Harry's predicament appears to be resolved, but then returns. His analyst tells him to look his problem in the face, and he finally jumps into a picture of the sea.

Scorsese's first short, with its jumpy, fast-cutting style, facetious verbal and visual punning, and self-conscious first-person narrative, could almost be seen as an early attempt to develop a style that was characteristically, neurotically of New York. That style might be defined as a hybrid of Godardian dislocation and the wiseacre comedy of the *Sid Caesar's Show of Shows* variety. In fact, Scorsese has identified the film's twin influences as being the New Wave on the one hand (although a closer equivalent than Godard might be Malle's self-consciously flashy *Zazie dans le metro*), and on the other, Ernest Pintoff's animated short *The Critic*, written and narrated by Mel Brooks, an alumnus of the Caesar script academy.

The narrative – such as it is – is largely an excuse for a febrile succession of gags, but the hero's name also alludes to its source in a story by Algernon Blackwood. The title is something of a red herring, too, referring solely to the party sequence in which Harry meets his painter wife-to-be, and romances her in parodic slow motion. The party scene is a typical trope of fast life in the big city, a theme on which Scorsese rings the changes with determinedly downbeat humour. The opening sequence flashes through a montage of stereotypical New York skyline photos, then proceeds at the same pace through the bland interior of Harry's apartment, which magically furnishes itself in a string of jump cuts.

To a great extent, the film seems to be a response to a dare, to see how much diverse material can be spliced together in ten minutes flat. But it also conspires to confound this purpose, cutting at one point to an extended interlude of a barbershop crooner on television, incongruously interpolated like an added attraction on the bill. Some of the better gags, in fact, are verbal, particularly the interventions of Harry's friend, who repeats verbatim what Harry has already told us in reported speech. The friend and Harry's excessively maternal analyst introduce a familiarly Scorsesean note of discomfort, exceeding the film's bounds as a skit. Significantly, they inhabit the dark, as does Harry himself at one point, staring around anxiously as the camera circles him with intent.

Essentially a clever tyro exercise, *What's a Nice Girl . . .* contains two telling ambiguities. First, Scorsese is working here as an urbane hipster in love with the myths of New York life, but also out to parody films that naively glamorise the city, and to signal his allegiance to the sophisticated, dislocated European school of urban filmmaking. And secondly, here is a Scorsese who brushes neurotic unease aside as simple material for a skit, while clearly signalling the fascination which that unease exerts. The spectacle of Scorsese learning to handle cinema is also the spectacle of his recognising the love-hate nature of his relationship with it. In the final analysis, the 'meeting cute' of the title is less between Harry and his wife than between a boy and his camera.

IT'S NOT JUST YOU, MURRAY!
Reviewed by Jill McGreal

Sitting in his New York office, businessman Murray leans into camera and announces the price of his tie, his shoes, his suit and, out on the street, his car. Inviting the audience to join him for a ride, he confides that his success in life is due to his pal Joe; Murray shows pictures of Joe, and scenes from his life trace his progression from one urban slum to another ('going places' says Murray) while his mother feeds him spaghetti. Joe sets him up in business as an illegal distiller of gin, until a raid ('a misunderstanding' says Murray) leads to a spell in prison. On his release, he goes back into business with Joe, this time as a producer of Broadway musicals, and meets his future wife, a pouting blonde nurse ('an angel of mercy' says Murray).

Murray tells us, to the accompaniment of 'Land of Hope and Glory', how they went to the top in business, while a montage sequence shows their racketeering. An indictment follows but Murray is acquitted; he returns triumphant and counts his wealth in the kitchen while his wife and Joe exchange caresses in the background. A further montage sequence shows Joe, Murray and Murray's wife and children ('Joe is like a second father') in happy harmony. Joe visits Murray in his office and a second 'misunderstanding' occurs, but Murray insists that the film's sound be turned off; Murray's voice-over informs us that Joe is telling it to him straight. Joe and Murray take a car ride to the waterfront and are joined by the whole cast in dancing to Italian carnival music. To a reprise of 'Land of Hope and Glory', Joe and Murray pose for a photograph; the 'shot' rings out.

It's Not Just You, Murray!, Martin Scorsese's second short, was made at the New York Film School in 1964, when he was 22. His film-buff credentials are evident: he was influenced by the French New Wave, Italian art cinema, the new Eastern European cinema, Fellini, Cassavetes ('What these films gave you was a sense of freedom, of being able to do anything . . . In my first movie, not one shot was a matched cut'). *It's Not Just You, Murray!* is not an experimental film, but it is vigorous and refreshing; the energetic direction coupled with the witty juxtaposition of Murray's guileless narration and scenes from his life as a small-time hood already announces a major talent.

In the way it traces a career path through Little Italy, it's also a sixteen-minute trailer for *Mean Streets* or *GoodFellas*. Murray's ultimate ambition is the attainment of 'the good life', which he measures in terms of the cost of his possessions. These clearly include his wife and children: 'She's still *my* wife, living in *my* home, going to parties with *me*,' expostulates Murray when Joe reveals her duplicity (a notion reinforced by her lack of any name other than 'Murray's wife'). In Scorsese's words, it's the corrupt version of the American Dream, 'according to which everybody thinks they can get rich quick, and if they can't do it by legal means, they'll do it by illegal ones.'

However, there is a difference between *It's Not Just You, Murray!* and Scorsese's later portraits of Mob and street life. In this film, there is a powerful irony which pumps out a clear moral message. If *GoodFellas*, in particular, left the audience in doubt as to Scorsese's attitudes, *Murray* clears up the doubt. When Murray relates how he and Joe put together one of the biggest 'syndicates' in America, his euphemisms are wittily juxtaposed with the realities of a hood's life: 'grants and foreign aid' (picture of Arab-style gunmen buying arms), 'the undertaking business' (picture of gangster being gunned down), 'improvements to the motel business' (picture of prostitutes plying their trade), and so on.

The ending at the riverside is the sole note of ambiguity. Murray, one presumes, is going for his last ride, though the closing shot is a play on the photographer's 'shot' and the executioner's: one a celebration of the gangster's life, the other its termination (see the similar effect of the 'exploding' flashbulbs in *Raging Bull*, also about friendship, marriage and jealousy). According to Scorsese, this final scene was a homage to *8 1/2* – 'Because I just couldn't figure out how to end it' – and elsewhere he uses Busby Berkeley-style sequences and gangster-movie references. Looking back from *Cape Fear*, the ultimate quotation movie, the 'guilty' reflection of the 1962 original, *It's Not Just You, Murray!* seems like the innocent, youthful, uncomplicated version of *Mean Streets* and *GoodFellas*.

THE BIG SHAVE
Reviewed by Kim Newman

A young man enters a blindingly white bathroom and, while Bunny Berigan performs 'I Can't Get Started' on the soundtrack, he shaves. Then he obsessively relathers his face and shaves again, repeatedly cutting himself, dripping bright red blood over the clinically clean bathroom fixtures and tile floor. Ultimately, he scrapes open his own throat.

This six-minute sick joke would seem, were it not for the ironic use of nostalgic music, more like the sort of thing one would expect from an early David Cronenberg than an apprentice work by Scorsese, concerned as it is with the wince-making process of self-mutilation. The humour and horror of the piece resides in the cool, methodical manner in which the shaver obliterates his own features, the realism of the effects – which mainly involves very red paint splashed on soap suds or gleaming bathroom fixtures – being totally at odds with the performer's attitude, which never remotely suggests pain or even pleasure, as each round of mutilation is followed by a close scrutiny of the mirror.

An *avant la lettre* instance of 'body horror', *The Big Shave* captures for the first time in colour what will become the all-important splatter-movie contrast between deep red and blinding white, later discovered by Dario Argento to be the ultimate image of sado-chic. With an end credit for 'whiteness – Herman Melville', it would be a mistake to take the black joke too seriously, even though those same credits also have a 'Viet '67' notation, linking this loving self-abuse with the South-East Asian situation. Scorsese's own comment on this is revealing: 'Consciously it was an angry outcry against the war. But in reality something else was going on inside me, I think, which really had nothing to do with the war.' The 'something else' probably reached its fullest, self-sacrificial expression – even to the hero who 'can't get started' – in *The Last Temptation of Christ*.

I CALL FIRST
Reviewed by Roger Ebert

There has been a long wait for an American film like Martin Scorsese's *I Call First*, which made a stunning impact in its world premiere Wednesday night at the [1967] Chicago International Film Festival.

As a film, it has something to say to everyone. As a technical achievement, it brings together two opposing worlds of American cinema.

On the one hand, there have been traditional films like *Marty, View from the Bridge, On the Waterfront* and *David and Lisa* – all sincere attempts to function at the level where real lives are led and all suffering to some degree from their makers' romantic and idealistic ideas, about such lives.

On the other hand there have been experimental films from Jonas Mekas, Shirley Clarke and other pioneers of the New York underground. In *The Connection, Shadows* and *Guns of the Trees*, they used improvised dialogue and scenes and hidden and handheld cameras in an attempt to capture the freshness of a spontaneous experience.

Both groups have lacked the other's strong point. The films like *Marty* are technically well done and emotionally satisfying, but they lack the flavour of actual experience. Films like *Shadows* are authentic enough, but often poor in technical quality and lacking the control necessary to develop character and tell a story.

I Call First brings these two kinds of films together into a work that is absolutely genuine, artistically satisfying and technically comparable to the best films being made anywhere. I have no reservations in describing it as a great moment in American movies.

Remarkably, writer-director Martin Scorsese is only 25 years old, and this is his first film. He tells a love story about two different kinds of people. His young man is from New York's 'Little Italy', has a strong Roman Catholic background, is intelligent but not very well-educated and divides the women of the world into 'nice girls' and 'broads'. The young woman is a college graduate, well read, more sophisticated and has probably had an affair or two. She loves him enough to try to explain that she is a 'nice girl' but not a virgin.

The divergent views of love and morality come into opposition, but they make a tremendous effort to understand and respect each other. In the end, they fail. Their story is told against a poetically evoked background of the young man's life with his friends, who were probably his high school and army buddies and will probably be his old age cronies. Two scenes – one in a bar, another at a party – are among the most evocative descriptions of American life I have ever seen.

I want to comment at length on the performances and details of the plot, but I will have to wait until the film begins its commercial run here. I hope that will be soon.

WHO'S THAT KNOCKING AT MY DOOR?
Review Analysis from *FilmFacts*

Who's That Knocking at My Door? is Martin Scorsese's first feature film (previously he made some prize-winning shorts) and was completed in 1967 when he was 25-years-old. Scorsese is a New York University graduate student who studied with Professor Haig Manoogian, one of the film's producers. (The other two producers are Manoogian's wife Betzi, who contributed 'additional dialogue', and Joseph Weill, an attorney who is also one of Manoogian's students.) After showing his film (under the title *I Call First*) at the 1967 Chicago Film Festival, Scorsese was persuaded to add a nude fantasy sequence in order to get commercial distribution. Follwing playdates throughout the US during 1969, the picture opened in Los Angeles in early 1970 under the title *J.R.*, a change which Professor Manoogian claims was made by the exhibitor.

Synopsis
J.R. grew up in New York's 'Little Italy' under the dual influence of a rigid Catholic upbringing and the tough law-of-the-jungle rule of the city streets. Rarely straying beyond the limits of his neighbourhood, he spends his time drinking with his buddies, playing cards and horsin' around with 'broads' until the time when he will marry a 'nice girl'. Then, while riding on the Staten Island ferry, he meets and falls in love with a young girl unlike anyone he has ever known. (She speaks French, reads F. Scott Fitzgerald, lives alone and doesn't own a television set.) As their relationship deepens, the girl offers herself to J.R. but, believing that she is a virgin, he refuses. Following an invigorating day in the country with one of his buddies J.R.'s high spirits are deflated when the girl tells him that some time before she was attacked and raped by a former boy friend. Feeling betrayed, J.R. walks out on the girl and attempts to resume his former life. However, his revulsion at a wild party leaves him disgusted with both himself and his world and he returns to the girl in the early morning hours. Awkwardly trying for a reconciliation, he tells her that he is willing

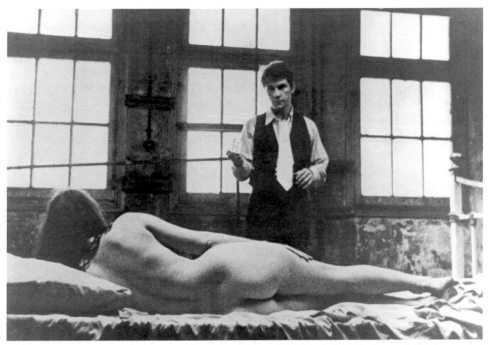

The youthful Harvey Keitel in Who's That Knocking at My Door? *(1969). Scorsese's highly personal first feature had this erotic dream sequence inserted for marketability.*

to forgive her and that he will try to overlook her loss of virginity. The girl, however, realises that J.R.'s forgiveness is proof that he is incapable of accepting her for what she is, and that they could never find happiness together. When she rejects him, J.R. flies into a rage and, from years of conditioning, returns to his Church. But the present has intruded upon the past and he finds no solace.

Critique
Martin Scorsese's first feature film was received kindly by many critics as, in the words of *New York*'s Judith Crist, a 'sincere and promising effort'. 'A very, very good and likeable movie,' wrote the *Los Angeles Times*' Charles Champlin, who, after comparing the picture favourably to *Marty*, concluded that 'we can welcome Martin Scorsese to the ranks of genuinely promising young talents.' Likewise, *Newsday*'s Jerry Parker hailed *Who's That Knocking at My Door?* as 'a most impressive debut', and called it 'a very personal film, in the way that *Medium Cool* and *Easy Rider* are personal films that express not only their creators' ideas about a certain aspect of modern life, but also reveal something of how the film maker came to form those particular ideas.' Such praise, however, was counteracted by those critics who ultimately agreed with Mrs. Crist that 'the over-all fuzziness of point and purpose leaves the work on the "promising" level'. Even harsher was *Cue*'s William Wolf who thought the film 'a forced, unconvincing quite banal drama' that 'emerges as little more than a sophomoric cinematic exercise', and *Variety*'s 'Robe' agreed that 'despite one or two moments of cinematic wit

and feeling', the film was 'more of a class exercise than a commercially sound film'. For both the *NY Daily News*' Ann Guanno and *Saturday Review*'s Arthur Knight, the principal fault was the same: the former complained (in her one-star review) that Scorsese 'has neglected to sustain interest in his characters and, while aiming for realism, has captured too much boring detail,' and the latter maintained that Scorsese 'never gives reason enough to care for 90 whole minutes whether the couple ever solve their difficulties.' Despite all these reservations about Scorsese's direction, almost all the critics agreed with Champlin that Scorsese had obtained 'remarkably fine' performances from the actors.

BOXCAR BERTHA
Reviewed by Roger Ebert

Boxcar Bertha is a weirdly interesting movie and not really the sleazy exploitation film the ads promise. It finds its inspiration in the exploits of Boxcar Bertha Thompson, an outlaw folk hero who operated in Arkansas during the Depression. I am not sure whether she was called 'Boxcar' because of the way she was built or because of where she liked to spend her evenings, but I can report that Barbara Hershey, who plays her in the movie, is built like the proverbial structure of brick. For that we can be grateful.

The movie is set in a murky Southern territory of sweat and violence, and gives us Bertha as a forthright young girl who gets involved in violence almost by accident. She falls in love with a certain Big Bill Shelley (David Carradine), who seems loosely modelled on the anarchist organiser Big Bill Haywood. The two of them meet other friends: Rake Brown, a slick young gambler with a yellow streak, and Von Morton, a sturdy black who wields harmonica and shotgun.

And then their gang is complete and their first murder just sort of happens when Bertha shoots a gambler who is about to shoot Rake. The movie's progression from young love to the most-wanted list reminds us of *Bonnie and Clyde*, and I suppose it was meant to. But there's a lot more going on than a remake or a rip-off.

I have the notion that Roger Corman, American-International's most successful producer of exploitation films, sent his actors and crew South with the hope of getting a nice, simple, sexy, violent movie for the summer trade. What he got is something else, and something better. Director Martin Scorsese has gone for mood and atmosphere more than for action, and his violence is always blunt and unpleasant – never liberating and exhilarating, as the New Violence is supposed to be. We get the feeling we're inhabiting the dark night of a soul.

The character of Bertha is developing along unexpected lines, too. She is promiscuous with her body and her mind, and when Big Bill is sent to prison, she remains

David Carradine (centre) as Big Bill Shelley, union activist turned outlaw, in Boxcar Bertha *(1972). 1970s icon Carradine later took a cameo role in Scorsese's* Mean Streets.

in love with him but goes to work in a whorehouse anyway. The way Scorsese choreographs this scene is interesting: The madam brings Bertha into the parlour. Bertha looks. Turns around to leave. Then turns around matter-of-factly deciding to stay. You have to adapt to survive.

There are some good visuals in the movie; a shot of convicts running between piles of lumber, a shot of the gang running down an apparent cattle chute, and the curiously circular use of the railway. Bertha and her gang are forever hopping freights, and once they even think they've made it to Memphis, but all of their train rides take them back to where they were before, as if Godot were waiting at the end of the line.

Scorsese remains one of the bright young hopes of American movies. His brilliant first film won the 1968 Chicago Film Festival as *I Call First* and later played as *Who's That Knocking at My Door?* He was an assistant editor and director of *Woodstock*, and now, many frustrated projects later, here is his first conventional feature. He is good with actors, good with his camera and determined to take the grade-zilch exploitation film and bend it to his own vision. Within the limits of the film's possibilities, he has succeeded.

Are You Talkin' to Me?

Extract from MARTIN SCORSESE SEMINAR
at The American Film Institute's Center for Advanced Film Studies, 12 February 1975

Do you think AIP and Roger Corman are still a viable way to go, a good place to use as a stepping stone for working with the majors? Early on, there were a lot of people who came out of there, like Coppola and Bogdanovich, and then it seems to me that there was a long lag. Now people find that once they've made a picture there, it's so much easier to continue to make those kinds of pictures.

Sure, I was going to make either *I Escaped From Devil's Island* or *The Arena*, about the gladiators in ancient Rome. I'm dying to make a picture about ancient Rome. I said, 'Gee, I can do a comedy and have some fun.' But luckily, we didn't do it. I can only tell you from my experience. My experience was the University, because I didn't have enough money to buy even an 8mm camera. I used to draw all my pictures. My first movies were all drawn, like storyboards, when I was a kid. Steve Spielberg used to have his own 8mm camera, used to do a lot of his own 8mm stuff. I couldn't do that. Eventually, I borrowed my friend Joey's camera, one of the characters in *Mean Streets*, and I shot some 8mm stuff.

The University was the place that got me the money, got me the chance to make the pictures. Then from there, Corman, really. I was killing myself in New York. Death. Pure death in New York. If it wasn't for Mike Wadleigh in New York, it would have been ridiculous. Mike was a student with me at the same time. That's when we started cutting the music films and we had some fun with that. But we would have died. I mean, guys I knew are dead now. Really.

Could you talk a little bit about how you financed **Mean Streets** *and how it came together? It was done independently, right? And then you sold it to Warner Brothers?*

Yeah, OK, I'll tell you. The first place I brought *Mean Streets* to was the AFI in New York. At that time, they were just starting a feature programme. I went over and gave them about a 50-page outline. It was ridiculous. The girl was nothing and had no character but it had all the basic elements. They told me they couldn't do it. They said, 'We should be doing this kind of thing but we can't do it.' Then I took it to Joe Brenner, who's a sex film distributor who distributed *Who's That Knocking?* with the sex scene in it. I was trying anything. I said, 'I'll shoot it in 16, anything.' He said, 'No.' So we put it away. One of my old professors at NYU told me, 'Hey, nobody wants to see films about Italian-Americans anyway so forget about it.' This was about a year before *The Godfather* was written as a book. Mardik and I wrote this thing with the *Godfather* image and all that in 1966, 1967. What happened was that we put it away for a long time. In 1968, I thought I had some access to some money and I got it out

De Niro and Scorsese confer outside the cab. The director's cameo as the passenger who wants to genitally mutilate his wife with a Magnum .44 is seared in the viewer's memory.

and rewrote it again. Another rejection. So I put it away, totally. Then I came to Hollywood to edit *Medicine Ball Caravan*, because I had edited *Woodstock* with T. Schoonmaker under Mike Wadleigh. Freddie Weintraub needed somebody to salvage *Medicine Ball Caravan* because they had a nine-hour cut – it was in three gauges – 35mm Techniscope, 16mm and 8mm. It was nine hours long and nobody knew what was happening. It had no continuity, nothing. He brought me out here and said, 'Try and see what you can do.' I thought I was going to be here two weeks and I've been here ever since. But what eventually happened was, the first week I got out here, *Who's That Knocking?* had opened in L.A. under the title *J.R.* It kept changing titles because the theatre distributor didn't like the title *Who's That Knocking?* It played at the Vagabond and he showed it as *J.R.* It got good reviews and Roger Corman went to see it. I met Roger the first week I was out here and he said, 'Would you like to do the sequel to *Bloody Mama*? It's got guns, it's got costumes.' I said, 'Yeah, I'll do it.' He said, 'I'll see you in six months with the script.' I said, 'Oh.' I figured in New York for nine years I'd been going through the same shit, everybody saying, 'Six months . . . Nine months . . . We'll be right back . . . Be back next week . . .' You never get a phone call back so I forgot about it.

The next thing I know, I go to work on *Medicine Ball Caravan*, which almost killed me, physically because it was a monstrous job and we did so many technical effects. I mean, you can only do so much when there's no content. A month later, after I finished *Medicine Ball Caravan*, I was helping Cassavetes do some *Minnie and Moskowitz* sound effects because John had seen *Who's That Knocking?* years ago in New York and loved it. Sure enough, it was nine months later and I figured Roger Corman was never going to call. So he called. He had a script. I read the script, liked it, went ahead and made *Boxcar Bertha*. Now *Boxcar Bertha* was finished seven months later and at that time I was scheduled to do one more picture for Roger Corman, *I Escaped From Devil's Island*. We were going to shoot in Costa Rica. Next thing I know, I showed a two and a half hour rough cut of *Boxcar Bertha* to a bunch of friends – Carradine and all the people in the picture and Corman and Cassavetes. Cassavetes took me aside the next day and spoke to me for three hours. He said, 'Don't do any more exploitation pictures. Do something that you really – do something better.' He was never a fan of exploitation pictures. I like exploitation pictures. But he was just never a fan of that kind of stuff. He never liked it. I said, 'The only thing I have is this *Season of the Witch*.' *Mean Streets* was called *Season of the Witch* at that time. So he said, 'Rewrite it.'

Sandy [Weintraub] and I got together and she read it. I said, 'What do you think?' She said, 'Well, you put more into description than what you told me about the neighbourhood.' In other words, there were stories that I used to tell her in *Mean Streets* about the mook scene and about the firecrackers and all that which were never in the original script. She said, 'Why don't you put those scenes in the picture?' I said, 'That's a good idea.' I did that and chopped out a little more of the religious stuff because there was a lot of religious stuff in it and trimmed it down a little and we started bringing it around. I brought it to Francis [Coppola]; he said he was going to read it but never did. He couldn't read it. He was in the middle of *The Godfather*, going crazy. We brought it to a lot of people. Roger Corman was the first I brought it to. His readers loved it. I said, 'Can we do it?' Roger said, 'Marty, I understand we got a script from you and everybody here says it's one of the best scripts we've received. However, I'd like to ask you one thing.' He said, 'I haven't read it. Has it got gangsters?' I said, 'Yes, it's got gangsters.' He said, 'Has it got guns?' I said, 'Yes, it's got guns.' He said, 'Has it got violence? Has it got sex?' I said, 'Yes.' He said, 'My brother just made a picture called *Cool Breeze*, which is the first time that my brother Gene is making money. It's making a lot of money.' He said, 'Now, if you're willing to swing a little, I can give you $150,000 and you can shoot it all with a non-union student crew in New York. The only thing is, I'd like the picture to be black.' I said, 'Roger . . . ' – goes to show you how much I wanted to make the picture – I said, 'I'll think about it.' I walked out knowing that I couldn't do it. That same week a good friend of mine, his name is Jay Cocks, his wife was out here doing *Old Times*, a Harold Pinter play, with Faye Dunaway – his wife is Verna Bloom – and she was out here alone and wanted to have dinner with me. She said, 'This young guy just came into town, his name is Jonathan Taplin; he used to be road manager for Bob Dylan and The Band and he wants to get into movies. He's 26 years old.' I said, 'Fine, we'll go for dinner.' At dinner he says, 'What scripts do you have?' I think: I'll just scare this guy away, so I say, 'I've got this script called *Season of the Witch*. You wanna see it?' He says, 'Yeah, I'll see it.' Then he said, 'During the week I'd like to see all your other films.' So I think, 'If the script doesn't scare him away, the films will.' Because all I had at the time was *Who's That Knocking?* and three shorts. What happened was that he read the script and called me up and told me that he liked the script, which I couldn't believe. I said, 'Oh, really? Well, wait'll you see the pictures.' He saw *Who's That Knocking?* and he saw *It's Not Just You, Murray!*, and he saw another movie and he saw *The Big Shave*. He called up and said, 'I like your pictures.' This was all in the space of one week. I said, 'OK. Sunday night we're having a preview of *Boxcar Bertha* at the Pantages. Sam Arkoff hates it. Roger Corman likes it but everybody at AIP hates the picture.' I said, 'Come to the preview with us.' And I figure we'll blow it right there. If the audience doesn't like it, we're dead.

So we go to the preview at the Pantages and it was the best preview they'd had since *Wild Angels*. Arkoff was outside and he told me, 'It's almost good now.' He smiled. He wouldn't give it all to me but he liked it. Afterwards, Jon and Sandy and I and some other people went to Chianti, the restaurant where this whole thing started, and we had a few drinks and he said, 'If Roger can get me a letter saying he'll distribute the film, I can get you money to make it in Cleveland.' Now Jonathan Taplin, his middle name is Trumball, he's related to the guy who painted George Washington crossing the Delaware – it's kind of odd, a person like this doing a picture like *Mean Streets*. So I said, 'OK, fine.' We went to Roger. Roger said, 'OK, you've got the letter.' We walked out and I was stunned. I said, 'We've got the letter, which means we can probably get the money.' He said, 'Yeah.' He went to Cleveland and he called me back a few days later and he said, 'Terrific news. They got the letter and they want to go ahead.' I said, 'How much are you going for?' He said, '$300,000.' I said, 'Terrific.'

Then what happened next is a little shady – not shady in the sense of the dealings – a little shady in my own mind because I'm not sure exactly what happened. He got the money from a guy named E. Lee Perry, who's got executive producer credit on the producer – a young guy, he was about 24 years old at the time and had just inherited a lot of money – we got the money from him and for about three weeks we were going strong. To make money, I was editing a picture for Roger that was directed by Vernon Zimmerman called *The Unholy Rollers* and I was also editing *Elvis on Tour* at the same time.

I was doing two pictures at once and we were also doing rewrites on the script, building up the girl's character, doing all kinds of things. Then he called one day and said, 'The money fell through.' I said, well, that's it. By that time, *Boxcar Bertha* had opened and a lot of guys knew me but they still felt it was a B picture, an exploitation picture, and they wouldn't have anything to do with me. They were offering me things like black exploitation pictures and they wanted to get me into that kind of stuff. I said, 'Gee, I don't know.' I was ready to do it but even then, some of those I couldn't get. They wouldn't give them to me. First they offered them to me, then they saw *Boxcar*, then they said, 'No, I don't know if it's right.' Anyway, I don't know how it happened but this guy Perry came back into town and we had dinner with him. It was him and his wife and Taplin and his girl friend and me and Sandy. It was very relaxed because I knew that the guy wasn't giving us any money so I didn't have to worry. We just told a lot of funny stories and had a good time and the next thing I know we've got the money back. What had happened was that the kid's family had called up Jon's family and said, 'Your son is trying to swindle our son.' That kind of thing, you know. But we got the money. I only found out last week in New York how much we really got and that was $175,000. That was it. The rest of the money came from a deferment from CFI labs. CFI rates the scripts they get and they rated ours a 90 or something like that and they gave us complete facilities – screening, processing, developing, opticals, answer print, everything – to be paid back a year after the picture was finished. So then I said, 'The only guys who can make this picture that I know' – because John had never made a picture – 'who can make this picture quickly and make it look like it was done for more money than it was made for are the guys that made *Boxcar Bertha* – Paul Rapp, who worked for Roger Corman for a bunch of years, Peter Fain and a bunch of guys.' He went to see Paul Rapp and Paul budgeted the picture and he called me up one day and said, 'In order to shoot this picture for $300,000, you're going to have to shoot it in Los Angeles.' I said, 'I can't shoot this picture in Los Angeles.' He said, 'Then don't make the picture.' I said, 'Well, what do you mean, shoot it in Los Angeles? What are we going to do?' He said, 'Go to New York, shoot some background stuff for four days and then come back here and we'll do all the interiors here. We can't crash the cars in New York. We can't pay the Teamsters so we'll have to find a place here at night.' I said, 'OK. I can write it into the script that they go to Brooklyn.' Which is what they end up doing, they go to Brooklyn. I shot the car crash in downtown L.A. at night. All the other exteriors are New York. Even the beach is New York because the water looks different at Staten Island than it does out here. It's true. We shot that in New York and all the interiors are L.A. except for the hallways. The hallway stuff is very important because we couldn't find a hallway to double. We shot those literally where the film takes place. In fact, we were working out of the lady's house who was the mother of the boy Robert De Niro was portraying. We worked out of her house and we worked out of my mother's house. But we only shot six days in New York. We kept stretching it to get more of the New York feeling. That also limited our shooting because the best I could do was put the people in the middle of the buildings and let the buildings do all the talking. Atmosphere-wise, you know. When De Niro's shooting his gun off the roof, the roof is New York because you see the Empire State Building, but the window is Los Angeles. When David Carradine gets shot in the bar, the guy falling in the street is actually in New York – that was a double – we shot that first. We blocked out his face just right so that he falls and hits the car, that sort of thing. The rest of the scene was shot in Los Angeles. The guys who were the doubles were all old friends of ours. His name was Larry the Box; he was a safecracker.

Did you screen the stuff you shot in New York before you shot stuff to match out here?
No, we had no time to look at anything. We had no time to look at rushes. I looked at rushes maybe on a Saturday and that was about it. The thing was done like a jigsaw puzzle. Like the scene where Bobby's up on the roof and he does this business [motioning], and all that. I set up the shot and then I had to go set up another scene so I said, 'Bobby, make sure you know exactly where you are so we'll get it.' The guys who shot the stuff in New York were a guy named Alec Hirschfeld, who's Jerry Hirschfeld's son, a cameraman, and many of them were students – Mitch Block and a bunch of guys. Dale Bell, who was the associate producer on *Woodstock*, set it up for us. We only shot six days in New York. The festival stuff was shot in October before we even started doing preproduction. At one point, Jon Voight was going to be in the picture. The night in New York that we discovered he wasn't going to be in it, I went right back to Harvey Keitel and Harvey did it that day. The stuff you see of Harvey walking through the feast was done right at the spur of the moment, when I said that he was going to be the lead. I got him a coat down at Barney's and we went. That was that. But there were a lot of crazy things like that on the picture. The blowing up of the mailbox was done in San Pedro by the second unit. Again, I drew the pictures for them and said, 'Get me this.' I went to the location and looked at it the night before. I said, 'Line it up over here.' I came back and told Bobby what I wanted, told the second unit cameraman what I wanted. David Osterhout, who plays one of the McIver brothers in *Boxcar Bertha*, was also my second unit director there too. He shot it that way while I was shooting another scene because I couldn't take the ride to San Pedro. It was too far. It would have taken me away for too long.

So it was done on time and on the money?
It was done in 27 days. We had to finish when we finished and that was that. But money no, we went over a little. I kept adding scenes. I added the backroom scene, the long improvisation. I added a scene in front of the gun shop in New York. I added the scene where they steal the bread in front of his uncle's shop. All that stuff. I added a lot of stuff like that. I kept pushing the limits of the budget and drove everybody crazy. But that was the only thing we could do because the more we got down there, the more fun we had and the more we realised the atmosphere we wanted to get. A lot of my old friends are in the film, a lot of guys who are now just hanging around, are there in the picture as extras. Where we really went over budget was in the music. The music killed us.

Paying for rights?
Yes. The Rolling Stones came to $15,000. Each. First it was $7,500 each, then they doubled it.

Did you have time to rehearse on **Mean Streets***?*
Yes, I had ten days rehearsal.

What about improvisation?
Oh, the improvisation took place in rehearsal. We taped it, wrote it down. We worked out of the Gramercy Park Hotel.

In your opinion, what influence did those limitations have on the final product of **Mean Streets***?*
The limitation is that the picture is sloppy, if you ask me.

Do you storyboard?
Every picture is on a storyboard so we know what we're doing in terms of camera. We know exactly where we're going. We can line up our shots totally. If we light all one way, we do all the shots from that angle. Then we switch around and do the other side. It's really like a jigsaw puzzle, the whole thing. That's what Paul Rapp and those guys are great at. In the morning I'd lay out all my storyboards and they'd juggle all the pictures, put them over here – but that doesn't mean you're shooting in sequence in scenes, you know. That means you're shooting your scenes out of sequence. Not only in one scene but you're shooting three lines that are in the middle first. It's very hard for the actors but it worked. It was the only way we could get the picture done on time. There are things in there where I would have liked to have held a two-shot but I had to cut, cut, cut, cut, cut. You know, it's a pain in the ass.

How do you account for the fact that **Mean Streets** *received almost unanimous critical acclaim and, as far as I know, it was not very successful at the box office? Could you talk a little about that?*
The picture opened at the New York Film Festival – was very successful in New York, still is, it plays in New York now – it was a combination of inexperience and circumstances. The inexperience came from the fact that Jon Taplin, my producer, said that because the picture got great reviews and we did such good business in New York the first couple of weeks, he wanted to open the film in 25 cities. Just like *The Last Picture Show* and *Five Easy Pieces*. He went to Bert Schneider and talked to him and he said, 'Do it because there's nothing opening in October except *The Way We Were* and that isn't going to make a cent.' Famous last words. I convinced Jon to only open it in San Francisco, L.A., Washington, Chicago and, I think, Boston. He said, 'OK, let's try it that way first.' Because I thought it was a good idea, too, but everybody was saying to be careful because *Five Easy Pieces* and *The Last Picture Show* were Americana – not just because *Mean Streets* was totally urban – but the other films had more of a universal appeal in terms of the whole country. That's probably why they did very well. Leo Greenfield, who's the head of distribution for Warner Brothers, felt that we were wrong. We asked John Calley and he said, 'OK, do it.' Naturally, they're not going to prove themselves wrong. They opened the picture in Los Angeles at the Plaza Theatre in Westwood and Leo said, 'It's a lousy theatre. You don't want to open there but we're going to have to open there. Do you want to open there?' We said, 'Yeah.'

See, we thought the New York Film Festival meant something out here. It does-n't mean a thing. Nobody even knew about the picture. We had nice, big full-page ads. Also, the ads were no good. We had no idea how to sell the picture. I had no idea how we were going to sell that kind of picture. How are you going to sell it? As *The Gang That Couldn't Shoot Straight?* That was our first concept – guys running around with shorts on with guns and hats because Johnny Boy takes off his pants at one point. It would have looked like a comedy. It is funny but it wasn't meant to be. The com-bination of not knowing how to sell the picture, the combination of opening in New York – and Leo Greenfield said to let it play in New York and he was probably right – we should have let it play in New York till 1974 and then opened it here in 1974.

Next thing I know, we opened in L.A., got nice reviews, did two weeks' business and that was that. Every place else, the same thing. At the same time, *The Exorcist* was coming in. That was $14 million and it was a company whose whole life depended on *The Exorcist* at that time because *Mame* they were a little shaky about. Naturally, they're not going to worry about a picture they paid $750,000 for and they didn't make anyway. They're not going to cover that and why should they? As they say, 'Why throw good money after bad?' In fact, they want us to buy back the foreign rights and we're in the process of doing that now. I'm trying to get them to re-release it in L.A. but they want to wait. At least they should show the damn picture in Los Angeles, you know. Because the only people that have seen it are in the Bel-Air circuits and the Beverly Hills circuits, in peoples' houses. That's the only place they screen it.

In a sense, it's not all their fault and it's probably our fault. It's inexperience and it's a damned hard picture to sell. How do you sell a picture like that? I remember we had two ads – one with a gun in it and one with a dead body in it. Don Rugoff said to me in New York, 'The ads that don't sell are the ads that have guns and dead bodies.' Those were our two alternative ads. What do I do? I said, 'Don, we just made two ads and those are our ads.' Then they tried a run in New York and they made it look like *Blackboard Jungle* and *The Amboy Dukes* which was OK with me. At that point I said, 'OK, run it off as a junior Mafia picture. I don't give a damn. Change the title. Do some-thing but the point is, I want people to see it.' I mean, it's got quite a following in New York. In the neighbourhood now, West Side and East Side, if there's any trouble they always say, 'Well, it's *Mean Streets* time, gentlemen.' It's really made its imprint there.

Which character were you in Mean Streets?
I was Charlie, the lead character, but there were other elements of a friend of mine because I never had enough money – I couldn't sign for those loans. All that was the other guy. The conflicts within Charlie were within me, my own feelings.

I know that some people see **Mean Streets** *and they are confused about what happened at the ending. What exactly happened? Did you make a decision whether he actually sold them out or not?*
Sold who out? Charlie sold them out? No, he never did that. Charlie just waited too long so that everything blows up in his face. He acts very irrationally by taking them out of town. It's the worst thing he could do. He takes his friend's car and he takes the girl which is the worst thing he could have done. He should have kept her out of it

Johnny Boy (Robert De Niro) at Tony's (David Proval) bar, in Mean Streets *(1973). In his first performance for Scorsese, De Niro stole every scene he appeared in as the recklessly unreliable anti-hero.*

totally. But he let everybody pressure him. 'All right, all right, all right.' Disaster. He's a character headed full on toward disaster. See, it's the idea of success – in fact, when I first wrote it, it was like an allegory for what was happening to me trying to make movies. Mardik and I were working together, writing scripts about ourselves at that time, trying to get things going. At that time, the sex films were coming out. We were going to do a film called *This Film Could Save Your Marriage* because in every one of those films that was a catch-phrase. We were going to do everything, anything we could get our hands on and we never got anywhere. We just did shorts and documentaries. It was frustrating. The picture was for me, I hate to use the word 'allegory', but that's what it was for me. I drew from personal experiences about a guy trying to make it.

And not making it?
Yeah. He learns something else, though. What that is is a kind of enlightenment of some sort. He realises something about himself which Johnny Boy knows from the very beginning. Especially when he sees him with his cousin and they have that fight in the street and he says, 'Hey, you didn't do anything for me.' Because he knows that Charlie is doing everything for himself, even when he's helping other people.

It's like the Pharisees, the guys who used to give money to the poor and blow trumpets so everybody could turn around and watch them give money to the poor. Christ said that they had already received their own reward because they had received their reward on earth. Something like that. We had tons of that in there, that kind of thing.

But wasn't there a moment when he changed the route on the ride out of the city or something like that?
That's because we had to make it match to L.A.

Right. That's why, anyway –
Oh yeah, when he said, 'Where are you going?'

Yes and he switched the road and the guys found them.
That's what happens when you shoot things in 27 days . . . What do you do?

What's a mook?
A mook. That scene actually occurred. Does anybody from New York remember the Fillmore East? There's a bar across from the Fillmore East – at the time the Fillmore East was called the Lower East Commodore, that's where I saw most of my movies when I was a kid – and they used to have a place right across the street from it called Foxy's Corner, on Sixth Street and Second Avenue. One night some of the neighbourhood guys went in with the Johnny Boy character and his older brother and they got into a fight. They were trying to settle an argument. That's exactly, literally, what happened in the film. In fact, it was written for a bar like Foxy's Corner but then we found this pool hall on Hollywood Boulevard and we wanted to do it there because I thought everybody running around throwing pool cues at each other would be funny.

    The guy said to Johnny Boy's older brother – everything was settled, everything was fine – and he said, 'The bartender called you a mook.' He said, 'Called me a mook?' And he got crazy. In the middle of his craziness, he was just about to throw a table up in the air and he said, 'What's a mook?' The guy said, 'I don't know.' Finally he threw the table up in the air and they started killing each other. Then they all made friends again. As they were walking out, the Johnny Boy character says, 'Hey, friends, huh?' And he says, 'Get your hands off me, you mother-fucker.' Bang! They're into it again. So it was a very funny story. But 'mook', I later found out in San Francisco, is a slang for 'mocha' or 'bigmouth' among the Neapolitan people. See, we were Sicilians and there was always some sort of rivalry. There was rivalry between the Neapolitans and Sicilians and Calabrese. There was rivalry between all three against the ones that lived on the East Side and the West Side. Whether you were a Sicilian on the West Side or the East Side, they all hated each other. Even down to buildings. They got into rivalries between buildings. It was always crazy that way.

Did I just read this into it or were you deliberately, consciously using every element you could in **Mean Streets** *to give us, the audience, the same feeling that these kids had growing up in that crazy world? I mean, I got really crazy in that film and I felt for the first time ever that I really understood New Yorkers. Before I never quite understood when they'd say, 'You don't know what it's like, you grow up in the gutter and you street fight and you know how – '*
Any place you go now, you can get shot for no reason. You get mugged. A car goes up the curb and hits you. It's the same thing out here but there's something extra-violent about New York. It's not only downtown but all over. Growing up in that neighbourhood, we used to go to school in the morning, carrying a little briefcase, going to Saint

Patrick's school around the corner and we lived a block away from the Bowery and there were always the drunks, the guys in the Bowery beating each other up with bottles. There was blood all over the street and you'd just step by. I mean, that's normal.

Were you using elements like the music and the harshness and the camera to make us all tense?
Oh, sure, yeah. But that was my own energy, though. I didn't say, 'Now we're really going to drive them crazy.' I had the camera move at a certain point because I felt that that was the way it should go. The music was very important because you can go by and hear the march from *Aida* and as you walk by another room you can hear 'Handyman', and then in another place you hear Eric Clapton and then in another place you hear an old Italian folk song, and you keep going and there's Chinese music. Especially in the summertime, it was incredible. I don't know if anybody here ever lived in tenements in the summer but in one building it was all one house, all the doors open, everybody would go in each other's houses, everybody would eat whatever everybody else had and there were always fights in the streets. They were always beating up Puerto Ricans and blacks. That was it. Nothing else to do.

What about the West Side?
Oh, the West Side always had a little more class. They had more class. They had the artists moving in. There was always Greenwich Village on the West Side.

Not around 36th Street.
No, no, you're right. Not around 36th Street. I'm talking about downtown. I always think of the West Side as the Village. The Village area is always a little more tolerant of other groups. That's why *Mean Streets* is set on the East Side in the Italian-American ghetto. That area is really very, very closed off, very secretive and sinister in a sense. That doesn't mean if you're living there now, a nice lady or a young kid or a student, that they won't take care of you. Because, as long as they know you're not pushing cocaine or something, they'll take care of you. If you're pushing cocaine, they want a piece of it. But it goes that way. It just goes that way.

I like the way you integrated the music into* Mean Streets *especially. I was wondering at what point you thought of the music?
The music was always in the original script.

I got that impression because the rhythm of the film was –
'Be My Baby' was the song. You can't beat that. I mean, that's 1963 or 1962 in New York. That's the Ronettes. We used to hear that late at night. There was always a social club stuck in the back of some building and that song was always playing, echoing in the streets. That sound – the Crystals, the Ronettes, Martha and the Vandellas, all the female singing groups of that time – that's what it was. Right before the Beatles.

Did that influence the way you shot it or was that in mind?
That was in mind. All that stuff.

MEAN STREETS: THE SWEETNESS OF HELL
By David Denby

Mean Streets, Martin Scorsese's independent, low-budget feature about four sub-Mafia punks in New York's Little Italy, was the hit of the Eleventh New York Film Festival (along with Truffaut's *Day for Night*), and has been widely described – even by people not much taken with it – as one of the most interesting American features of 1973. By common consent, 1973 has been a dull year for American movies, so perhaps this accolade conceals an insult; nevertheless, the movie has built up considerable good-will. People want to like it, they want to be generous towards it, an impulse that has led to a certain genteel condescension among several of the American reviewers.

Yet no movie deserves condescension less. Certainly it's a 'little' New York film ($550,000 budget), with no stars and not much variety or glamour in the settings – in some respects the movie is the culmination of the lonely-streets-and-sullen-bedrooms style of student films produced in the last decade at New York University, where Scorsese, now 30, was once a student and then a film teacher. But emotionally, *Mean Streets* is grandiose and amazingly intense – 'operatic' (as Pauline Kael has said) in the manner of mid-Visconti, yet peculiarly American in its speed, energy, obscenity and humour. And Scorsese is no sweet little talent, but a large, dangerous and deeply flawed talent.

The Godfather revealed the crime aristocrats building their empires and plotting against one another; perhaps one reason for its fantastic popularity was that it brought us close to the kind of total amoral power that obsesses the age, and gave us the illusion of understanding that power. Yet *The Godfather* was disingenuous in so far as it implied that all Mafia operations took place on this exalted level and that the Mafia had no victims outside its own ranks.

Mean Streets shows what *The Godfather* left out – the neighbourhood chisellers, loan sharks and screw-ups who prey on their own community and each other, sucking money out of ordinary people, hustling for $10 bills. Scorsese's Mulberry Street punks are only hanging on to the edges of organised crime, but the Mafia provides the system of values they live by and even a certain legitimacy, should they want it. For Charlie (Harvey Keitel), the film's hero, torn between disreputable friends and a stern Mafia uncle, 'maturity' would mean running a restaurant that has been extorted from its rightful owner. But Charlie isn't really committed to crime, it's simply the easiest, most congenial activity in his neighbourhood – a way of staying close to friends. Thus the first effect of Scorsese's revision of the classical gangster film is to take crime out of the semi-mythical realm of monstrous ambition and the moralistic realm of low-life despair. In *Mean Streets*, crime is just a way of getting by.

As Scorsese introduces his people in short, character-revealing vignettes, for one dismaying moment you might think he was making a conventional 'wacky' caper picture about bumblers who want to be gangsters, or possibly an American *Big Deal on Madonna Street*. But it turns out that he doesn't need satire to ingratiate his characters with the audience; Scorsese, who grew up in Little Italy and obviously knows the scene, discovers the humour in the life itself and in the characters' naturally obscene idiom. And because he doesn't see these bums as 'little' people, but rather as very familiar friends who got bogged down, his film has none of the patronising, sentimental tone of bourgeois American movies about the working class (e.g. *Marty*). Pursuing his friends relentlessly in and out of bars, bedrooms and restaurants, up and down streets, stairways and hallways, he creates a life of crazy restlessness that we soon realise is totally satisfying to the characters, even though it's oppressively enclosed, barely touching on the world outside. They do little but drink, brawl, hassle over money and pick up girls who wander downtown, but their lives are inherently dramatic none the less because of the violent way honour, obsession and guilt bind them to one another. 'Why should we care about these working-class hoods?' asked some of the film's colder reviewers. But it's hard to see in this question anything but class bias and squeamishness; the reasons for caring are there in almost every scene.

Scorsese and his co-screenwriter Mardik Martin are weak on narrative construction, but they have a preternatural instinct for the psychology of dependent relationships. For once, the male friendship theme is developed with enough psychological richness to explain the emotions it generates; this time no one will suspect something embarrassing has been left out (as people did suspect in the case of *Midnight Cowboy* and *Scarecrow*). The hero, Charlie, is a suffering, masochistic Catholic, a man who constantly must sin to fulfil his sense of unworthiness. Eternally guilty, eternally repentant, Charlie works out his pain by taking care of two troublesome friends – Teresa (Amy Robinson), an epileptic girl who loves him, and the reckless, perverse, tragically incoherent Johnny Boy (Robert De Niro).

For each of these two men, the other's character becomes a necessary fate. Charlie, the Mulberry Street Jesus, needs that lying, cheating punk Johnny Boy for personal absolution just as Johnny Boy needs Charlie to keep himself alive; the men's edgy, murderously unstable love for each other holds the film in tension. Charlie tries to protect Johnny Boy from another friend, Michael (Richard Romanus), who wears suits and long dark coats with felt collars and has pretensions as a very deadly *mafioso*; the trouble with Michael is that he's as much a punk as any of the others, although he doesn't know it. Desperately eager to impress his friends, Michael turns to violence when Johnny Boy contemptuously refuses to pay a debt – if the film has a villain it's prissy, status-conscious Michael, who denies the bum's humanity they all share. Only Tony the bartender (David Proval) stays out of the mess; self-protective, responsible for no one, Tony is the obvious survivor, a mediocrity.

As these four bounce off one another – enraged, derisive, hilarious, sentimental – it becomes clear that their energy has no goal or purpose, certainly not love or career or even style (they are much less conscious of style, for instance, than the silky urban swashbucklers in recent black movies). Scorsese is celebrating emotional verve as a moral quality in itself, and this is something new in American movies and takes some getting used to. The reforming, punishing instinct dies hard, particularly in an American. In the late 1930s there were the Dead End Kids, cuddly juvenile delinquents who snarled for a couple of reels and then performed good deeds. Even Marlon Brando, as Terry Malloy in *On the Waterfront*, stopped being a punk in the

Harvey Keitel as Charlie in Mean Streets. *Reminiscent of J.R. in Scorsese's first feature, Charlie lives on the edge of the underworld and is haunted by desire to do the right thing.*

end; redeemed by a priest and a girl, he paid for wasting his potential (a prime American sin in the moral economy of the 1950s) by accepting a beating. The punks of *Mean Streets*, however, will never shape up; if they survive, they'll simply become *ageing* punks. As American idealism declines, and there's no longer a single type of optimistic, useful American that we all must aspire to (most of the recent models having turned out to be frauds or poltroons), film-makers are increasingly able to allow characters their own reality without imposing a moral destiny on them. Scorsese's *Mean Streets* is remarkable, I think, for its moral realism – realism without cynicism.

The mood of independent New York features of the 1950s and early 60s was modest, sombre, 'downbeat', featuring black and white cinematography in muted lyrical-documentary style, and original jazz scores, mournful and elegant, rather than studio strings. The city emerged as a grey, unhappy place; its inhabitants as weary, repressed, violent. To some this may have looked like the truth, although now it appears as artificial as any other style, a dour, often unimaginative way of appearing serious.

Scorsese goes completely in the opposite direction; the film is bursting with noise, colour, movement, and the mood is consciously over-ripe – what shall we call the style, operatic naturalism? His characters don't perceive the city as dull and grey; yes, the neighbourhood may be crummy, but up on the roofs the ever-astonishing skyscrapers of New York twinkle on all sides, incredibly beautiful and powerful at night, and the local bars, admittedly lousy and stale, give off a satisfying glow. The film opens during the Feast of San Gennaro, a yearly outdoor confluence of grease, fragrance and overpowering crowds. Scorsese's point, I think, is that Little Italy has this suffocating, sweetness-of-hell atmosphere all the time, and that it's gotten to Charlie and the others and corrupted them. By immersing us in the voluptuous pleasures of the neighbourhood, Scorsese, while never suggesting that the city is a benign place, punctures the liberal view of the city as an unrelieved nightmare for poor ethnic groups. His city is hypnotic, irresistible, and for us to pretend that some people aren't drawn to the rottenness is sheer cant.

Scorsese's neighbourhood bar is a proletarian descendant of those white-on-white movie nightclubs of the 1930s and 40s where the hoods met to trade insults and listen to a girl sing. A home away from home, the bar is a pleasurable and infinitely dangerous place where wildly destructive young men get viciously drunk, brawl over impassive young women, and pass out on the floor. One man uses the bathroom to shoot heroin; another is assassinated while taking a leak. With cinematographer Kent Wakeford, Scorsese has worked out a dark reddish lighting for this place, both lurid and soft, and a floating camera style – the camera moves in behind Charlie as he greets his friends and women, tracks up and down the bar, turns a full vertical circle as a man spirals to the floor, and after a while we begin to feel drunk and dislocated ourselves, as if we were under water in a red grotto or gliding around one of the upper circles of hell.

As the friends gather for the evening, Robert De Niro as Johnny Boy makes his appearance with a girl on each arm and without his pants. I'm not sure why he has no pants – I think they're holding a pair for him at the bar or something – but De Niro makes such an outrageous show of this potentially disastrous, TV-comedy entrance – preening and posing and carrying on – that he pulls it off triumphantly. As an actor he has that kind of supreme self-assurance (or it may be desperation – at the moment it's hard to tell) that goes beyond technique and preparation; at times he reveals Johnny Boy's unconscious so effortlessly that his performance hardly seems like acting at all, but rather like some sort of super-naturalistic *presence*.

He's not conventionally handsome in any way: dark, stringy hair, a seemingly dumb smile and small, rather mean-looking eyes are hardly ideal physical equipment for an actor. Like Cagney, he dances through the performance, but whereas Cagney was always graceful, no matter what role he was playing, De Niro's dancing has a clumsy, swaggering rhythm to it; he reminds me of the Italian and Puerto Rican men who dance by themselves on subway platforms at three in the morning and dare you to snicker.

Yet despite the bravura, there's something touchingly selfless about him. He's always completely submerged in the character and the scene, and he's very quick and decisive, never holding the camera, for instance, through a long, dreamy pause like Warren Beatty or Robert Redford. The exuberance and physical detail of his performances are unique in American film acting at the present moment. Our leading men are either cool and withdrawn, working within a narrow range of gesture and emotion, or they become specialists in sympathetic anxiety (Dustin Hoffman, George Segal or Richard Benjamin). De Niro doesn't have much physical beauty or an ingratiating smile to fall back on, and he won't truckle to an audience. In an earlier film of 1973, *Bang the Drum Slowly*, he played a stupid, ugly, inarticulate baseball catcher who was also dying (Christ, what a bum role!), and with his hair slicked up in a foul pompadour, tobacco spittle hanging from his lips, he was almost perversely unattractive. Clearly he doesn't care if an audience thinks he's an ugly sot; it will be interesting to see if a man this intransigent can survive in the commercial cinema.

In his first big scene with Harvey Keitel, De Niro hasn't been given much to work with in terms of script – some near-gibberish about gambling debts and a man named Joey Clams – but he improvises around the lines, and with his dancing and obscenity and terribly convincing incoherence he gives a stunning demonstration of how much an actor can do when he has his freedom. The performance is verbally disorganised to an incredible degree, but the psychological underpinning is flawlessly clear.

Scorsese counts on our familiarity with improvisation and our approval of it as a method, and I feel he uses it better than anyone in American movies so far. At one point Keitel emerges from a movie theatre and we see posters for *Point Blank* and *Husbands*. It's a very unlikely double-feature, so I assume *homage* is intended. I can't see much of *Point Blank* in *Mean Streets*, apart from the way De Niro handles a gun in one scene (like Lee Marvin, with the arm held out stiff and high and the gun muzzle pointing down), but the linkage with Cassavetes is obvious. We hear the same explosiveness and repetitions, the talk circling back to a given point, then lurching ahead in a sudden flash of anger only to come back once again. But the resemblance is only on the surface. Scorsese's improvisation conveys none of the solemnity about communication, the ritual stripping away of defence to find 'the truth', that has become Cassavetes' stock in trade. 'Directing actors means, above all, liking people, liking certain things about people,' Bertolucci has said. Despite all the evidence of Cassavetes' ready embrace of his fellow men, I find it hard to believe he likes people very much. There's something terribly aggressive in the way the camera bores in for the kill in *Husbands*, particularly in the hotel-room scenes. The super-close-ups isolate the characters from the support of their surroundings and each other, putting them interminably on the spot; in these circumstances improvisation becomes a kind of punishment.

Scorsese, on the other hand, stays back from his people, letting them move around in their own space, which he respects, allowing them to draw strength from the streets, the music, their friends; and since these working-class characters don't repress much to begin with, there's no need for laceration or emotional striptease. Thus Scorsese's improvisation becomes a fast, explosively funny way of extending the actors' expressiveness. The near-musical texture of obscenity, for instance, would be impossible without improvisation; no one could possibly get down on paper the lunatic obsessiveness of the swearing, with its infinite variety of meanings conveyed through minute variations in rhythm and inflection. The mood of the dialogue is almost ecstatically high-pitched; Scorsese uses improvisation to make his people sound as free as possible, not stricken, like Cassavetes' sufferers. But when he has an actor who can't pull it off he's in trouble. Amy Robinson has an impossible role to begin with (the adoring epileptic girl friend), but her anxiety and self-consciousness in the semi-improvised scenes makes the character seem unnecessarily pathetic – not even on the same existential plane as these ecstatic male talkers.

Scorsese is already a master of film texture and expressive atmosphere and directing actors, but as I said earlier, his narrative sense is weak. Once he sets up his relationships and moods, he's incapable of developing them. The endless quarrels and fistfights don't lead anywhere; the Charlie-Johnny Boy dependency doesn't accumulate new meanings as the movie goes on, it's simply stated over and over with increasing vehemence. For a while, in the middle, you don't think the story is ever going to move forward again, and a terrible depression sets in; afterwards it seems as though the middle sequences could be shifted around without damage and some of them dropped altogether. The tension never sags, but since the actors rather than the narrative supply all the urgency, we get tired of being worked up emotionally only to learn what we already know. It's as if we were starting at the beginning each time, as if Scorsese didn't trust the audience to absorb or learn anything; he wants to recapitulate the movie in every scene, like a mad composer who can't relinquish a good melody.

We come out grateful for this experience but also feeling a bit mauled. Don't Italian-Americans ever communicate without slapping and shoving and brawling? Aren't there any quieter forms of intensity? Scorsese knows how to reach an audience in the gut, but some of his demands are obtuse. The scene in which Teresa has an epileptic fit in the middle of a furious argument between Charlie and Johnny Boy is supposed to be powerful and tragic, but it comes out as ludicrously overwrought and flatly unbelievable, particularly since the men run off and leave her to continue their argument. It's an abuse of the audience because there's no possible way we can relate to the scene emotionally, and Scorsese must know that at some level, because he doesn't stay with that girl writhing on the floor either.

These terrible mistakes (and there are others) are so forgivable because they emerge out of the same violent sincerity that makes the film exciting: Scorsese's impulse to express all he feels about life in every scene (a cannier, more prudent director wouldn't have started his film with that great Keitel monologue), and thus to wrench the audience upwards into a new state of consciousness with one prolonged and devastating gesture, infinitely hurting and infinitely tender. *Mean Streets* comes close enough to this feverish ideal to warrant our love and much of our respect.

Extract from SCORPIO DESCENDING:
IN SEARCH OF ROCK CINEMA
By Howard Hampton

Nearly a quarter of a century has passed since Martin Scorsese opened *Mean Streets* (73) with the fated beat of 'Be My Baby'. The film stands as the most enduring, not to mention thrilling, union of film and rock sensibilities. It's an infinitely seductive vision of a world where human and musical passions are one, the soundtrack elaborating and intensifying the movie's meanings. We first see Harvey Keitel's Charlie waking abruptly from a nightmare, as though for the thousandth time. When he goes to the darkened mirror, the reflection could be his double looking back at him from the confessional or the grave: his stillborn twin. Charlie returns to bed and falls to the pillow in exquisite slow motion as 'Be My Baby' begins, the sound of time standing still. The heart-rending staccato drumming might be coming from Charlie's sweaty chest, even as the teenage Veronica Bennett's wet-dream voice smothers him in its plaintive embrace. Produced a decade earlier by Phil Spector (a 'one-man millennium', as Nik Cohn put it) and sung by the Ronettes, 'Be My Baby' is a breathless utopia of self-fulfilling desire where to wish for something is to make it so. Thus it's the sound of everything Charlie's divided, self-cancelling life is not.

Under the titles, the song orchestrates Scorsese's home-movie snippets of Charlie (the director's dark, altarboy-ego) and it sucks the viewer straight into Charlie's penny-ante world of duty and crime: 'I'll make you so proud of me,' the fabulous Veronica sings in her unsteady, riveting voice, as on screen Charlie moves like a marionette supplicant for whom the Church and the Mafia are indistinguishable. 'Be My Baby' gives these 8mm memories a radioactive glow – Spector's 'wall of sound' closes in around Charlie and the audience, until its ardour turns back on itself to reveal the doubt secretly inscribed in its promise of total gratification. A lover's plea turns into last rites: beneath the tenderness of 'Be My Baby' lies a claustrophobic undertow of dread. And that is the bittersweet rhythm *Mean Streets* moves to, a pulse of impending chaos, the rapt trance of waiting damnation.

This was the first film to truly integrate rock into its narrative, transforming Kenneth Anger's iconographic abstractions (which bordered on camp) into a new form of heightened, pop-operatic naturalism. Scorsese's images were extensions of – and commentaries on – the music. He turned the jukebox smile of the Marvelettes' 'Please Mr. Postman' inside out by shooting a wild brawl to it in real time, as a kind of eroticised *cinéma vérité*. (Putting a lithe, high-kicking Robert De Niro on a pool table, Scorsese turned him into a hoodlum Iggy Stooge: the first punk Rockette.) The doomsday purr of 'Jumpin' Jack Flash' served as Greek chorus to a barroom Hades, while the graveyard romance of 'Pledging My Love' and the crazed jive of 'Mickey's Monkey' foreshadowed looming disaster – the movie's dance with death growing ever more intimate and feverish. But 'Be My Baby' established the tone, holding up a teen hallucination as the sign of unattainable grace, the pleasure that only intensifies the pain of eternal guilt.

In paying such homage, Scorsese alluded to something else: namely that rock had replaced Hollywood as the source of America's most deeply felt representations of itself. A Spector was haunting Hollywood: the spectre of the cultural upheaval the movies had yet to come to terms with. *Mean Streets* drew on late-show film noir and the new wave of European cinema as well (not to mention other kinds of music – Scorsese was an omnivorous sensualist), but filtered through a deep sense of what had been excluded from American cinema in the wake of rock. *Mean Streets* has a funky city-of-night sheen that echoes rock's synthesis of the mythic and the quotidian; it reinvents film in terms of rock as much as the contemporaneous early works of Bruce Springsteen reimagined rock in terms of Kazan, Dean, and Brando, of *West*

Side Story as *Scorpio Rising*. Indeed Springsteen's 'Backstreets' was itself a kind of answer record to Scorsese, a tale of two Charlies: Keitel's as well as Steiger's from *On the Waterfront*. 'Remember all the movies, Terry, we'd go and see,' he sang, the cab ride in the latter dissolving into blood brothers Keitel and De Niro sharing a bed in Little Italy. 'Backstreets' and *Mean Streets* intersect in the subterranean life where myth is transmitted and then lived out, where movies, songs, guilt, and desire all come together in what Pauline Kael called 'a witches brew'. One where the miniskirted Ronettes stirred the cauldron Charlie was drowning in.

THE ETHOS OF *MEAN STREETS*
By Leonard Quart and Paul Rabinow

In the past decade, historians have been uncovering and discovering whole new areas of inquiry: the family, immigrants, women, working class, popular culture. So, too, the film has begun to deal with aspects of the American past and present that Hollywood has either ignored or twisted out of recognisable shape.

In the main, the films that have dealt with Italian immigrant and second generation life – *Marty, Brothers Rico, Pay or Die, House of Strangers* – have been bound to melodramatic conventions or comic stereotypes so broadly drawn that little of the complex concreteness of the culture could seep through. Italians were seen as amoral or venal racketeers; loving, hysterical mommas; earthy authoritarian patriarchs; and dialect comedians named Luigi. They were exotics whose distinctive patterns and customs were portrayed merely externally as superficial trappings or colourful flaws, but never as people with a distinctive consciousness and tradition which could not be discarded easily and which provided much of the substance of their everyday life.

In its shallow treatment of the Italian-American ethos, Hollywood was just sticking to its own commercial principles: don't tamper with successful formulas, and don't risk alienating the mass and ethnic audience by creating a complex and possibly controversial social universe. For to deal with the community honestly would mean that real empathy and criticism would have to be extended; that the limits, mores, oppressions, as well as authentic strengths, of the culture would have to be painfully drawn. It would also implicitly challenge the powerful strain in American mass culture and mythology that holds that we are all really the same – that adulteration and assimilation has been so thorough that only a few dialect jokes and foods have been left as a pop residue.

Martin Scorsese's *Mean Streets* dispenses with the largely apocryphal community of street vendors and earth mothers, aglow with warmth and humanity, and explores one aspect of the real community in a manner that has not been encountered in American film before. *Mean Streets* is Martin Scorsese's third film, and though somewhat uneven

Charlie in bed with Teresa (Amy Robinson), Johnny Boy's cousin. His attitude toward women is typically complex, moving from tenderness to misogyny in an instant.

artistically, it profoundly subverts most of Hollywood's Italian-American fantasies.

The film's aims are as limited in scope as the neighbourhood (Little Italy) itself, but that turns out to be its very strength. It focuses almost exclusively on 'the boys' – that male universe hovering uneasily between adolescence and the ultimate integration into marriage and family life. *Mean Streets* is devoid of parental figures except for the august personage of Giovanni, the neighbourhood's Godfather. But the treatment here differs markedly from other films in that the Mafia figure is viewed from a dual perspective: Charlie's adulation and Scorsese's light mockery. First, he is seen through the eyes of 'the boys', primarily Charlie (Harvey Keitel), the film's protagonist and anti-hero who romanticises his uncle and relates to him in the most formal and submerged manner. For Charlie, Giovanni is like the Church, a source of transcendental authority, held distant to better keep his aura unblemished. The film's texture is less involved with the internal processes of 'the boys' than with the cultural symbols that bind the community together. There is a code and Uncle Giovanni is an enforcer of one part of it, just as the Church serves this function for higher realms.

However, parallel to this exalted vision of Giovanni, Scorsese almost imperceptibly demonstrates his fallibility. The limits of Giovanni's code are laid bare by his analysis of the epileptic girl, Teresa, as 'touched in the head', or his clichéd self-perception as a man of honour especially in relation to the corrupt politicians who needed the Mafia during WWII – quietly mocked by Scorsese. The world depicted in this film is prescriptive and the Uncle, though the dominant figure, is as limited by and tied to it as 'the boys' are – even more so. The code is his whole life, and both his self-esteem and profit are entwined with it. That this adds up to something far from heroic is clearly what Scorsese is telling us by the final image of Giovanni, this Mafia aristocrat, with his roses and cigar, sitting alone near his TV watching *The Big Heat*.

Every ash can, clothes-line, and huddle of men on Little Italy's streets is etched by Scorsese, as are the lights, booths, crowds and movement of the San Gennaro Festival. But they are not the subject of the film. They are background, cultural geography, for 'the boys' and their narrow turf – Tony's bar, Charlie's apartment (he still lives with his mother who provides clean monogrammed shirts) – are what obsess Scorsese. Uptown is a vague abstraction except for the 42nd Street movies; the sea and sun are alien elements; and one of the characters cannot find the South Village, an Italian neighbourhood some ten blocks away. Tony's Bar is their special spot. It is not a particularly realistic place; the red filters provide an all too obvious imagery of hell. It is dim, complete with incessant rock on the juke box, cigarette smoke, ritualistic fights, pick-ups, black go-go dancers, lion cubs, bouncers and even murder. Though at times an emotional atmosphere is fully realised, Scorsese's more explicit attempts to evoke a living hell are crude, and fail. He falls into Peckinpahesque clichés of violence, blood spurting everywhere, overly elongated death scenes, as well as a silly sense of vertigo, created by a revolving camera. He is falsely literary: Tony doesn't read Blake; Scorsese does. However, all these are signs of a young director still trying to achieve full control over his style and vision.

The strengths of the film come in the almost ethnographic portrayal of the ritual interaction and acting out of the codes which the community had handed down to them. The use of curses and nicknames – Joey Clams, Frankie Bones, Jimmy Mook, 'Scumbag', 'Douchebag' – are artfully strung throughout the film and give it its real texture. The endlessly repetitive games of 'sounding' pass the time but, in a deeper sense, are the almost obsessive substance of 'the boys' lives. They continually put one another down, attempt to achieve temporary symbolic dominance over each other, drink, fight, go to the movies, and start all over again. The key ritual here is, 'Let's have a drink'; this is both the entree to all of these ritual scenarios and the leitmotif of their world. Drinking itself is neither an obsession nor a sign of their maleness (Charlie passes out on several occasions); it is a cultural form. 'What'll you have?' is the socially rhetorical question: the only answers are 'Seven and Seven' or 'Johnny Walker'; there is no Tequila in this world, as the Jewish girls from the Village find out. If drinking Scotch is the sign that all is in order, then 'bullshitting' is what occupies the other dead periods. As Tony says at the party for the Vietnam vet: 'Are we drinking or bullshitting?'

Their life ambitions are limited ones. Tony seems serene in his neighbourhood bar. Michael, who looks like Tony Curtis, is a petty con man and loan shark (and somewhat of a 'jerk off' – buying Japanese adapters instead of German lenses). Charlie's vision extends to the vague promise his uncle has made him of a club, possibly uptown. The most complex of 'the boys' is Charlie; pasty-faced, bags under his eyes, glad-handing and passive, he still clings to the older symbols of fire, blood and water. His benedictions with Scotch are only half mocking. His hand in the fire has meaning to him but not to his buddies. His Saint Francis fantasies and guilt-ridden nightmares take their shape within his world as a petty numbers runner and gain expression only in his relationship to Johnny Boy. As his Uncle Giovanni makes clear, it's against Charlie's interest to be so close to Johnny. But Franciscan moral imperatives coupled with a passivity which feeds off Johnny's aggression and self-destructive games (the role played flamboyantly, manically, and brilliantly by Robert De Niro), triumph over self-interest. The emotional complexity of this relationship comes through with a dramatic impact which goes beyond the structure of explanation which either we or Scorsese could impose.

Johnny and his cousin Teresa are at the other fringe from Giovanni in the world Scorsese evokes for us. For them their needs come first. They are not tied either to the symbols of the Church or to the code of the bar. Yet they are driven to the edge of hysteria by the lack of an alternative vision. Teresa wants Charlie and an apartment uptown; Johnny Boy wants the moment and to hell with the consequences. Johnny compulsively betrays the code of obligation and respect that the community of petty thieves and well-dressed punks lives by. He flaunts his debts and jokes his way from creditor to creditor, capitalising on his persona of dimness. He both plays on and resents Charlie's protective and saintly fantasising, using him as a shield but raging against his smothering amiability. Johnny has no future and knows it; Teresa goes beyond the stereotype of the nice protected Italian girl, in her flashes of bitchiness and spite (displayed to the black maid) that could grow, one feels, into a matronly tyranny over Charlie. Both are denied the seemingly warm, ritual interactions of 'the boys', but have no other options. Teresa's parents still need Giovanni's advice about her supposed desire to move out and get her own apartment. Only Johnny and his violence (though it seems less willed than fated) force the codes of honour and revenge to their logical conclusion; but it's a conclusion that must be forced, for Michael is a reluctant murderer.

Although only sketchily drawn, some incisive portraits reveal the relationship of 'the boys' to outsiders. Homosexuals are seen with contempt as 'screaming queens', blacks are taboo but also idealised and seductive (the black go-go dancer excites Charlie but he's a bit frightened by her). Jews are erotic (easy lays), close to the fringes of the community; though still 'other', one can joke, drink and screw with them.

In an attempt to expand his scope, Scorsese has a scene with a Viet vet that intimates that the outer world is a demonic jungle with even more irrational violence than the world of the bar. The vet is told affectionately by Tony to calm down, for: 'This is America, Jerry.' However, though such grand themes may be part of Scorsese's ultimate intent, the film's prime strength lies in his ability to mine his own world and past for more than local colour, nostalgia, and overly precious lyric images. Scorsese has moved us down a road, which seems truly promising for American directors: to dramatically evoke and probe the codes, rituals, and myths which are the stuff of everyday life in America. That he falls into standard melodramatic clichés and overly baroque flourishes should not disguise the authentic power and originality of the film. By narrowing his focus on the world of 'the boys', he has at times really opened up a past that was banal and complex, ritualised and aimless, and warm and thoroughly destructive.

Extract from MARTIN SCORSESE SEMINAR
at The American Film Institute's Center for Advanced Film Studies, 12 February 1975

Did you have any problems when you were shooting the movie about your parents? I thought it was just wonderful and a very appealing thing, to do a movie about your parents. What was their reaction?

The film came about through a series called *The Storm of Strangers*, being done by the National Endowment for the Humanities. This guy called me up and asked me if I wanted to do a picture on the Italian section. They were doing one on the Greeks, the Jews, Armenians, blah, blah, blah. It's going to be for bicentennial TV, 1976. They all have to be a half-hour long. So I said, 'No,' because we were in the middle of shooting *Alice* [*Doesn't Live Here Anymore*]. A day later, I called back and said, 'Wait a minute, I think I would do it if you want to do it my way.' Which was to go to my mother's house, my mother's apartment on the Lower East Side, and to shoot while we were having dinner and I would ask my parents questions about my grandparents. He said yes. What he had in mind was, of course, a still of the people getting off the boat and the camera zooming in and the voice saying, 'So the Italian got off the boat,' and that sort of stuff. I wanted to do it a little differently.

They first got a little nervous. We set it up when I was in Cannes. I set it up with Dale Bell, the same crew that shot most of the New York stuff in *Mean Streets*. I called them from London and when I got there on Saturday, they had it all set up for me. Mardik Martin, in the meantime, had written up all the questions because my parents know him well. He used to go to our home to eat. What you see first in that film is the warm-up. I tried to get them to warm-up but what happened was that they didn't need it, obviously. I don't know if anybody has seen it here, except for you. But the point is that they really got into it and we wound up with a picture that was really much more than about immigration.

The picture is about 48 minutes long and now I think they're going to make a truncated version for TV, a 30-minute version, which I'm not too happy about. People want it for commercial distribution and the government is sort of bureaucratically holding back so we have to be very careful. Hopefully, it will get released. But my parents didn't give me any trouble, no. My father didn't go see the picture at Lincoln Center at the New York Film Festival because he had a hard time watching *Mean Streets*, you know, because he went through all the palpitations of it's your movie up there and 2,000 people are seeing it for the first time. He got the same feeling. Now with *Italianamerican*, the fact that he's on screen and he hadn't seen it and he imagined seeing it for the first time in front of 2,000 people – he felt he'd come off terrible so he saw it privately. That was OK. My mother went instead. I couldn't be there, my mother took over anyway. She threw kisses to everybody, signed autographs. That was like a blueprint for the third part of *Mean Streets*, which is going to be about Charlie when he gets married, settles down, has a couple kids and lives on Staten Island. That's a picture to be done years from now but Mardik and I are working on that now.

ITALIANAMERICAN
Reviewed by Tom Milne

The problem with this engaging documentary, filmed after *Alice Doesn't Live Here Anymore* and edited simultaneously, is that it is either too long (as a profile of Scorsese's parents) or not long enough (as an account of the immigrant's world). Although Mardik Martin and Larry Cohen are credited as writers, according to Scorsese the script was prepared mainly to get the project off the ground with its sponsors, and subsequently used simply as an *aide-memoire* recalling the proposed questions: everything Catherine and Charles Scorsese say is unscripted. Filmed at home and pretty much at ease, both emerge as enormously likeable and as vivid talkers. But their reminiscences remain essentially scattershot, occasionally evocative (as when Charles recalls going over to Delancey Street on Saturdays as a boy to earn a few coppers by lighting gas jets for Jews forbidden to light their gas on the Sabbath) and often touching (like Catherine's memory of the year her elder brothers started work and they bought their first Christmas tree, a hitherto unknown joy since their parents' traditional celebration was Midnight Mass and family dinner the next day).

But mostly, interspersed with scraps of 8mm home movie and old footage of Hester Street, their stories add up to little more than the familiar immigrant picture of cramped housing conditions, ethnic mixtures first clashing then co-existing, hard times in the days of coal stoves and hand laundry ('our poor mothers worked'). It has a certain generalised relevance to Scorsese's work, sketching in the family environment that is largely taken for granted in *Who's That Knocking at My Door?* (where Catherine Scorsese played Harvey Keitel's mother) and *Mean Streets*. At a pinch, a case might be made for it as describing the painful building of a way of life which the next generation (the heroes of Scorsese's films) scornfully turned their backs on. But basically it stands or falls as a programme-filler. Funded by a grant from the National Endowment for the Humanities, and commissioned as part of a television series about immigrants called *Storm of Strangers*, it is said to be streets ahead of any of the other episodes in originality and execution.

MARTIN SCORSESE
By Mark Carducci

Our conversation took place in his suite at the Hotel St. Regis; the very same room where he, actress Ellen Burstyn and his associate producer, Sandra Weintraub, improvised, rehearsed and wrote the character of Alice. Like every Italian worth his pasta, Scorsese uses numerous hand gestures as he speaks. He is short and slim, almost to frailty, yet in his voice and very quick speech there is great vitality and self-assertiveness. His full beard makes his eyes stand out, and they too belie his seeming weakness, for in them one can see some of the strength that allows him to 'hold on', to have tenacity. The quality most critics lauded in Mean Streets, *that nervous electric energy, is very much a part of the personality of Martin Scorsese. The director operates under a slight handicap: since he was a child he has had recurring attacks of asthma. Only recently he was hospitalised in Los Angeles, preventing his acceptance of a New York Film Festival award for a short about his parents and the Italian heritage, the film called* Italianamerican.

Up until relatively recently you were considered a New York filmmaker. What led you to Los Angeles to work?
I had cut *Woodstock* for Fred Weintraub, and he had a picture called *Medicine Ball Caravan* he needed edited. He asked me to come out to the coast and do it for him in 1970. I remember Fred had a nine-and-a-half hour rough cut, so I really had to re-direct the whole picture; it had no concept at all. My first week in L.A. I met Roger Corman through a friend at William Morris. Roger is always interested in features by young film-makers, and he had seen *Who's That Knocking?*, which had just opened. What he did was to say, 'Here's a couple of thousand dollars; I want you to direct a picture. Every fifteen pages it has to have nudity, a little violence here and a little action there, otherwise you can do what you want with it.' Roger gives you great freedom as long as you stay within the 'Corman genre'. *Boxcar Bertha* had guns and costumes, so I accepted.

In relation to that film, John Cassavetes was quoted in* Esquire *as telling you that you had spent a year making three hours of bullshit and not to do it again. Was that actually his reaction to the film?
That fucking thing is such a misquote. Kit Carson called me three times to apologise for it. For the record, John did not like *Boxcar Bertha*. But he saw my two-and-a-half hour rough cut. The film works very well at 90 minutes; not so well at 150. John resented me doing an exploitation picture, something he has no interest in. At the time, he lectured me for several hours about it and gave me the encouragement to try and produce a script I had written years earlier originally called *Season of the Witch*. John advised me to revise it and do whatever I had to do to get it into production. So I took editing jobs and wrote *Mean Streets*, and as I had gotten to know people like Francis Coppola, the script was seen by people. The money finally came from a man named Jonathan Taplin, a road manager for The Band. I showed him my films and

Ellen Burstyn sings her nervous heart out in Alice Doesn't Live Here Anymore *(1975). Her career as a barroom chanteuse is a hybrid of movie romanticism and grimy realism.*

the script; he liked both and went with us as producer.

The violence in* Mean Streets *came easy to you?
Yes.

Did you ever kiss a gun?
Yes, actually that scene came from two sources – partially *The Wild Bunch* and partially from an experience I had. I once saw several Puerto Ricans fight at a baptism. They were all family, but one of them knelt in the middle of the street, made the sign of the cross and put a vendetta on his brother. You knew he meant business.

What about Harvey Keitel's burning his fingers all the time?
That was something they used to make us do on religious retreat to help us imagine the pains of hell. That was in 1960 though.

How was the long tracking shot of Keitel walking through the bar achieved?
That was devised by my cameraman, Ken Wakeford. We put a body brace on Harvey and put his coat over that. As he walked we had a grip hold the camera in balance with a board. We shot it three times, and that was it.

Getting away from **Mean Streets,** *I wonder whether you feel there are negative aspects to film school?*

It can do one basic harm. You can make a film that receives recognition, and you graduate thinking you should be given a feature to direct. It happened to me; I got a little ambitious and made a feature which didn't quite work. I know many ex-students who have the attitude that they won't come out to L.A. without a definite job. I've heard things like, 'I'm too good for that. I won't work in a lab. I won't carry that box.' If you won't, then fuck it; you won't be able to do anything. The idea is to hang around as many people as you can with your eyes and ears open and your mouth shut and to once in a while ask a question. You can't be too proud to edit for someone like Roger Corman.

So you feel L.A. is where it's at production-wise?

Yes, absolutely. Get that first picture made any way you can, then go to the place where it's all happening.

What is the general reaction to independent features in Hollywood?

They are looked down upon, especially independent features made in New York. They look down on most non-Hollywood-produced stuff except foreign films. They have that aura of 'art'. For a joke I felt like subtitling *Alice* and running the track backwards. Take a guy like Carrol Ballard – he's made some great documentaries, and he's only now getting the opportunity to direct his first feature, *Stallion*, through Francis and Cinema V.

What do you feel is wrong with Hollywood?

Tons of things, the situation will never be ideal. Though working with the studio on *Alice* meant no financial hassle, the studios have other ways of pressuring you. The worst of the pressure comes in having to use all your time and effort in making 'the deal'. I've never experienced the kind of hassles I'm going through right now – the aggravation, the fighting . . . I can't begin to tell you. Then some part of a deal falls through and all that fighting becomes meaningless. We're facing this on every project now: the deal isn't right or the actor isn't available or any one of a million other things is wrong.

How do you succeed against all this?

By tenacity – the ability to hold on. A good business sense is nice to have too. I don't have one, but I have people who take care of those things for me.

What was the impetus for your involvement in **Alice Doesn't Live Here Anymore**?

It was the result of a dinner Ellen Burstyn had with Francis Ford Coppola. She had asked him to recommend a good, young, New York filmmaker for a picture David Susskind owned. David went with her, because she told him Warners was anxious to make a film with her right away. Ellen and I met; I read the script and told her how I felt about it; we more or less agreed, and we had a picture.

What intrigued you about the script?

It dealt with a woman, and I wanted to better understand my relationships with women – to better understand the whole male-female thing. It was a form of therapy for me.

What kind of relationship did you have working with David Susskind?

None at all. The extent of his involvement was that he owned the property. We had a few meetings, but that was it.

It has been suggested that the sensibility in **Alice** *is quite different from the sensibility in* **Mean Streets,** *or at least superficially.*

I would agree with that. I wanted to make a film that was radically different from *Mean Streets* on a superficial level, but that was the same if you looked deeper into its emotions and feelings. That's where the two films are similar.

What kinds of things formed in your mind as you read the script as regards your conceptualisation of the finished film?

I'll tell you about my concepts for *Alice* by example. I grew up in a very structured family life, and my mother was always having people over to the house – for coffee or this or that – so in *Alice* you have a scene where Alice's girlfriend comes over for coffee. I used that to get across a feeling of being home. That's why Alice's house is filled with so many small details – some so small as to have merely a subliminal effect. The cups have names on them: Alice, Tommy, Donald. In one scene Alice is wearing an apron with little eggplants on it – eggplants because I'm Italian. Even the kitchen curtains have eggplants on them, though you may not notice them. The point is that all that detail was good for the actors and for me and consequently for the film as well. The actual visual 'look' of the picture formed in my mind when I saw Tucson for the first time. I usually get a lot from the locations themselves, and my first feelings about Tucson were that there was a lot of light and a lot of space. The amount of sunlight was tremendous. I come from New York where everything is kind of grey, and that's the way I like it. In Tucson I always had to wear huge sunglasses.

Adding to your visual look was a great deal of camera movement.

Right away I felt we should keep the camera moving, because the picture was on the move. That was my intention, and the moves were all worked out in advance. Whenever Alice is most confused or upset, the camera is kind of sliding to communicate an uneasy feeling to the audience. We used hand-held cameras for this on occasion. Sometimes we were forced to shoot hand-held, because the rooms were too small to shoot with a static camera. When Alice is feeling most secure, as in the kitchen scene with Kris Kristofferson, the camera hardly moves at all. As a matter of fact, it only moves twice: once when she rises to show him how she used to act as a kid, and again in a point-of-view shot when she's walking towards him. The camera is tracking in on Kris, because for many reasons Alice is moving in on him. The musical sequences were especially well-planned. Those numbers had to be mini-musicals.

In making the film, was there any improvisation with the actors, or did you rigidly follow a script?

It usually worked like this. Me, Ellen and Bob Getchell, the writer, would come up with new ideas. Ellen and I and other actors would meet in my hotel room, here in New York, and we would rehearse and improvise on videotape. Ellen would do an improvisation of Alice ten years after the movie ends, things like that. Then we would structure these tapes into new dialogue and scenes and give it to Bob to rewrite. The end of the picture was rewritten many times. The scene between Ellen and Diane Ladd in the bathroom was totally improvised, mostly in sessions beforehand and some on the set. A perfect example of an on-the-set improv was when Diane says, 'My husband hasn't spoken to me since the day Kennedy got shot.' Ellen came back with, 'Why, did he think you had something to do with it?' That was perfect for the character, and it kept the sense of humour we were after. But more often than not even improvised scenes were written down beforehand.

Could you talk about the Harvey Keitel character in **Alice**?

Harvey's character changed the least from the way it was originally written. He was the most accurately delineated. Some things were written to make him funnier, crazier. But he stayed pretty close to our original conception. I cast Harvey against the grain. It was unusual for him to play a non-Italian, even though he's Jewish. [*laughs*]

Some critics have called the character of Alice's husband the weakest character in the film.

He's the weakest for me as well. It's a pity, because Billy Green Bush is a fine actor. Since the first cut of *Alice* was three hours and fifteen minutes, we had to delete a great deal. We discovered that the picture really became the movie it was supposed to be when Alice got on the road. I had wanted to take the picture in one direction for twenty minutes and then have one of the main characters die, allowing the picture to go in another. But the sooner we got Alice moving, the more favourable were the preview audiences' responses. We had to keep compressing the beginning of the picture without losing too much. As a result the only realistic element we kept was when Billy and Ellen are in bed and she starts to cry a little, so he puts his arms around her and she understands. That's what's left of their relationship after thirteen years. We had many sequences between him and the kid – there's a whole dinner sequence lasting several minutes. That scene was like a battlefield, but it was all cut except for the tail end of it.

As an actress, what was Ellen Burstyn like to work with?

Ellen is the movie. The way Alice reacts is the way Ellen does. She is fantastically inventive and helpful. She doesn't let a director do all the work, but instead offers suggestions and variations. I got a lot of input on the character from Ellen. The film is practically a documentary of her.

Do you consider the film a woman's picture?

Not really. I wanted to make a picture about a person who is a woman and not the other way around. It's not a feminist picture. It's about people first and women second.

Why do you think there are so few good roles for women?
There aren't that many good scripts around. You wouldn't believe some of the stuff
I've been reading lately. One contained a scene for a major actress to play in, and she
was being tied to a toilet. There's just nowhere to go so a lot of actresses are developing their own ideas now. Ellen is writing something – so are Diane Ladd, Lee Grant
and Shirley MacLaine.

Can you talk about your writer, Robert Getchell, a bit?
Finding a guy like Getchell writing today is really interesting. His work is like thirties
stuff, with all that snappy dialogue and all. That was the idea in terms of tying the rest
of the picture in with the opening scene, which is that William Cameron Menzies-
type set. We used it to indicate Alice's aspirations – to show how much her mind was
into movies. Shooting on that set was great fun for me. The whole picture was fun,
because we tried crazy, experimental things like that.

How were you involved in Marlon Brando's Indian film?
I can't talk about that. I can talk about the Indian situation, but not the film situation. I think Marlon's picture has got to be made. You wouldn't believe the things we
saw when we got into the Indian way of life in America. It was like visiting a concentration camp. Living conditions were unbelievable . . . pitiful. Somehow the picture
has got to be made. That's all I can say.

Do you physically cut your films?
I cut all my pictures except *Alice*. I did cut a few scenes myself, but basically I left it
up to Marcia [Lucas]. I would go over her edits, and then she would re-cut until I was
satisfied. We worked very closely in these sessions as it was the first time I'd ever used
an editor.

Did you have final cut?
Nobody I know has final cut, not even Alfred Hitchcock. I am promised three pre-
views, however, and that's pretty fair. If at each succeeding preview the people continue walking out on the picture, you know you're going to have to talk to the studio
and make some changes their way. Sometimes their suggestions can be quite helpful.
Susskind gave me several good suggestions on cuts. He didn't say, 'Cut that,' or in any
way force me to, he just asked me to think about certain things.

Do you find yourself influenced by other directors, either American or European?
I guess when I was a student I was. I got a lot of input from France and Italy – and
Russia. *Mean Streets* has more in common with Wajda's *Ashes and Diamonds* than with
the gangster film. But I've gotten those influences out of my system.

Who are the directors you most admire?
John Ford is my favourite director. Of the directors working today that I admire,
many are my friends – Coppola, Cassavetes, Lucas, DePalma, Milius, Altman . . . I

don't know. I liked *Thieves [Like Us]*, *The Long Goodbye* and *McCabe and Mrs. Miller*. That's three, isn't it? I guess I like Altman.

Bogdanovich?
For me he's too classical, too straight. I admire his work, but I can't get emotionally involved in it, something I demand from any film I watch.

Do you draw some kind of line between art and entertainment?
I try not to. I hope *Alice* works as both. *Mean Streets* perhaps works more as entertainment.

How do you feel about film criticism?
I deal with criticism in a very simple way – I take it all personally. [*laughs*] No, not really. There's little you can do about the critics. I read a review which said my camera movements have no 'internal truth'. I guess I have to go through some mystical experience before I move my camera again! My main complaint with critics is that they often like pictures for the *wrong* reasons. They fail to grasp correctly what a film is saying and like it without ever really understanding why.

How valuable is critical acclaim?
Not very. Critical acclaim and money mean a great deal. And money alone means a great deal; that's all the distributors are truly interested in. Look at *The Exorcist*. It was pretty much destroyed critically and yet it is one of the biggest money-grossers of all time.

What do you think of the film?
I got scared. But not as scared as I got as a kid watching a film called *Isle of the Dead* by Mark Robson. *The Haunting* also scared me. I remember sitting in the third row at the Paramount Theatre late at night with all the guys from *Mean Streets* watching that. I also like some of Corman's stuff – *Tomb of Ligeia* is my favourite. Also Mario Bava's *Black Sunday*.

***Have you seen* Chinatown?**
I loved it. It's freaky . . . a really marvellous picture. Bob Towne, the man who wrote it, wrote *Tomb of Ligeia*, you know. I didn't know that until he told me one night when we had dinner together.

Any possibility you might be working with him in the future?
No, we're just friends. He's working on some things of his own right now. I know he's writing a beautiful script based on *Tarzan*, using the actual story.

What projects are you working on for the future?
Several I could talk about. One is called *Taxi Driver*, which Mike and Julia Phillips are going to produce. It'll be a low-budget New York picture. It's about a Mid-Western guy who's spent several years in Vietnam. He's asked why he drives a cab at night, and

he answers he can't sleep. It's based on the diaries of Arthur Bremer, the guy who shot [Governor George] Wallace. Paul Schrader wrote the script, and we hope Bobby De Niro will be in it. I'm also planning a musical called *New York, New York*. We'll be using existing music, forties music. The picture is about the decline of the big-band era, 1945 to 1952. We haven't cast it yet, but we need a good actress who can sing, like a Streisand. It should be a great deal of fun doing a musical. And if we do the picture, I'll shoot it all on sets; open it with a stock shot of the New York skyline, then go to the studio for the rest.

You've achieved that dream so many have: great success as a feature filmmaker. Do you feel any great pressure now to stay on top?
Yes, but success is mainly a matter of chance. To play it safe, you can take less risks. If I played it safe it wouldn't be hard at all to stay on top. All I'd have to do would be to direct the best properties of the year – you know, film that book. But that's wrong. You should make the pictures you want to make, and also those that you will learn from. *Taxi Driver* will be a kind of exorcism for me. That's why I have to make it. The key words are always 'have to'.

ALICE DOESN'T LIVE HERE ANYMORE
Reviewed by David Denby

Martin Scorsese's last film, *Mean Streets*, was so highly praised (in some quarters) and so poorly attended (almost everywhere) that it's already on the way towards achieving a kind of legendary lost-classic status. Critics loved the intentionally overripe texture and emotional hyperbole, but audiences felt oppressed, imprisoned, battered. The excesses of Scorsese's style – the cruel repetitions, the verbal (but not psychological) incoherence, the claustrophobia of the street, bar and bedroom nightworld – were more than many people could handle. Warners' incomprehensible ad campaign (the picture appeared to be a late forties/early fifties Richard Conte melodrama) and half-hearted distribution never allowed *Mean Streets* to find its proper audience, and the movie died.

Those who feared Scorsese might give in to industry pressures had nothing to worry about. *Alice Doesn't Live Here Anymore* is a lesser film than *Mean Streets*, an engaging, inconsistent movie with some stunning scenes and some others that don't work at all, but the director's feverish personality and style are unmistakable. They transform what might have been a feeble exercise in liberal conscientiousness (the film was produced by David Susskind) into a fitfully exciting (and perhaps controversial) movie.

At first glance, *Alice* would seem to be an entirely new direction. Set in the unfamiliar territory of the Southwest, it's a feminist-era, new-style 'woman's picture' and

Alice (Ellen Burstyn) abandons her ambition for the love of a good man. 1970s Country & Western /movie star Kris Kristofferson's role belies Alice's reputation as a 'feminist film'.

star vehicle (Ellen Burstyn) about a 35-year-old woman's search for a new life – on the road, singing, waiting on table, taking care of her twelve-year-old son – after her husband dies in an accident. Indeed, the picture begins disastrously, and it seems that Scorsese may have lost his way. A rather meaningless prologue sends up the flaming-sunset-and-plastic-wood style of 'farm' settings in late thirties/early forties musicals (i.e. *The Wizard of Oz*); Alice as a young girl, walking home on an intentionally phony path, dreams of singing better than Alice Faye, and we wonder what is being ridiculed: a girl's dreams? The unreality of old movie musicals? Everything in Scorsese's style tells us that life is chaotic, difficult, 'real', so the latter is hardly necessary. A quick cut to Alice's uneasy domestic life in Socorro, New Mexico 25 years later, and the feeling of discomfort and lack of focus persists. Husband (Billy Green Bush) is surly and unresponsive, son (Alfred Lutter) annoyingly infantile, and Alice thoroughly fed up, but the camera style is so zany and hyperactive (every shot is either a pan, a dolly, or a track) that we never get much of a fix on the relationships. The sequence appears to have been cut to the bone, and its intentions aren't always clear: when Alice mimics her husband's voice at the dinner table, we don't know what she's reacting against because we've barely heard him say a word.

Finally, husband dead, and mother and son launched on the road to Arizona, Scorsese's assurance returns and the picture takes hold. Still, it's odd material for him. What does he bring to it? Ellen Burstyn, who was determined to make the Robert Getchell screenplay (owned by David Susskind), reportedly requested Scorsese after seeing *Mean Streets* because she knew he would 'roughen' the material. As it turns out, one of the fascinations of *Alice* is the conflict between material that is very much in the Susskind mould of liberal, up-beat family drama and Scorsese's frenetic, life-is-a-battle sensibility, in other words, between 'dignity' and one possible kind of authenticity.

What did Burstyn mean by 'roughness'? First of all, Scorsese's characterisation. His people all seem to burn on a very short fuse; at any moment they might start screaming and cursing, throw themselves around the room, clobber someone, smash furniture. The instant rages, the explosive obscenity and charged-up, semi-improvised dialogue give the films their moments of grandeur and hilarity. Some of us get high on the style; for many others, it's like walking through a minefield. However, I think those who complained of the repetitiveness of the violence in *Mean Streets* will agree Scorsese has it under control in *Alice*.

One scene seems clearly to represent his feeling of how close, how omnipresent, violence is: as Alice and her son sleep one night in their motel room the sounds of a terrible fight come through the wall. The moment is frightening and oddly mysterious in its combination of violence and safety. Who hasn't held on to someone at 4 a.m., wondered at the sounds in the next room or the street, and felt the precariousness of the moment's shelter and peace? Soon enough, in *Alice*, the intrusion comes. An attractive woman travelling without a man is considered fair game by men of all sorts – this we know, and it could easily become a feminist commonplace. In the person of Harvey Keitel (the star of *Mean Streets* and *Who's That Knocking at My Door?*), playing Ben, the man who 'puts powder in bullet cases', the male threat is both hateful and scarily convincing. A grinning, idiotically self-assured young Westerner with cowboy hat, string tie, and scorpion pendant, Ben can't take no for an answer and Alice, weary of resisting, starts an affair. When his wife comes to protest, Ben arrives, too, and humiliates her in front of Alice, kicking her out the door and then wrecking Alice's room. Keitel's rage and cruelty here is extremely shocking: the silly young man has become a tyrant only because he knows he can get away with it. Scorsese directs (and Marcia Lucas cuts) the scene so we identify with Alice, sensing her humiliation at the sordidness of the affair, her outrage that the man can act this way and still imagine that he means something to her. The idiocy of men's using their physical strength to terrorise women and women's growing contempt for it has never been captured so powerfully on screen. A smoother, more tasteful director would have hesitated at the kicks, the screaming, snarling infantilism; the scene works precisely because Scorsese is willing to take Ben's macho lunacy to its limits.

What else did Burstyn mean by 'roughness'? Perhaps the way Scorsese works a set, exploring it, opening it up, charging through it until we know it like home. In *Mean Streets*, the neighbourhood bar, with its rituals of friendship and rivalry, becomes a complete world, as vivid in its own way as Rick's café. Here it's the cheap, greasy diner in which Alice becomes a waitress. Scorsese has an instinctive comic feel for the noise and chaos of the workaday world (I'd love to see him work in New York's garment district!). With dishes and obscenities flying back and forth, harassed, collapsing waitresses and miserably unsatisfied customers, the scenes in the diner achieve a kind of hilarious, heightened 'normality' just short of farce.

For the first time in his career, Scorsese is shrewd enough to play off against the riotous stuff with the kind of tenderness that wins an audience over. The friendship of Alice and the waitress Flo (Diane Ladd) is the best thing in the movie. (It's also the first real female friendship in movies in many years.) Diane Ladd, a blonde of a certain age with an infectious laugh and an Army sergeant's pleasure in obscenity, plays the slatternly, unromantic Flo with great panache; she's a worthy heir to Helen Broderick or Aline McMahon, the sceptical, tough-tender, never-met-the-right-man good broads of the thirties. For Flo, sex has been completely emptied of romance, and men are just silly slobs good for a laugh now and then; but Alice, younger, and still hoping, can't live alone, can't live without a man. Neither is satisfied with what she is, and yet together they seem to define the limited possibilities for a woman alone. Their friendship culminates in a potentially maudlin laughing/crying scene which is saved by the two actresses and Scorsese's perverse choice of a toilet as a location. Bad taste saves the day once again.

In other words, give Burstyn credit for sensing that Scorsese's intentional messiness and rather violent sincerity would bring to the feminist screenplay the conviction it lacked, the 'roughness' breaking through the conventional, right-minded attitudes. Indeed, it's heartening to see Scorsese move out of the macho world of his previous films without turning his heroine into a martyr or ideologue. The ending, when Alice settles down with a new man (the extraordinarily attractive Kris Kristofferson, in another effortlessly self-assured performance), may not please some of the militants, but it's right for this woman and this movie.

Ellen Burstyn, in her largest role, is an eminently likeable actress of obvious talent and clear ambition. Her technical skills are impressive. When she dresses up like a fancy prostitute for her singing audition, there's a wonderful slump of depression in her back as she enters a cheap bar; and her amateur singing is exactly right: thin, bodiless, rather well-mannered and pleasant but basically lifeless – Julie London without the necessary vulgarity, the show-biz seductiveness. Yet despite her skills there's something annoyingly facile about Ellen Burstyn. She runs through her emotions too quickly, and none of them seem to stick. Her all-too-flexible face is strangely unmemorable. Along with Gena Rowlands, another actress who acts too many emotions, it's hard to recall what she looks like in-between her movies.

She isn't quite a major actress and certainly not an old-style star. In *The Last Picture Show*, *The Exorcist*, and *Alice*, she has played basically the same role: the lonely young mother, 35-ish, soured on men but still looking. Her performances have plenty of bite (and before Burstyn it was rare to see a movie mother curse or go to bed with a man) but not the kind of stylised temperament that would make us care about her when the movie was over. I suppose her up-front, no-shit manner works against her chances to be a star. She's reassuringly normal and human, when what we really want (no matter how much we praise normality and humanity) is myth, glamour, personality. In this respect, she may have lost out on her chances for stardom in *Alice* by choosing to work with Scorsese – a-de-mythicising director if there ever was one. Her choice was courageous and intelligent, and she deserves honour for it.

CABBIN' FEVER
By Richard Goodwin

When he first conceived the idea for *Taxi Driver* back in 1973, aspiring screenwriter Paul Schrader was in a bad way. Not only had he lost his job at the American Film Institute, the L.A.-based film critic had been kicked out of his house by his wife. Schrader's homelessness and unemployment brought with it alcoholism and depression. His spirits sank so low that he even considered suicide; instead he wrote a bleak study of urban alienation that came to define the brutality of life on the American streets.

Taxi Driver told the story of Travis Bickle, a naïve, psychologically unstable loner whose loathing of the city's low-life inhabitants leads him to take arms against pimps and politicians alike. Dark and unrelenting, Schrader's script passed through the fingers of director Brian De Palma and producers Julia and Michael Phillips before it reached Martin Scorsese, a director from Roger Corman's stable who had just enjoyed his first critical success with *Mean Streets*. Scorsese loved the script and knew that *Mean Streets* star Robert De Niro was just the man to play Travis.

Twelve months after he contemplated suicide, Schrader signed his first major film contract. But although closing the deal solved some of Schrader's problems, it also marked the beginning of Scorsese's. The casting of fourteen-year-old Jodie Foster as child prostitute Iris raised charges of paedophilia, resulting in the presence of a social worker during the shoot. Scorsese quarrelled with producer Julia Phillips over the casting of Cybill Shepherd as Travis's fantasy woman, Betsy, and filming went way over schedule as leading man De Niro asked Scorsese about his 'motivation' for everything – from killing Harvey Keitel's pimp character Sport to such simple tasks as setting his cab's meter.

Even after filming wrapped, questions continued to be asked about *Taxi Driver*. Although the film was partly inspired by Jean-Paul Sartre's existentialist novel *Nausea*, it was also informed by the diaries of would be assassin Arthur Bremer, who shot and paralysed right-wing Governor George Wallace on 15 May 1972. Ironically, the film was later cited as a key influence on John Hinckley Jr., the deranged Jodie Foster fan who tried to impress his idol by shooting president Reagan on 30 March 1981.

While the debates over its political and sexual agenda continue, *Taxi Driver*'s power remains beyond question. An outstanding movie from one of the most creative eras in US cinema, Scorsese's film represents the high points in the careers of its leading participants. The film also had the rather dubious distinction of being grouped in with the glut of vigilante movies that followed 1974's *Death Wish*, although *Taxi Driver* undoubtedly contains a redemptive quality glaringly absent from its rivals. As Schrader once explained: 'There are warning signs in the film that could help to prevent someone who is isolated from becoming like Travis Bickle. If you are on the edge, this is the film that could pull you back from the precipice. It certainly did it for me.'

Paul Schrader: In 1973, I had been through a particularly rough time. My marriage broke up and I had to quit the American Film Institute. I was out of work; I was out of the AFI; I was in debt. I fell into a period of real isolation, living more or less in my car. One day, I went to the emergency room in serious pain, and it turned out I had an ulcer. While I was in the hospital talking to the nurse, I realised I hadn't spoken to anyone in two or three weeks. It really hit me, an image that I was like a taxi driver, floating around in this metal coffin in the city, seemingly in the middle of people but absolutely, totally alone.

Martin Scorsese: The whole film is very much based on the impressions I have as a result of growing up in New York and living in the city.

Paul Schrader: At the time I wrote it I was very enamoured of guns, I was very suicidal, I was drinking heavily, I was obsessed with pornography in the way a lonely person is, and all those elements are up front in the script . . . Right after writing it, I left town for about six months. I came back to L.A. after I was feeling a little stronger emotionally and decided to go at it again. I was a freelance critic at the time. I had written a review of *Sisters* and interviewed Brian De Palma at his place on the beach. That afternoon we were playing chess and somehow the fact that I had written a script came up. So I gave it to him and he liked it a lot and wanted to do it.

Brian De Palma: I loved the script. Paul said he had based it on Arthur Bremer, the psychopath who had tried to assassinate [right-wing Alabama Governor] George Wallace. But it was the script's autobiographical quality that made it truly compelling.

Julia Phillips: After I read the script I refused to be alone in the house with him. He was following [John] Milius around and had bought his own .45, an act of romantic adulation.

Martin Scorsese: Brian told me Paul had this script, *Taxi Driver*, that he didn't want to do or couldn't do at that time, and wondered if I'd be interested in reading it. So I read it and my friend read it and she said it was fantastic: we agreed that this was the sort of picture we should be making.

Julia Phillips: Schrader always scared me. When we first met him, after Brian De Palma gave us *Taxi Driver*, he was so shy he talked into his armpit.

Martin Scorsese: *Taxi Driver* was almost like a commission, in a sense. Bob was the actor, I was the director and Paul wrote the script. The three of us – Schrader, Bob and I – just came together. It was exactly what we wanted, it was one of the strangest things.

Paul Schrader: *Taxi Driver* was as much a product of luck and timing as everything else – three sensibilities together at the right time, doing the right thing. It was still a low-budget, long-shot movie, but that's how it got made.

Martin Scorsese: That year, 1974, De Niro was about to win the Academy Award for *The Godfather Part II*. Ellen Burstyn won the award for *Alice Doesn't Live Here Anymore* and Paul had sold *The Yakuza* to Warner Brothers, so it was all coming together. Michael and Julia Phillips, who owned the script, had won an award for *The Sting* and figured there was enough power to get the film made, though in the end we barely raised the very low budget of $1.3 million. In fact for a while we even thought of doing it on black-and-white video!

Paul Schrader: At one point, we could have financed the film with Jeff Bridges, but we elected to hold out and wait until we could finance it with De Niro.

Brian De Palma: It's true, Neil Diamond screen-tested for *Taxi Driver*. Neil wanted to get into movies and someone thought this would be an appropriate vehicle. Then Jeff Bridges got an Oscar nomination and he became the preferred choice. Bob was always in the frame, though. He was Travis Bickle.

Julia Cameron: In Martin, Bobby found the one person who could talk for fifteen minutes about the way a character would tie a knot. I saw them go at it for ten hours non-stop.

Martin Scorsese: Paul said, 'What about De Niro? He was great in *Mean Streets*.' And it turned out Bob had a feeling for people like Travis.

Julia Phillips: I think Travis is someone people should know about. I know he is out there, created by American culture and etched in stone by the Vietnam War.

Robert De Niro: There are underground things about yourself that you don't want to discuss. Somehow these things are better expressed on paper or on film.

Jodie Foster: At first I didn't want to do the part, but only because I was worried my friends would tease me about it afterwards. I thought, 'Wow, they've got to be kidding'. It was a great part for a 21-year-old, but I couldn't believe they were offering it to me. I was the Disney Kid.

Martin Scorsese: I never had any doubts about Jodie. She's always very fresh and very clear in her personality. She takes direction exceptionally well and has a natural craft, a natural capacity when acting, which is a delight.

Jodie Foster: I spent four hours with a shrink to prove that I was normal enough to play a hooker. It was the role that changed my life. For the first time I played something completely different. But I knew the character I had to play – I grew up just three blocks from Hollywood Boulevard and I saw prostitutes like Iris every day.

Harvey Keitel: When we did *Mean Streets* I was living in Greenwich Village and by *Taxi Driver* I had moved to Hell's Kitchen. I had seen a lot of pimps in my neighbourhood.

I just put a number of them together, and out came Sport.

Julia Phillips: Marty's misogyny was apparent from his casting of Cybill Shepherd as Betsy. We had interviewed just about every blonde on both coasts and still he kept looking. I liked Farrah Fawcett, her fine bones, her aquiline profile, her big teeth and her thin body. Marty picked Cybill for her big ass; a retro Italian gesture, I always felt. In the end he had to give her line-readings and De Niro hated her.

Martin Scorsese: The process of making the film, for me, was more important than the final result.

Paul Schrader: Bob was so determined to get the character of Travis down, he drove a cab for a couple of weeks. He got a licence, had his fingerprints taken by the police and hit the streets. He made quite a lot of money.

Martin Scorsese: I drove with him a couple of nights. He said he got the strangest feeling when he was hacking, like he was totally anonymous. People would say anything, do anything, in the back of his cab, as if he wasn't there at all.

Robert De Niro: I am normally a fairly quiet man, but I chatted with my passengers, keeping within the character I was about to play.

Martin Scorsese: One time he picked up a guy who happened to be an actor. The guy was like, 'Jesus Christ, one year you're winning an Oscar and now you're driving cabs? Guess it's hard to find a steady job?' Bob explained what he was doing. The guy just put a hand on his shoulder and said, 'It's OK, Bobby, I've been there too.'

Harvey Keitel: I worked with a pimp for a few weeks in creating the role. We wrote nearly all of the dialogue, me and this pimp. I recorded the improvisations we did. He'd play this pimp and I'd play the girl; I'd see the way he'd treat me, then I would play the pimp and he'd play the girl. We did that for a few weeks over at the Actors Studio.

Jodie Foster: There was a welfare worker on the set every day and she saw the daily rushes of all my scenes and made sure I wasn't on the set when Robert De Niro said a dirty word.

Martin Scorsese: Everything was story-boarded, even the close-ups, because we had to shoot so fast. It would have to be, 'Get this shot!' Then, 'OK, got it.' Then, 'Go on, OK, next.' That's the way it had to go.

Jodie Foster: You rarely have a director like Martin Scorsese or a co-star like Robert De Niro, who rehearses and rehearses until you get the feeling that for the time you're with him he is the character. It's so real it's frightening.

Martin Scorsese: The scene I did in the taxi cab was filmed during the last week of shooting. I learned a lot from Bob in that scene. I remember saying, 'Put down the flag, put down the flag.' De Niro said, 'No. Make me put it down.' And Bobby wasn't going to put down the flag until he was convinced that I meant it. And then I understood. His move had to be a certain way and if he didn't feel it, the move wasn't going to be right. For me, it was a pretty terrifying scene to do.

Jodie Foster: Marty chews his nails, scratches his head, pulls his shirt out, worries and worries and worries. He worries so much about moviemaking that at the end of every movie he winds up in the hospital with ulcers.

Martin Scorsese: I was accused in *Mean Streets* of just showing the garbage on the streets. When I was shooting *Taxi Driver* it was filthy because of a garbage strike and everywhere I aimed the camera there were mounds of garbage. I said, 'They're going to kill me! Guys, take some of the garbage.' In L.A., with *Mean Streets*, we had to put garbage in the street to make it look like New York.

Paul Schrader: The dialogue is somewhat improvised. The most memorable piece of dialogue in the film is an improvisation: the 'Are you looking at me?' part. In the script it just says, *Travis speaks to himself in the mirror.* Bobby asked me what he would say and I said, 'Well, he's a little kid playing with guns and acting tough.' So De Niro used this rap that an underground New York comedian had been using at the same time as the basis for his lines.

Martin Scorsese: Victor [Magnotta, a friend of Scorsese's from NYU] came back from Vietnam and we went with him one night for dinner. He told us some of the things he had done or had happened to him. Horror stories. During dinner, Bob was asking him questions about Special Forces. [Victor] told us that, in Saigon, if you saw a guy with his head shaved – like a little Mohawk – that usually meant those people were ready to go into a certain Special Forces situation. You didn't go near them. They were ready to kill. They were in a psychological mode to go.

Jodie Foster: Actually, I think the only thing that could have had a bad effect on me was the blood in the shooting scene. It was really neat, though. It was red sugary stuff. And they used Styrofoam for bones. And a pump to make the blood gush out of a man's arm after his hand was shot off.

Robert De Niro: I once told Marty that we should put together a movie of outtakes. That whole slaughter scene in the hallway took us about four or five takes to shoot. Things went wrong technically. There are a lot of special effects and with those things something always goes wrong. You have this sort of serious, dramatic kind of carnage going on and all of a sudden somebody drops something or the machinery breaks down. It just blows the whole thing and it turns out to be funny. Oddly enough, in that sort of scene – I guess because it's so gruesome – everybody's ready to laugh. There was a lot of laughing and joking during the shooting between takes. I remember that. It was a lighter period, even though the material was very heavy.

Albert Brooks: My role was only indicated in the script, so I had to write it. Paul Schrader once said the funniest thing to me. He said, 'Thank you, I didn't understand that character.' And I thought, 'That's the character you don't understand? You understand Harvey Keitel and Travis Bickle perfectly, but the guy who works in the campaign office you're not so sure of?'

Martin Scorsese: I never thought *Taxi Driver* would make a dime.

Paul Schrader: There was a very good feeling around the making of the film, everything felt right about it, and I remember the night before it opened we all got together and had dinner and said, 'No matter what happens tomorrow we have made a terrific movie and we're damn proud of it, even if it goes down the toilet.' And the next day, I got up and went over to the theatre for the noon show. There was a long line that went all the way around the block, but I absolutely had to be let in. And then I realised that this huge line was already for the two o'clock show, not the noon show! So I ran inside and watched the film and everyone was standing at the back and there was a sense of exhilaration about what we had done. We knew we'd never repeat it.

Robert De Niro: The whole alienation thing probably affected people. That's the thing with movies. You do them in a personal way and people are affected and you never know why.

Paul Schrader: Jean-Luc Godard once said that all great movies are successful for the wrong reasons, and there were a lot of wrong reasons why *Taxi Driver* was successful. The sheer violence of it brought out the Times Square crowd.

Martin Scorsese: I was shocked by the way the audiences took the violence. I saw *Taxi Driver* once in a theatre, on opening night, and everyone was yelling and screaming at the final shoot-out. When I made it I didn't intend to have the audience react with that feeling – 'Yes, do it. Let's go out and kill!'

Jodie Foster: I was literally skipping across the Yale campus with my friend when I heard Reagan had been shot [30 March 1981].

Martin Scorsese: In terms of the John Hinckley shooting, people ask me how I feel about it. Well, I'm a Catholic. It's easy to make me feel guilty.

Julia Phillips: Hinckley had three obsessions: Jodie Foster, writing and Nazism – he's one of the few people to have read *Mein Kampf* cover to cover. Before he shot Reagan, he'd planned to shoot Jimmy Carter.

Martin Scorsese: I got to the [1980] Academy Awards and we were the first ones let in. Then I had to go to the men's room and suddenly these three big guys came with me. Three big guys with jackets. I said, 'Gee, this security is incredible tonight.' A few years earlier, when Jodie and I were nominees, I had received a threatening letter about *Taxi Driver* – 'If Jodie Foster wins for what you made her do, you will pay for it with your life.' So we got the FBI then. So now I said, 'Well, this security is even better than the last time, this is fantastic.' I went backstage with Robert Redford to put some sort of statement together. The FBI didn't want me moving around. Everybody knew why but me. Redford told me that a connection to *Taxi Driver* had been made in the shooting of the President. I never thought in a million years that there was a connection with the film. It turned out even the limo driver was FBI.

Julia Phillips: I ran into [*Easy Rider* executive producer] Bert Schneider at a soiree. 'See, *Taxi Driver* wasn't such a bad movie,' I smiled. And Bert said, 'If it was really great Hinckley would have killed him.'

Martin Scorsese: Movies don't kill people. People kill people. I do not regret having made *Taxi Driver*. Nor do I believe it was an irresponsible act – quite the reverse. Bob and I are at one on this.

Paul Schrader: I'm not opposed to censorship in principle but I think that if you censor a film like *Taxi Driver* all you do is censor a film, not confront a problem. These characters are running around and can be triggered by anything. A few years ago, they did a study about incitement to rape, and the thing that cropped up most often was the old Coppertone suntan oil ad – it had a little puppy tugging at a girl's swimsuit. It had just the right mixture for these rapists of adolescent sexuality, female nudity, rear entry, animals, violence . . .

Jodie Foster: *Taxi Driver* completely changed my life. It was the first time anyone asked me to create a character that wasn't myself. It was the first time I realised that acting wasn't just this hobby you just sort of did, but that there was actually some craft.

Paul Schrader: When I talk to younger film-makers they tell me that it was really the film that informed them, that it was their seminal film, and listening to them talk I really can see it as a kind of social watermark. But it was meant as a personal film, not a political commentary.

Jodie Foster: I think it's one of the finest films that's ever been made in America. It's a statement about America. About violence. About loneliness. Anonymity. Some of the best works are those that have tried to even imitate that kind of film, that kind of style. It's just classic. I felt when I came home every day that I'd really accomplished something.

Additional material: *Schrader on Schrader & Other Writings* edited by Kevin Jackson (Faber & Faber); *Taxi Driver* by Paul Schrader (script, Faber & Faber); *Scorsese on Scorsese* edited by David Thompson and Ian Christie (Faber & Faber); *You'll Never Eat*

Lunch in This Town Again by Julia Phillips (Heinemann); *Untouchable: Robert De Niro Unauthorised* by Andy Dougan (Virgin); *Martin Scorsese: A Journey* by Mary Pat Kelly (Secker and Warburg); *Jodie Foster: The Most Powerful Woman in Hollywood* by Philippa Kennedy (Macmillan); *Martin Scorsese* by Andy Dougan (Orion Media).

SCORSESE ON *TAXI DRIVER* AND HERRMANN
By Carmie Amata

You're very good in **Taxi Driver***. Did you dream about becoming a movie star when you were a child?*
I'm not an actor; I only did that part because the actor cast in it couldn't get away from another picture he was doing. It's a short scene so we postponed it until the last two days of shooting. When he still couldn't do it, I did it because it was too late by then to get another actor.

How do you feel about the criticism the violence in your work receives from some quarters?
No matter what you've learned in terms of dramatic structure and all, you ultimately make a film on your own. No school can teach you how to make a film. In other words, you have to know who you are, or you can't really have your film mean anything to you, or to anyone else. Knowing who you are is a major necessity, and once you've fulfilled that requirement, you've got to make a picture the best way you know how and you can't really think in terms of how to make it palatable for everyone. With *Taxi Driver* I wanted a reaction from everybody who sees it because I do feel very strongly about the film.

But is anger an acceptable reaction to you?
Who wants to make people angry all the time? You don't really want to do that, but we know that anger is bound to be there. It's something that comes from very harmless things, too. I mean, a lot of people were angry about *Alice Doesn't Live Here Anymore*.

Why?
The film was presented by the distributor [Warner Bros.] as a feminist tract, which it was not. People went to see it as that –

And reviewed it as that.
And reviewed it as that. Actually it was a film about relationships and it stands on its own merits in that area, despite the fact that it was not a strong feminist tract.

Was anyone in the old neighbourhood angry about **Mean Streets***?*

Most of my friends – the friends that the picture is really about – liked it. The other guys, the ones who knew me and talked to me about it, well, they were offended by the film at first, but eventually they came around. In the long run, the neighbourhood took pride in it.

There's a lot of violence in the world today, and in one form or another it all seems to crop up in your films. Why is that?
I hate it. I hate violence, I've never ever been in a fight, although I grew up in a very volatile area. That, by the way, is what I tried to get into *Mean Streets*. But as much as I hate violence, I know that it's in me, in you, in everyone and I want to explore it. That means the small violences, too. There are a lot of small violences, too. In *Taxi Driver* they come through in a lot of the dialogue, like when Bobby [De Niro] and Harvey [Keitel] are talking in the doorway for the first time. They're playing with each other when Bobby asks him about the young prostitute [Jodie Foster], but there's a very violent undertone when they talk about doing it with girls. There's such a degrading violence about the way those two human beings are talking about each other and about other human beings.

The scene has an incredible spontaneity about it. Was it improvised?
The only thing that's totally improvised, that came in about an hour before we shot it, are the scenes with Peter Boyle. Albert Brooks' part needed to be built up so we worked on them, built them up through improvisation and had Paul [Schrader] come in to re-write them for organisation before we shot them. Of course there's improvisation throughout with a couple of natural lines and reactions, but basically everything was written in Paul's script. He wrote a great script. I did the film in the first place because it came very close to saying what I'd have probably said if I'd written it.

I'd like to thank you for not using slow motion during any of the killings.
Thank you. I'm pleased you agree that killings are not pretty and that violence isn't pretty.

I think most people would agree that they aren't, don't you?
I hope so! But what I mean is that I think those things should be shown as being ugly and awful. At least that's how I see them and how I must, therefore, present them. Actually, the climactic slaughter wasn't entirely realistic. We shot it slightly off-speed, not only to show bullets going through people, but to show reactions. A lot of the picture is like that, slightly off-edge and a little paranoid; like the camera will always move in the opposite direction from what you'd expect. That's just to throw you a little off, the way Travis does, because he's full of contradictions. Also, many of Bobby's close-ups aren't at the usual 24 frames per second. They're at 36, which makes them a little slower, more deliberate and off-kilter than the rest.

Travis isn't really so 'off-kilter' from the rest when you consider the sequence where the store owner beats up the black boy who was trying to rob him. The boy had already been shot, he was helpless, and yet –

Yes. Certainly. That's the point. It's very important there to realise that the store owner has probably been robbed five or six times and he's very angry. He says, 'Now! Now's my chance to get even.' It's not very nice, but that's the reality of the situation. It is utterly sickening, sure, but while we were shooting that scene, a man was killed just around the corner at 86th and Columbus. All that stuff is real. We didn't know which cops were for us and which were for the real killing around the corner. Everything got mixed together and we really couldn't tell, so we just shot whatever was happening around us. Certainly, you don't condone or excuse any of that violence; you just present it.

And offer no solutions?
I don't see that as my prerogative. Another big reason why I did *Taxi Driver*, beside the fact that Paul's script was one of the best I'd read, is to say, 'Look! It's not pretty, but this is it. What can we do about it?'

What would you say to people who don't want to see similarities between themselves and the Travis Bickles of the world?
You mean what *do* I say to them. A lot of my friends are like that. A couple of them say to me, 'Yeah, yeah, people are all a little crazy these days, but nobody wants to go to the movies and see that they are!' I say don't go to see the movie! If you can't or don't want to face that about yourself, that's your problem. What can I say? All I can do is try to present, as closely as possible to the truth, what we're like as I see it. And in a picture like *Taxi Driver* or *Alice* people start relating to themselves in all kinds of ways. Yet they still keep missing each other. I don't know; I don't have the answers. It's disturbing, but then, life can be disturbing. It really can be and who has the answer to that?

The fact that Bernard Herrmann finished recording his score for Taxi Driver *only hours before he died makes the film a particularly important one for film music lovers, who realise that his death has left a void which may never be filled; certainly not with anyone so colourful and talented as he was.*
When I asked producer Michael Phillips to add his comments on Herrmann to those of Martin Scorsese's, he was more than eager to do so, for he, like the director, was as awed by the composer's consummate talent and unerring judgement as he was proud to have known him.

When did you decide that you wanted Herrmann to do the score?
Scorsese: At the very beginning.
Phillips: We really discussed the use of Benny long before we started the film. [*Taxi Driver* was shot in New York in July and August of 1975.]

Was it very difficult to get him to do it?
Scorsese: He didn't want to work in this country ever since his break-up with Hitchcock over *Torn Curtain*. Hitchcock wanted him to do that score, but at the time [1966] they wanted hit tunes coming out of film scores, and Lew Wasserman [head

of Universal] wanted a hit single. Benny said, 'I don't do hit singles; I write music!' And Hitchcock said he'd have to get someone else then, because Universal was where he did his films. It was his life, so to speak.

Phillips: Benny worked out of London from that time on. Although in 1973, when he did *Sisters* for Brian De Palma, he went to New York briefly, when the film was cut, to meet with Brian. *Sisters* was an independent production, shot in Canada I believe, so they could record the score in London without any union problems. But we were financed by a major studio [Columbia] and we were locked into using American musicians. Union demands state that a film shot in America must be scored by American musicians. Benny wrote the main theme, the love theme, and made a sample tape in England with eleven musicians and sent it to us. But the entire score was finally recorded in California.

De Palma wrote a tribute to Herrmann in **The Village Voice** *about the time that* **Sisters** *was released in the US, wherein he said that he found him loud, brutally frank and almost invariably right. Would you agree with De Palma?*

Scorsese: I knew Benny for about two years and we got to be very, very friendly. He was fine to work with if you just talked to him, explained it to him . . . like I'd say, 'Benny, I really think it needs this, or it needs that, but I'm not quite sure of exactly what.' If he respected your work, he'd come up with it on his own and he wouldn't give you a hard time.

Phillips: His understanding was uncanny. For example, we were on the recording stage and, if you remember at the end of the slaughter, there's a reprise of the main theme, the love theme, only this time it's done in a very brutal fashion. Throughout the film, whenever you see a woman you hear [*humming*] da-da-dada-da. But at the end of the slaughter it's DA-DA-DADA-DUM-M-M! We heard that for the first time on the recording stage and Benny explained that the reason he did it that way was to show that this was where Travis' fantasies about women led him. His illusions, his self-perpetuating way of dealing with women had finally brought him to a bloody, violent outburst and Benny's music certainly illuminated that to me. I had never thought of it in terms of what Benny said, but Bobby [De Niro] and I both said, 'God, he's right.' Absolutely. Perfect.

Scorsese: The score works because Benny understood, and I mean *really* understood, the picture so well.

Whose idea was the last credit – 'Our gratitude and respect; Bernard Herrmann, June 29, 1911 – December 24, 1975'?

Phillips: Marty and I talked about it and I just wrote it.

According to the wire service reports, Herrmann finished recording the score only two hours before he died. Is that true?

Phillips: Actually, we had two days set for recording. We finished the main score in one-and-a-half days and we were supposed to come back the next day to re-record the love theme. We'd already recorded it, but we wanted to do it again. But out of consideration for Benny's health – it was very bad and he was very feeble – we were going to postpone re-recording for another day. But he said, 'No, let's do it today.' We knocked it off in one-and-a-half hours and we were finished by five p.m. He died that night in the middle of his sleep.

Do you think that his coming back to Hollywood may have had something to do with it?
Scorsese: He'd been ill for years of course, and it was an emotional homecoming in many ways. The first day on the recording stage, all the musicians came around just to greet him and pay their respects.
Phillips: There's a very historical feeling in the fact that he died in Hollywood. I'm still trying to digest, to gain a perspective on his coming back to California and dying there. I do feel the trip contributed to his death. And he knew it might; he didn't want to come back. He complained about his health. He didn't like Hollywood and he was careful to stay away. But, ultimately, he chose to come back when we told him what the situation was, that we couldn't – not wouldn't – but that we were not permitted by the union to have him record his music himself unless he did it here. All of this played a part in his dying.
Scorsese: It's the first time he ever really used jazz in a score; he was very proud of the entire thing.
Phillips: When he died, his wife said that he was very happy with his work. She said that he felt that *Taxi Driver* was his best score in at least a decade. Considering what happened, that's a nice thing for us to remember.

TAXI DRIVER
Review Analysis from *FilmFacts*

Synopsis

'Loneliness has followed me my whole life.' – Travis Bickle

Travis Bickle is a 26-year-old ex-Marine from the Mid-West who drives a cab in New York City. Unable to sleep, he works an extra-long night shift (twelve hours, six days a week) and is willing to take any type of passenger to any type of neighbourhood. A loner incapable of communicating with even his fellow cabbies, he usually spends his off hours in porno movie houses eating junk food, or sitting alone in his dingy room and describing in a notebook diary how he hates the city – how he'd like to see all the scum and filth, all the hookers, pimps, muggers, queers and junkies, flushed off the streets into the sewers. Then one day he sees an attractive blonde in a white dress who somehow seems above it all. Following the young woman, Betsy, to where she works, the storefront campaign headquarters of presidential candidate Senator

Drug-using child whore Iris (Jodie Foster) takes breakfast with Travis, in Taxi Driver *(1976). 'Do you ever look at your own eyeballs in the mirror?' she asks the No-Doz-popping paranoid.*

Charles Palantine, Bickle spies on her from his cab until he musters up the courage to invite her out for a cup of coffee. Intrigued, she accepts, and later agrees to go with him on a date. But when he takes her to a 42nd street porno theatre, she walks out in disgust and refuses to answer his phone calls or acknowledge his flowers. Furious at the rejection, Bickle barges into the campaign office, creates a scene, and lashes out at Betsy for being just like 'all the others'. Two other individuals also leave their mark on Bickle: a twelve-year-old prostitute named Iris whom Bickle sees being roughly treated by her lover-pimp, and a bearded passenger who tells Bickle how he intends to blow apart his faithless wife with a magnum .44. As 'the bad feelings' in his head intensify, Bickle buys a small arsenal of guns and embarks on a rigid training program: he exercises daily, eats only food that will 'purify' his body, perfects his marksmanship, and devises a special sleeve holster for a gun as well as a boot holder for a commando knife. Motivating this discipline is Bickle's decision to assassinate Palantine; and while familiarising himself with the candidate's pattern of public appearances, Bickle visits a campaign site in a park – unaware that his conversation with a secret service agent has aroused suspicion. Eventually, he gets the chance to prove his expertise with a gun when a black hoodlum attempts to rob a grocery store and Bickle coldly shoots him down (but flees because he lacks a gun permit). Upon once more spotting twelve-year-old Iris, Bickle approaches her, makes a fifteen-minute booking with her pimp Sport, and goes to her room. But he will not permit sex; instead, he urges her to return to school and her parents. When she dismisses the idea and calls him square, and repeats it the next day at a breakfast shop, Bickle formulates the final plan for the mission he now believes is his destiny. After mailing Iris a note and all his money, he sets out to assassinate Palantine. His head shaved like a Mohican and wearing dark glasses, he edges into a crowd gathering to hear a Palantine speech; but before Bickle can draw his pistol, he is recognised by a secret service man and forced to run. His crusade thwarted, Bickle returns to his room, changes his shirt, and goes to rescue Iris from her bondage. After firing a bullet into Sport's stomach, he storms into Iris' tenement and erupts into a frenzy of killing. Superficially wounded by the pursuing Sport, Bickle kills him with several more shots, blasts the hand off a collector-hood outside Iris' door, fires round after round into the hysterical girl's mobster customer, and culminates the bloodbath by firing point blank into the head of the collector-hood. Finally out of ammunition, the exhausted Bickle slumps onto a couch and greets the arriving police by lifting a hand dripping with blood to his temple and firing an imaginary bullet. Ironically, he emerges from the carnage as a public hero who saved a victimised teenager from a life of degradation; laudatory newspaper articles and a letter of gratitude from Iris' parents in Pittsburgh adorn the walls of his room, and there is a distinct change in the attitude of his fellow cabbies. Finally, Betsy gets into his cab one night, and, as he drives her home, she tells him she has heard the news about him. But when she tries to pay her fare, Bickle refuses the money, slams down the hack's meter flag, smiles at her, and drives his cab toward the blazing neon lights of Times Square . . .

Critique

'*Taxi Driver* is the first important American movie of the year, and it should become a legitimately controversial hit,' asserted the *Washington Post*'s Gary Arnold; and Arnold's evaluation of what he termed 'a powerfully envisioned and detailed study of a psychotic personality' was confirmed by the film's generally laudatory notices and outstanding business in its first wave of US engagements. 'What finally makes the movie so compelling is director Martin Scorsese's scathing vision of New York as a fiery inferno of neon lights and relentlessly hostile populace,' noted the *NY Daily News*' Kathleen Carroll in her three-and-a-half star review, and the *San Francisco Chronicle*'s John L. Wasserman agreed that '*Taxi Driver* is riveting from beginning to end – superlative in its seedy, gutter atmosphere, awesome in the flair of a dozen different sequences and terrifying in a climactic scene of human carnage next to which Sam Peckinpah's work appears positively pastoral.' Additionally, most critics not only seconded the verdict of *Variety*'s 'Murf' that the 'powerful film' was 'an excellent credit for Scorsese', but also concurred that it was 'a terrific showcase for the versatility of star Robert De Niro'. Discussing the actor's work in his second collaboration with Scorsese,* *Cue*'s William Wolf raved that 'De Niro gives an astonishingly convincing, many-faceted performance of award stature,' Wasserman predicted that 'De Niro will probably win the Best Actor Academy Award next year for this portrayal,'

Miss Carroll praised his 'altogether devastating performance,' both *Time*'s Richard Schickel and *Saturday Review*'s Judith Crist called his work 'stunning', and *Newsweek*'s Jack Kroll labelled him 'the most remarkable young actor of the American screen'. Apart from hailing the film's direction and star, the majority of critics also cited the other performers and craftsmen whose contributions yielded what Wolf dubbed 'a jolting film to remember'. 'Top acting honours,' according to *The Village Voice*'s Andrew Sarris, 'have to go to Jodie Foster's breathtakingly goofy teenage hooker who inspires the film's ultimate bloodbath,' while *The Hollywood Reporter*'s Arthur Knight (who found the picture 'chilling' and 'horrifying') offered 'a special word for Cybill Shepherd' – 'I seriously doubt whether any other young actress could have caught so well all the shadings of her Betsy.' Mrs Crist said that 'Harvey Keitel is smashing, Miss Shepherd is perfect and Scorsese himself does a fine bit as a masochistic cuckold,' and Kroll added that Peter Boyle was 'the embodiment of the cab driver as ponderous philosopher'. While Michael Chapman's cinematography was widely praised for having 'caught the grimly garish look of the city by night, the grey sterility by day' (the *Los Angeles Times*' Charles Champlin), the most frequently mentioned technical contribution was the late Bernard Herrmann's score. Among those who admired it, Knight said 'it's one of his best, filled with shivery, anticipatory drum beats, lush saxophone rides at the appropriate moments, and Miles Davisish astringent trumpet tones to underscore De Niro's growing madness.' However, this adulatory outpouring from many critics was offset somewhat by a sizeable minority of reviewers with major reservations, although only *The New Republic*'s Stanley Kauffmann felt these demurrals weighed heavily against the film. The principal objection to *Taxi Driver* was what Champlin called the 'ambiguous coda following the bloodbath'; stating that the ending of this 'nerve-scraping new film' 'seems curiously tacked on and unconvincing,' Champlin felt the coda presented the 'currently fashionable and idiot thesis that violence is good for what ails you, a right rite of passage to maturity and mental health.' Likewise, Mrs Crist found this 'ironic twist' a 'fuzzy-headed, grabbed-at conclusion that smacks of last-minute lack of inspiration', and even the otherwise favourably disposed Wasserman complained that the 'almost trick ending is so "ironic" that it changes the film's entire thrust and, in trying to Make Us Think, compromises that which has gone before.' On the other hand, while Schickel felt it 'a nice irony that this outburst of extraordinarily gory violence could convert an individual who was within a hair trigger length of becoming a national horror into a local hero,' he otherwise faulted the film's 'shocked innocence' and 'easy sociologising'. *The NY Times*' Vincent Canby was more specific than most of his colleagues in affixing blame for the film's seeming 'less than the sum of its parts' – 'The original screenplay by Paul Schrader, one of Hollywood's new young hopes (writers' division), imposes an intellectual scheme upon Travis' story that finally makes it seem too simple' and 'robs the film of mystery.' And while Sarris 'didn't mind the sordidness, the violence, or the mock-ironic ending,' he did object to the film's 'life-denying spirit, its complete lack of curiosity about the possibilities of people. Between Scorsese's celebrated Catholic guilt and Schrader's celebrated Protestant guilt even a Checker cab would groan under such a burden of self-hatred.' But where Sarris complained that 'De Niro's Bickle baffles me,' the *Chicago Sun-Times*' Roger Ebert countered that '*Taxi*

Driver is a brilliant nightmare,' and, therefore, 'like all nightmares, it doesn't tell us all of what we want to know.' Further, Ebert applauded Scorsese's film as 'a masterpiece of suggestive characterisation' and De Niro for being 'as good as Brando at suggesting emotions even while veiling them from us.' And even the less admiring Canby leaned toward the majority vote by concluding that while 'you may want to argue with *Taxi Driver* at the end, and with good reason, it won't be a waste of time.'

*When De Niro previously worked for Scorsese in 1973's *Mean Streets*, his performance won the Best Supporting Actor award from both the NY Film Critics and the National Society of Film Critics. The following year, De Niro won the 1974 Academy Award as Best Supporting Actor in Francis Ford Coppola's *The Godfather Part II*. The 31-year-old actor's prior screen credits were *Greetings* (1968), *Bloody Mama* and *Hi, Mom* (1970), *Born to Win* and *The Gang that Couldn't Shoot Straight* (1971) and *Bang the Drum Slowly* (1973).

AN INTERVIEW WITH MARTIN SCORSESE
By Susan Morrison

Charlie in **Mean Streets** *seems to be seeking redemption through self-inflicted punishment – again the lighted matches, votive candles, taking care of Johnny Boy.* **Taxi Driver** *picks up on similar religious imagery – Travis' hand held over a flame, references to hell, Betsy as an angel. Iris' room filled with candles.*
Oddly enough, that image of the hand held over the flame came directly from Schrader's script for *Taxi Driver*. You see, that's why I said it's almost as if I'd written it. He's a Calvinist and I'm a Roman Catholic – it's very interesting. That image was Paul's; mine [the lighted matches] was in *Mean Streets*.

Can the massacre at the end of the film be seen as a catharsis purifying Travis? Is there any chance of redemption for him?
Oh, I don't know, I never thought of that. I mean I never thought of that, *of course* I've thought of it. But what I'm saying is that Schrader has his own ideas about that and I have mine, I guess. It's like a catharsis, yes, but at the same time he's like a time bomb just waiting to go off again. That's what I always felt.

So it's a really open ending?
It's an open ending because I just think it will happen again and again and again. He's not the only one that it's going to happen to, too. In New York yesterday a guy on the Staten Island Ferry just killed two people with a knife and injured eleven. Before he attacked them he said, 'Viva Islam.' He's a Cuban refugee and he is also

evidently mad, schizophrenic, who was let out. So this you have almost every day happen.

It's just part of everyday life then.
Well, in a way. It doesn't mean that there's no reason for it. The reasons with each person change. And who knows what the reasons are, really, I don't know. I just think the catharsis . . . a blood letting of that kind, I don't think it's ever fully quenched. Do you?

CITIZENS OF HELL
By Jake Horsley

'I'm God's lonely man.' – Travis Bickle, *Taxi Driver*

Taxi Driver is that rarest of things, the full flowering of a movie auteur possessed (however briefly) by genius. The apotheosis of Scorsese's vision with *Taxi Driver* is particularly apparent when juxtaposed with his *Mean Streets* of three years earlier: by using the same actors and the same location, and by dealing with basically the same themes, the filmmaker's preoccupations – his obsessions – carry over from one film to the next so that, in a unique, quite mysterious way, the two works seem to flow into one another. *Taxi Driver* not only develops and extends the ideas and characters from *Mean Streets*, it completes them, bringing them to their full and final form.

Taxi Driver unfolds with all the force and inescapable logic of an authentic nightmare – it makes a sense beyond sense. Like Polanski's *Repulsion* (and later *The Tenant*), it puts us squarely and wholly inside the point of view of its slowly deteriorating protagonist, dragging us steadily deeper into his feverish dementia. Unlike *Repulsion*, however, the film has the breadth and scope of vision to create an actual all-inclusive world for us to inhabit – the world of a tormented soul.[1] With its poetic consistency and dramatic, psychological depth, *Taxi Driver* may be closer in spirit (and stature) to great literary works (of the Russian novelists and the French existentialists for example) than it is to most other American movies. In her review of the film, Pauline Kael cited Dostoyevsky's *Notes from Undergound*,[2] an astute comparison, as both Scorsese and Paul Schrader (who wrote the script and is not Catholic but Calvinist) were at the time admirers of Dostoyevsky. Like Scorsese, Dostoyevsky was a deeply religious artist with an apocalyptic vision of suffering. He perceived the criminal as having a twisted relationship – an affinity – with the saint, and he favoured madness as a subject because it was fertile ground to develop and explore his ideas in. Like Scorsese (and like his protagonist Travis, who lacks artistic release and becomes a killer instead), Dostoyevsky saw the world as a kind of madhouse, an 'everyday inferno' in which we are all burning.

For Travis Bickle (Robert De Niro), isolation and anguish are one. Travis isolates himself primarily in order to suffer, it would seem, and yet he suffers above all because he is alone. (He writes in his diary, without the slightest irony: 'I do not believe one should devote himself to morbid self-attention. I believe one should become a person like other people.') His similarity to Raskolnikov of *Crime and Punishment*, and to the abject, tortured protagonist of *Notes from Underground*, is above all in his solipsism: the way he twists everyone and everything to fit his own sordid vision of the world, and slowly turns his madness into a kind of divine inspiration, and finally, a demonic calling. Travis is Raskolnikov without intellectual faculties; Raskolnikov kills the old pawnbroker out of conceit, his theoretical superiority rendering her expendable to his own advancement. This 'theoretical superiority' is Raskolnikov's Napoleon complex; he believes that superior beings (e.g., Napoleon) have the right to destroy inferior ones whenever it should be necessary to their advancement, for the fulfilment of their destiny. He kills the old woman (and, in an unforeseen complication, is forced to slay her young half-sister too) ostensibly in order to rob her; really it is to test his theory, to act upon the thoughts that are tormenting him, and to satisfy his morbid, self-destructive curiosity. The moment it is translated into action, Raskolnikov's theory falls apart, however, taking him along with it, because in actual fact, in was only ever a theory, a justification for his inner rage and self-loathing. Really, he kills the old woman out of frustration and doubt, and so suffers the corresponding guilt and torment. Raskolnikov's theory may have held true for Napoleon, but if so, he will never know for sure, because Raskolnikov is not Napoleon, any more than Travis is an avenging angel sent by God.

Like Travis, Raskolnikov is a solipsist who can only see his acts in terms of himself, never in terms of those affected. There are no victims in the solipsist's perception, and when Travis destroys Sport and the others, he is, like Raskolnikov, lashing out at his own demons, demons which he has (in true schizophrenic fashion) projected onto the world. The greatness of *Taxi Driver* is how completely it communicates this process. Above all, Scorsese achieves total identification with Travis (and his inner demons) through a pure, expressionistic style. Like *Mean Streets* only more so, *Taxi Driver* has the consistency and visual richness of a painting – a mixture of Bosch, Francis Bacon, and Jackson Pollock, with some of the sensuality of Blake – and no other film looks quite like it. This is how Travis sees the world, and we never get a sense of anything beyond such a fevered perception; it's Scorsese's vision, but it's Travis's point of view, and Scorsese never rubs our noses in the squalor or asks us to judge it or condemn it; on the contrary, he draws us into this world seductively, like a master, and bathes us in its colours. The movie is a hellish baptism.

Through the combined work of Schrader, Scorsese, and De Niro (artists at their peak whose talents converged into an uncannily unified vision), Travis is an authentic movie creation, a killer-saint and self-obsessed martyr, descending into Hell like some pulp Dante to save his Beatrice (in this case, Iris, the twelve-year old prostitute played by Jodie Foster). The bittersweet irony of the film is that Travis is saving her principally from what turn out to be his own demons. Travis is no poet and Iris no saint, and in fact the film bears less resemblance to Dante than it does to (a more fittingly 'lowbrow' source) John Ford's *The Searchers*. Its monstrous loner-hero, a reactionary crusader and self-claimed 'lonely man' of God, ironically invokes both John Wayne and – the seventies version of the moral avenger – Harry Callahan. Scorsese's film has far more dimensions to it than either *Dirty Harry* or *The Searchers*, however. It depicts Travis's acts not as heroic, or even anti-heroic, but as simply deranged, excessive, and motivated not by nobility or justice but by madness and rage.

Much has already been written of the parallels between Scorsese's film and Ford's, so I won't go into it too much here, except to mention the key difference, thematically speaking, which is the inclusion of what Scorsese and Schrader referred to as 'the Scar scene'.

A word of exposition is required first: *The Searchers* involves John Wayne as Ethan, the lone gunfighter, tracking down his niece, who was taken and adopted by the Apaches who slaughtered her family many years earlier. Ethan is committed to tracking her down and destroying the Apaches; we discover during the course of the film, however, that he is also resolved to destroy his niece as well, whom he considers contaminated by her time with the Apaches. When he finally finds her, just as he feared, she has been taken for a wife by the Apache chief, Scar. Ethan wastes no time killing Scar, but at the last moment he has mercy on his niece – played by Natalie Wood – and spares her life. At the end of the film, Ethan is seen from inside the house of the reunited family, framed in the doorway, outside; he watches briefly, then turns and walks away into the desert. The doorway closes on him, and the screen goes black. This closing shot is justifiably celebrated, and may well be the single most powerful image of 'God's lonely man' – the wandering hero/killer condemned to the desert plains – in American movies. Perhaps better than any other image, it sums up an entire mood, beyond genre, of modern movies (what Robert Philip Kolker called a cinema of loneliness, I have called poems in blood).

The 'Scar-scene' which Scorsese and Schrader devised for *Taxi Driver* (Harvey Keitel's Sport being the Scar to Travis's Ethan) is meant to correct what they perceived as a central weakness of Ford's film, namely, that we are never allowed to see Ethan's niece within the Apache community; we are not asked to imagine her relationship with Scar, nor allowed to feel the slightest sympathy for Scar himself. In *Taxi Driver*, this thematic weakness is avoided with a single scene taking place outside the perceptions of Travis (the rest of the film being almost entirely inside his point of view). In this scene, Sport (Iris's pimp) and Iris dance together in the seedy, sultry gloom of Iris's apartment. The scene, a remarkable blend of sleaziness with hypnotic dreaminess, allows us to see Sport outside Travis's perception of him as a monster, and as the 'lowest sucking scum' that ever walked the earth. It also communicates why Iris is so drawn to Sport and his world, a world which, for all its sordidness, is a necessary refuge for her. Travis's 'saving' Iris, his murder of Sport (and the others), can then be seen as much as an invasion of Iris's world – provoked by what *he perceives* as iniquity and abomination – as a rescue mission. Ditto, Ethan's slaying of Scar and abducting his niece from her (presumably quite content) life with the Apaches. Quite plainly, exactly like Ethan in *The Searchers*, Travis is going after his own demons.

The most celebrated bloodbath in movie history: Mohawk-shaven Travis (De Niro) storms the hotel where child prostitute Iris is being abused, in Taxi Driver *(1976).*

'The idea had been building up in my mind for some time: true force. Here is a man who wouldn't take it any more, a man who stood up. . .' – Travis Bickle, Taxi Driver.

The above words, for all the conviction with which they are uttered, ring horribly false. For a moment it seems like the film is about to go grotesquely wrong, to degenerate into a macho fantasy of vigilante justice, to become as trite and contrived as Travis's speech. Right after the words 'stood up', however, Scorsese cuts to one of the most eloquent images in the film – an overhead shot of Travis, splayed out on his bed, fully dressed and armed to the teeth. He looks like a catatonic rag doll. Drained of all vitality, dignity and purpose, he is a lost soul. All his bravado, his new-found sense of direction, are reduced by this single image to an insane man's desperate reaching for sanity, a drowning man's last grasping for the straw that will break the camel's back.

Before Travis decides to vent his religious wrath upon the venal world of street scum, he bizarrely directs it first at the political candidate, Palantine. Travis's attempt at political assassination seems motivated solely by the fact that Palantine is associated in his mind with Betsy (Cybill Shepherd), the vision of perfection who rejects him and turns out to be 'like all the rest – in Hell.' The film doesn't really explore Travis's reasons at this juncture, wisely, since he is slipping slowly deeper into psychosis where motivations are of secondary importance. Travis is split in his moral outrage and his nausea: he can't decide whether to strike at the top or at the bottom of this rancid, irredeemable hellhole 'society' (it's his own hell, of course, one that he's made and is now stewing in). He appears to see a hit on Palantine as an appropriate response to the candidate's ineffective mincing, and perhaps as a fitting challenge for the guerrilla skills he learned in Vietnam (in the Marines, where shaving the hair into a Mohawk, as Travis does, signified a kamikaze-style attack mission). Apparently, as his Mohawk suggests, Travis fully expects to die on this mission, and it seems fair to say that his motive is really a suicidal one. Lacking the clarity or courage (or honesty) to destroy himself, Travis redirects his destructive energy outward at a more or less random target, knowing it will assure his own death. This is one of the film's most profound observations (barely even implied, but it's there) – that all brutal acts are essentially deviated violence against the self, and that many killers are really failed suicides. Travis does attempt to end his life in a dramatic fashion after he has committed the grand carnage of the finale, but by then all his guns are empty, leaving him no choice but to survive.

It's particularly curious if we look at these two alternative options of attack – of Palantine and then of Sport and the other hoods – in the light of two real-life events that followed *Taxi Driver* and would appear to have been at least partially inspired by the film (in the first case directly, and in the second case indirectly). I refer to the John Hinckley, Jr. assassination attempt on Ronald Reagan, and, several years later, the Bernard Goetz shooting of several black youths on the New York subway. In the first case, Hinckley claimed to be haunted by the film *Taxi Driver* and to have fallen in love with its adolescent heroine, Jodie Foster (he wrote her love letters).[3] In a truly uncanny case of life imitating art imitating art imitating life (a sort of endless loop, like mirrors inside mirrors), Hinckley was 'inspired' (or possibly coerced, since the 'lone nut' theory is always open to doubt) to imitate a movie 'hero' who was in actual fact a psychopath who was in turn inspired – albeit unconsciously – to act out his fantasies of heroic behaviour by a culture gorged on infantile ideas of manliness and heroism, as propagated by John Wayne films and the like.[4]

Hinckley's reasoning (if such it was) was as incoherent as Travis's – there was no possible relationship between his 'love' for Foster and his attempt on Reagan's life, nor was there any conceivably *heroic* motive for such an act (save politically speaking, which as a motive seems as beyond Hinckley as it is beyond Travis). Hinckley claimed he'd done it 'to prove his love' (or some such, I'm guessing here) to Foster; but, as far as relations to *Taxi Driver* go, Travis was never in love with Iris, only infatuated with Betsy, on account of whom he took a shot at Palantine. Maybe Hinckley was obsessed with the wrong actress (either that or he made an attack on the wrong 'scum')?! Regardless of the true meaning or motive behind the Hinckley affair, it proved one thing beyond all doubt – *Taxi Driver* was an uncommonly powerful film, the kind that affected people deeply, and, if the media was to be believed, could incite them to murder. Poor Martin Scorsese, I'll wager, has had a few sleepless nights wrestling with his own 'artistic responsibility' over the affair.

The Bernard Goetz case is another matter, and it establishes something even more remarkable about *Taxi Driver*. Anyone who has seen the film knows that it is an impressive work; what might have been in doubt (before Goetz exploded onto the scene) was that it is also a prophetic one. At the ending of the movie, Travis's explosion is interpreted, by tabloid journalism, as authentic heroism, and Travis himself is not only exonerated but hailed as a modern-day crusader – a crime fighter along the lines of *Death Wish*'s Charles Bronson or Batman. This was received by some critics as a dubious 'liberty' – an essentially implausible, ironic resolution. The intention seemed to be to raise the possibility that Travis's insane fantasies might not be aberrational, but merely a product of the society and culture in which he existed. If so, it doesn't seem so far-fetched if this society would – to the extent that it shared in such fantasies – accept and even embrace Travis as the hero he imagined himself to be. (The movie slips into outright fairy tale in the last scene however, when the ice-angel Betsy 'comes back' to him.) Whatever our original feeling about the irony and the insight of the film's ending, the Bernard Goetz case put any doubts to rest, proving that truth is indubitably stranger – and more twisted – than fiction.

Goetz exploded one day on a New York subway car, drew a pistol and shot down several young black 'hoodlums' who he claimed were trying to rob him; the young men denied Goetz's claim and at least one of them sued for damages.[5] There seems ample reason to assume that, like Travis, Goetz acted out of personal rage and frustration, and simply snapped one day and started shooting. The media and the general public, however – fed-up with the ever increasing crime rate and street violence of New York – reacted with ambiguity and even, in some quarters, outright approval. Quite literally, 'Here was a man who wouldn't take it any more, a man who *stood up!*' The actual resolution of the case was by no means so simple or unambiguous as that of *Taxi Driver* – Goetz served eight and a half months for possession of an illegal weapon – but (and this is the most important point) in the eyes of the public, parts of it anyway, he was a hero. His actions were viewed not with horror or disgust as the acts of a madman, but as those of a brave, justifiably indignant citizen of Hell (where any kind of action is permitted, so long as sufficiently provoked). There's no telling what kind of man Goetz was (or if he'd ever seen *Taxi Driver*), but in the end it really doesn't matter. Like Travis, he may as well be Everyman: just one more downtrodden, dejected nobody with delusions of grandeur (he carried a gun, obviously), who reached the limits of his patience – or sanity – a little before the rest of us. As Pauline Kael wrote of *Taxi Driver*: 'part of the horror implicit in this movie is how easily he [Travis] passes. The anonymity of the city soaks up one more invisible man; he could be legion.'[6]

Scorsese's vision of New York City as a microcosm of the world, an ordinary inferno burning with ever greater intensity and rage, no longer seems (if it ever did) to be hyperbole. At this early stage of his career, Scorsese was an artist of expressionism, with a visionary gift close to madness, and that was exactly what qualified him for his subject. His art was to take us where we all – and the world along with us – must some day go. *Taxi Driver* and *Mean Streets* simulated the experience of urban apocalypse for our edification and education; meanwhile, the Bickles and the Hinckleys and the Mansons and the Goetzes (and the Reagans and the Bushes and the Palantines), and all the other citizens of Hell, keep busy making reality of the nightmare. *Taxi Driver* and *Mean Streets* give us the American Dream exploded – what America looks like when the 'Dream' comes true. Who can blame us, in that case, for going back to sleep?

'We have reached the turning point.' – Charles Palantine, *Taxi Driver*

As Travis, Robert De Niro gives a cagey, evasive, strangely haunting performance; he makes us feel at all times his internal anguish, growing desperation, and overwhelming sense of isolation. Travis is alienation incarnate, and when he's up there on the screen, we don't feel disgust or superiority – our hearts go out to him. What De Niro accomplishes here goes beyond standard screen acting: Travis being a secretive, introverted and above all *lost* soul, most of De Niro's work is internal. It's not a showy performance, like his Johnny Boy (or like Brando's Kowalski), yet neither is it a work of restrained grandeur like his (and Brando's) Vito Corleone. Yet it is I think even more remarkable, not only De Niro's finest performance but one of the finest in the brief history of movies. De Niro and Scorsese work so closely together here that it's impossible (and unnecessary) to separate their work. Between the two of them (working from Schrader's script) they have created a modern archetype – a 'hero' for our times. The irony of this is that Travis is both a nobody and an Everyman: he is the archetypal stereotype. What Scorsese and De Niro have done, however, is to make him into a living, breathing person, the most fully realised picture of a sociopathic killer that the movies have ever provided.

The other players in the film, though incidental to Scorsese's vision and peripheral to Travis's viewpoint (everyone is peripheral, finally – he's got tunnel vision and there's only darkness at the end of it), are collectively inspired, right down to the bit parts given to Peter Boyle and Harry Northup (as Wizard and Doughboy, Travis's cabbie associates), Cybill Shepherd as Betsy, the urban angel Travis becomes obsessed with, Albert Brooks as her nebbish co-worker, and most of all Harvey Keitel and Jodie Foster, as Sport and Iris, the pimp whom Travis pits himself against and the whore he 'saves'. It's in the scenes between these characters that we see Travis more or less as he is: this is *his* world, though he can never admit it to himself. In his 'date' with Iris in the coffee bar (for noonday breakfast – she's wearing two pairs of sunglasses), Travis, for a brief moment, actually seems to relax and forget his morbid brooding, to become an ordinary person at last. There's no possibility of redemption here (Iris and Travis are as impossible a couple as Travis and Betsy), but there is something approaching relief – for us at least, if not for Travis.

Conversely, in his meeting with Sport, we get to see Travis as the street warrior he imagines himself to be. (Sport seems vaguely aware of Travis's fantasies, calling him 'cowboy', and briefly convinced that Travis is a cop.) In their first scene together (they have only two, the meeting and the stand-off, and they are the high points of the film), Travis seems dazed and bewildered – he hardly seems to know what Sport is talking about (though he registers just fine). For his part, Sport is amused and a little bit baffled by Travis. He instantly senses that Travis is not quite all there, but being a pimp he's used to dealing with weirdos. Ironically, Sport's playfulness helps Travis to set Sport up in his mind as his adversary, and finally his victim. (Sport's reference to guns and his playful gestures with his fingers – simulating a pistol, just as Charlie does in *Mean Streets* – ominously foreshadow the showdown.) When he talks in lurid detail about Iris's 'services', for example (Keitel superbly improvises the scene), Sport is tragically unaware of feeding the fires of Travis's demented rage, and how the flames will soon devour him. (Travis's demons, once released, turn not on himself but on everyone else.) Sport is actually one of the most likeable characters in the film, and along with Iris he seems to be the only 'real' personality; the rest of them, being repugnant or at best irrelevant to Travis in his isolation, seem more like shadows.[7]

And amid these shadows walks Travis, a man crucified by his own fear and loathing, a martyr to modern alienation, himself no more than a shadow, a suffering phantom with no chains to rattle (the soundtrack rattles them for him).[8] Travis's hell of loneliness and enforced celibacy comes most of all from his incapacity to connect with women: either he wants to be saved by them (as in the case of Betsy), or else he wants to save them (Iris). In both cases, there's no possibility of equality or understanding between them, and so he feels betrayed when these women don't act according to his fantasy-view of them. When he says of Betsy, 'I realise now she is just like all the rest, cold, distant. Many people are like that; women for sure. They're like a union,' he is diagnosing his own disease. To Travis, women are a force unto themselves, gathered against him, refusing him access to their world. Travis is so isolated inside his own world that all his efforts at communicating – at sharing – are doomed to failure from the start. Only when he literally blasts his way out of his shell and into the real world does the world sit up and take notice. And when Betsy 'comes back' to Travis in the final scene, it might be Travis's ultimate fantasy fulfilled. He's not only slain the dragon – he's won the maiden. What's more, he gets to reject her (gently), thereby proving his superiority and righteousness. She is 'in Hell, like all the rest,' and, now that she realises it too, she comes back to him, her saviour; but it is too late, he has moved beyond her. (Iris, on the other hand, who always knew she was in Hell, was willing, and therefore able, to be saved.) The film actively shares in Travis's fantasy here, and in his madness and alienation: it's a poetic fairy tale, written in blood.

The tragedy of *Taxi Driver* – and of perhaps all solipsist sociopaths driven to violence – is that Travis only becomes real (to himself and to a world of indifference) when he kills. Travis is one of an unknown legion for whom 'murder is the only door, through which they enter life.'[9] And when the film leaves him pacified, vindicated, strangely complacent, chatting with his cabbie buddies, it's the most disturbing image in the film. The heat that sent him past boiling point is still on, and it's only a matter of time until the next explosion comes.

Travis is a man whose inner hell has seeped out into the world around him. His mentioning having served in the Marines (in the opening scene with Joe Spinell) and the scar on his back are the only indications of his war experience, and for those of us who don't register the symbolism of the Mohawk, there's no overt suggestion that these experiences are responsible for the state of his mind, or for his finally coming off the rails.[10] And yet the film is, I think, the first to deal – in a non-symbolic fashion – with the horrors, the psychological consequences, of Vietnam. Of course, the war is neither seen nor mentioned in the film, but neither does it need to be. Travis brings the war with him, and wherever he goes he's in a state of total paranoia – of fear and loathing. Travis has transposed the 'gooks' of Vietnam onto the junkies and pimps and pushers of New York City, and he sees them as every bit as alien, inhuman, and threatening as (presumably) he was conditioned and trained to see the Vietnamese.[11]

Travis's internal conflict – his tension and dread – is so intense, so overwhelming, that he *needs* a visible enemy to placate him, as a means of releasing and directing the pressure. And when it comes, the bloodbath – Scorsese's idea of a baptism – is Travis's redemption, damnation, and sexual consummation all wrapped up into one twisted paroxysm. (As Kael writes, it's 'the only real orgasm he can have'.[12] This idea is also anticipated in *Mean Streets*, when Charlie describes his dream to Teresa: 'I come, only I come blood.') The final orgy of killing is anything but pleasurable to watch, but it *is* strangely orgasmic in effect. It presents the only relief that the film has to offer, for Travis and by extension for us. Scorsese has taken us too far by now to let us down gently. The whole of *Taxi Driver* is expressionistic, but never more so than when Travis's madness finally comes into its own and his inner hell spills out, in a surge of agony and ecstasy. The film remains to this day one of the most relentlessly savage and virtuoso blood poems ever written on the American screen.[13]

Apart from the shooting of the black hold-up man in the grocery store, these last five minutes constitute the only violence in the film; the rest of the film depicts the steady build-up of pressure, dread, and nausea in the protagonist, and it is essential that the explosion be worse than anything we could have anticipated. Anything less than a full-fledged massacre at this point would have been anticlimactic.[14] As it is, these images of wanton destruction stay with us, haunt us, even as all great works of art stay with us – as images from the unconscious that we can't quite get free of. Unable to decide if they are beautiful or ugly, such pure expressions of souls in torment make beauty out of terror, and atrocity out of art. That's the privilege of the damned, after all, and the *sine qua non* of every artist, chosen by Hell to represent it.

That Scorsese is of such divinely demonic ilk is best evidenced by the director's choice to play the role, midway through the film, of the backseat driver with fantasies of vaginal destruction. His performance (as disturbing as anything in the movie) gives us the best clue we could ask for as to Scorsese's true artistic intentions. Because it is this racist, malignant, wife-hating imp who indirectly awakens Travis's gun-mania and inspires him to 'get *organizized*' (soon after he meets Andy the gun salesman and assembles his arsenal). The scene is Scorsese's way (albeit unconsciously) of confirming the allegiance of the artist to the evils of his imagination. When Scorsese – the director of the film and therefore Travis's primary creator – appears as a grinning demiurge inside his own *mise en scène* in the back of Travis's cab, he is there with *specific purpose*. He is there to get the show on the road, to ignite the spark that will set fire to the cinder block and lead to the final apocalyptic movement. And, as Kael so poetically observes of Scorsese's performance, '*he burns a small hole in the screen.*'[15]

This creative intrusion from one realm to the next is the ultimate artistic conceit or hubris, perverse and inspired in precisely equal portions. It is the film director as *deus ex machina* – the *auteur* who intervenes in the life of his own creation, not for its salvation but for its damnation. As ever (and as Blake said of Milton), the poet is exposed – has exposed *himself* – as of the Devil's party. Scorsese's wicked snickering at his own devilry will linger in our ears long after the show is over.

1. The difference between *Taxi Driver* and *Repulsion* is above all the difference between a religious and an atheist vision of madness. Polanski's film suggests the hell of the mind; Scorsese's goes further by far, into the hell of the soul.

2. Kael called the film 'a raw, tabloid version of *Notes from Underground*', in 'Underground Man', *When the Lights Go Down*, p.131.

3. It's also possible that Hinckley was responsible for a death threat which Scorsese received several days before the 1976 Academy Awards ceremony, at which *Taxi Driver* received several nominations, including one for Jodie Foster for best supporting actress. The letter Scorsese received warned him, 'If little Jodie wins on March 29 for what you made her do in *Taxi Driver*, you will pay with your life. I am serious. I am not a sicko. I love little Jodie. I would never do anything to hurt her. Never, never, never.' As a result of the letter, the FBI were called in and Scorsese was given a personal guard at the Oscars ceremony. (Foster did not win, no doubt much to Scorsese's relief.) Whether the letter was written by Hinckley has never been established, but seems a distinct possibility.

4. Robert Philip Kolker calls Travis 'the legitimate child of John Wayne and Norman Bates', and writes that 'the more deeply he withdraws, the more he comes to believe in the American movie myths of purity and heroism, love and selflessness, and to actuate them as the grotesque parodies of human behaviour they are.' *A Cinema of Loneliness*, p. 194.

5. He was eventually awarded $43 million in damages. Goetz claimed to have been 'threatened' by the teenagers' 'body language', but when he was arrested, the only words he recalled any of them saying to him prior to the shooting were, 'How are you?' In the same interrogation, Goetz admitted that before firing a second round into victim Darrell Cobey, in true Hollywood vigilante fashion he quipped, 'You seem to be all right: here's another.' Three of the teens were found to be carrying long screwdrivers at the time they approached Goetz, however, and partly as a result of this, a grand jury declined to indict Goetz of attempted murder. In 1987, he was found guilty in criminal court of an illegal weapons charge and nothing more.

6. From 'Underground Man', *When the Lights Go Down*, p. 133.

7. Scorsese himself appears as one of these urban fiends, in a particularly disturbing but sickly hilarious performance as a jealous husband in the back of Travis's cab, fantasising out loud about destroying his wife's vagina with a .44 Magnum. The joke turns sour, however, when we see Travis specifying this very weapon while choosing his arsenal.

8. Bernard Herrmann's music is a deeply ominous, overwrought percussive score which fortunately, much like the film itself, has improved with age. It no longer seems obtrusive to the film, and its excessive augmentation of the already gothic atmosphere of dread seems less an intrusion and more a simple accompaniment. Actually, the score, having matured and mellowed with age, seems somehow ironic in effect – it's like Travis's own idealised soundtrack by which he pumps up his existential angst, and romanticises his torments. In a strange way, it is even relaxing, its threatening quality so obvious and unsubtle that it nullifies itself, while Travis's deceptive calm and inhuman passivity is what builds the tension.

9. From the Tom Waits song, 'Murder in the Red Barn', on *Bone Machine*.

10. Part of the film's subversion and inversion of the old conventions of the Western hero and moral avenger (a subversion that began with *The Searchers*) can be traced through the superficial details. The 'scar', for example, such as it is, is now on Travis himself – a war wound across his back (he was 'stabbed in the back' by America?). Likewise the Mohawk. Apparently Travis

himself has become the adversary; he's fallen prey to Nietzsche's axiomatic trap of self-immersion and vengeance—by battling with monsters he has become a monster, and he's been gazing at the abyss so long that it's all he sees. Travis sees enemies – corruption – everywhere: 'all the animals' that 'come out at night – whores, skunks, pussies, buggers, queens, fairies, dopers, junkies.'

11. There is a scene in *Mean Streets* which anticipates *Taxi Driver*: a returning Vietnam vet Jerry – Harry Northup – goes to a party in his honour, is presented with an American flag, gets drunk, and explodes in apparently unmotivated rage and violence, attacking one of the girls, being dragged off by his friends.

12. *When the Lights Go Down*, p. 135.

13. It is also one of the very few cases that transcends the law of 'less is more' (a law which so particularly applies to screen violence). Irate studio heads, who found the final holocaust scene too much for their palates, insisted Scorsese do something about it in order to avoid an X rating. Scorsese came up with a demonically inspired 'solution': 'To really stop Columbia from redoing things, I suggested the idea of draining the colour out of that scene. I had wanted to do that originally, because I wanted to do an experiment in draining colours out of the shots like John Huston did with *Moby Dick*. But it was also a way of making it appear that I was doing something to tone things down in the scene. When I finally saw the scene with Julia [Phillips, the producer] the toning down of the colour made it look even worse!' (Scorsese, quoted in *The Scorsese Picture*, by David Ehrenstein.) Columbia went along with the changes, as the only thing they *could* do (the little devil made them do it), since the extreme violence of the climax is integral to its meaning, and any attempts at diluting its savagery and power would be futile. To interfere with the sweeping, tidal force and rhythms of this scene would be to render it impotent; instead Scorsese 'washed' the images, not with water but with blood. The final tint that the images assume is a dirty, reddish brown that actually makes the sequence, if perhaps less powerful and searing, even more grotesque and nauseating in effect.

14. Though Scorsese shot equally brutal and even more nasty scenes in later films (*Goodfellas*, *Casino* and *Gangs of New York* in particular), he has never equalled the horror which he creates here. Scorsese naturally possesses more power to shock and revolt audiences than most other directors will ever learn; of late, he hasn't lost his edge, exactly, but his more recent depictions of violence lack the depth, troubling beauty, and intensity of *Mean Streets*, *Taxi Driver* or *Raging Bull*, all of which have the raw splendour and passion of an urban crucifixion.

15. Italics mine, *When the Lights Go Down* pp. 130-35.

Americana

GUILTY PLEASURES (1978)
By Martin Scorsese

This is the film lover's list. It's like a cushion: you can fall asleep thinking of these pictures. If you're uncomfortable you can lean over and rest on *Land of the Pharaohs*.

SPECTACLE

Land of the Pharaohs (1955, Howard Hawks). When I first saw it, as a kid, *Land of the Pharaohs* became my favourite film. I'd always been addicted to historical epics, but this one was different: it gave the sense that we were really there. This is the way people lived; this is what they believed, thought, and felt. You get it through the overall look of the picture: the low ceilings, the torchlit interiors, the shape of the pillars, the look of the extras. There's a marvellous moment when the dead are being taken away from battle in their coffins, and someone says, 'Let us hear the gods of Egypt speak.' The camera pans over to one of the statues of the gods, and it talks. That's it – the statue talks! You don't see the mouth moving, you just hear the voice. Then they pan over to the other god – and now he talks. Soon there are about four gods talking. You're never told, 'This is how they did it: it was a joke, a trick.' In a sense, you're taken into confidence by the Egyptians; you're let in on a religion. I watch this movie over and over again. I put it at the top of the list because it's my favourite.

Khartoum (1966, Basil Dearden). I like anything about the British in the Sudan; I love the 1939 version of *Four Feathers*. In *Four Feathers*, the British are out to avenge the killing of Chinese Gordon in Khartoum by the Mahdi, the holy redeemer. *Khartoum* takes place ten years earlier. Charlton Heston, as Gordon, is marvellous; and Laurence Olivier has a lot of fun as the Mahdi, with a space between his front teeth. It isn't very good filmmaking, but it has a mystical quality about it. This was a holy war. At the end – when Mahdi killed Gordon, and then six months later he died himself – it was as if the two of them cancelled each other out, religiously and historically. It a story I want to be told, over and over again, like a fairy tale.

The Ten Commandments (1956, Cecil B. DeMille). I like DeMille: his theatricality, his images. I've seen *The Ten Commandments* maybe 40 or 50 times. Forget the story – you've got to – and concentrate on the special effects, and the texture, and the colour. For example: the figure of God, killing the first-born child, is a green smoke; then on the terrace while they're talking, a green dry ice just touches the heel of George Reeves or somebody, and he dies. Then there's the red Red Sea, and the lamb's blood of the Passover. DeMille presented a fantasy, dreamlike quality on film that was so real, if you saw his movies as a child, they stuck with you for life.

Giant (1956, George Stevens). I've seen this film over 40 times. I don't like the obvious romanticism, and it's very studied, but there's more here than people have seen.

The love between Francine (Liza Minnelli) and Jimmy (De Niro) doesn't survive in New York, New York *(1977). Scorsese's tribute to 1940s/50s musicals is bittersweet.*

It has to do with the depiction of a lifestyle through the passage of so many years. You see people grow. I like James Dean; I like the use of music, even though Dmitri Tiomkin did it; I like Boris Leven's image of the house, and the changes in the house; I like the wide image of Mercedes McCambridge riding the bronco, then cut to an extreme closeup of her hitting the bronc with her spur, then back to the wide image. As far as filmmaking goes, *Giant* is an inspiring film. I don't mean morally, but visually. It's all visual.

The Silver Chalice (1954, Victor Saville). *The Silver Chalice* is one of the reasons I hired Boris Leven to design *New York, New York*. *Giant* and *The Silver Chalice*: any man who could design those two films . . . that's it, I had to have him. *The Silver Chalice*, which is a bad picture, has no authenticity. It's purely theatrical, and this is mainly due to the sets. They're clean and clear; it s almost like another life, another world. We don't know what ancient Rome was like, so why not take the attitude Fellini had with *Satyricon*: make it science fiction in reverse? *The Silver Chalice* came close to that, fifteen years earlier.

WAR

Hell's Angels (1930, Howard Hughes and James Whale). The dialogue sequences, directed by Whale, are atrocious; there's no excuse for them. But I was amazed by the aerial footage: real planes, real houses being bombed, overhead shots of barns exploding and things flying up in the air. What I've seen of *Wings* just couldn't compare to it. I showed *Hell's Angels* to John Milius and Steven Spielberg during the preparation of *Close Encounters of the Third Kind*. After seeing the film, Milius made a speech: 'This is the kind of film that should be made these days.'

The Counterfeit Traitor (1962, George Seaton). Before *The Counterfeit Traitor*, most war-related movies were in black-and-white – the neorealistic, Rossellini influence. You got used to it. Then, suddenly, comes this film: intelligent, beautifully made, expensive, its plot twists based on true incidents, terrific performances by William Holden and Lilli Palmer – and all in vivid colour. For kids brought up on the black-and-white battlegrounds of newsreels, the use of colour here – especially the colour red, which is very important – gave the film a presence and an immediacy that frightened us.

Play Dirty (1969, André de Toth). In the opening sequence, Michael Caine is driving a dead body on a jeep, and there's Italian march music on the soundtrack. Right away you know you're in for something unique. *Play Dirty* isn't a sadistic film, but it's mean. The characters have no redeeming social value, which I love. In one sequence, they pretend to be Italian soldiers to fool some Arabs; one of the Arabs spots something on them, so they take their guns and shoot all the Arabs. They don't think, they just act. They have a job to do, and they're going to do it. The nihilism, the pragmatism – it's frightening.

Twelve O'Clock High (1949, Henry King). I know all about Gregory Peck, don't read any further, Gregory Peck is Gregory Peck, when he's in a film you accept it for what it is, it's a given, like a theorem in geometry, okay, Gregory Peck. But here he's a man in war, dealing with his conscience and his fears. You figure, this guy's so tough he can take anything. But then comes the moment when he has to get into the bomber, and the machismo breaks down. He can't get in the plane. And I love it. The movie deals with a man of war on the human level. Because this guy can't take anything. That's the point. That's why he's so tough.

In Harm's Way **(1965, Otto Preminger).** The ships are out there in the Pacific at night, and the combination of image and music gave the scene a foreboding, a danger, a horror of the war. Until finally everything explodes in the last battle sequence: glass starts to break on the bridge, and it's frightening the way it intrudes on your privacy. John Wayne is the complete American in the film: they ask him if he'd like a scotch, and he says, 'No, a Coca-Cola.'

MUSIC AND COMEDY

Lady in the Dark **(1944, Mitchell Leisen).** Leisen went all out here. The whole film is so vulgar and outrageous, there's got to be something to it. The dime-store psychology is ridiculous, of course, but the dream sequences are marvellous kitsch. I love the fantasy element. I love the Kurt Weill-Ira Gershwin songs. I love 'Jenny'. For me, the whole film builds to the point where Ginger Rogers sings, 'Poor Jenny, bright as a penny' – and she opens her dress, and it's fur-lined and red. The film has influenced a lot of my movies. I screened it before shooting *New York, New York*, to look at the colour and the use of lipstick, etc. Liza Minnelli was named after the Ginger Rogers characters; her godfather was Ira Gershwin.

My Dream is Yours **(1949, Michael Curtiz)** and *The Man I Love* **(1946, Raoul Walsh).** Both are musical *films noirs* about nightclub singers; they had a lot to do with *New York, New York*. When we asked Doris Day about *My Dream is Yours*, she said, 'That's my life story.' The style, the colour, the décor, I took it all for *New York, New York*. For the opening titles I wanted a New York skyline – the one from *The Man I Love*. We wound up painting the film.

Always Leave Them Laughing **(1949, Roy Del Ruth).** Milton Berle is the archetype of the comedian who's really tough and nasty. This film depicts in no uncertain terms on the kind of character Milton Berle – the real Milton Berle – is. I find comedians fascinating; there's so much pain and fear that goes into the trade, and this is one of the most honest films about comedians. I admire the guts it took for Berle to make this autobiographical film about a completely dislikeable guy. In fact, I believe Berle completed direction of the film after Roy Del Ruth got sick about three-quarters of the way through.

The Road to Zanzibar **(1941, Victor Schertzinger)** and *Blue Skies* **(1946, Stuart Heisler).** I like most Bing Crosby films. I was fascinated by his character. He's charming, he sings all the time – and meanwhile, he's swindling everybody. In the *Road* pictures, he takes advantage of Bob Hope from beginning to end – and still winds up with the girl. He uses Hope so badly, but with such integrity, such confidence. I used a variation of that in the *Mean Streets* relationship between Robert De Niro and Harvey Keitel. In *Blue Skies*, Crosby is a marvellous, dangerous character, because he's too restless to stay in one place. Every time he makes a success with one of his nightclubs, he sells it, goes on to another one. Fred Astaire is the stable good guy. And Crosby is the hero: unstable, irrational, maybe crazy, and such a charmer. It influenced the De Niro character in *New York, New York*.

Lost in a Harem (1944, Charles Reisner) and ***Abbot And Costello Go To Mars*** (1953, **Charles Lamont**). *Lost in a Harem* has one of the great Abbot and Costello comedy routines: 'Slowly I turned . . . step by step . . . inch by inch . . . I took my revenge.' When they do their word-play routines, nobody can come near them. They take the English language, dissect it, throw it up in the air, fiddle it around; they find absurdity in the English language. This film is really Theatre of the Absurd: Beckett, Ionesco, it's all there. *Abbott and Costello Go to Mars* was recommended to me by Michael Chapman, my cameraman, while we were doing *Taxi Driver*; he used to show it to his kids on Sunday mornings. It becomes very avant-garde during a 'weightless' sequence. Two gangsters have a fight, and when they're weightless they talk in slow motion. One of them fires a gun, and the bullet goes in slow motion, and finally it just drops. It's total surrealism, the whole picture. These guys took a lot of chances and, in doing that, stumbled over something they didn't expect. The movie is worth seeing, at least on a Sunday morning.

HORROR AND WESTERN

House of Wax (1953, André de Toth). It's the best 3-D film ever made – and André de Toth had one eye! Throughout the first third of the film, the camera keeps tracking around Vincent Price, and around the wax figures – who look very much like real people. And every time somebody comes into a frame, you don't know whether it's a dummy or a real person. When the wax museum burns, and the eyes start to fall out of the dummies' eye sockets, it's tremendously effective. The whole movie is so outlandish, so outrageous. And I like that it takes place on Mulberry Street – my old neighbourhood.

The Uninvited (1944, Lewis Allen). *The Uninvited* is even scarier than *House of Wax*. In fact, it's the best ghost story ever made. It's so frightening that Ray Milland has to crack a few jokes now and then, just to keep everybody in the theatre.

Frankenstein Created Woman (1967, Terence Fisher). I like all Hammer films. If I singled this one out, it's not because I like it the best – it's a sadistic film, very difficult to watch – but because, here, they actually isolate the soul: a bright blue shining translucent ball. The implied metaphysics is close to something sublime.

Exorcist II: The Heretic (1977, John Boorman). Again, we're dealing with metaphysics. The picture asks: Does great goodness bring upon itself great evil? This goes back to the *Book of Job*; It's God testing the good. In this sense, Regan (Linda Blair) is a modern-day saint – like Ingrid Bergman in *Europa '51*, and, in a way, like Charlie in *Mean Streets*. I like the first *Exorcist*, because of the Catholic guilt I have, and because it scared the hell out of me; but *The Heretic* surpasses it. Maybe Boorman failed to execute the material, but the movie still deserved better than it got.

One-Eyed Jacks (1961, Marlon Brando). It's a shame this movie has to be included here. It's unique: so extraordinary and so personal a vision, I can't see how it could have been a flop. Brando even has the guts to ride off into the sunset, waving, on a white horse – and he gets away with it. Even in its cut version, it's an amazing achievement – one of the best Westerns ever made.

TOUGH GUYS

I Walk Alone (1947, **Byron Haskin**). In the late forties, Paramount released a series of *films noirs* unlike others at the time. They were produced by Hal B. Wallis, and usually starred Burt Lancaster or Kirk Douglas. In *I Walk Alone*, Lancaster comes out of prison after ten years – he took a bum rap for his friends – looking to cash in on his part of the nightclub his pal Douglas bought with the loot. But everything's changed; he can't fit in. He has only one way to deal with his problems: brute force. *I Walk Alone* is a very intelligent movie about a man totally perplexed by the new postwar world. And this world became the new world of filmmaking, too. The gangster of the thirties became the gangster of the forties.

Night and the City (1950, **Jules Dassin**). This was an important film for me, in terms of the background for *Mean Streets*. There's a good sense of emotional violence in the film. Richard Widmark is a character obsessed, a hustler, all night running, panicked, desperate – like Charlie in *Mean Streets*. And he winds up ruined, like Charlie – doom written on his face.

Station Six – Sahara (1963, **Seth Holt**). A group of men live alone in an oil station in the desert. There's a strong suggestion of homosexuality among the men – and then, in an extraordinary sequence, this siren (Carroll Baker) drives into the scene, with her husband, and all the men try to kill each other. The desolation and the overall lurid quality make the movie better than anything *The National Enquirer* could come up with. The editing and the use of overlapping dialogue are marvellous; Seth Holt began his movie career as an editor. Here you get that palpable sense of being in a place – stuck in a place. And you learn what it's like in a society of people who live on the outside. Way on the outside.

Dark of the Sun (1968, **Jack Cardiff**). This movie – Rod Taylor vs. the Mau Maus – was the most violent I'd seen up to that time. There's a scene where Taylor fights an ex-Nazi with chainsaws. In another scene, a train full of refugees has finally escaped the Mau Maus in the valley below – and just as it's about to reach the top of a hill, the power fails, the train goes all the way back down, and the refugees are slaughtered. It's a truly sadistic movie, but it should be seen. I'd guess that because of its utter racism, a lot of people would have found it embarrassing, so they just ignored it. The sense of the film is overwhelmingly violent; there's no consideration for anything else. The answer to everything is 'kill'.

Guns Don't Argue (1957, **Bill Karn and Richard C. Kahn**). On an incredibly low budget, this movie told the entire FBI story, with Pretty Boy Floyd, Ma Barker, Bonnie and Clyde, etc. It's very episodic, very documentary. There's a moment when Ma Barker knows she has to kill her husband. She tells him to go off in the woods; he goes; dissolve to a machine gun; dissolve back and Ma's in the car. It's an amazing film. It's to be studied, because it shows you how to make a film on a low budget. Twenty cents.

Murder by Contract (1958, **Irving Lerner**). This is the film that has influenced me most. I had a clip out of it in *Mean Streets* but had to take it out: it was too long, and a little too esoteric. And there's a getting-in-shape sequence that's very much like the one in *Taxi Driver*. The spirit of *Murder by Contract* has a lot to do with *Taxi Driver*. Lerner was an artist who knew how to do things in shorthand, like Bresson and Godard. The film puts us all to shame with its economy of style, especially in the barbershop murder at the beginning. Vince Edwards gives a marvellous performance as the killer who couldn't murder a woman. *Murder by Contract* was a favourite of neighbourhood guys who didn't know anything about movies. They just liked the film because they recognised something unique about it.

And . . .
The Magic Box **(1951, John Boulting).** I saw it as a child. It was the film that taught me a lot about the magic of movies. (Specifically, it taught me how to do flip books.) The scene where Robert Donat shows Laurence Olivier his film is a scene that says everything about movies; it opened the whole magical quality of filmmaking. The magical and the mad: a man who would continue to try and try – at the expense of his family, his career, everything. The obsession of it! It makes you want to sign up. When you're eight years old, it makes you want to be a filmmaker.

Martin Scorsese's 100 Random Pleasures

On the whole, these films are not good. They're **guilty**.

But there are things in them that make you like them, that make them worthwhile. *The Agony and the Ecstasy, Alexander the Great, Barabbas, The Bible, Black Magic, Blood on Satan's Claw, The Brothers Karamazov, Captain Kronos – Vampire Hunter, Carry On Cleo, Circus of Horrors, The City That Never Sleeps* (or any John Auer film), *Damn Yankees, Elephant Walk, The FBI Story, Fantasmi di Roma, The Flesh and the Fiends, Forever Amber, The Golden Mask, The Halls of Montezuma, Helen of Troy, Honour Thy Father, Horrors of the Black Museum, Invasion USA, The Iron Maiden, King of Kings* ('61), *The Last Valley, The Legend of Hell House, The Man from Colorado, The Man Who Never Was, Middle of the Night, Mr. Sardonicus, The Naked Jungle, Ocean's Eleven* ('60), *One Million BC* ('40), *Pal Joey, People Will Talk, Pete Kelly's Blues, The Pride and the Passion, Prince of Foxes, The Proud and the Beautiful, The Purple Heart, Quo Vadis?, Raintree County, Sands of the Kalahari, The Scent of a Woman, The Snows of Kilimanjaro, Sodom and Gomorrah, The Streets of Laredo, The Three Musketeers* ('48), *Vampire Circus.*

These are **unguilty** pleasures, films that I love, even though something spoils them. *Al Capone, Arsenic and Old Lace, Autumn Leaves, Battleground, The Big Lift, Blanche Fury, Canyon Passage, The Chapman Report, The Climax, The Comic, Corridors of Blood, The Desert Fox, Don't Make Waves, Drums, The Easy Life, The Flight of the Phoenix* ('65), *The Girl Can't Help It, The Guns of Batasi, The Haunting* ('63), *Hill 24 Doesn't Answer, Idiot's Delight, Insect Woman, Invaders from Mars* ('53), *It's in the Bag* (or any Jack Benny film), *Jason and the Argonauts, The Jungle Book* ('42), *King Solomon's Mines* ('50), *Kill, Baby, Kill* (or any Mario Bava film), *Leave Her to Heaven, Living It Up, The Long Ships, The Macomber Affair, Mafioso, The Man Between, The Man in the Iron Mask* ('39), *The Man Who Could Work Miracles, The Maze, The Naked Prey, Pandora and the Flying Dutchman, Pay or Die, The Picture of Dorian Gray, Pork Chop Hill, The Purple Plain, The Razor's Edge* ('46), *The Red Tent, Shake Hands with the Devil, Take Care of My Little Girl, Too Late Blues, Il Viaggio, Where's Poppa?*

Extract from 'EASY RIDERS – RAGING BULLS'
By Peter Biskind

New York, New York went into production without a finished script. 'They started shooting because [Liza] Minnelli had a commitment to go to Vegas or something,' recalls Mardik Martin, whom Scorsese called in to rewrite Earl Mac Raush's draft. Scorsese knew the script wasn't ready. He explains, 'You get a big head. You think, "Oh, I don't have to make up a script, I can work it out on the soundstage when I'm there." Sure. A lot of guys work that way. Evidently, I couldn't.' Adds Sandy Weintraub, 'After *Mean Streets*, the critics called Marty "The King of Improv". And he decided that he *was* "The King of Improv". So on *Alice*, he was just gonna have everybody improv up a storm. That continued through *Taxi* and obviously the result you see is *New York, New York*, where it got out of control.' Continues Martin, 'It was a nightmare. I was writing up till the final frame. You don't make movies like that.'

Scorsese says he used coke as a creative tool: 'I didn't know how to get to these feelings. I kept pushing and shoving and twisting and turning myself in different ways, and I started taking drugs to explore, and got sidetracked a lot of the time. We put ourselves through a lot of pain.' One day, he kept over 150 fully costumed extras waiting while he talked to his shrink from the trailer. He was sick a lot, and late to the set. Says Martin, 'I blame all that on coke.'

The movie was intensely personal, for both Scorsese and De Niro. Consciously or unconsciously, De Niro's jazz musician (Jimmy Doyle) – the artist as a young man – was very much Scorsese at that time, torn between the claims of his family and his art, intoxicated with his own talent, and honeycombed by self-hatred. Doyle rejects his baby just like Scorsese rejected his. The Minnelli character is a version of [Scorsese's second wife] Julia Cameron, Sandy Weintraub, and other women Scorsese knew. Scorsese called it a $10 million 'home movie'. Cameron continued to irritate Marty's friends. Says Martin, 'She conned her way into doing a lot of rewriting, then told everyone she wrote *New York, New York*, which is total bullshit. She was a really bad drunk, a Jekyll and Hyde. I had a brand-new, beautiful Cadillac Seville, and I used to pick her up when she was drunk, and take her home. She threw up in my car twice. Marty said, "I'm sorry, I'm sorry."'

Cameron was pregnant, but Scorsese, mimicking the De Niro character, was carrying on an open affair with Minnelli, who was married to Jack Haley, Jr. (whose father played the Tin Man in *The Wizard of Oz*), and herself having a liaison with Mikhail Baryshnikov. Running into her with Haley on the street one day, Marty is supposed to have berated her about Baryshnikov. 'How could you!' he shouted, while Haley looked on. On another occasion, according to Andy Warhol's *Diary*, Minnelli appeared on Halston's doorstep pleading, 'Give me every drug you've got,' while Marty, ever dapper in his white suit, but shaking badly – apparently from the coke he'd taken – waited in the shadows. Halston gave her four 'ludes, a Valium, a vial of coke, and four joints. The couple went off into the night.

In the middle of the pregnancy, Marty realised it wasn't going to work out between him and Cameron, and when the baby was born, a girl named Domenica, he left her. Fuelled by an I-am-a-genius ego and surrounded now by an adoring circle of friends, with *New York, New York* shaping up as an unprecedented triumph, Scorsese had begun to change. Says Chris Mankiewicz, who had been in Europe and hadn't seen Marty since he had known him in New York in the sixties, 'By the time I came back I was surprised to see how much more – I won't say arrogant, but self-assured and bordering on arrogance – he had become. He was already a superstar director, and it was clear that he didn't tolerate [criticism].' Adds [Willard] Huyck, 'De Palma, who I always thought of as Marty's best friend, thought that Marty was so egocentric that he just became very difficult to relate to. [At one point, Brian] hadn't seen him in years, and there was no interest in anything that Brian had gone through. It was all what Marty was doing. I never liked him personally, but compared to everybody else, I always felt that Marty was the artist.'

TAXI DANCER
Martin Scorsese interviewed by Jonathan Kaplan

This interview took place May 25, 1977 during a break at Goldwyn Studios, where Martin Scorsese has been dubbing his new film, New York, New York.

Hello, I've had two hours sleep. I'm exhausted

Well, here we are. How do you feel about the picture?
This picture, *New York, New York*? I got pretty much what I wanted on the screen. More so actually. I got things as the picture developed that I didn't expect. Once I got the lean of it, in other words, where it was going to, it became more a dramatic story, and I took more of the music out. This wasn't even in the editing, I'm talking about the shooting.

What initially attracted you to the picture?
I liked the whole idea of the premise – a love story set in the big band era in the forties. For whatever reasons, I liked the idea. It was just one of those things. I planned to do it before *Taxi Driver*, but because of commitments, whatever, I had to do *Taxi* first. In fact, I started work on *New York, New York* before *Taxi*. When we got back to *New York, New York*, it became a little bigger than we thought because of this concept I had of doing the picture in the old style, which is, you know, sound stages and back lots. A movie called *New York, New York* shot entirely in Los Angeles. Made in Hollywood, USA, which reflects back to the old films I used to see as a kid, which

reflected a part of New York – I was really living in New York, but that was a fantasy of New York up on the screen. So in the picture, I tried to fuse whatever was a fantasy – the movies that I grew up with as a kid – with the reality that I experience myself.

Can you describe your working method on this picture?
The working method was kind of strange because Earl Mac Rauch worked on the script for a long time, but Earl, he is a very interesting writer. He is more of a novelist. Whenever we would ask for a change of two or three pages, he would bring twelve pages in and they were terrific. A whole new direction, whole new character things. He is a good writer and what happened was it became unmanageable in terms of making a shooting script. So eventually, at a certain point, my wife, Julia Cameron, started working with him and then about a month before the picture started shooting, Mac felt that he had given as much as he could to it. He couldn't go any further. He worked on it for two years. So then, Bobby De Niro and I had some ideas about some improvisations, and I had known Liza Minnelli for about a year and a half and we could feel comfortable in terms of the improv, but you just can't do a whole picture on improvisations. We needed the structure. So Mardik Martin of *Mean Streets* came in. Mardik structured it with Julia. He wrote some scenes, some key dialogue.

And this went on during the whole picture?
Yeah, fourteen weeks became 22 weeks. Mainly because of the fact that it was a musical. Irwin Winkler and Bob Chartoff and I had never done a musical before so we under-scheduled the picture mistakenly.

You mean in terms of the production numbers?
Actually, the big musical number 'Happy Endings' was perfectly scheduled. It was shot in ten days. Of course, eventually, it was cut out of the picture.

Not entirely . . .
Well, there are two shots left – the staircase and the popcorn. It works much better. But the entire 'Happy Endings' number, along with all the other scenes we liked, are in the television version, which is three to three-and-one-half hours. Tom Rolf just cut it. So what happened was that when we started making the picture, I did this all-out work on the production number. I made it as good as I could because I didn't know what the script was eventually going to turn out like. Even though I had a feeling at that point that it was going to be more personal than I had thought, and I was going to base it on myself, our relationships, our marriages. Sure enough, in the picture, the character [Jimmy Doyle/Robert De Niro], his wife [Francine Evans/Liza Minnelli] was pregnant, my wife was pregnant, Bobby's wife was pregnant, it was crazy time.

Art imitates life imitates art –
Imitates life. It was just madness. It went on and on like that. It was fun, it was crazy, it was upsetting, it was terrific; what eventually happened though, the improvisation procedure cost some time. We couldn't have done without Mardik supplying the structure, and Julia helping out. Also Irwin, too, helping out a great deal. Of course, with-

out Mac's script – I mean, he worked two years on it – we wouldn't have had anything.

What does Mac think of the film?
I don't know. I don't think he has seen it.

I don't know of another film that has been so widely screened during the editing process. How did you deal with all that feedback? I mean constantly being inundated with differing opinions, etc.
Well, at a certain point, you have to leave it. I left it for about three weeks. I left in a way that was not leaving it. I mean nobody knew I left it. They sensed I wasn't around as much. 'What's Scorsese doing? What's he playing the fuck around? What is this? Isn't he serious about the picture?' I mean when they got to that point, I just said, 'Leave me alone for a goddamn three days. Let me goddamn think about the goddamn movie. Everybody's given ideas, ideas, ideas, I appreciate it all, but at this point, it's total clutter. I can't see the picture and I don't know what the hell anybody is talking about anymore.'

The first cut was what? Four and a half hours?
Four and 29. And it worked.

It worked great.
But it wouldn't be for the theatrical audience. Once we started cutting it down and finally got it down to two hours, 45, that was when we were in the ballpark area. I reshot the key things, a couple of things at the end, because up until that point, I had been so close to the subject matter, the characters, that I couldn't see how they should end as characters.

It's a very organic process.
Yes, exactly. Really, in a way, I didn't shoot an ending, and we knew it. So we just waited. It was really that kind of a picture.

You rely so much on improvisation. What would you do if you found yourself confronted with an actor who couldn't improvise?
A lot of it has to do with casting. There are certain people who are just immovable. You try to stay away from them, but sometimes, you get stuck. The majority of actors, I find, give them the script and say, 'This is the dialogue,' or, 'I'll write the dialogue for you in a minute,' which automatically gives them a feeling of great insecurity and/or a feeling of great looseness and they can be relaxed to a certain extent. And you say, 'Here's the idea, and here are the sections – you go from here to here to here. Maybe you could think of how you want to say it. Why don't you say it in your own way?' And so you're stumbling around and you find new things and you write them down.

So you have an improvisation and now you set it.
Yes, you finally set it. You do it four or five times, but you finally set it.

Left: Big Band vocalist Francine Evans is based in part on Scorsese's former wife, Julia Cameron. Singer/actress Liza Minnelli would also become one of the women in his life. Right: De Niro as saxman Jimmy Doyle, a white man in thrall to the emergence of bebop jazz.

You do it four or five times in rehearsing, or on film?
You do it in rehearsing. But what happened eventually in *New York, New York*, the rehearsing caught up with us. So you are standing around the set rehearsing. That is where a lot of the time went to a certain extent.

Can you talk about a scene, a moment, a piece of business, anything, that was not scripted at any point that is in the final theatrical cut?
The breaking of the glass, when Jimmy knocks on the door.

In the proposal scene, at the Justice of the Peace?
Yeah, I got that idea at the end of the day. We had been rehearsing the shot all day. I kept thinking when he would knock on the glass that he would put his hand through it by accident. I said to myself, 'Gee, this is terrible. Bobby's going to cut his hand. We have to be careful. I'll tell him not to knock the glass so hard.' And then I thought, what if he actually *does* put his hand through it? So I asked about the window. I asked the A.D. and other people. They said 'Oh, that will take time. You know, the windows, it's a big deal.' Within fifteen minutes, we had two of them [breakaway windows], and then, of course, when we had the two, we got five more. And it went on like that, and we did it, and it worked. That kind of thing works. It was 5:30 in the afternoon, and we were trying, but we hadn't even taken a shot. So by the next day, we developed the point in the scene where he literally gets on his knees and tells Francine that he doesn't want her to be with anybody else. That element was added,

see, totally unscripted. That's what we were looking for. The scene in the script at that point was a farce scene. We said we needed something else.

Something real.
Yeah. Something where maybe this is the area where we can 'lock-in', 'lock-in' meaning that we could get a certain kind of honesty between the characters. And we asked, 'Will it work with the humour and everything?' and I said, 'Yeah, I think it will,' and then Bobby came up with the idea of putting his head under the car. But then he said he thought it was too much. But I said, 'Let's shoot it anyway.' You know, that's how it went, like that.

In general, if you had the time, you shot more than one alternative for a given scene?
Yes I really covered myself, and that came in handy, you know.

What are some of the problems of doing a musical?
The playback system.

Staying in synch?
The singing and dancing, staying in synch. And the way I shoot the music – every eight bars or four bars or twelve bars, there is a new shot.

This is all choreographed beforehand?
Drawn pictures, everything. I mean other people shoot it differently.

All in one master?
Yeah.

What else?
Well, Bobby learned to play the saxophone in synch. And it had to be in synch. The shot may have been beautiful, but the technical adviser would say, 'I'm sorry, the fingering was way out there,' and we would have to shoot it again.

The fight in the car, how long did it take to shoot?
Two days. One day for the masters, and then we had to stop.

Because they were both so bruised?
Yeah. Everyone was tired. The next day we did some close-ups and *that* is when we all went to the hospital, really. Liza almost broke her arm, Bobby hurt his knuckles, I hurt my knuckles. Of course, I wasn't in the car, it was from something else, I don't remember. But we all got x-rayed.

And what was scripted in that, was there scripted dialogue?
Yes, there was scripted dialogue. Some of the dialogue is in there. But the emotional thing became mainly improvisation. At one point I was with Bobby and I said, 'You know what, I think she should hit you here.' He said, 'Yeah, yeah, that's good.' The

next day when the three of us got together, Bobby had an idea for rearranging the scene. I said no, I didn't want to rearrange the scene, but we knew something heavy was going to happen. But Bobby said, 'Look at it this way,' and I said, 'Yeah yeah, it might work,' and I remember thinking to myself I shouldn't say this, and I started laughing to myself. Liza said, 'What?' and I said, 'But then, if we are going to do it that way, *he* should hit *her* at this point, towards the end, you know, six months, seven months pregnant, it doesn't matter.' And that's the way it happened. It happens in the first takes, and if you want, you tone it down, that's all, or you bring it up.

Let's talk about sets for a minute. Particularly the trees set at the Meadows Club. Did you anticipate the kind of reaction where people are going to say, 'What is it supposed to be? Real? Fake? What's going on?'
Yeah, I knew that was going to happen. We showed the film to a bunch of students and one of them said, 'Did you intend for that set to look realistic or the way it looks?' I said, 'Yeah, yeah, well, the whole film is on sets, do you realise that?' They all said no.

Of course some sets look very –
Real. I know. But if you look closely, they are all stylised. Boris Leven did that – the production designer.

What was the most common reaction you got from all the rough cut screenings that you had? Was there one scene, one character, plot point, something that people –
Liked?

Or didn't like.
The biggest thing was the 'Happy Endings' production number. But a lot of people felt it overbalanced the picture. I mean it was eleven minutes long, and eventually I realised it *did* overbalance the picture, and I had to cut it, and I did, and it was very painful. We made a short of it and it's also in the television version. But it does over-balance the film, because at the end, people felt in the montages in the end, Bobby's character was weakened.

But the production number was in a way a stylised microcosm of the whole picture.
Of course, I know. But they don't want to see it. Believe me. We like it. We are just crazy film buffs. It was a direct homage thing, a loving thing to the fifties, early fifties production numbers. Forties, whatever, but they don't want to watch it. Even if they like it, you could sit in the back of the screening room and see them moving around – restless. They want to know what is going to happen to the characters. And you know what happened, actually, was that the characters became stronger than the music.

So what are you up to now? What's next?
I've got two more films that will be done by the end of this year: *The All American Boy* about a friend of mine, Steve Prince, and *The Last Waltz*, you know, with The Band. Now, I'm going to do a play with Liza – almost like an extension of *New York, New York*.

The same Francine Evans character. Only after she has made it, and now she has to find a new image. A where-do-I-go-from-here sort of thing, at age 31, I've had it. That kind of character.

This might be sort of a strange question, but how are you going to put yourself in it? I mean is there a character that you can hang yourself on?
Herself.

Her?
Yeah, herself. The character. She's a workaholic. Complete crazy, crazy person who ruins everybody who comes near, marries her, disaster. Right? Another person, disaster. Always with the wrong person, and gets crazy and finally winds up alone. And likes it. [*laughter*] I don't know if I like it, but I wind up alone when the time comes. But that way I am undertaking a fantasy. This is going to be my first fantasy film –

Play.
[*laughter*] Play, play, whatever.

Extract from 'EASY RIDERS – RAGING BULLS' By Peter Biskind

New York, New York opened on June 21 [1977]. It was a darker movie than UA wanted. They thought it was going to be some sort of breakthrough musical of the old MGM school. Marty refused to change a frame. He was stubborn, and convinced of his own vision . . . . The plot was ragged and desultory, overwhelmed by the big, static production numbers. Even the critics, whom Scorsese had always been able to count on, deserted him. The lukewarm reception of *New York, New York* devastated him. He had gone from hit to hit. This was his first taste of failure, and he didn't like it. He says, 'I was angry, especially about being treated as if I had gotten a comeuppance – for what? For making *Mean Streets*? *Alice* and *Taxi Driver*? It wasn't the criticism, it was a lack of respect, so what I did was to behave in such a way that you could be guaranteed no respect at all.' Later he admitted, 'I was just too drugged out to solve the structure.' He was put on lithium in an effort to dampen his anger and control his violent outbursts. He took it for four months, but his drug of choice remained coke. It was as if he were lost in another world, Luke Skywalker stumbling about the ice planet Hoth in the opening scene of *The Empire Strikes Back*, lost in a blizzard of snow.

Not even De Niro could bring him back. He was still carrying around his well-thumbed copy of Jake La Motta's book, which he brought to Irwin Winkler. Winkler agreed to produce it, if they could get Marty to commit. But De Niro had a hard time getting his attention. Scorsese read a couple of chapters, gave the book to Mardik.

He had no interest in boxing, never went to fights. Besides, La Motta wasn't much of a boxer. His singular talent lay in his ability to absorb punishment. Mardik read it, told Scorsese, 'The trouble with *Raging Bull* is that the damn thing has been done a hundred times – a fighter who has trouble with his brother and his wife, and the Mob is after him. I don't want to do another brother-fighter story because that was done in *Champion.* And *Rocky* is out, same company. Same producers! Plus, I think this book is full of shit. It's made-up stuff, looks like a PR job.'

Scorsese, depressed, was more than willing to be discouraged. All the New Hollywood directors believed that being an auteur meant making personal movies. If they didn't generate their own material, they couldn't proceed until somehow they had made it their own. Through his affair with Cybill Shepherd, Bogdanovich experienced the vertigo of adolescence, which was the subject of *The Last Picture Show.* Francis Coppola *became* the Godfather. 'I really didn't want to do *Raging Bull,*' Scorsese says. 'I had to find the key for myself. And I wasn't interested in finding the key, because I'd tried something, *New York, New York,* and it was a failure.' . . . .

'We poured all of ourselves into one movie, and if it didn't hit, our whole career went down with it. There are directors who, after certain titles, didn't have anything more left, any more fight.' – Martin Scorsese

By the late seventies, there was a hard white snow falling on Hollywood. Coke was so widespread that people wore small gold spoons around their necks as jewellery. Drug connections became intimates, friends, and boyfriends. You went out to eat, you'd leave a line of coke on the table for the waitress as a tip. Scorsese, exhausted, in poor health, and fuelled by a perpetual coke high, tried to do everything. He promiscuously took on several projects at once. Then, toward the end of *New York, New York,* producer Jonathan Taplin called. The Band was going to break up, and he asked Scorsese to shoot a documentary about the group's final concert on Thanksgiving Day 1976, which would become *The Last Waltz.* Without giving it a second thought, Scorsese agreed. 'He never could resist Robbie Robertson and The Band,' says Irwin Winkler, who produced *New York, New York.* In the frame of mind he was in, he figured he could cut the film at night while he edited the feature during the day. Adds Taplin, 'Marty was just so wired he could show up at any hour of the day or night, go into the editing room, do a sequence, and go on to the next thing.'

After Julia Cameron moved out in January 1977, Robertson left his family to move into Scorsese's Mulholland Drive house. He had delusions about becoming a movie star, and Marty was his ticket. 'We were the odd couple – looking for trouble,' says Robertson. Reflects Sandy Weintraub, 'It was a shame that Marty wasn't gay. The best relationship he ever had was probably with Robbie.'

The Mulholland house was barely furnished, and notable for a seventeenth-century wooden crucifix concealing a dagger that hung over Marty's bed. His friends puzzled over the symbolism. The house looked like a hotel for transients, filled with the hangers-on, visiting filmmakers, musicians, and druggies who made up Scorsese's circle. The regulars, Steve Prince, Mardik Martin, Jay Cocks, and assorted hangers-on, used to gather in Scorsese's projection room in the garage – which doubled as

Robertson's bedroom – and watch four or five movies a night. 'Marty's house was blacked out with blinds,' says Robertson, 'soundproofed, and he installed an air system so you could breathe without opening the windows. We only had two problems: the light and the birds.'

'We were like vampires,' recalls Martin. 'It was like, "Oh no, the sun is coming up." We never got to sleep before seven, eight a.m., for six months.' Marty had also put in an elaborate security system, which invariably malfunctioned, bringing unwelcome visits from rent-a-cops. Outside of watching movies and doing drugs, Marty's only relaxation was playing with his collection of toy soldiers.

Marty had been taking pills since he was three, so by this time it was second nature to him. He took drugs like aspirin. He was still going up and down in weight. Coke depresses the appetite, but after going without food for two or three days, there was a lot of binge eating, a lot of junk food, anything that was at hand. Moreover, he and his friends needed booze to come down, so they knocked back a couple bottles of wine or vodka just to get to sleep. According to Taplin, 'They would call the editor of *The Last Waltz*, Yeu-Bun Yee, in the middle of the night with ideas. They were so stoked they thought everyone else was up all night too.'

'At first you felt like you could make five films at once,' Scorsese recalls. 'And then you wound up spending four days in bed every week because you were exhausted and your body couldn't take it.' He had been in and out of the hospital a number of times with asthma attacks. 'The doctor would say, "Take these pills. You're suffering from exhaustion,"' says Robertson. 'But we had places to go, people to see.' The rule was, live-fast-and-leave-a-good-looking-corpse. Scorsese was convinced he wouldn't see 40. 'It was a matter of pushing the envelope, of being bad, seeing how much you can do,' he continues. 'Embracing a way of life to its limit. I did a lot of drugs because I wanted to do a lot, I wanted to push all the way to the very very end, and see if I could die. That was the key thing, to see what it would be like getting close to death.' This kind of recklessness lent his work a high passion that hoisted it above the ordinary, but it was dangerous. 'I've always felt that there's something self-destructive in directors,' says Ned Tanen – himself no slouch in that department – contemplating the sorry spectacle of the New Hollywood directors careening pell-mell down the mountain, arriving in a heap at the bottom, careers shattered, marriages sundered, friendships broken, lives in ruins. 'I once asked Howard Hawks, my former father-in-law, about it, and he said, "The studio system worked because we couldn't be excessive, we couldn't just do what we wanted to do."'

One day there was a party at Winkler's home. Scorsese, Martin, and Robertson came late, stoned out of their minds, hung out by themselves at the far end of the pool. Scorsese was dressed in the crisp white suit he favoured above all others. All of a sudden John Cassavetes walked up, pulled Marty aside, started in on him for doing drugs. 'Whatsamatter with you?' he growled. 'Why are you doing this, ruining yourself? You're fucking up your talent. Shape up.' Scorsese broke out into a sweat. Cassavetes was a notorious drunk himself, but no one could call him on what he said, because they knew it was true.

De Niro had not given up on *Raging Bull*. But he was still having a hard time getting Scorsese's attention. Marty's personal life was in such turmoil he couldn't concentrate on his work. Despite his success, Scorsese was still extremely fragile, emotionally speaking, a state of affairs that doubtless stemmed from the aggravations of his childhood: his diminutive stature, his frailty, his perception of himself as unattractive. His feelings were easily hurt; he was quick to feel slighted and slow to forgive. He nursed grudges for years. He built a wall around himself. 'He was lost personally,' says Martin. 'Secure as he was on a film set, he was very insecure with himself as a man, dealing with people.' Martin once invited him to a party. 'I said to him, "We'll have a lot of fun, girls, orgies . . ." He said, "Nah . . . somebody will know who I am . . ." I said, "You don't have to tell them who you are. Nobody cares." He said, "No, no, no, I can't deal with a woman who doesn't know who I am." He had to be "Martin Scorsese" for him to deal with a woman, but then he worried she would only like him because he was "Martin Scorsese".'

'I was making love to different women, but I didn't find that very interesting,' Scorsese recalls. He was doing it more, enjoying it less. He got into a tempestuous relationship with an assistant, and one night he went to a party where he encountered her, Liza Minnelli, and Julia Cameron, all at the same time. She was the kind of woman who always had another man in her life, which drove Marty insane with jealousy. She threatened suicide every other day, which is to say, she was perfect for him. 'Marty sort of likes a little bit of drama, and if it's not there, he creates it,' says Martin. 'It was a typical living-dangerously mentality. She brought out the worst in him.' Scorsese could never stand to be alone. One night, he drove her out and then ran naked down Mulholland after her screaming, 'Come back, don't leave me.'

Scorsese knew he was acting badly, driving people away from him, but he couldn't help it. He says, 'I was always angry, throwing glasses, provoking people, really unpleasant to be around. I always found, no matter what anybody said, something to take offense at. I'd be the host, but at some point during the evening I'd flip out, just like when I'm shooting.' He began to have paranoid hallucinations. He'd say, 'I think somebody's watching me,' or, 'Somebody's trying to get in.' Marty had a one-night stand with Yeu-Bun Yee's girlfriend, who looked like a model, and was afraid that he would come up in the middle of the night and kill him. One of Steve Prince's jobs was to protect him from real or imagined dangers.

Scorsese and Robertson took *The Last Waltz* to Cannes in the spring of 1978. Fuelled by coke, Marty was doing back-to-back interviews, but even he eventually ran out of words. And coke. He joked, 'No more coke, no more interviews.' He couldn't score in Cannes, so a private plane was dispatched to Paris to bring back more coke.

'It hit me finally, when I was watching the end credits crawl of *The Last Waltz* at the Cinerama Dome, that I didn't enjoy it anymore,' says Scorsese. 'There was nothing left. I knew when I broke up the second marriage – I had a child, I knew I was not going to see the child for a while – but I always had a bottom line: the work, and felt good about having been able to say something in a movie, but this one day, it was like rock bottom. I thought, I've lost my voice.'

Scorsese kept everyone at bay, just yessing them to death, but refusing to move forward on *Raging Bull*. He was emotionally and spiritually tapped out. 'We were just circling the globe constantly, going from party to party, trying to find what it was that would inspire us again to do work,' he recalls. 'I knew what I wanted to say in *Mean*

Streets, like I knew what I wanted to say in *Taxi Driver*. I even knew what I wanted to say in *New York, New York*. But I know I didn't know what the hell *Raging Bull* was about.' He had done three straight pictures with De Niro. 'After a while, you want to do movies just on your own, especially after the unhappy experience with *New York, New York*,' he adds. 'I just didn't want to play anymore.'

Mardik was already on salary at Winkler's company, in which he was partnered with Robert Chartoff. Winkler told him to go ahead anyway, write a script. Mardik did a draft, which Scorsese couldn't even bring himself to read. One day, after Mardik pestered him for the hundredth time, the director asked, 'Okay, whaddya got?'

'I got one good scene that you're gonna like. You have these gladiators, see, just like in Rome, two guys, fighting each other, and you got all these rich people, fur coats, tuxedos, sitting in the front row, and Bobby gets punched in the face, and his nose starts to squirt blood, and it splatters all over these rich people's clothes and furs.'

'Whew, that's great, I love that. Lemme read the script.' Scorsese read the script, told Mardik, 'I wanna make it more personal.' His grandfather, who used to live on Staten Island, owned a fine fig tree, and one day he said, 'If the fig tree dies, I'm gonna die.' And sure enough, the fig tree died, and he died. Recalls Mardik, 'He wanted me to put that in the movie, a lot of crazy stuff that had nothing to do with Jake La Motta. I didn't want him to say no, so I catered to his whims and bullshit. It was driving me crazy. I said, '"Marty, I don't think this makes any sense, Bobby's gonna kill me."' Indeed, De Niro hated it, said, 'What's going on? This is not the picture we agreed upon.'

Continues Mardik, 'One day, Marty said to me, "Whaddya think of Paul Schrader coming in for a polish." Because Marty was not listening to me anymore, he was doing his Godfather bit. I said, "Sure, why not." Paul didn't even come to me. He sent somebody to get all my research, all my versions, three of them. I gave it to the guy, said, "Good luck."'

THE LAST WALTZ
Reviewed by David Bartholomew

On the basis of *The Last Waltz*, as well as his earlier films, it doesn't seem to me that Martin Scorsese knows much about, despite his obvious interest in, rock music. But perhaps that is part of the reason why he has fashioned one of the best rock films made thus far in this fledgling genre. That the movie is a documentary, a visual and aural recording of The Band's farewell concert, staged at San Francisco's Winterland on Thanksgiving Day 1976, seems secondary to its larger purposes. (Coincidentally, the only other rock documentary that brings intelligence to its form and content is also a 'farewell' film, Richard Heffron's *Fillmore*, chronicling the final concert, on July

4, 1971 – another patriotic American holiday – at Bill Graham's Fillmore West. Graham also produced the Winterland concert for The Band.) *The Last Waltz* was released at just the right time, before the spate of dumb, prepackaged music shows, geared around potential best-seller sound-track albums, like *FM* or *Thank God It's Friday*, and the summer extravaganzas, *Grease* and *Sgt Pepper's Lonely Hearts Club Band*.

I had suspected that Scorsese's tastes in music centred in forties Big Band jazz, judging from how that music impels, and in some sequences actually structures much of *New York, New York*. That film ambitiously sets out to criticise as well as memorialise an entire now deceased film genre, the forties movie musical, emblemised by MGM product, through intelligent usage of its every stylistic characteristic, not least the music. The pacing of this film, along with *Alice Doesn't Live Here Anymore* (in which Ellen Burstyn's piano bar rendition of 'Where or When' and the controversial opening 'flashback' using Alice Faye's 'You'll Never Know' [from *Hello Frisco Hello*, 1943] directly evoke the forties), and *Taxi Driver*, none of which substantially employs rock music, is notably different from the feverish, hypertensive quality of the (fiction) films that do: *Mean Streets*, in which the nonstop music serves as an occasionally ironic, nearly wallpaper-like indicator of mood and emotion, as well as its student-film-précis, *Who's That Knocking at My Door?* In these films, the rock music, without Scorsese's ever really confronting or analysing the form, is the determinant of the films' hopped-up style.

But certainly a nostalgic fondness for *New York, New York*'s world, which never really existed outside the Hollywood sound stages and the nation's movie theatres, is evident in Scorsese. At a press conference for the New York Film Festival, I had a chance to ask Scorsese about his musical preferences. He responded that his introduction to music was with forties Big Band music (just as his desire to direct films came from watching forties and fifties movies, which also accounts for much of the warm feelings in New *York, New York*), but that that music has led 'as a progression' to rock, which he now prefers.

But apart from the music itself, I think what interests Scorsese in rock seems to be its phenomenological accoutrements: the energy it so nonchalantly contains, slowly releases, but never consumes; the awesome power it exerts over audiences, often in a mass sense, which is a bit frightening, as anyone who has been to a 'busted' rock concert – one that has gone wrong and soured – may attest. He seems fascinated with probing the particularly American rock myth and raucous lifestyle – the unceasing, rootless touring, the rabid adoration of fans, the drugs and boozing and easy multi-city groupie sex, the ostentatious display of wealth, the wielding of power, via music, incorporating a space-centre-worthy array of electronics, whether for art (Dylan) or commerce (Kiss), and the creation in-concert of a seamless fantasyland. Even the negative elements entail an attractive vulgar glamour like that of glossy potboiler movies like *The Betsy*, *The Other Side of Midnight*, or *The Greek Tycoon*. That myth, an evenly designed, clear-headed creation of concert promoters, the rock press and record companies, and facilely perpetuated in movies like *Performance*, *Welcome to LA*, *Payday*, and the Kristofferson half of *A Star is Born*, is one of the last great Romantic notions. As an all-encompassing, all-sense enveloping experience, the only thing to come close to the power of in-concert rock is . . . the movies.

Scorsese is also interested in longevity, its traits, values and problems, and in the

Old Band mates (l-r) Richard Manuel, Rick Danko and Robbie Robertson during the filming of The Last Waltz *(1978). Robertson moved in with Scorsese during the most self-destructively hedonistic stage of his life.*

impact of passing time, which is often computed in his films in terms of physical distance, as in *Alice Doesn't Live Here Anymore*, or in the incessant, even neurotic movement of *Mean Streets*. (It's also no accident that Travis Bickle drives a cab.) When Scorsese met them for the film, The Band had played together, cut records, and toured for more than sixteen years. It was a group decision to call a halt; they had developed other interests (one of them, Robbie Robertson, decided to produce *The Last Waltz*). In one of the film's many interview sequences, cut in between the musical numbers, Robertson, The Band's lead guitar and voice vocalist, sums it up: 'The Road has taken a lot of the great ones.' He mentions Joplin, Presley, Morrison, Holly. 'It's a goddamn impossible way of life.' Earlier, he had looked away from the camera, saying, 'Man, I couldn't have handled twenty years.' He laughs incredulously at the thought of it. (It is perhaps not so unusual to note that Robertson, who produced the film, dominates the movie's interview footage – he learns fast.)

The Band – the simple name was deliberately chosen to repudiate the garish psychedelically named groups (Strawberry Alarm Clock, Ultimate Spinach, et al) prevalent in the sixties – has always been composed of Robertson, Rick Danko (bass), Garth Hudson (organ), Richard Manuel (piano) – all Canadians – and Levon Helm (drums), from Arkansas. As a group, they actually go back to the late fifties when they toured for six years in seedy one-night-stands through Canada and the rough-and-tumble US South and South-West, working their asses off as 'the Hawks' behind Rompin' Ronnie Hawkins, one of rock's great madmen/legends, who fits the more negative, self-destructive dimensions of the rock star myth, albeit an early version – so early that he was never able to take advantage of it and become famous. Together, they were a loud, cutthroat, rockabilly bar band and seldom were afforded the luxury of recording. Hawkins was responsible for forging them into a band (he proudly comes out to do the film concert's first number), but they left him when Dylan, in 1965, shocking his fans by 'going electric', asked them to tour as his backup. It was a move that most rock critics dub the beginning of the folk-rock movement. They worked on their songs in a ranch house (the 'Big Pink' of their first album title) in West Saugerties, NY, then migrated a bit north to Woodstock to rejoin Dylan in 1966 during his 'creative rest period', when he was recuperating from his near-fatal motorcycle accident. Dylan eventually left them to return to Greenwich Village and other forms of music. But The Band kept on, together, and their second, and probably best-known album, released late in 1969, is a classic; it put them, as well as country-rock, on the charts. The fans and media fell to – including a *Time* cover story on January 12, 1970, and they've been up there, without even a brief decline in popularity, ever since. Until 1976, when The Band disbanded.

About midway through *The Last Waltz*'s repertoire of 26 numbers, featuring a parade of 'friends' – guest artists who signed on for the final concert – Scorsese works a cumulative small miracle that continues to deepen in impact through the rest of the film. The artists, ranging from the Staples to Dr John to Eric Clapton and Ringo Starr, emblemise the sixties to early seventies, and the film becomes a moving testament to that tumultuous time, a non-nostalgic chronicle and summation of where we and they have been, and what we've all gone through. The songs are exactly the same as when they were first performed, indigenous and locked into that specific time period, but we and the singers are different, changed. Looking at them now, we can see the rough passing of the years. Neil Diamond, singing 'Dry Your Eyes,' is pudgy with Top-40 success and verges on Tom Jones-y, self-parodying macho kitsch; Neil Young, hollow-eyed, looking as if he's felt the draining torment of the raw, brilliant songs he wrote and sang in album after album since his easy-going Crosby-Stills-Nash days, cuts loose on 'Helpless'; Joni Mitchell, large-eyed, thin and bony, sings 'Coyote'; Van Morrison, puffy, clean-shaven, double-knitted, working on a second chin, like a has-been Vegas lounge lizard, comes on for 'Caravan'.

Several of the performances are utterly electrifying: Neil Young's, and the changeless Muddy Waters – the man who has seen and survived more of the Road than most of these people put together – and his exuberant rendition of his classic 'Mannish Boy'. Dylan himself, the grand mentor, a sixties icon, appears near the end; the camera slowly coasts down over his white rock-star hat, searching for his face hidden behind the brim (like David Bowie's in the last shot of *The Man Who Fell to Earth*).

Somehow Scorsese has managed to avoid the multitude of clichés of the rock concert film; after all, the raw material – a group on a stage – is largely the same, film to film. He has also managed, particularly in the interview sequences, to defeat the childish, ego-bound pretensions of many rock stars and their films (e.g. Led Zeppelin's *The Song Remains the Same*), pretentious by their very venturing into film, a move too easily and stupidly taken (most rock stars take their god-likeness very seriously). Not surprisingly, Scorsese has achieved a formal quality in the film's visuals and editing, resulting in an even blending of concert, studio and rehearsal numbers, interview and offstage footage. Some of the concert material is intricately detailed;

Bob Dylan sings at the farewell performance of The Band, The Last Waltz *(1978).*

for instance, during Neil Diamond's song, the camera suddenly discovers, then zeroes in tight on Diamond's lips caressing the surface of his microphone.

The film is beautifully photographed by the likes of Laszlo Kovacs and Vilmos Zsigmond (the credits list them as well as four others as directors of photography, along with eleven first assistant cameramen). The images are steady, including several from a crane – I'm not sure how they ever got one in there in the midst of the swirling mob of an audience, let alone manipulate it. The photography eschews the *vérité* feel – the concert film cliché – which results in a slightly distancing effect, often overpowered by the music, not to mention eyestrain headaches. It is Scorsese's intention to examine, not stimulate, a concert experience. The sound recording, utilising a 24-track Dolby mix, is superb, rivalled only by that of *Renaldo and Clara*, Dylan's recent mammoth self-indulgence.

Surprisingly, Scorsese doesn't come off all that well as an on-camera interviewer. He seems nervous, as if he knows he's at the wrong end of the camera. In one scene, gently photographed at night outside a quiet, rural-like pool hall, a tableful of musicians linger over some beers and talk about the origins of their music, how it all came together. Amongst the group, Scorsese seems puzzled after listening for a while, asks what this new kind of music is called. They look at him in amazement. 'Rock and roll,' they say. Scorsese mumbles, 'Oh, yeah. Of course.' In another scene, Robertson leads Scorsese and the camera through a labyrinthine series of hallways and rooms and points out that the building, now used for offices, was once a bordello. Still moving rapidly, after a few seconds of silence, Scorsese numbly observes, 'I guess that's why there are a lot of rooms.'

Movies Are My Life, a 59-minute documentary on Scorsese by British director Peter Hayden, perhaps sheds some light on this curious aspect of Scorsese. The film was shot with Scorsese's full cooperation, which probably accounts for Hayden's getting on-camera interviews with most of Scorsese's actors, including the notoriously publicity-shy Robert De Niro. Many of them comment on Scorsese's extreme nervousness while shooting. Jodie Foster says he was especially nervous during *Taxi Driver* (as opposed to *Alice*) since he feared that 'there were cops always around the corner ready to arrest him because I was so young.' (She also off-handedly mentions his downing pills 'for his ulcers'.)

This nervousness could also account for his seeming on-camera naiveté. The second of Scorsese's planned one-hour films on various individuals (the first, *Italianamerican*, dealt with his parents) was recently shown in New York. *American Boy* is an extrapolated portrait of the sixties through a series of funny but increasingly harrowing stories told by one of his friends, Steven Prince, described as an actor and producer (he played the jittery junior-businessman-type gun salesman in *Taxi Driver*). In this film, Scorsese occasionally interrupts Prince's rambling to ask him what various drug names and slang mean. (Is it possible, for instance, for anyone as old as Scorsese was during the sixties *not* to know what a 'shooting gallery' was?) Watching this film, it ocurred to me that Scorsese's odd naivité on-camera may be merely feigned to overcome the possible ignorance of his eventual movie-theatre audience.

The Hayden film, incidentally, which features a long predawn interview with a semidrunken Robbie Robertson, also provides information on the development of *The Last Waltz*. The two men apparently met for the first time at the legendary Woodstock Festival, for the film of which Scorsese was principal editor. When it came time to make *Waltz*, Scorsese 'was the only person I knew who knew enough about movies to do it. I didn't know anything about movies, plus he loves the music and grew up with it, so he could relate to the whole fucking experience. The movie was supposed to be simple, a recording of the concert,' but as Scorsese got more and more involved in it, 'he talked us into doing some additional numbers in the studio and also all the interview stuff. It all just grew out of a very simple idea.' Perhaps referring somewhat incoherently to the stylistic effect of music on films, Robertson, who doesn't use Scorsese's name and addresses him only as 'Maestro', says that 'the man is a conductor', and describes a shot (apparently the last one in the film) during which he suddenly looked up in surprise to see Scorsese, riding on the camera crane, eyes half closed, 'conducting' the music they were playing. Later he mentions that often during the filming of the interview segments, Scorsese would be 'on the chair opposite, moving his arms to what I was saying to him. He was "conducting" our conversation!'

The Last Waltz is the most movie-free of Scorsese's pictures. Still, the opening credits sequence features a formally dressed waltzing pair, which recalls the subway *pas-de-deux* from *New York, New York*. You can't tell from the film, or from Hayden's film, or the Prince short, which deals by implication with the time period, what Scorsese really thinks about the era, whether he regrets the decade and its excesses or accepts its lessons. After all, those years have been kind to him. In and after them, he found success as a movie director, his dream from adolescence. Whether that success also includes wealth is problematical; certainly he hasn't achieved it on the scale of Lucas and Spielberg, the West Coast branch of his generation, who traded each other points on *Star Wars* and *Close Encounters of the Third Kind*, thus becoming millionaires on *each other's* films alone.

In that context of sixties-seventies evaluation, the final sequence of *The Last Waltz* becomes less a conceit than a quietly moving statement. On a small, empty stage, The Band is playing the film's theme song. Beginning with a close-up of the organ pipes, the camera cranes down over them and out until the group is squarely framed. They are suddenly brightly illuminated against a dark green background. (The bright light coldly symbolises their long-term success, literally, somewhat banally, time in the spotlight?) Then the light is extinguished, and the camera continues to move backward, the group still playing, now dimly lit. The camera moves further and further back, past two long lines of large soft globes of light, at opposite ends of the frame, extending from the stage like a night-time airport runway. Implying a creative permanence, they continue to play, softly.

AMERICAN BOY
Reviewed by Tom Milne

At George Memmoli's home in Hollywood, Martin Scorsese – making a film about Steven Prince, his friend and associate since 1968 – is already filming when Prince bursts in and picks a playful fight with Memmoli. Prince is then encouraged to tell stories (which are interspersed with brief 16 mm clips of him as a child), and begins with his encounter, while stoned on grass and working as road manager for Neil Diamond, with a toilet-trained gorilla in a straw hat and short pants. After talking about his father (an army colonel and gun expert), his mother ('her cooking had no taste at all'), and his grandmother ('a real Russian Jew, a real ballbuster', who ran a paper company until she was 84). Prince tells more stories. HOT BAGELS: Aged sixteen, he ran a business importing hot bagels to the Jewish quarter. ON THE SOUND: He was run aground while sailing with a drunken skipper on Long Island Sound at night. IN THE PARK: A child was electrocuted while playing with electric cables in Prince's charge. BACKSTAGE: Exhausted from overwork as head technical student on a stage production, he was galvanised by an amphetamine injection. THE DRAFT: He was graded 4F by the army after claiming to be a homosexual. JACK THE COP: Drawing a gun on a mugger while making a night deposit, he was advised to shoot the thief to save paperwork by a cop arriving on the scene. COCOA JACKS/SHOOTING GALLERY: His experiences as a heroin addict for five years before he kicked the habit. ETHYL AND REGULAR: Holding a vacation job at a gas station, he shot and killed a thief coming at him with a knife. SURVIVING: A telephone conversation with his dying father, who asked if he was happy.

There are several possible ways of looking at this home-movie documentary, filmed by Scorsese after *Taxi Driver* and while editing *New York, New York*. The least interesting is probably as the chronicle of disenchantment suggested by the use of Neil Young's song 'Time Fades Away' to open and close this downbeat account of what became of the all-American child whose innocently beaming face was so faithfully filmed on each of his birthdays. Only marginally more interesting is the 'Profile of Steven Prince' (as the film describes itself), since it emerges as a sort of *reductio ad absurdum* synthesis of every aspect of the protest generation of the sixties, from drugs and violence to conning the draft board. It may all be true, but there is a heady whiff of mythomania here. To judge by the constant cries of 'tell the one about . . .', accompanied by a beatific grin of anticipation on Memmoli's face, Prince has a local reputation as a storyteller. That this is not really upheld in the film, that the stories sound as if they had become embellished in the telling, and that Prince himself sometimes seems more the party bore than the priceless raconteur, is not entirely his fault, since the film was apparently shot in one extended session: one senses an increasing hysteria that does not help much with the credibility.

But it is at this point that the film becomes fascinating as a gloss on Scorsese's work, since the edgy ambivalence of Prince's persona, as a junkie who has kicked the habit but still comes on with the unpredictable violence of the junkie, is a sort of bridge spanning *Mean Streets* and *Taxi Driver*. An explosive mixture of shaggy and mad dog, Prince might (superficially, at least) be a model for De Niro's Johnny Boy in *Mean Streets*. The opening scene of *American Boy* even playfully suggests a parallel with the tortured Catholicism of Harvey Keitel's Charlie in the same film when Prince (sitting in a jacuzzi with Scorsese) jokingly says, 'I'm guilty, huh?', and a voice-off answers, 'We're all guilty, God knows.'

Scorsese tries to carry this parallel a stage further at the end when Prince is describing a conversation with his dying father, who asked him if he was having fun in what he did. Scorsese intervenes twice to ask Prince to rephrase the question exactly as he had told it before filming began. Obediently rewording both question and answer, Prince then says, 'I told him I was happy, yeah,' and the camera holds on his impassive face until the film ends. But it doesn't really take, because the quasi-theological distinction between having fun and being happy, which would mean everything to Keitel's Charlie, clearly means nothing to Prince. From there one battens on ethnic differences: a long way from Scorsese's underprivileged Little Italy, Prince is privileged middle-class Jewish. And throughout *American Boy*, one senses Scorsese's fascination – almost his uncritical admiration – for attitudes so alien to his own experience as Prince talks of death and violence from the standpoint of a dilettante gun collector and expert. If one then thinks of Prince's performance as the fanatical gun salesman in *Taxi Driver* and his kinship with Travis Bickle, one comes closer to understanding why the violence in that film – moving away from traditional Mafia-oriented criminality into fashionable urban apocalypse – seems so unconsidered and unassimilated by comparison with *Mean Streets*.

Extract from 'EASY RIDERS – RAGING BULLS'
By Peter Biskind

During the last week of *Hardcore*, when De Niro paid a visit to the set, Schrader knew something was up. The actor was not the sort to casually drop by. He told Schrader that UA wouldn't make *Raging Bull* with Mardik's script; he asked Schrader to rewrite it. He also told him he was fed up with Scorsese's indifference to the project. By that time, Schrader had firmly established himself as a director, and he was not eager to work on other people's scripts. At a dinner with Bob and Marty at Musso and Frank's Grill in the summer of 1978, he agreed to do a polish, but he made sure they knew he was doing them a favour. This did not sit well with Marty.

After reading Mardik's drafts, Schrader concluded that more was needed than just a fix. He knew he had to go back to the sources, do his own research. It was then that he discovered Jake's brother, Joey. Recalls Schrader, 'They were both boxers. Joey was younger, better looking, and a real smooth talker. It occurred to Joey that he could do better at managing his brother. He wouldn't have to get beat up, he'd still get the girls, and he would get the money. And having a brother myself, it was very easy for me to tap into that tension. I realised there was a movie there.' *Raging Bull*, among other things, became a version of Schrader's relationship with Leonard.

Meanwhile, the movie was coming together for De Niro. One day, at Scorsese's suite in the Sherry, La Motta just got up and banged his head against the wall. Recalls Scorsese, 'De Niro saw this movement and suddenly he got the whole character from him, the whole movie. We knew we wanted to make a movie that would reach a man at the point of making that gesture with the line, "I'm not an animal."'

Schrader wrote at Nickodell's, a bar on Melrose next to Paramount that, in [Don] Simpson's words, 'was a great place to get fucked up, because it was dark and cavernous.' He remembers Schrader retiring to the bathroom for some moments, then emerging to take a seat at the bar, where he feverishly scribbled on a napkin. It was a scene in which La Motta, in jail and at the nadir of his fortunes, tries to masturbate. But he can't get off, because his mind is flooded with guilt, memories of how terrible he's been to the various women in his life. This was Schrader at his best, going places nobody else would go, raw and fearless.

But material of this kind was way too rich for UA. Winkler met with the executives at Eric Pleskow's apartment on Ocean Avenue in Santa Monica, near the beach. 'We'd just done a boxing movie, *Rocky*,' recalls [Mike] Medavoy, 'and this was a real downer.' According to Winkler, the company wanted no part of *Raging Bull*. Still, the producer had a trump. 'We were in a unique position, 'cause we owned the rights to *Rocky*,' he says. UA had released *Rocky* in 1976. It was one of the coming crop of post-New Hollywood feel-good films, a throwback to the fifties, and a peek at the eighties, a racist, Great White Hope slap at Muhammad Ali – on whom the character of Rocky's opponent was all too obviously based – and everything he stood for, the generation of uppity black folk and the antiwar, 'nigger-loving' white kids who admired him. *Rocky* was a huge success, taking in about $110 million before it played out, making it the fifth highest grossing picture of all time. So all Winkler had to say was, 'Want to make *Raging Bull?* No? Want to make *Rocky II?* Yes? Okay, let's make a deal.'

Even the writer of *Taxi Driver* found the characters repellent. Schrader told Marty, 'We have to give Jake a depth, a stature he does not possess, otherwise he's not worth making a movie about.' He says Scorsese didn't get it. For Scorsese, Jake's Neanderthal sensibility was the whole point. 'Bob and I sort of pushed each other in terms of how unpleasant a character could be, and still people cared for him,' he says. 'Because there's something in Bob as an actor, something about his face, that people see the humanity.'

Scorsese, De Niro, and Winkler met with Schrader at the Sherry to discuss the script. It was a tense meeting. Marty thought Schrader's new draft was a breakthrough. He too responded to the sibling aspects of the script. Still, both he and De Niro had reservations. Recalls Schrader, 'De Niro was baulking at a lot of the heavier stuff, the raw, controversial stuff, the cock and the ice and all that, "Why do we have to do these things?" Marty wasn't going to take on Bob, because he had to work with him, so he was letting me fight those fights. It was a bold, original kind of scene. But looking at it from De Niro's point of view, it was pretty hard to make it work, sitting there with your dick in your hand.' To Marty and Bob, Schrader's attitude was, 'Here's your script, I don't need this, I want to get back to my own projects.' At one point, Paul threw the script across the room, yelling, 'If you want a secretary to take dictation, hire one. But I'm here to try to write a real story about someone that people care about,' and stormed out. Says Scorsese, 'I'll do anything and say anything to get what I want on the screen. Throw something at me, curse at me, do what you want to do as long as I get what I want. I sit there and smile and take it and run, which is what I did. He broke the icejam and gave us something special. But I certainly couldn't embrace the person afterward. Not after years of slights and insults, it was just too much.'

But Scorsese's world came crashing down around his ears right after Labor Day 1978. He had been living with Isabella Rossellini since early summer. Rossellini, De Niro, and Martin, went to the Telluride Film Festival. 'We didn't have any coke, somebody gave us some garbage, it made us sick,' recalls Mardik. That weekend, Scorsese started coughing up blood, and blacked out for the first time in his life. From Telluride, he went to New York, where he collapsed. 'He was bleeding from his mouth, bleeding from his nose, bleeding from his eyes, ass. He was very near death,' Martin adds. Rossellini had to go to Italy for work, and when she left, after that weekend, she thought she was never going to see him alive again.

Steve Prince took Scorsese to New York Hospital. A doctor came running down to the ER carrying a sample of his blood, yelling, 'Is this your blood?'

'Yeah,' Scorsese replied, blankly.

'Do you realise you have no platelets?'

'I don't know what that means.'

'It means you're bleeding internally everywhere.'

'I want to get back to work.'

'You can't go anywhere, you may get a brain haemorrhage any second.'

Scorsese's condition appeared to be a result of the interaction among his asthma medication, other prescription drugs, and the bad coke he had taken over the weekend. He was down to 109 pounds. The doctor stopped all the drugs and pumped him full of cortisone. He was put in a palatial room previously occupied by the Shah of Iran, but he couldn't sleep, and the first three nights he stayed up watching movies, among them, *Dr. Jekyll and Mr. Hyde*, appropriately enough. Eventually, the cortisone worked, and his platelet count started to rise, stopping the bleeding.

'Finally,' says Robertson, 'Marty got a doctor who conveyed the message that either he changed his life or he was going to die. We knew we had to change trains. Our lives were way too rich. The cholesterol level was unimaginable. I went back to my family, hoping they would overlook my fool heart.'

De Niro came into Scorsese's room, said, 'What's the matter with you, Marty? Don't you wanna live to see if your daughter is gonna grow up and get married? Are you gonna be one of those flash-in-the-pan directors who does a couple of good movies and it's over for them?' He changed the subject to *Raging Bull*, said, 'You know, we can make this picture. We can really do a great job. Are we doing it or not?' Scorsese replied, 'Yes.' He had finally found the hook: the self-destructiveness, the wanton damage to the people around him, just for its own sake. He thought: I am Jake . . . .

Like Arthur Krim and company, the new production heads at UA, Steven Bach and David Field, found the *Raging Bull* script scabrous and depressing, thought it made *Rocky* look like a dust-up between two sissies in the sandbox. One of Winkler's jobs was to keep bad news away from his volatile director. Scorsese had no idea the project was in jeopardy. He recalls, 'I thought I could get any picture made, particularly with De Niro. He was a big star. I was naïve about that.'

Winkler finally called Marty, said, 'We better have a meeting with the UA guys. Just say hello and talk about the script.'

'What do they want to know? What do we have to talk about?'

'Just say hello. It's a hello meeting. It's just something so they feel part of it.' At the end of November 1978, just after Thanksgiving, Bach and Field accompanied Winkler to Scorsese's co-op in the Galleria on East 57th Street in New York. De Niro was there as well. Winkler wasn't worried. He still had the *Rocky* trump. But Scorsese startled them by announcing he wanted to do the film in black and white. He wanted *Raging Bull* to have a tabloid look, like Weegee. Bach and Field demurred, eventually gave in, but came up with a series of objections to the script.

'This picture is written as an X, and I don't think we can afford that,' said Bach.

'What makes you so sure it's an X?'

'When I read in a script "close-up on Jake La Motta's erection as he pours ice water over it prior to the fight," then I think we're in the land of X . . .'

'Look,' interrupted Field, 'it isn't about the language or the things the writers wrote that you probably won't shoot anyway. It's the whole script. It's this *man*,' Field said, quietly. 'I don't know who wants to see a movie that begins with a man so angry, so . . . choked with rage, that because his pregnant wife burns the steak, he slugs her to the kitchen floor and then kicks her in the abdomen until she aborts.'

'We'll find a writer who can lick it,' said Winkler, blandly.

'It's not finally about the writer,' said Field. 'Can any writer make him more than

Jake La Motta (De Niro), in Raging Bull *(1980), soaks up punishment from Billy Fox, throwing the fight without taking a dive. Scorsese's fight scenes are beautifully choreographed and grotesquely expressionistic.*

what he seems to be in the scripts we've seen?'

'Which is what?' asked Marty, brows knitted.

Field regarded him with a faint smile. 'A cockroach.'

A suffocating silence fell over the room like a blanket. De Niro, in jeans and bare feet, slumped in an easy chair, had said nothing. He roused himself, and said, quietly but distinctly, 'He is not a cockroach . . . . He is *not* a cockroach.'

Bob and Marty took off for St. Martin, and completely reworked the script. Scorsese didn't like islands, his asthma was killing him. He was taking Tedral to clear his lungs, but it sent him into bouts of trembling. De Niro nursed him, made him coffee in the mornings. They knew this was it; either they came back with a usable screenplay, or the project was history. But right away they found the zone. Once again, Scorsese dipped into himself. He recalls, 'The key thing was the writing of the scene where Jake is fixing the television, and he accuses his brother of sleeping with his wife. What I took from myself was the tenacity of a man who is so paranoid and so self-destructive that even though he knows nothing, he will conduct an investigation of the person closest to him as if he knows exactly what happened, and he will not accept no for an answer, which means he sets up everything to destroy himself.'

Weeks later, UA approved it . . . .

Scorsese went into *Raging Bull* twisted into a knot of bitterness, defiance, and self-doubt. He was overwhelmed by a sense of fatality, a certainty that this was his last movie. 'I was dead serious about it,' he says. 'I was throwing it back at them, like, This is what I think I can do, and I don't know if I have any more in me.' He was lucky he never had the huge hits, *The Godfather, Star Wars*. He had nothing to protect. 'After *New York, New York*, I thought, I'll never have the audience of Spielberg, not even of Francis. My audience is the guys I grew up around, wiseguys, guys from Queens, truck drivers, guys loading furniture. If they think it's good, I'm fine. Maybe I'm crazy. But rather than compromise the story and make ten other pictures afterward, I'd rather leave it alone and not make any more movies after this. So what the hell!' The conviction that he had cut himself loose from conventional Hollywood filmmaking, that he had nothing to lose and nowhere else to go, freed him to do the best work of his career.

Raging Bull commenced principal photography in April of 1979, the same month *Heaven's Gate* went into production. Scorsese was edgy and irritable as ever, prone to sudden outbursts of anger. He got frustrated waiting for the DP, Michael Chapman, to set up shots. He would go into his trailer, put on The Clash at top volume, and sit there, revved up by the music, pacing back and forth, counting the seconds. After 45 minutes, he'd come storming out yelling, 'It's more than one side of The Clash, Michael. What are you doing?' Then he picked up a folding chair and heaved it against the side of the trailer, making big dents and chipping the paint. The beefy Teamster driver tried to stop him, shouting, 'Hey, you can't do that.' Scorsese's tiny mother, Catharine, sprang to his defence. 'Leave him alone,' she snapped. 'He's waiting, he's upset.'

They took a break while De Niro ate his way through Tuscany and Rome for two months to gain the 50 pounds he needed to impersonate La Motta in his decline. 'He stuffed himself with ice cream and spaghetti every night until he looked like a pig,' recalls Martin. Scorsese and Rossellini got married in Rome on September 30. Sandy Weintraub joked that he was sleeping his way through the daughters of his favourite directors. The couple went to Japan where she had two weeks of work. Scorsese had such a severe anxiety attack on the bullet train from Kyoto to Tokyo that he couldn't catch his breath and was convinced he was having a coronary. They took him from the train to the hospital in Tokyo in an ambulance. A doctor asked him to breathe into a paper bag. The next day, he was fine. But it was in a disturbed frame of mind that he returned to shoot the last two weeks of the picture.

MARTIN SCORSESE FIGHTS BACK
By Thomas Wiener

Mid-July in Manhattan. Outside, the temperature hovers around 100, but inside it is cool and quiet. It is 1:30 p.m. and Martin Scorsese's day is winding down. The blinds and curtains in both bedrooms of his midtown apartment are drawn. In one bedroom a visitor is watching a videotape projected onto an oversize television screen; in the other Scorsese and his editor are making last-minute cuts on his new film.

Martin Scorsese is worried. For several months, since he began editing, his schedule has been to work through the night and morning, go to bed in the afternoon, sleep until nightfall, and then get up for more work. 'Except that I haven't been sleeping well lately,' he admits. 'I watch a movie on the television, I try to read, but I can't seem to fall asleep. Nerves. I'm just so involved with this picture.'

The film is *Raging Bull*, and it stars Robert De Niro as boxer Jake La Motta. The title refers to La Motta's 1970 autobiography, but according to Scorsese, the film, which was shot in black and white, is not an adaptation. 'It is Bobby's [De Niro] and my view of him,' says Scorsese.

Scheduled for release this month, *Raging Bull* is Scorsese's first feature since the critical and box-office disappointment of *New York, New York* three years ago. Before that, Scorsese's career was riding high from the successive triumphs of *Mean Streets* (1973), *Alice Doesn't Live Here Any More* (1975), and *Taxi Driver* (1976). With *Raging Bull*, there is renewed excitement about what Scorsese is up to. Some observers of the film scene see the movie as his big comeback. And in a year of cinematic letdowns, there is hope that *Raging Bull* may be the genuine article, a film that provokes serious critical discussion and possibly sells a few tickets along the way.

The world of boxing seems a natural place for Scorsese, whose films have succeeded so well in capturing the unpredictable violence of urban America. Jake La Motta grew up poor in the Bronx, landed in reform school, and there became a boxer under the guidance of a kindly priest. After a stormy professional career, which included charges that he threw a fight, and a short reign as middleweight champion, La Motta retired to face even more tumult. His second wife, Vickie, left him after eleven years, and in 1954 La Motta was arrested in Miami on what is politely referred to as a morals charge. The ex-champ found himself where he had begun his boxing career – in jail.

It was not Scorsese, however, who originally was attracted to La Motta's story. 'Bobby De Niro brought me the book about five years ago,' Scorsese recalls, 'and said he wanted to play this guy.' At first Scorsese balked; for one thing, he had never been to a prizefight. Attending a few bouts with De Niro did little to change his mind, but after reading about La Motta and talking with people in the boxing world, Scorsese began to sense something about boxers in general and La Motta in particular that fascinated him.

Scorsese saw La Motta's life as one of personal redemption, 'of a guy attaining something and losing everything, and then redeeming himself.'

In a new book, *Martin Scorsese: The First Decade*, Scorsese tells writer Mary Pat Kelly what attracted him most to La Motta. 'He's on a higher spiritual level in a way, as a fighter. He works on an almost primitive level, almost an animal level. And therefore he must think in a different way, he must be aware of certain things spiritually that we aren't, because our minds are too cluttered with intellectual ideas, and too much emotionalism. And because he's on that animalistic level, he may be closer to pure spirit.'

The story of *Raging Bull* is really the story of two men: a boxer whose determination to become a champion nearly destroyed him and a director with a consuming devotion to film. The movie opens in 1941, the beginning of La Motta's boxing career, but the intense drama of La Motta's life actually began on June 16, 1949, when, as a once-promising contender for the middleweight title, he took on popular champion Marcel Cerdan.

There was a growing feeling among sportswriters and boxing fans that La Motta's star had begun to fade. In February of that year, he had been beaten badly by Frenchman Laurent Dauthuille. Moreover, many fans remembered La Motta's November 1947 fight with Billy Fox, which Fox won on a technical knockout. La Motta's effort had been so feeble in that bout that he was subsequently questioned by the New York State Boxing Commission.

Part of the problem was La Motta's style as a fighter. Working from a crouch position, he bore in on his opponent, always probing, willing to take punishment in order to dish out what he could. (Amazingly, in his thirteen-year career, La Motta, nicknamed the Bronx Bull, was never knocked down.) So when he seemed to be waltzing instead of fighting with Billy Fox, the fans smelled something fishy. And they were right.

As La Motta later recounted, he threw the fight on orders from the Mob, which, he claimed, controlled the boxing world. For years, in fact, La Motta had wanted a shot at the middleweight title, only to be denied the crucial match because of his refusal to throw in with organised crime. Years of frustration finally took their toll, and the Fox fight proved his willingness to cooperate.

The Cerdan championship bout was no less controversial. In the first round, Cerdan went down, some said by a hard La Motta punch; others claimed it was a slip. Whatever the reason, Cerdan pulled a muscle in his right shoulder, and by the tenth round, he could not answer the bell. La Motta had his championship. There were cries for a rematch, but before it could be fought, Cerdan was killed in a plane crash.

It was July 1950 before La Motta defended his title, against Tiberio Mitri, the European middleweight champion. One reporter noted that 'in a year's time, La Motta had become more hated than any two other boxing champions.' The fans had come to resent La Motta's chest-thumping routines, his flashy leopard-skin robe, and his mugging at opponents and crowds. Nevertheless, La Motta's unpopularity meant money in the bank for promoters, who were only too happy to have a champ that everyone would like to see lose.

La Motta finally lost his crown seven months later, on February 14, 1951, to Sugar Ray Robinson. The bout was a classic demonstration of both men's skills: La Motta fought out of his familiar coiled crouch, while Robinson used quickness and an awesome assortment of punches. The fight was called in the thirteenth round, with La Motta dazed and bleeding. He was also still on his feet.

La Motta's decline after the Robinson fight was swift. In 1954 he retired from boxing, having already moved to Florida with Vickie and their three children. La Motta opened a bar in Miami Beach and, no longer constrained by the rigours of training, began gaining weight. Disgusted by his heavy drinking and affairs, Vickie filed for a divorce.

Then La Motta was arrested on charges that he allowed a fourteen-year-old girl to operate as a prostitute in his bar. Although he claimed to be innocent, La Motta was fined $500 and sentenced to six months in jail. The brutality of his stay in jail frightened him much more than any fighter he had faced. Once free, he took up acting, made a few movies and is now living in New York, not far from Scorsese's apartment.

Martin Scorsese, wearing an Oriental robe, sits cross-legged on his bed in a room that is dominated by huge posters of *Children of Paradise* and Cocteau's *Beauty and the Beast*. It is 10:30 p.m. Awake for an hour, he is about to attack his first meal of the day. The television screen in the corner flickers with silent, ghostly images.

Scorsese is quick to point out that *Raging Bull*'s action is not confined to the boxing ring. Fight scenes make up only about fifteen minutes of the film's two hours. The emphasis, he maintains, is on La Motta's life outside the ring and, in particular, on his relationships with Vickie, and his brother Joey, a sometime fighter who also worked in Jake's corner.

In a sense, La Motta, who alienated virtually everyone around him in his determination to become a champion, is not unlike other Scorsese protagonists – characters whose determination and single-mindedness are potentially self-destructive. De Niro's Travis Bickle in *Taxi Driver* comes immediately to mind, but there is also Harvey Keitel's Charlie in *Mean Streets*, Ellen Burstyn's Alice Hyatt in *Alice Doesn't Live Here Any More* and De Niro's Jimmy Doyle and Liza Minnelli's Francine Evans in *New York, New York*.

If these characters are all fighters of a sort, it is because they reflect in no small way their creator. In anything he pursues, Scorsese is persistent, determined, and, above all, intense. 'I can't do anything I'm not interested in,' he says in a rare instance of understatement. Whatever he *is* interested in will consume his time, his health, and the people he works with. (More than one person who worked on *Raging Bull* spoke to me of the 'incredible experience' of working with Scorsese – the long hours, devotion to the tiniest details, and demands for intense concentration.)

At first glance. Scorsese does not seem the stereotype of the autocratic Hollywood director. Short, slight, his face framed by a neatly trimmed beard, he can also be the deferential host. 'If you really want to know about *Raging Bull*,' he tells me, 'ask Bobby, or [cinematographer] Michael Chapman, or [casting director] Cis Corman, or . . . ,' and he continues to list names as if to say: Look, this is a collaborative art; I'm not the only one who worked on this film. Of course, he is right, but as you talk with him, you sense that the source of tremendous energy and vitality his films exude is Scorsese himself.

First, there is his speech: The words come tumbling out so fast you have to lean forward to catch every one. His attention always seems divided, particularly if there is a television on or a videotape playing. He will jump up in the middle of a sentence and scurry over to a videotape recorder. '*Hell is for Heroes* is coming on at 11:00,' he says, 'and I want to tape it. You don't mind . . . ?'

The truth is, Scorsese is a media junkie. 'I just have a feeling,' Scorsese told Mary Pat Kelly, 'of how I loved films so much when I saw them as a child and growing, and how much they influenced me and my growing.' Scorsese's youth was spent in movie theatres; his first heroes were John Wayne and Roy Rogers; later they would be John Ford and Howard Hawks. As fellow director Michael Powell has said, 'He breakfasts off images

La Motta, bloated and out of condition, with his second wife and their children. Eighteen-year-old unknown Cathy Moriarty was remarkable as the put-upon Vickie La Motta.

[and] eats tapes for lunch.' A Scorsese film is crammed with film references and even clips from his favourites, among them a fight scene from *The Searchers* which the young hoods in *Mean Streets* watch appreciatively from the balcony of a 42nd Street theatre.

Music is also a Scorsese passion. One of the elements in *Mean Streets* that attracted so much acclaim was its score, a mélange of rock 'n' roll and Italian opera. It is no surprise, then, that Scorsese served his film apprenticeship as an editor on three rock documentaries, including *Woodstock*. Scorsese's great empathy for music led him to explore the world of jazz and pop musicians in *New York, New York*, and led rock musician Robbie Robertson to ask him to direct a film of The Band's farewell concert. The result, *The Last Waltz*, was compared favourably, by many film critics, to *Woodstock*.

What may have finally swayed Scorsese to take on *Raging Bull* was the type of film he saw in the moments of Jake La Motta's life. This would not be a big-budget picture to be shot on sound stages with an all-star cast, but a story of raw immediacy filmed largely on location, with non-professional actors. 'Until *New York, New York*,' Scorsese once said, 'I had never had a dressing room. Before that, I stayed on the streets of New York while Bobby De Niro changed in a Winnebago.' *Raging Bull* held the promise for Scorsese of a return to the streets and to the filmmaking *experience* that resulted in his best work.

He assigned Mardik Martin, who collaborated with him on *Mean Streets* and *New York, New York*, to write the script. Martin laboured for two years, doing extensive research into La Motta's fight history. But Scorsese and De Niro were not pleased with the results. They decided to see what Paul Schrader, who wrote *Taxi Driver*, could do. 'I hated to do it after all the time Mardik spent,' Scorsese says, 'but there was much more boxing than we wanted.' Schrader's draft was closer to what they were looking for, but they still weren't entirely satisfied. So Scorsese and De Niro took off for the Caribbean to work on the project.

Before he left, Scorsese requested that the film's casting director, Cis Corman, avoid familiar professional actors and go for unknowns. She immersed herself in the boxing world, interviewing fighters, trainers, and ring announcers for small parts in the film. As a result, virtually all the faces outside of De Niro's will be unfamiliar to film audiences. (Many of La Motta's opponents are played by amateur and professional fighters whom De Niro met while he was training.) Joe Pesci, who plays Jake La Motta's brother Joey, was an actor Corman spotted in an independent feature. And Cathy Moriarty, who plays Vickie La Motta, was a non-professional who was found after an extensive search.

The original plan was to shoot most of the film in New York using gyms and boxing arenas from La Motta's era. A training gym for De Niro was found on Fourteenth Street, but nearly all the small halls were gone. In Los Angeles, however, they discovered the legendary Olympic Auditorium, which was still used for boxing and wrestling matches.

After the script problems were resolved, De Niro literally went into training as a professional fighter. Scorsese shot some footage of the training sessions in 8mm, and one evening he showed it to Michael Powell. As the film ended, Powell turned to Scorsese and said, 'But the gloves are *red.*'

Powell's comment, says Scorsese, led him to consider shooting *Raging Bull* in black and white. Today's fighters usually wear red gloves and pastel-coloured trunks, but our memories of boxing in the forties and fifties are in black and white, partly because of grainy newsreel films and newspaper photographs. Boxing was then a very popular sport, conducted in smoky, dimly lit halls all over the country. To hype a gate, promoters would often turn a match such as the La Motta-Cerdan fight into a struggle of evil vs. good, or black vs. white. (By the forties, race was less of a factor, with the rise of such popular black champions as Joe Louis and Sugar Ray Robinson.)

There were two other considerations. One was the problem of colour preservation, an issue with which Scorsese has become publicly identified: the other was that several forthcoming movies featured boxers – *Rocky II, The Champ, The Main Event,* and *Matilda.* Scorsese admits. 'We just wanted to be different, to have a different look.'

Filming began in April 1979 in Los Angeles. The Olympic was used for shots of the ring and the crowd, and of fighters climbing in and out of the ring. The fights themselves were filmed in a studio. According to cinematographer Michael Chapman (who worked on *Taxi Driver* and *The Last Waltz*), 'We treated the fights like a dance. Shooting them was somewhat like shooting the performers in *The Last Waltz,* in which we had everything extensively choreographed ahead of time.'

In most recent boxing films, Chapman points out, the bouts were photographed with several cameras from outside the ring, and the variety of angles was later orchestrated in the editing room. For *Raging Bull,* however, one camera was used, and it was placed *inside* the ring, with the fighters.

It was there that De Niro's months of training paid off. He and his opponents were able to 'dance' around the camera while maintaining the realism that such close shooting demanded. He could imitate perfectly La Motta's charging style, his stance, his punch combinations.

That summer, the company moved to New York, where it began filming in locations which had virtually not changed in 35 years, from a miniature golf course on Long Island to tenements in the Bronx. 'That was the easiest part of the film,' recalls Chapman. After the gruelling work inside the studio ring, De Niro and Scorsese were back on the streets of New York, shooting in many neighbourhoods familiar to them.

By August, the only scenes remaining to be filmed were those of La Motta's early years of retirement, when the ex-champ had put on a considerable amount of weight. Shooting was suspended until mid-November, while De Niro put on over 60 pounds. 'It was Bobby's idea,' Scorsese says, 'and when he told me about it, I thought it was great.' De Niro, who normally weighs around 145, swelled to over 200 just to portray La Motta the bloated bar owner and accused pimp. 'We did have to be careful,' Scorsese recalls. 'Bobby would get tired pretty easily from carrying that weight.'

As of July, Scorsese had not shown *Raging Bull* to Jake La Motta. The ex-champ had acted as adviser for the film's fight sequences, and he and De Niro had had long talks in preparation for the film. But Scorsese was scrupulous about staying away from La Motta for the rest of the filming. 'It might be difficult for him to see the film,' Scorsese admits. 'We've changed some things, and it's hard to tell how someone might react to that.'

In *Raging Bull*, he contends, the important thing is to convey a sense of what La Motta and his times were all about. The film may not be completely factual, but, Scorsese points out, what film about a real person's life ever is? 'Even a documentary can't be objective,' he says. 'There's the footage you select, there's the way it's edited.'

Scorsese has made two documentaries since *New York, New York*: *The Last Waltz* and a 48-minute film called *American Boy* which was shown at the 1978 New York Film Festival but has never been released. The latter is easily Scorsese's least-polished film; it is also his most disturbing. The film records one night with Steven Prince, a friend of Scorsese's who appeared briefly as a slick-talking gun salesman in *Taxi Driver*. Prince spins out a series of stories about his life that start out as amusing anecdotes of growing up Jewish, but end up as horrifying yet oddly touching tales of a heroin addict. Intercut is actual footage from the Prince family's home movies. Scorsese has carried over this technique to *Raging Bull*: He uses clips from La Motta's home movies, which also are the film's only colour sequences.

Scorsese is excited by film's ability to document people's lives in their own words. In a 1974 documentary, *Italianamerican*, he affectionately recorded his parents' recollections of emigrating from Sicily and making a life in New York. He plans to do a series of these film portraits, beginning with Michael Powell and with his own wife, Isabella Rossellini (the daughter of Roberto Rossellini and Ingrid Bergman, and a reporter for RAI, the Italian state television network).

It seems fitting that Scorsese should turn to Powell; his friendship with the British director is a reflection of the intense affection and concern he feels for directors who have influenced him and who, in some cases, he feels are unjustly neglected. Last year, Scorsese agreed to donate money toward the release in this country of an uncut version of Powell's classic *Peeping Tom*. When it was mistakenly reported in the *New York Times* and *American Film*, among other places, that Scorsese was distributing the film, he was upset by the implication that he was gaining financially from the arrangement. Then last summer, Scorsese organised a petition, signed by several hundred prominent names in the film industry, that was presented to Eastman Kodak. The subject was the preservation of colour films, and the letter urged Kodak to 'recognise its responsibility to the people it services' and to 'assume a major role in the research and development of a stable colour film stock.' Since then, Scorsese has met with several Kodak representatives, presented a clip show at the New York Film Festival to illustrate the colour crisis, and has begun organising, with the AFI, a conference on the subject, to be held in the spring.

Martin Scorsese is not a rabble-rouser; he is a concerned filmmaker and filmgoer who has decided to fight back against the years of complacency with regard to the preservation of colour films. His devotion to this cause is no different in intensity from his friendship with Michael Powell or his approach to making *Raging Bull*. Martin Scorsese doesn't back off. He moves ahead, sometimes taking punches, but never letting up. He can't. He doesn't know any other way.

Extract from 'EASY RIDERS – RAGING BULLS'
By Peter Biskind

Raging Bull was in post-production throughout the spring, summer, and fall of 1980. The sound mix alone took six months. According to Winkler, while Scorsese was editing, UA was quietly trying to sell the picture, but none of the studios would touch it.

If Scorsese was in fragile emotional and physical shape when he started *Raging Bull*, he was a mess when he finished it. He says, 'I didn't achieve any of the peace that Jake had with himself in the movie where he could sit down and look at himself in the mirror calmly and recite those lines. I just didn't.'

Scorsese showed the picture to Albeck, Bach, and a few other people in the middle of July at the MGM screening room on 55th Street and Sixth Avenue. As Bach described it, 'The lights came up slowly in a room full of silence, as if the viewers had lost all power of speech. Nor was there the customary applause. Martin Scorsese leaned against the back wall of the screening room as if cowering from the silence. Then Andy Albeck rose from his seat, marched briskly to him, shook his hand just once, and said quietly, "Mr. Scorsese, you are an Artist."' Scorsese asked a young woman after the screening what she had thought. She burst into tears and ran down the hall. The director knew he was not making a 'likeable' movie. He says, 'The poster with the picture of Bob's face all beaten and battered – I mean, if you're a girl, nineteen years old, I don't know if you'd say, "Let's go see this one."' But he didn't realise just how unlikeable it was, just as he never seemed to understand how disturbing the ending of *Taxi Driver* was.

Raging Bull opened on November 14, 1980, at the Sutton Theatre in New York. Jack Kroll called it 'the best movie of the year' in *Newsweek*, and Vincent Canby gave it a rave in the *New York Times*. But it was Kathleen Carroll in the *New York Daily News* who struck the prevailing note when she called Jake 'one of the most repugnant characters in the history of the movies', and went on to criticise Scorsese because the movie 'totally ignores [La Motta's] reform school background, offering no explanation as to his anti-social behaviour.' Worse, UA was too preoccupied with *Heaven's Gate* to give it a proper promotional campaign. Scorsese's movie bombed.

Although *Raging Bull* was later selected in a *Premiere* magazine poll as the best movie of the eighties, it was very much a movie of the seventies, very much a beached whale on the shores of the new decade. It was an actor's movie, a film that valued character over plot, that indeed contained no one to 'root for'. With its unromantic, black and white, in-your-face tabloid look, its ferocious violence, and its pond scum characters layered with ghostly images of Italian Renaissance pietas and echoes of *verismo* operas such as *Cavalleria Rusticana* and *Pagliacci*, it was at the furthest remove from the smarmy, feel-good pap of the coming cultural counterrevolution. Scorsese had refused to get with the program, had made an anti-*Rocky*, thumbed his nose at *Star Wars*, and he would pay for it.

RAGING BULL
Reviewed by Steve Jenkins

1941. Middleweight boxer Jake La Motta, married with a child and managed by his brother Joey, is gaining a reputation as a championship contender. As his career progresses he becomes involved with fifteen-year-old Vickie and marries her, after divorcing his first wife Irma. Jake becomes obsessed with a belief that Vickie is being unfaithful, and asks Joey to watch her when he is away. Joey is involved in a night-club brawl over Vickie with Salvy, one of the hoods who have for some time been trying to involve themselves with Jake's career. The two men are later reconciled by Tommy Como, a powerful underworld figure, who tells Joey that Jake must throw a fight if he wants a chance at the world title. Jake complies, and after deliberately losing a match with Billy Fox, he defeats Marcel Cerdan to become world middleweight champion in 1949. Jake has weight problems, and his increasing suspicions as to Vickie's promiscuity drive him to the edge of madness. Finally he physically attacks both her and Joey, accusing them of having an affair, and Joey walks out. After being brutally defeated by 'Sugar' Ray Robinson, Jake retires from boxing, and in 1956 opens a night-club in Miami, where he performs as MC and stand-up comic. After Vickie has told him she is leaving and taking their children, Jake is arrested when a fourteen-year-old girl is found in his club. Unable to raise the money needed to beat the charge, he spends time in prison, where he is mistreated by the guards. In 1958, while working in a New York bar introducing strippers, he meets Joey and attempts, unsuccessfully, to renew their relationship. 1964 finds Jake performing in a club, reciting extracts from the works of (among others) William Shakespeare, Budd Schulberg and Paddy Chayevsky.

In a recent interview (*American Film*, November 1980), Scorsese describes how Paul Schrader became involved with *Raging Bull* because Mardik Martin's original script contained 'much more boxing than we wanted.' In terms of the end product, the question is more one of structure than quantity. The boxing scenes function as brief, explosive and almost entirely discrete units, marking out the chronology of Jake La Motta's rise, fall and, for Scorsese, ultimate redemption. They are rendered as an astonishing, dialectic combination of physicality and abstraction, where every blow landed in bloodied close-up seems matched by a moment of slow motion or loss of focus. This tendency is brilliantly deployed on the soundtrack, which plays off punches as much heard as felt against a bizarre, welling tide of baying animals and rolling thunder. What this formal bravado effectively precludes is any sense of the fights as *dramatic* entities, as struggles designed to aid the definition of La Motta's character. Precisely the opposite, as is made clear by the montage which juxtaposes the development of Jake's relationship with Vickie in incoherent snatches of home movies (the film's only colour sequences) with a succession of briefly glimpsed fights, sometimes reduced to a single still image. The simple colour/black and white opposition succinctly underlines the impossibility of any easy equation between events in and out of the ring, while the basic impenetrability of both private and public strands points to a crucial difficulty of 'knowing', of 'understanding'. Which in turn leads straight to the biblical quotation before the final credits: '"Whether or not he is a sinner, I do not know," the man replied. "All I know is this: once I was blind and now I can see."' The difference between seeing/showing and knowing/judging is the central tension in Scorsese's conception of violence and character, whether it be the ebullient, dangerous craziness of *Mean Streets*' Johnny Boy or the obsessive passion-as-ritual of *Taxi Driver*'s Travis Bickle. Both are the exploitable but ultimately indefinable, unknowable centres of the narratives they drive. *Raging Bull* comes closest to using its central character's profession as an explanatory focus for his destructive impulses in the fight with Tony Janiro, where La Motta's specific intention is to ruin his opponent's good looks. Ostensibly this springs from psychotic jealousy, a result of Vickie's casual mention of the boxer's 'pretty face'. But this moment of self-understanding (later contrasted with Jake's hysterical breakdown after 'knowingly' throwing the Fox fight) is undercut with ambiguity. Joking in a night club with the hoods who impinge on both his career and his exclusive possession of his wife, Jake remarks of Janiro (apropos his looks) that he doesn't know whether to 'fuck him or fight him'. The link between sexuality and aggression is here decidedly double-edged. The doubt emerges elsewhere in the way the script is obsessively littered with derisory references to 'faggots', or (a more specific example) in Jake's worry that he has small hands, 'girl's hands'. These fears lead with inexorable logic to the nightmarish climax of his boxing career where, in a stun-

Jake La Motta (De Niro), the eponymous Raging Bull *(1980), as a nightclub MC. The disgraced ex-champ still has further to fall, and will be jailed on a 'morals charge'.*

ning single shot from Jake's point of view, his opponent ('Sugar' Ray Robinson) becomes a monstrous black demon, a gross caricature of the Otherness which throughout the rest of the film is rigorously sexual. In this sense the inevitable, effortless evocation of a *noir* ambience, achieved largely through Mike Chapman's outstanding photography, is perhaps deceptive. Key filmic references lie elsewhere. *Raging Bull* is poised somewhere between *Night of the Hunter* and *Bigger than Life*. The compulsive, religion-soaked (two-fisted) sexual violence of Mitchum's preacher is instantly conjured as La Motta stands over the recumbent Vickie in a room become a cave of shadows, while Jake's decisive eruption into Joey's home rips apart the family unit with all the mysterious fury of James Mason's drug-induced, violently aggressive egotism. Much of *Raging Bull's* fascination lies in its binding of modes (*film noir*, biopic) which are embraced but inflected to the point where they cannot define the object. Thus when Vickie, with Jake jealously watching, crosses the Copacabana Club to talk to Tommy Como and his cohorts, the characters, setting and narrative tension are pure *film noir*. But the *meaning* of the moment is essentially signified by the 'excessive' use of slow motion, linked with Jake's gaze, through which the representation of aggressive subjectivity becomes the only real issue. Similarly, the focus on Jake, the biopic thread, is consciously disrupted by *Joey's* crazed attack on Salvy, where character, action and motivation instead become linked in terms of filial loyalty as psychosis. Jake and Joey become interchangeable functions; 'character' is definable only as degrees of repression in Scorsese's Catholic family romance, which ensnares its protagonists at every stage. For Scorsese, La Motta's story is that of 'a guy attaining something and losing everything, and then redeeming himself'. But within the film's heavily deterministic scheme, redemption can ultimately only be the denial of self. Jake's plunge into the darkness of a prison cell, the walls of which he batters with head and fists, is the summation in negative (loss of light, loss of the crowd's gaze, loss of opponent) of the career through which self-definition was violently possible if always illusory. His 'redemption' is depicted as an ironic grasping at a projected self, as *other*, as lost: gazing at his bloated reflection in a dressing-room mirror, reciting Brando's *On the Waterfront* 'contender' speech, the very image of Jannings in *The Blue Angel* (another significant reference), his identity destroyed. *Raging Bull* may prove to be Scorsese's finest achievement to date. Certainly the visceral intelligence on display, the radical awareness and *use* of his own cinephilia, the creation of a fractured biography productively shot through with his personal obsessions, make it a powerful contender.

Extract from 'EASY RIDERS – RAGING BULLS'
By Peter Biskind

The commercial failure of *Raging Bull*, on top of *New York, New York*, was a crushing blow for Scorsese. 'Marty wanted the kind of success that Lucas and Coppola had,' says Sandy Weintraub. 'He was afraid he would always be the critics' darling, but the American public never would love him.' He was terrified that he wouldn't be allowed to continue making movies if he didn't make money. She adds, 'There was nothing in his life besides movies. What would he do?'

Later, when *Ordinary People* beat out *Raging Bull* for the Oscar, Scorsese was bitter. He always thought he could work within the system and maintain his vision, and for a while, he had. 'When I lost for *Raging Bull*, that's when I realised what my place in the system would be, if I did survive at all – on the outside looking in.'

After *Raging Bull* landed with a resounding thud, Scorsese directed *The King of Comedy*, which he did as a favour to De Niro. He regretted it: 'We had explored everything that we could with each other on *Raging Bull*. I should not have done *The King of Comedy*, I should have waited for something that came from me.' It turned into another troubled production. He says, 'I found that I had to convince myself every day to be a pro and go into work, and I disappointed myself, like very often I was late in the morning and that sort of thing, and the picture went over budget.'

During the editing, Scorsese hit a stone wall. 'It was partly because I shot so much footage, almost a million feet of film I had to sit through. There were 20, 25 takes of one shot, 40 variations on a line. For the first two months, I just couldn't do it. At the same time, from November '81 to March '82, my marriage with Isabella was breaking up.' When Scorsese met her, she was a TV journalist. He had not been pleased when she decided to become an actress, and when she divorced him in 1983, she complained to *Time*, 'he wanted me to spend life between the cookstove and the kids.'

'That left me flat, and crazed,' continues Scorsese. 'I sought out a doctor, and that started very intense therapy, five days a week, and phone calls on weekends, all through '82 and '83, '84, into '85. I got myself into such a state of anxiety that I just completely crashed. I'd come downstairs from the editing room, and I'd see a message from somebody about some problem and I'd say, "I can't work today. It's impossible." My friends said, "Marty, the negative is sitting there. The studio is going crazy. They're paying *interest!* You've got to finish the film." Finally, I began to understand a lesson I learned when I went to NYU. It was up to me. Nobody cared, ultimately, even your closest friends. You're gonna act crazy? You're gonna get into a situation where you can't work? Nobody gives a damn. And you wind up alone. You face yourself anyway. It's Jake La Motta looking in the mirror at the end of *Raging Bull.*'

MARTY
By Carrie Rickey

Alert, with a bird of prey's darting eyes and the tautness of an overwound watch, Martin Scorsese delivers a mock-pedantic lecture on the four stages of making a movie. His intense, bearded face belongs in a Renaissance altarpiece by Masaccio, but his staccato diction and flailing-arm body language are strictly from Jimmy Cagney. Suppressing a grin, though the corners of his mouth curl upward, talking and gesturing in double time, he states: 'The first part of the film is preproduction, preparation. Then you shoot it. Part three's the postproduction, the editing.' He adds, with a diabolical giggle, 'Then comes the depression.'

Now in stage three of *The King of Comedy*, a fantasy-meditation on show biz starring Jerry Lewis and Robert De Niro, Scorsese, though fearful of the postpartum stage four, seems much more calm and less depressed than in October 1981, when I visited him on the set. Whether dashing around the Manhattan studio in which *King* was filming or 'relaxing' – that is, inhaling sushi in his trailer before a day's shoot – Scorsese was totally frazzled. He was only just wrapping up four months of shooting. He had become appalled by the escalating cost of filmmaking, and whatever patience he had held in reserve to orchestrate his cast and associates, and satisfy the demands of New York unions, was wearing thin. 'It's a tough grind,' he said with a sigh. 'Sustaining interest is so hard. There's this languor on the set . . .'

Scorsese – now ten months into postproduction – is a man transformed. Admittedly, he prefers the editing stage. 'More control,' he cackles, but a number of events outside his control have reshaped his life, making stage three different from what he had anticipated: the death of Dan Johnson, his friend and domestic main-stay, and the estrangement of his wife, Isabella Rossellini, which coincided with a move from 57th Street downtown to the formerly mean, now funky-chic streets of Tribeca. I assumed I'd find a flummoxed Scorsese in an advanced state of disequi-librium. But no. In an orderly loft – residence on the upper two floors, editing facil-ities below – he is neither manic nor panicky, just civilly pressured. It is Wednesday evening, and at Friday noon he has to show Sherry Lansing and the rest of the Fox brass a segment of *The King of Comedy*. Replacing Scorsese's native apocalyptic pes-simism is a relaxed, almost impish sense of the absurd.

Like David Bowie's alien in *The Man Who Fell to Earth*, Scorsese lives and works sur-rounded by video monitors and audio equipment. His stereo speakers stand as tall as he does. Videocassettes line his bookshelves, making for a cosy, polyresin wallpaper. In the lacunae unfilled by movie books, cassettes, or hardware are movie posters, stills, and awards yet to be hung. It is hard to tell whether he is proud of or puzzled by the Finnish and German citations for *Raging Bull* – probably both. The vintage one-sheets of Michael Powell's films are the most conspicuous in Scorsese's collec-tion, with *The Red Shoes* dancing, *Tales of Hoffman* stair-climbing, and *Colonel Blimp* fly-ing off the walls. Pearl and Lewt (Jennifer Jones and Gregory Peck in *Duel in the Sun*) cast overheated glances across the room at another Texas Lone Star, Jett Rink (James Dean in *Giant*), teetering in a French poster blazoned *Le Gigante*.

There's virtually no decorative difference between Scorsese's editing room and his living quarters: These are the surroundings of a professional who lives, breathes, and dreams movies. Love and work are one. For a moment I think of asking him whether he's familiar with the Degas plaint: 'There is love and there is work but there is but one heart.' Instead I ask if he knows the Michael Powell lament overheard at a recent soiree: that even though he made *The Red Shoes*, all about the incompatibility of romance and art, 35 years ago, it took him until this year to realise he'd been right. Scorsese roars with laughter. 'It's true! It's true! Powell's right!'

Wearing 3-D glasses and watching John Agar's girlfriend being devoured in *Revenge of the Creature*, Scorsese throws off a deadpan aperçu: 'Agar always senses something wrong.' The way this workaholic lives, totally absorbed in movieland – its history, aes-thetics, and ephemera – is in a sense identical to that of Rupert Pupkin, the protag-onist of *The King of Comedy*. Rupert, an aspiring stand-up comedian (played by Robert De Niro) surrounds himself with stacks of comedy lore in his Union City basement. From roaming around the set last year, I remember Rupert's lair vividly. Designed by the legendary Boris Leven, the room was littered with comedy tomes – Will Rogers and Charlie Chaplin biographies, Joey Adam's *From Gags to Riches*, a book about Florenz Ziegfeld called *Showmen and Yuksters*.

Rupert fantasises celebrity by identifying with talk show host Jerry Langford (Jerry Lewis, in a composite of himself and Johnny Carson) and dreams of hosting Jerry's talk show, of *becoming* Jerry.

When Scorsese first read Paul Zimmerman's script for *The King of Comedy* in 1974, while finishing *Alice Doesn't Live Here Any More*, he recalls, 'I didn't go for it. Didn't understand it. I was writing something then with Jay Cocks about comedy from a different angle; we wanted to do something about Borscht Belt comedians.'

It was only after he passed the script on to De Niro that 'I realised Rupert's an extension of me inasmuch as he'd do *anything* to get what he wanted. When I realised he was to comics as I was to the movies, I understood. Rupert reminds me of the hunger I had in the sixties.' Scorsese sees Rupert as the outsider-huckster angling to get on the inside, eager to bask in the limelight. This is a characteristic shared by virtually every Scorsese protagonist: Johnny Boy in *Mean Streets*, Alice Hyatt in *Alice Doesn't Live Here Any More*, Travis Bickle in *Taxi Driver*, Jimmy Doyle in *New York, New York*, and Jake La Motta in *Raging Bull*. Hunger for celebrity is the dominant motivation for their cocky, cockeyed professionalism, and a self-screwing mechanism – usually the feeling of inadequacy – is the key to their fluky success or disastrous downfall.

New York, New York was compelling because of Scorsese's empathy for both of his antipathetic leads: Jimmy Doyle, the jazz vanguardist who shies away from conventional success in the belief that if the public accepts his music, it isn't experimental enough, and Francine Evans, the swing songstress who believes music has to be popularly appreciated to be worthwhile. The two reflect the split in Scorsese's persona, a fondness for both the avant-garde poetry of a Michael Powell and the hallucinatory but ultra-accessible fantasies of a Vincente Minnelli. Split allegiances to characters are also a feature of *Raging Bull*, where Jake's and Vickie's needs are clearly incompatible. *The King of Comedy* promises to be vintage dialectical Scorsese; Rupert and Jerry demonstrate that although lonely at the top, it's lonely at the bottom, too.

Scorsese is afflicted with the dilemma of celebrity, not unlike the conflict between aspirant and achiever that characterises *The King of Comedy*. An outsider whose reputation has made him an insider, he feels hamstrung by success. On the one hand, he presents himself as a recluse, a movie monk sequestered in a cinema cloister, the New York filmmaker who made *Mean Streets* on the cheap, from his own flesh and blood. The other Scorsese is the Hollywood director, hassling with unions, meeting his deadlines, the adult businessman dealing with the real world. He wants it both ways, but is frustrated that his fame has made it impossible for him to make movies cheaply and simply. A quote from *Sweet Smell of Success*, hand-printed on a three-by-five-inch card, is tacked to a column in his loft, reminding him of the contradiction: 'Are we kids, or what?'

At 40, Scorsese is too old and accomplished to play the prodigy-amateur, too young and unpretentious to play the prodigal-professional. Although he claims to identify with the success-starved Rupert Pupkin, isn't there more than a little of Jerry Langford in him, too? Last fall, on the set, Scorsese described a scene where Langford returns, after a tough day, to his high-tech high rise: 'So here's Jerry, alone in his apartment, picking at his food. People are gonna say, "It's lonely at the top." But I'll tell you, believe me, make a film and you *wanna* eat alone.' This is the resignation of a man who is an adoring fan, but resents the burden of being adored by fans, and displays the Peter Pan lament of 'I don't want to grow up.' Every time I ask Scorsese a serious question, such as how he feels about *Taxi Driver*'s relation to John W. Hinckley, Jr.'s attempted assassination of the president, he moans or evades, unwilling to admit the power of his movies, shy of being quoted because he's afraid his opinions will be engraved in stone. He doesn't want to be anybody's guru.

Will *The King of Comedy* be funny? On the set, cast and crew were studiedly vague.

'Better king for a night than schmuck for a lifetime.' In The King of Comedy *(1983), tenacious creep Rupert Pupkin (De Niro) fails to see that he can be both simultaneously.*

It won't have much of Scorsese's characteristic violence: Phil, the makeup man, complained that his most complicated job was to paint De Niro's hand to look as though it had been cut. And what of the audacious casting of Jerry Lewis opposite Robert De Niro? *Disorderly Orderly* meets *Taxi Driver*? Mr. Explosion ignites Mr. Implosion? Scorsese gets animated on the subject of Lewis. A natural mimic, the director makes his body paraphrase Cinderfella as he remarks, 'Jerry Langford's based on a Carson-type character, and we actually thought of using Johnny, but Jerry, who's done everything in show biz, has more to draw from.'

Did Lewis's extroverted acting inhibit De Niro's sometimes tortured method of improvising within the confines of the screenplay? Carefully, not wanting to speak for or about De Niro, Scorsese answers only the Jerry Lewis part of the question. 'The less Jerry does, the better he is; the less he does, the more he acts, I mean, because he's naturally so effusive. Being Jerry Lewis, effusion is self-protection.' As Scorsese describes Lewis, I have the feeling he's also talking about himself.

Did he pick up any directing tips from Lewis? (Lewis, after all, was the first film-maker to use video playback to get a sense of the take – a technique Scorsese employs as well.) 'I asked him for help a coupla times,' Scorsese confided when I visited the set. 'I get confused sometimes technically and Jerry knows how to move his body precisely – you know, I just found out that every time I say "left" I mean "right".' Dyslexia? 'No,' Scorsese said, grinning. 'High living.' Scorsese's publicist, Marion Billings, added: 'Jerry will kibitz and Marty says, "Great, great, I want that kind of input."' *The King of Comedy* crew reciprocated Lewis's generosity by donating $10,000 to his favorite charity, the muscular dystrophy telethon.

It's not unusual to ask Scorsese a question and be answered by one of his loyal colleagues. The crowd on the set is less an entourage than an extended family. And a biological family. The first thing I saw when I walked onto the West 59th Street *King of Comedy* sound stage was Catherine Scorsese, Martin's mother, perched on a director's chair at the top of a scaffold, ad-libbing her off-camera part as Rupert's mother, The Voice. 'Oh, the things my son does to me,' Catherine cheerfully kvetched after descending from her parrot's loft, a curious combination of pedestal and prison. 'I'm supposed to say whatever's on my mind, but I'm running out of thoughts.' (She would consult notes, a rough outline for her ad-lib.) She explained that Marty built such an aerie because he wanted the sound to come from 'upstairs'. Rupert lives isolated in the basement, the underground. His parents and Jerry Langford, the adults, live on a literally higher plane.

There was no reign of terror on the set; it was like a Passover Seder, or, rather, a convivial Easter dinner. No one pulled rank. If there was temper, it was well concealed. After one intense scene, in which De Niro had been improvising on a closed set, Scorsese and De Niro emerged, visibly exhausted. Catherine asked Marty if he remembered to cover the close-up with a master shot.

At another point – during a lull – De Niro somnambulated through, wearing an electric-sky-blue vested polyester suit and improbable white patent-leather loafers. I shuddered for a moment at the thought of the acid blue of the suit being shot against the Japanese-style red-and-black lacquer of Rupert's basement. Kind of a vulgar colour scheme – Fourteenth Street meets the Ginza – but one not unfamiliar in televisionland, the subject of the movie. A costumer muttered something about Rupert's 'dream' suit. Apparently, the film ends with Rupert's fantasy monologue, where he's dressed in a scarlet version of his three-piece ensemble.

At the mention of fantasy monologue, I was jolted out of my *Godot*-like Waiting for Marty. Scorsese doing dream sequences! His movies are about the hallucinatory quality of daily life, never the transcendence of daily life through fantasy. Wouldn't this be taking his empathy for Vincente Minnelli a little too far? Or would *The King of Comedy*, with its wacky cast and excursions into dreamland, be like *Stardust Memories*, using surrealism to contrast the hunger for success with the realisation that status doesn't sate the appetite? Then, thinking of the opening shot of *Alice Doesn't Live Here Any More* – that fantastic, rosy image of idyllic things past – I imagined a Scorsese dream sequence as part and parcel of his intensified realism: looking at the past through rose-coloured glasses or projecting the future in a scarlet suit.

The next day, in his trailer (which, like his Tribeca home, provides him with basic needs: cassettes and vitamins), Scorsese answered my questions in monosyllables, as though being cross-examined, until Boris Leven joined us. My questions were then deflected toward this design visionary, who created the look of movies as different as *The Shanghai Gesture* and *West Side Story*. Scorsese's logorrhea, suddenly in gear, was the perfect foil for Leven's epigrammatic diction and aesthetic; the rapport between the two was palpable. Leven explained, 'I open my mouth and Marty starts talking.' Scorsese deferred to the graceful, trim man who looks like an informal Marcel

Duchamp: 'Boris gives me all of the ideas and I just execute them.' Leven returned with, 'But Marty inspires me, he lights the match.' Working with the *éminence grise* designer has further connected Scorsese with movie history and given him a fresh perspective on the present.

Leven's conversation about directors he's worked with ranged from von Sternberg to Preminger ('Preminger got bored so fast on *Anatomy of a Murder*, but Marty? Never.'). In the hurly-burly world of filmmaking, he lamented, 'nothing is simple. That's why when you get simplicity it's so wonderful.' Scorsese barked in appreciative laughter.

Leven, while admitting daytime shots look ludicrous when filmed on a set, said he prefers the studio to location work. In *West Side Story* a real location was matched to a studio set, a Leven audacity that contributed an original, surreal effect. When I mentioned this to him, he smiled, confessing, 'Only the' – he snapped his fingers in imitation of the Jets' hand jive – 'was shot outside, everything else is inside the studio!'

Although the television-world setting of *The King of Comedy* required interior shooting – production stills show a *Jerry Langford Hour* featuring Liza Minnelli and Dr. Joyce Brothers – the company also had to shoot many exterior scenes. 'There's no control outside,' Leven quietly moaned, echoing Scorsese's exhaustion during location shooting. Scorsese said he had planned for *The King of Comedy* to be a cheap and simple movie, 'like *Mean Streets*'. But with a major studio financing a film by a director of his reputation, simplicity and speed turned into complication and slowdown. Scorsese complained, 'Movies now aren't fun to make anymore.' Leven, with a tolerant smile, said, 'You're not doing so badly for a young man.'

Ten months later I ask Scorsese, at home and editing the film with Thelma Schoonmaker, whether he thinks productions of the old-style studio system were more efficient than the free-form, deal-to-deal independent arrangements he has wrought for himself. He starts listing the pros and cons: The positive aspects of a studio, where makeup, scenery, and costume departments don't have to start from square one, are appealing, admittedly, but are outweighed by the hierarchical format in which movies are generated by executives, not filmmakers. Scorsese laughs. 'They got you either way – I don't know who "they" are – there's good and there's bad either route. It's a case of perfect paranoia.'

Schoonmaker, Scorsese's longtime friend, and his editor on *Raging Bull*, recalls first meeting Scorsese twenty years ago at New York University. She was a philosophy student who answered an ad in the *New York Times* for an assistant editor, and went to NYU for an intensive editing course in which Scorsese was also enrolled. 'He was incredibly intense, hadn't slept for days, and sat, wide-eyed, next to the editing table. I thought he was awake, but he was sleeping with his eyes open.' (Quite a metaphor for filmmaking, dreaming and open-eyed at once.)

Though on the set Scorsese groaned when I asked him about upcoming projects, now he animatedly acknowledges the future. One effort is *The Last Temptation of Christ*, featuring a libertine Jesus – 'It doesn't pay attention to the known landmarks of the story,' Scorsese says with a chuckle – from Paul Schrader's adaptation of the 1960 novel by Nikos Kazantzakis. Would De Niro play Christ? 'It's, like, wide open,' he says evasively. 'I want to do the thing simple and cheap,' insists Scorsese in the same words he used to describe how he wanted, and failed, to make *The King of Comedy*. Is Scorsese too big to make a small picture?

His modus operandi has been to wind up a feature film by zapping out a documentary. *Italianamerican* (a profile of his parents), *The Last Waltz* (documenting The Band's last concert), and *American Boy* (a chronicle of his pal, the gun salesman in *Taxi Driver*) were made in between *Mean Streets, New York, New York*, and *Raging Bull*. And there might be a documentary in the cards after he finishes editing *The King of Comedy*. Michael Powell is producing *Thirteen Ways to Kill a Poet*, an omnibus of short films on the deaths of great artists, and Scorsese proposes to profile Ernie Kovacs, poet laureate of television.

Other plans? For someone so wrapped up in his work, it's not surprising that the man who makes movies for his business watches them (on cassette, mostly) for pleasure. Among the films he has been watching while editing: *From the Life of the Marionettes, Oh, God!, Street Scene, The Chapman Report, Shack Out on 101*, and a PBS documentary on Caravaggio. 'I don't know much about painting,' Scorsese confesses, 'but I like him.' Caravaggio-style chiaroscuro and crimsons are prominent elements in *New York, New York* and *The King of Comedy*. (Scorsese's eyebrows arch in surprise when I mention this.) And, fittingly, even his activism is related to the movies: He's playing a lead role in the crusade for colour film preservation.

I ask the movie monk if he's seen any recent movies. 'No,' he says, then corrects himself: *Poltergeist*, which he likes, and films by David Cronenberg (*Scanners, Rabid, The Brood*), about whom he's wildly enthusiastic. 'Cronenberg's got a vision, a sensibility,' says Scorsese, gesturing with open hands to convey his admiration. He likes Mel Brooks's *History of the World Part One*, and does a wicked impersonation of Brooks's Roman stand-up comedian bombing at Caesar's Palace: 'When you die here at the Palace, you *really* die,' mimics Scorsese, who has a Borscht Belt in joke karate.

Somewhat offhandedly I mention that he seems happier and more optimistic than on the set. '*I'm* sounding optimistic?' Scorsese demands in mock rage. 'You're ruining my whole image.' He reflects for a millisecond. 'I'm not that much of an optimist, because I believe: Why be disappointed?'

The cable-connected Advent screen, which was displaying an ethnographic film moments earlier, is now doing the horoscope rundown. We study the screen. Scorsese, of course, is a Scorpio (remember Harvey Keitel in *Alice* with his Scorpion ring tie?), and his astrological forecast is the perfect admonition for his Friday meeting with the Fox brass: 'Collect facts to convince those you need to impress.' Quaking with laughter, Scorsese and Schoonmaker sit down at the editing table to do just that, geared up to work around the clock until the Friday deadline. The workplace is charged with atmospheric adrenalin. As if to prove Degas and Powell wrong, Scorsese may have successfully grafted love and work together: Instead of bisecting his affections, it looks as though he's doubling his pleasure.

THE KING OF COMEDY
Reviewed by Ed Sikov

In *The Total Film Maker*, his book on film technique, Jerry Lewis wrote, 'Emulsion has the strangest capacity to react. It's almost like infectious hepatitis, only germ known to medical science that can't be sterilised off a needle. It picks up information germs.' This bizarre simile, like the best of Lewis's films, reveals a certain outrageous truth underlying the inanity. The cinema and infectious hepatitis – information carriers, contagious beyond control. The virulence of the cinema was even presented as medical fact in the trial of John Hinckley, whose defence rested to a great degree on the notion that film images intruded into his already diseased mind – images from another Martin Scorsese film starring Robert De Niro. *Taxi Driver* was by no means the first cultural product accused of spreading cultural disease, but what was shocking was that it communicated its most decisive message to Hinckley in the form of strictly iconic images, narrative gestures which could be, and were, mimicked in an absolutely straightforward way. Certain 'information germs' which *Taxi Driver* had picked up had zeroed in on a receptive subject, germs which catalysed a spectator's murderous obsession with actress Jodie Foster. According to her confessional testimony in *Esquire*, Foster's initial reaction to the assassination attempt was to laugh herself silly.

The King of Comedy was already in pre-production at the time of the shooting, but it can hardly escape its own context. Its audacity lies both in its comic treatment of obsession and in its refusal to offer any explanation for its characters' behaviour – any explanation, that is, outside of the domain of images and their effects. Unlike *Taxi Driver*, which tries in a very literal way to examine what kind of nut would drive a cab in New York, *The King of Comedy* avoids ethnography by challenging the distance between audience and character, by centring its story on the relationship between spectator and fiction. Unlike the exotic Travis Bickle, firmly categorised as a psychopathic Other, Rupert Pupkin shares with his audience an intense desire to look at images, participate in them, and be gratified by them. Instead of being a nut-out-there, Pupkin is very specifically a nut-in-here as far as the audience is concerned. What pushes him over the brink is his compulsion to extend his vicarious participation in an on-screen world into action. Scorsese and Paul Zimmerman, the screenwriter, steadfastly refuse to pry into Rupert's psyche and, by so doing, control him. His fantasies are not traced back to some psycho-sexual misfire and are therefore not packaged away. Without this explanatory gesture and the moralism it would entail, the joke of *The King of Comedy* – an aspiring comedian kidnaps and threatens to kill a talk-show host unless he, the comedian/kidnapper, gets a spot on the show – is played first on the comedian, then on the victim, and finally on the spectator. If Pupkin is the brunt of the first joke because he's crazy, and the talk-show host is the brunt of the second because he's kidnapped, it is the spectator, whose vicarious entry into narrative the film both demands and ridicules, who ends up the laughingstock. Pupkin, the hero, becomes less of a character than a *deus ex machina* designed to turn an audience's perceptions back on itself.

On the level of performance, both De Niro and his co-star, Jerry Lewis, could hardly be said to effect well-roundedness; as a matter of fact, the film depends on quite a different conception of character. First, both actors are cast somewhat against type, with Lewis's casting being particularly perverse since he is the object of a character's obnoxious interest rather than being the obnoxious character himself. His explosive persona is kept under such tight control that he becomes sinister – forbidden to scream, to roll his eyes, even to gesture wildly or contort, he becomes a sort of hollowed-out reproduction of himself, an image never able to do what is expected of it. Similarly, De Niro never indulges the dynamism with which he made a career. Though he plays an obsessive character, he denies himself the psychologising quality associated with his screen persona by expressing only its outer shell. Having a psyche which only perceives a limited amount of the information presented to it, Pupkin remains a two-dimensional character, as flat as a television or movie screen. In one scene, Pupkin sits between cardboard cut-outs of Liza Minnelli and Jerry Lewis (as Jerry Langford, the talk-show host) and conducts a conversation with them. That he acts as if the cut-outs were real is only half the joke; more to the point is that Pupkin fits right in. Like Lewis, De Niro suppresses any sense of emotional anarchy, and his character's single-mindedness is horrifying precisely because there seems to be absolutely no governing intelligence behind it.

With Lewis in particular, the idea of an autonomous, well-rounded character gives way. The role of Jerry Langford, obviously modelled on Johnny Carson, was actually offered to Carson, whose fear of life imitating art made him turn it down. Instead of just having Carson play Carson, an image made in its own image, Scorsese then had the opportunity to play one image against another while also playing it against itself. The opening shots of *The King of Comedy*, marked visually as video, are likewise the opening shots of *The Jerry Langford Show*, a point by point imitation of *The Tonight Show*: titles against a multicoloured curtain, an announcer named Ed, the star walking through the curtains and ending up in 3/4 shot, a shot of the band leaders, and into the star's monologue. Dependent not only on the familiarity of Lewis as a comedian and telethon-host, the opening sequence rests on the recognition of the structured and inviolable opening of a popular television show. It is this familiarity, so readily accepted by anyone even remotely acquainted with American popular culture, which propels the obsessive Rupert Pupkin into action. In other words, it is a symbolic familiarity which both star and presentation encourage but which Rupert accepts without qualification – entering the living room every night in exactly the same way, Jerry Langford becomes a houseguest, a friend, in a certain sense a possession.

But for the fan, possessing a star's image is only the first step toward actually possessing the star. The second stage, wanting a relic, takes the form of autograph hounds who form a violent mob outside Langford's stage door. Scorsese introduces Pupkin, as well as his equally obsessive friend Masha (Sandra Bernhard), in this context, and the violence of the scene contrasts with the hermetic organisation of the Langford show. Aside from the tonal contrast, though, these two scenes are consequential – the images presented on television and in films already contain the seeds of an unrequited and potentially violent desire. On every level from commerce to form, the screen compels pleasure and then refuses to gratify it completely; Langford's image, carefully and cosily situated in its regular format, encourages as much attention as possible without ever foreclosing the option of appearing the next day, without ever exhausting the attracted viewer's desire. Langford himself, however, resists any intrusion into his life and is appalled by the attention he receives. Retreating into a limousine and then into a steely apartment, the real Jerry Langford seeks only isolation.

His fans, meanwhile, are quite out of control. Not content with the image as it is offered on the television screen, they demand the icon himself, hoping to find in him a final consummation. In Frank Tashlin's 1956 film, *Hollywood or Bust*, a similar quest toward meeting a star forms the basis of the whole story. There, Jerry Lewis plays a film buff driven toward meeting his idol, Anita Ekberg. For Lewis's character, the screen appearance of the star is merely an incomplete substitute, and his failure to make the gratifying conceptual leap from the iconic to the symbolic, to locate desire within the image itself, leads to tremendous fear and frustration. The star exists above him, and the unsatisfying nature of the relationship he has with her by way of the movies is due, he thinks, to his own inadequacy. In *The King of Comedy*, though, the obsessive fans evidence no fear at all. Unlike Lewis in *Hollywood or Bust*, they see no qualitative difference between themselves and the star and therefore have no hesitation in approaching him. Since he has, after all, been in their homes every night for years, they see Langford as being no different from themselves. By turning the tables on that crucial separation between spectator and star which film and television tend to maintain, they refuse to be content with the passive role assigned to them and, in their dissatisfaction, become a bit subversive.

Through the complex interactions of star and fan, familiarity and violence, Scorsese exposes the contradictory forces at work in audiovisual narration: his obsessive characters are unable to reconcile their attraction toward images with the fact that images are not substantial. But while Masha's obsession takes the form of hysteria, Rupert channels his energy creatively into becoming an image himself. Unfortunately, Scorsese does not take this sexual and ideological aspect into account at all. Fashioning himself a talent, Rupert aspires to become a comedian, but more impressively, he writes his own narrative as he goes along since Scorsese incorporates scenes of his fantasies into the seemingly objective narrative of the film. After the scene in which Rupert meets Langford, Scorsese cuts directly to a scene in which Rupert and Langford have a congenial business lunch to discuss Rupert's future as a comic. There are no stylistic clues that the lunch scene is only taking place in Rupert's mind – the cut, like any other, serves to develop the narrative by joining one fiction to another. Structured classically with two-shots and over-the-shoulder shots (Langford on the left, Rupert on the right), the lunch scene proceeds with Langford offering one compliment after another to the magnanimous Rupert until Scorsese cuts abruptly to Rupert alone in his basement, still carrying on the conversation, still on the right side of the screen. Then, by cross-cutting back and forth between restaurant and basement, Scorsese implies not just that Rupert is deluded but that in this case the delusion takes the form of a classical film dialogue sequence in which Rupert includes himself in every shot. Rupert creatively transgresses the bounds of space and time by constructing and conjoining images; further, he places himself prominently in the images, thereby becoming spectator, author, and actor.

The scene concludes with Rupert laughing at his own joke, a joke which is told

Rupert enjoys an imaginary friendship with chat show host Jerry Langford (Jerry Lewis). Johnny Carson reputedly turned down Lewis's part out of fear of all the real-life Ruperts.

in two-shot and at which Langford laughs as well. Rupert's laughter, a controlled show-biz laugh, the kind stars use on talk-shows, continues into a shot of Rupert alone in his basement, still on the right of the frame. Abruptly, Rupert switches sides – he takes Jerry's place on the screen, laughs for him, becomes him in a visual twist that neatly foreshadows his literal replacement of Jerry on the show.

From this point on, each consecutive scene is called into question in terms of both content and contiguity. Just as Pupkin simply cuts to a scene he'd like to see, Scorsese turns the progress of the narrative into overt wish fulfilment. When Rupert, sitting at a bar, asks the barmaid out of the blue if she'd like to go out on a date with him, Scorsese cuts directly to the date in progress. Since the event is exactly what Rupert wants, the cut is nearly as outrageous as the one which transported him into a luncheon with Jerry, though the date turns out to be 'real' within the story. To his credit, Scorsese is not much interested in separating Rupert's perceptual problems from those of the audience by signalling Rupert's visions as unacceptable; what Rupert sees and what the audience sees are not all that different. There is one shot which distances the audience from Rupert's perceptions, and it occurs while Rupert makes a tape of his comedy routine to submit to Langford's office. Even here, though, the shot is ambiguous. From a shot of Rupert sitting in front of his recording equipment beginning his monologue, Scorsese cuts to a shot of Rupert standing in front of a huge blow-up photograph of an audience laughing. Their deafening laughter is heard on the soundtrack, and the camera tracks back to reveal a grey, tunnel-like room. On the one hand, the room is clearly a fiction within the fiction – photographs do not laugh; on the other hand, Rupert has already shown himself to have made life-size reproductions of Liza and Jerry, the difference being that the stars' blow-ups exist in the basement while the audience exists in a foreboding netherworld which, ironically enough, rather resembles Jerry Langford's apartment.

In a scene taking place at a row of pay phones in Times Square, where Rupert has stationed himself to receive calls from Langford's assistant, Scorsese dresses up an otherwise event-free scene – a character waiting for a call he probably won't get – by injecting a little violence. Suddenly all the other phones are broken, the receivers dangling, a hostile crowd closing in on Rupert. Just as suddenly, the phones are back in order and the crowd is gone. Whether the scene 'really happened' or whether it is Rupert's paranoia at work makes little difference. The scene contains no reassuring explanation, no phone repairmen, no skewed camera angles to represent Rupert's perceptual error. The events are visible but not necessarily factual.

By failing to distinguish between representation and truth, by conflating image with icon, Rupert leads himself first to betrayal but then to success. He believes that Langford has invited him out to Long Island for the weekend, but Langford throws him out and insults him. His only choice is to take matters literally into his own hands and kidnap Langford, thereby consummating his desire to possess the star while also furthering his career goals. Strapping Jerry to a chair, Rupert then mummifies him with adhesive tape, an action Scorsese records in an overhead shot. Here, the restraints on Jerry Lewis's persona find a physical correlative; it is as if the dream of many a hostile film critic has come true. Bound and gagged, Lewis is forced to sit and watch as another borderline maniac threatens his life. Moreover, Rupert's circular movement around Langford becomes metonymic – in his desire to reach Jerry, Rupert goes round and round him and finally displaces him on TV.

According to the kidnapper's demands, Rupert's monologue must be broadcast or Langford will be killed. In other words, Rupert must see himself become an image in his own right or he will destroy the source of his frustrated desire. That the gun is loaded with fake bullets and that the monologue turns out to be funny are in the final analysis less humorous than the fact of Rupert's success and the manner by which he attains it. The final sequence of *The King of Comedy*, like the first, appears as video. A newscaster begins to tell Rupert's story; images of Rupert appear on the screen; his face appears on magazine covers; he becomes the talk of the town. The video broadcast then switches time frames, skipping several years without a break in structure and continues with Rupert, now released from prison, having written a bestseller. Hundreds of copies of his book appear in a store window, and finally Rupert himself appears on a television sound stage to tremendous applause. Every element of ignominious pain – Rupert on trial, Rupert in jail, Rupert actually sitting at a typewriter writing a book – are excised from the sequence, leaving only glory presented in the form of objective news. This extraordinary slide from a newsroom to Rupert as a star appearing in front of television cameras, a scene which is itself being recorded by a television camera, resolves the narrative by disintegrating it. For the spectator, unable to make a safe judgement between the fiction film and the fictions Rupert lays on top of it, Rupert's confusion becomes his or her own. From a newscast, that trusted source of seemingly unmediated facts, to Rupert Pupkin live on television, the sequence's profoundly ironic tone reveals the nature of images to be deeply perverse. The banality of content together with its sequential logic expose any transmission of information as being fraught with distortion and ambiguity.

Acutely aware of the complexities of image production and transmission, Scorsese's is an analytical comedy which tries to come to terms with its own consequences. In revealing Rupert's disturbance as being connected to the effects of representations, and in treating the information contained in every image as being highly manipulative and yet beyond control, Scorsese turns a scandal back on itself. Not a sociological battle between nuts and celebrities, Scorsese's conflict is played out on the screen, any screen, right in anyone's own home.

MARTIN SCORSESE:
Who the Hell Wants to Make Other Pictures
If You Can't Have a Relationship with a Woman?
By Roger Ebert

Walking back to my hotel after dinner with Martin Scorsese, I asked myself how much longer he would go on driving himself up the wall with his obsession of finding happiness with a woman. For all of his adult life, Scorsese has been searching for love and serenity with a woman, and he has never found those comforts for very long. Out of his pain, however, he has directed some of the best films ever made about loneliness and frustration. Pausing for a stoplight, looking up at the Manhattan canyons where lonely people sleep on shelves all the way to the stars, I reflected that Scorsese's hurt has at least inspired great films. If he stays miserable, I thought, he might make some more masterpieces like *Taxi Driver*. On the other hand, he might simply go off the deep end into bitterness and despair. We had just talked for three hours about *The King of Comedy*, Scorsese's problematical new film – a movie the studio was ready to give up on, until some good reviews started coming in. For Scorsese, the making of the film coincided with a painful period of his life, a time when he fell in love with Ingrid Bergman's daughter, Isabella Rossellini, was married and was divorced. Although it is easy to see *The King of Comedy* as the most barren and unemotional of all Scorsese's films, that is not the way he sees it. Maybe that's because each scene is connected in his memory with a hurt in his life.

'The amount of rejection in this film is horrifying,' Scorsese said. 'There are scenes I almost can't look at. There's a scene where De Niro is told, I hate you! and he nods and responds, Oh, I see, right, you don't want to see me again! I made the movie during a very painful period in my life. I was going through the Poor Me routine. And I'm still very lonely. Another relationship has broken up.'

Since Isabella?

'Since. I'm spending a lot of time by myself now. I go home and watch movies on video and stay up all night and sleep all day. If I didn't have to work I'd sleep all the time. I've never had such a long period when I've been alone.'

Just the way he said that, quietly, without emphasis, much more softly than he usually speaks, places it in a special category. Perhaps it gives an additional dimension to *The King of Comedy*, a movie about a man so desperately isolated that even his goals do not include a relationship with another human being.

The character, Rupert Pupkin, played by Robert De Niro, has constructed a set for a talk show in his basement, and he sits down there night after night, holding chatty, condescending conversations with life-size cardboard cut-outs of Liza Minnelli and Jerry Lewis. Rupert Pupkin doesn't feel cut off from life – he feels cut off from talk shows. His life consists of waiting. He waits outside stage doors, outside office buildings, in waiting rooms and on telephones. He wants to be on television, He wants to be on first-name terms with Liza and Jerry and Tony and Joyce and the other members of America's amorphous extended family of television 'personalities', who all seem to know each other so very well.

Rupert does not know how to have a conventional conversation, but he knows the form for talk shows; he has studied talk-show host 'Jerry Langford' (Jerry Lewis) so carefully that he even knows how he dresses, and what his credo for beginning comics is: 'Don't tell them it's the punch line, just tell them the punch line.'

Scorsese says that both Rupert Pupkin and Jerry Langford remind him of himself. Pupkin is young Marty Scorsese, camped out in agents' offices, scrounging loans to finish his student film, hustling jobs as an editor in between directing assignments. Langford is Martin Scorsese at 40, famous, honoured, admired, besieged by young would-be filmmakers asking him for a break.

'Last night,' Scorsese said, 'I went to the 10 p.m. show of *King of Comedy*. On the screen, the scene is playing where Rupert pushes into Jerry's limousine and says he's gotta talk to him. He's out of breath. Take it easy, kid, Jerry tells him. Meanwhile, in the back row of the theatre, a kid grabs me by the arm and he's saying he's got to talk to me. He's out of breath I tell him to take it easy. It's the exact same scene that's on the screen!'

Time. What that story is about is time. There was a time when Marty Scorsese was an intense, asthmatic, talented kid from New York University who wanted to make movies. He had a lot of self-confidence. Now time has passed and Scorsese has achieved all the things he dreamed of. There are those who believe he is the greatest of American directors, the most personal, the most obsessed. But if he once thought that success would bring him happiness, he now thinks again. Since famous film directors are supposed to be able to have whatever they want, the fact that Scorsese is famous and yet still unhappy must seem to him a terrible irony.

Scorsese at 40 is bearded, slight and often cheerful, despite the burden of his unhappiness. He comes to dinner dressed like a successful undertaker, wearing an expensive dark-blue suit and a double-breasted navy-blue topcoat. Perhaps he looks like the well-dressed Mafioso who ran New York's Little Italy when he was growing up there. He was in Israel recently to scout locations for a project called *The Last*

Temptation of Christ, and when they took him out in the desert in a helicopter, he wore the blue suit and the blue topcoat and the expensive black shoes. Most directors wear desert jackets to dinner. Scorsese wears a suit to the desert.

'The studio was ready to give up on *King of Comedy,*' he said. 'They sneak-previewed it. The response was not great. Good, but not great. I told them this was not the kind of movie where preview audiences meant anything. If you are not prepared in your mind to see this movie, it can be a very strange experience. The way to sell this movie is, basically, on the track records of De Niro and myself, and on the story line. The studio was ready to put the movie on the shelf. It was dead and buried. Then some of the good reviews started coming in, and they reversed themselves. Now it looks like it might do all right.'

One of the reasons the studio was afraid of the movie (Scorsese did not add) was that the subject matter is extremely touchy. In the movie, Rupert Pupkin kidnaps Jerry Langford and holds him for ransom. The ransom demand is a ten-minute slot for a standup comedy routine on the talk show. Since it is well known that Scorsese's *Taxi Driver* (about an alienated assassin) was seen by John Hinckley before he shot Reagan, *The King of Comedy* seemed in some circles almost like an invitation to trouble for someone like Johnny Carson.

Such fears were not alleviated by Paul Zimmerman, the onetime *Newsweek* film critic who wrote the movie, and who brashly told a New York press conference, 'It is not the job of art to serve as a security system for celebrities.'

For Scorsese, though, the movie does not precisely seem to be about kidnapping a celebrity. That is simply the plot line, in a screenplay that Zimmerman wrote twelve years ago and that Scorsese originally turned down six years ago. 'It seemed like a one-joke movie at the time,' he said. 'But then I began to see that it wasn't about kidnapping, it was about rejection. It required a new visual style for me. I'm known for my moving camera. I'm usually all over the place. This film has very little camera movement, and when the camera moves, it means something. Look at the scene where the receptionist tells Pupkin that Jerry won't be back until Monday, and Pupkin says he'll wait. Look how the camera moves. It moves to show how solidly planted Rupert is. It's a nice move.'

But it comes, I said, out of your sense of loneliness and rejection?

'Yes.'

Simple as that?

'Simple as that.'

Scorsese's first movie, *Who's That Knocking at My Door?,* was about an Italian-American kid from New York who fell in love with a blonde on the Staten Island ferry, and wanted to marry her before he discovered that she was not a virgin. Angry and confused, he rejected her, and at the end of the movie they were both alone and we had the feeling that he would stay that way. Freud wrote about the 'Madonna/whore complex', the hangup of men who have only two categories for women: First they idealise them, and then, when they discover that their perfect woman is only human after all, they rigidly reject them.

Without getting into your personal psychology, I said to Scorsese, are you still replaying the same scenario?

'I'm still stuck at the *Who's That Knocking?* stage,' he said 'Except it's not so much that I reject, as that something goes wrong. Maybe I'm impossible to be with.'

The same pattern, of idealisation and rejection, turns up in Scorsese's other movies, including *Mean Streets, Taxi Driver* and *Raging Bull* (where Robert De Niro, as Jake La Motta, marries a sixteen-year-old sexpot and then is driven mad with jealousy when other men look at her). I could only guess at the forms that Scorsese's own obsessions take, and I did not want to really press the subject, although he seemed willing to talk about it.

What eventually happened, toward the end of our dinner, was that I discovered by accident how deeply he was hurt. I mentioned a new film named *Exposed*, by James Toback, starring Nastassja Kinski. I said I thought Kinski possessed whatever rare magic Marilyn Monroe had; that whatever Kinski appears in, good or bad, she commands the screen.

'I can't bear to see Kinski in anything,' Scorsese said. 'She reminds me too much of Isabella. It tears me apart. I can't even go to see a film by the Taviani brothers, because Isabella and I had a little courtship on the set of one of their films. I can't ever go back to the island of Salina, where Visconti's *The Leopard* was shot, because we were there. In fact, I can hardly even watch a film by Visconti without growing depressed.'

By memories of Isabella?

'By memories of a period when I thought I was happy. I'll put it that way. A period when I really thought I had the answers.'

OK, then, I said. I've got a new movie that can't possibly depress you or bring up any old associations. It's called *Say Amen, Somebody*, and it's this wonderful documentary about gospel music.

'Can't see it.' Scorsese was grinning, but he was serious.

Why not?

'It's distributed by United Artists Classics.' He sighed.

You mean you can't see a film that is distributed by a company that is connected to a woman you once loved?

He smiled. 'I'd see the United Artists logo and it would ruin the movie for me.'

Maybe you could come in after the logo had left the screen?

'I'd know.'

With some directors, you fear that they will lose their early fire and obsession, and, in middle age, turn to directing safe and cheerful commercial projects. With Martin Scorsese, I don't think we have that to worry about.

1980s Interlude

NIGHT OF THE LIVING DEAD
By Chris Peachment

There is a thumping irony, not much publicly, expressed, in the non-appearance of so many Americans at this year's [1986] Cannes Festival. Of course, as every major star from Stallone downwards was at pains to explain, it was *impossible* for them to put in an appearance simply because they were all working so hard on their next projects. This raises the speculation, however, in the doubter's mind as to how they ever manage to arrive during other years, when perhaps the Libyans just across the water are not making such threatening noises and muttering about the 'Line of Death'. It is always instructive to place people in a 'money-mouth situation' and watch the result. But the real irony must be apparent to any visitor to New York. Never mind Libyans. Go south from Fourteenth Street after dark, and your best companion would be a flak jacket and a Remington twelve-gauge.

This is a journey undertaken one dark night by Paul Hackett (Griffin Dunne), a computer yuppie from uptown whose only armament is a $20 bill. When this blows away out of the taxi's window he is left helpless in the SoHo area, and thus begins one *very* long dark night of the soul as he becomes a human pinball, rebounding from chance encounters with the sort of kooks who are all very definitely both paddles out of the water. 'It's a Comedy of Paranoia,' says Scorsese, a man who knows all there is to know about paranoia. If *Taxi Driver* was about a paranoid man who believed that all the city had turned against him, then *After Hours* is about an ordinary man to whom it is proved that the city has indeed done that very thing.

Scorsese is currently doing the fine tuning on his latest film *The Color of Money*, a sequel by Walter Tevis to his previous book *The Hustler*, in which Paul Newman is once more roped in to play the same character, Fast Eddie, some 30 years on from his triumph over Minnesota Fats at the pool tables, and now instructing Tom Cruise in the same art. After the critical success but disastrous fiscal failure of *The King of Comedy*, Scorsese spent some time trying to set up his next project *The Last Temptation of Christ*. In spite of managing to find exactly the right sort of 'warm, human Christ' he was looking for in the shape of Aidan Quinn, nonetheless the project foundered, possibly because the large sums of money required tended to prove daunting. Or as Scorsese puts it: 'You know, people kept *disappearing* . . . The times are rather conservative.'

Left high and dry for a period of nearly eighteen months, he began to experience that frustration common to any director used to racking up at least one a year. 'I was like a race horse. Raring to go, but no race.' A studio-developed project did not appeal for the simple reason that there was so little in any of them that accorded with his personal view of the world – and Scorsese is the most *personal*, as well as the most talented, of his generation of non-mainstream filmmakers. The answer came one day

Paul (Griffin Dunne), a man adrift in night-time SoHo, with neurotic waitress Julie (Terri Garr). After Hours (1985) is a rare Scorsese excursion into comedy, albeit of a dark hue.

in his lawyer's office. When his legal eagle handed him a script that was hanging around that had been written by Joseph Minion, a 26-year-old film-school graduate, as part of his final thesis. 'It had something of myself in it.

'I read it, it struck me that here was the way people really talked. I became fascinated by the coffee-shop scene.' This is the early moment when Hackett becomes launched on his odyssey. Sitting alone at a late-night coffee joint, he is ostentatiously reading Henry Miller's *Tropic of Cancer*, which just happens to catch the eye of Rosanna Arquette. They exchange pleasantries, then they exchange phone numbers, but he doesn't have a pen and so borrows one from the cashier who is busy doing pirouettes behind the counter for his own amusement. He is first in a long line of bystanders, all of whose elevators don't go quite to the top. Indeed, to judge by the look in Rosanna Arquette's, the lights are on there, too, but no one's at home.

'I read this scene halfway through, when I went upstairs to do something else. And I kept wandering about upstairs, wondering what was going on downstairs.'

What was going on downstairs in fact was Griffin Dunne's fateful journey to Arquette's SoHo loft, which she shares with one Kiki (Linda Fiorentino), a dead-eyed sculptress who does her work clad in fetching black underwear, tends to fall asleep while Dunne is massaging her shoulders, and later turns out to be an enthusiastic bondage freak. But her first act is to throw the keys to the apartment down to Dunne, which are then photographed as if they were an avenging Stuka, raining down destruction on a fuddled refugee. Anyone who has ever regularly visited a friend who lives five storeys up will testify to the truth of this particular menace. 'Yes, I liked that touch too. I wanted to photograph almost every normal detail, so that it somehow implied *dread*. It also happens with ordinary things like light switches. Dunne is often panicking in the dark, and he thinks, "If only I can find a light switch, everything will be all right," and so I shot all the lamps and the switches to be really out of the way, or rather sinister in some way. And of course when he hits them, *nothing gets any better*. The poor guy is like a man with tunnel vision. Everything he looks at, turns sinister.'

And everything that he then does turns out even more sinister. It is not giving too much away to point out that, somehow, one is howling with laughter as Arquette takes an overdose, and Dunne then falls in with three more apparently sweet-natured females, all of whom exhibit more menace and destruction than Godzilla. There is Julie (played by Terri Garr), a weepy barmaid who is still stuck in some sixties time-warp, addicted to the Monkees, and keeps an array of mousetraps around the bed. There is Gail (Catherine O'Hara), an artist who also drives a Mr Softee truck in which she leads a gang of gay vigilantes in pursuit of Dunne whom she believes to be the neighbourhood mugger. And finally June (Verna Bloom), another sculptress who saves Dunne from the marauding band of queens by encasing him in plaster and turning him into a living statue, much in the fashion of Corman's famous *Bucket of Blood*. There is an amusing little aside at one point when Dunne gazes with a look of crazed vacancy at a piece of lavatory wall graffiti, of a man having his member vigorously chewed by a shark. This little reminder of what I believe Freud named *vagina dentata* is nothing compared to what Dunne goes through in this territory far from home. Even the doughnuts have teeth down there.

And so do the nightclub acts. Scorsese himself makes a brief appearance as the militarily clad follow-spot operator at some hellish dive called the 'Berlin', into which Dunne strays little knowing that it is 'Mohawk' night. To the cry of 'Mohawk him,' he is set upon by the denizens and only just manages to struggle free after a sizeable patch of hair has been removed from his scalp. 'Oh sure, that happens,' says Scorsese gleefully. And all the rest? 'Oh yes, much much worse.' Finally, broken like a doll, soaked to the skin, penniless, dispossessed of all human contact, eyes like bloodshot saucers, Dunne sinks to his knees on the pavement, arms stretched to heaven like Job at the final break point, and cries, 'I'm just a word processor, for Christ's sake.'

'He's a very nice guy,' says Scorsese. 'He kind of came with the dinner, so to speak. I mean it was his project all along, he produced it with Amy Robinson, with whom he had already done *Chilly Scenes of Winter*. We met and I liked the way he told stories. He's got this manic charm which makes him a great raconteur.' All the other actors also came with the dinner, since many had worked with Dunne before; John Heard from *Chilly Scenes*, and Rosanna Arquette from John Sayles's *Baby It's You* which Dunne produced. They each of them only worked for two weeks at a time on the film, partly because this was all that was necessary for the mosaic structure of the film in which only Dunne is on-screen for most of the picture, and partly because it's a lot cheaper that way. Dunne himself is the offspring of a talented confederacy. His father Dominick is a movie producer and journalist, and his uncle is John Gregory Dunne, which makes Joan Didion an aunt.

From *New York, New York* onwards, Scorsese has been used to taking some 100 days to shoot a picture. Here he got 40. He has in other words found the courage to go small again. In this time schedule he was considerably helped by his cameraman Michael Ballhaus, onetime operator for Fassbinder, who in Scorsese's words, turned in a 'gutchurning' experience of something like seventeen set-ups a day. (A 'steady eight' is the industry norm. Kubrick probably does one a week.) Originally budgeted at the paltry sum of $3.5 million, the picture finally went up to $4.5 million when the ending was completely reshot after the original failed to satisfy both Michael Powell and Scorsese's father, two of his sternest critics and best advisers.

'I rewrote much of the original script from about three quarters of the way through to the end. However, the picture finished with Dunne encased in the statue simply being carted off into the night on the back of the truck.' He has been stolen at this point by two charming and energetic thieves played by Cheech and Chong. 'The camera just followed his capture and then swooped up into the night. But no one seemed to like that, so we came up with another ending whereby he escaped and is seen wandering down the road, stopping the cars and crying, "They're coming, they're coming," which of course is a *homage* to *Invasion of the Body Snatchers*.' But again it was too dark an ending. It was, in fact, Michael Powell who came up with the present much brighter notion, which it would be unfair to reveal, but does at least give the picture a very satisfying circularity by returning Dunne to his starting point as if he were waking from a nightmare. 'Mickey [Powell] was saying that Dunne's only sympathetic connections were with computers, which is a concept I don't really understand, but as usual, he was right.'

Griffin Dunne's computer operator with Gail (Catherine O'Hara), a loft-dwelling artist who drives an ice cream van. Dunne took After Hours *to Scorsese as work for hire.*

This may well be the first true black screwball comedy. Of course the best screwballs, like Howard Hawks' *Bringing Up Baby,* have been surrounded by darkness, forever on the brink of succumbing to the encroaching madness of the participants. But their tone has ever been light. *After Hours,* like all the best city films, is shot entirely between the hours of dusk and dawn. It is a movie of great formal elegance, with each episode slotting together as neatly as a jigsaw to provide a perfect whole. And it is audacious in the sense that Scorsese, as always, never panders to any possible instincts for commercialism or self-promotion. If it is marked by the unmistakeable sound of the man falling off a log, that is still a noise I would rather hear coming from Scorsese than from any other of his contemporaries, who all, even Schrader with his last, *Mishima,* seem to be straining after effect. And Scorsese after hours? 'It's renewed my faith.'

AN INTERVIEW WITH MARTIN SCORSESE
By Susan Morrison

What was working for Steven Spielberg's **Amazing Stories** *like, where you were working in the commercial medium?*
I did that as a discipline. To discipline myself to make a film very quickly.

Did you have any input in the actual story?
Not really, no. It was Steve's story. He told me at dinner one night. He said he was going to direct it, but if I wanted to do it, I could do it. I said, 'Oh, great, I'll do it.' That's how he got me. Then he got all the other directors, too, from that. He said, 'Marty's doing one.' 'Oh, okay, we'll do one.' He caught me that way, because he told the story. It was a great story, I thought. It was funny. And then they wrote the script and basically, I just changed the script a little bit here and there, that's all. And just basically tried to get something that's disciplined, with the least amount of control as possible and still see if I could survive in the making of it.

How did you feel working in the horror genre?
Oh, I love it.

You did? It's so different from all your other films.
I don't think so.

I don't mean the content, but I meant, in terms of using make-up and special effects and all that stuff, the monsters . . .
Oh, that, make-up and stuff, I don't know, the monsters, I don't know about that. I just made him look like the professor in *House of Wax*, I thought that was funny. I liked that, with the cloak and the hat. I thought that was fun and the lighting, we really didn't have time to play around with the lighting on the monster. But the really interesting aspect about that half-hour show was the camera moves and the idea of the piece, of a man slowly losing his mind, a man who is having a nervous breakdown. And having tight camera angles and moves. There was hardly any dialogue in the piece. And the comforting that the Helen Shaver character tries to give him. Those are the really interesting scenes. I don't know. Has anybody seen it?

*It was advertised here in Toronto, in **TV Guide**. It gave you a credit for it, and so people I know watched it.*
Oh, I see. So somebody *did* see it.

Yeah, some people have seen it.
The problem is that *Amazing Stories* didn't do well. NBC put it on too late in the season. It was anticlimactic by that point. If they had put it on earlier, when expectations were higher, it might have done better. We would have gotten a bigger blurb in the TV guide and things like that. And people would have known that I did it. Even though they put my name in there, it didn't have a special little 'Close-up' section and that sort of thing, where people would say, 'Oh, there's the one.' Because everybody kept asking, 'When's it going to be shown?' By the time it was shown, people missed it.

It's really too bad. Maybe they'll re-run it over the summer.
Yeah.

*After the unfortunate experience of **The Last Temptation of Christ**, all the projects you've* *worked on have been initiated by other people:* **After Hours** *by Amy Robinson and Griffin Dunne,* **The Color of Money** *by Paul Newman,* 'Mirror, Mirror' *by Steven Spielberg. Has this made any difference to you in terms of your approach to these films? Are they less personal as a result?*

No, I don't think so. But again, it's you people who tell me that. In a sense I just try to get the most personal kind of film made within this Hollywood system because I'm an American. I can't go over to Italy and England and France and make pictures. Yes, I could. I physically could. They would probably be good films, but I don't know the language, I don't know, I can't hear it in my ear, you know what I'm saying? I mean, there'd be something intrinsically missing, unless I'm doing *Anna Karenina* or something, where it's a different thing. Then it's purely a job as a director where it's almost like just pure *mise-en-scène*, where you tell the person to move from there to there, which is the thing I hate. I hate that the most.

I was going to ask before about whether you could make a film about a protagonist with whom you had nothing in common, like **Anna Karenina,** *I guess, unless you could find something . . .*

Yes, I think I could, but then I would be taking the role of a real director. And I really don't want to be a director.

What do you want to be?

I just want to be a filmmaker. An American filmmaker, and I just try to make my films. And if, for example, I could utilise Paul Newman, and if he could utilise me, we would both mutually get something out of it. Then it's the best of both possible worlds, which I think the new picture, *The Color of Money*, is that way.

It is? Even though it wasn't yours to begin with, you feel that you've really got your touch on it?

I think that I've got my touch on it. That's what I liked about it. And at the same time he's got his and then we just came together with it. And we got Richard Price, I got him involved, and with Richard Price, the three of us worked on the script for a year, before we decided even to make the picture.

You've just finished working on it now?

Yeah. We're finishing the fine cut right now.

When will it be released?

Christmas. It's my first Christmas movie.

Not until then? Is it a 'Christmas Movie'?

No. It's a Christmas movie in terms of performance. Paul Newman is terrific, he is great. Tom Cruise is terrific, Helen Shaver is wonderful, Mary-Elizabeth Mastrantonio, I mean everybody is just great. It's a nice movie. As I say, I have some projects that are generated by me and if they can't get made, in the meantime the trick is to try to find, I think, staying within the limitations, the limitation being I'm an American, and not wanting to go make, immediately anyway for now, to make pictures in Europe, then you have to stay within the game plan here. One of the ways of staying within the game plan is to see if a major star can get something out of you, and you can get something out of a major star. The other thing is doing something so low budget, like *After Hours*, and so unique and so different, so unique in the sense that it's hardly like anything else made, that it's going to get some attention.

Well, it certainly got you the attention in Cannes.
Yeah, it did! I was very pleased.

Were you?
Yeah, sure. They can give me any award, I'm pleased. I'll take any award. To get that kind of recognition . . . The funny thing is, ten years ago I got the Grand Prize. But I wasn't there either.

What happened ten years ago?
Well, ten years ago, we arrived and we only did a day's worth of work, a day and a half worth of work. Tennessee Williams was the head of the jury and he came out and said in print, in one of the periodicals that come out every day in Cannes, that he felt that *Taxi Driver* was too violent a film. He hated it. He was the head of the jury, so we left. A week later they called up in the morning and said we won the Grand Prize. So it must be good luck not being there.

So for next year when **The Color of Money** *comes out . . .*
Oh, I don't know. These days travelling all around kills me.

CHALK TALK
By Peter Biskind and Susan Linfield

Martin Scorsese's new film, The Color of Money, *picks up the story of Fast Eddie Felson, the pool shark played by Paul Newman who we last saw 25 years ago in Robert Rossen's* The Hustler. *Scripted by novelist Richard Price (author of* The Wanderers, Bloodbrothers, *and* The Breaks*), the film stars Newman as an older and perhaps wiser Eddie, and Tom Cruise as the young player who becomes his protégé and eventual rival.* American Film *spoke with Scorsese and Price in New York about the making of* Money.

How come Marty Scorsese is making a sequel?
Martin Scorsese: It's not a sequel. Let me give the rundown. I was in London for about a week in September of 1984, after the shooting of *After Hours*. Paul Newman called me while I was there and asked if I'd be interested in this project. When I first

spoke to Newman on the phone, he said, 'Eddie Felson.' I said, 'I love that character.' He said, 'Eddie Felson reminds me of the characters that you've dealt with in your pictures. And I thought more ought to be heard from him.' I asked, 'Who's involved?' He said, 'Just you and me.' I said, 'OK, what have you got?' He said, 'I've got a script.' So he sent it to me and the next day I read it. I had a lot of reservations about it. I felt that it was a literal sequel: There were even a few minutes of film inserted in it from the first picture. It had its own merits, but it certainly wasn't the kind of thing I wanted to do. And so I made an appointment to see Newman when I got to New York.

Now, I know that he's not afraid to play people who are not necessarily 'nice'. Many characters in my pictures are also what we would call unsympathetic. So, I like the guy and he likes me and we respect each other's work – maybe we can find a common ground. And this character of Eddie Felson is the only common ground that we have. And, of course, Fast Eddie lives and thrives in my favourite places, which are bars and pool rooms. But I have to ask myself: Can I, from my generation of filmmakers, work with somebody from his generation? I've admired and appreciated the guy since I was twelve years old and in a movie theatre. But can this happen?

At about the same time, I found out that there had been a book called *The Color of Money* by Walter Tevis, who wrote *The Hustler*. I read the book, but I didn't really think it had anything in it in terms of a film, either. So I thought: Let's drop the book, just keep the title. I asked Richard if he would get involved in it. It was totally starting from scratch.

Richard Price: To write the script, I spent a lot of time travelling with pool hustlers. If I'm doing a movie about pool hustlers, and if pool hustlers are sitting in the audience opening night, I don't want anybody getting up in disgust. I don't want anybody saying, 'This is bullshit.' I want people to say, 'This is true.' As true as drama and fiction can be true.

The nature of pool is such that on one night, if there's a $7,500 pot, 60 of the 100 top pool hustlers in the nation will be under this tin roof. You can go and say, 'Hey, I'm doing a movie,' and they're all your friends, they all want to show you the inside, because they're all dreamers in a way. They all knew *The Color of Money*, the book, and they all knew the movie *The Hustler* because that was a romanticised version of their lives. You can be like one of those guys in a red vest playing in the lobby of the Roosevelt Hotel and writing little pamphlets on trick shots, too, but you know, pool is really just hustlers. It's kids in Members Only clothing with those sort of long, outdated hairdos and those marshmallow shoes.

What's the thrust of the script?
Scorsese: I felt that Eddie Felson was a very strong guy. I thought if something that bad happened to him in the first film, he would get stronger. He says, 'You want to see bad, I'll show you bad.' In 25 years he's become a sharpie and a hustler of a different type. He doesn't play pool anymore; he doesn't have the guts to do that. But he sees young talent, takes it, and makes money with it. He takes this young kid under his wing and corrupts him. And then somewhere along the road, in the education process, he reeducates *himself* and decides to play again. It's about a man who

Paul Newman and Tom Cruise keep their eyes on the ball in The Color of Money *(1986). Newman wanted Scorsese for the continuing story of* Fast Eddie *from* The Hustler *(1961).*

changes his mind at the age of 52.

The first time I met Paul Newman, I asked him why this guy would start playing pool again at 52. I asked Paul, 'Why do you race if you don't win every time?' There is really no answer. We looked at each other for a while and I said, 'That's the picture.'

There's no ethnic material in this script. But both of you have frequently dealt with Italians and Jews.
Price: This is more urban stuff than ethnic stuff. But I feel like everybody's a Jew in the world.
Scorsese: I feel everybody's Italian.
Price: But all Italians are Jews.

How did the three of you work together?
Scorsese: In writing sessions, it was the three of us constantly reworking, constantly coming up with and batting ideas back and forth. Eventually, the writing sessions took on the aspect of rehearsals. So by the time we did the picture, I'd already had two weeks of rehearsal – it was the most preplanned film I had ever made. This was also the way that I've worked with Bob De Niro. We'd get something we'd be interested in – maybe he'd be interested first, or I'd be – and we'd get together and see if both of us could find ourselves in it. And then we'd get a writer. It always comes down to whether I can see myself in the film, if I can express myself in it through the mouthpiece – in this case, through the persona of the Paul Newman character. And

could Paul express himself in it.

Price: I know this: If these guys had left me alone to write what I wanted (because I'm a novelist and all that), it would not have been as good a screenplay by any stretch of the imagination. I'll be the first to admit that. It would have been different, and it would have had its merits, but in terms of the requirements of the film, it would never have been as good.

Scorsese: Remarkable meetings.

Price: Four o'clock. 'Why does this guy have to play pool, anyhow?' Paul says, 'Guys, I don't know, I have to go race, so I'll see you in about a million years.' He'd come back with a big steel bowl of popcorn.

Scorsese: I gained seven pounds.

Price: That's because you put butter on it.

I learned a lot about writing dialogue from working with Marty and Paul. I've always taken pride in writing these great lines, but it was literary dialogue, an urban literary dialogue. An Elmore Leonard line or a George Higgins line looks great on the page, but when somebody is saying it, you feel like you have to stand up and say, 'Author! Author! Perfect ear!' It sounds like a David Mamet thing. You just look at each other and go, 'Wow, that is really true dialogue.' And everybody is at the mercy of the dialogue because the dialogue is so, like, perfect.

So, they sort of decalibrated my dialogue. I didn't go for the razor every three lines. It's like, instead of acres of diamonds, let's just make it a tomato box of diamonds.

Scorsese: How about one diamond? I'd say, 'It sounds like it's written.' Very blunt. Paul would say, 'It sounds like a *bon mot*.'

Price: A what?

Scorsese: It means it's written. Sounds like a play.

Price: *Now* my problem, frankly, is going back to a book. Because I had to unlearn a whole lot of novelistic stuff to do a screenplay. I've got to go back to baseball from softball, which I'm playing now. For example, I don't know how to write a sentence more than five words long.

Scorsese: Working with me – any word longer than two syllables is no good!

Price: It's not just from you, but it's the momentum, the pace. I feel like I'm Leroy Neiman and there's a camera over me and I'm doing a quick sketch of horses neck and neck. I can't go into depths of character, because everything has to play out one-dimensionally on the screen. There's no internals. You can't stop and sniff the roses; you're playing beat the clock. My pacing is all off. My thought processes are jacked up too high. I've got to go back to a slow pace and think: Now, what do I really want to say?

The other phrase of Newman's that was great was when I would have an idea, but it was sort of unformed and obscure and it existed exclusively in my mind. Newman would say, 'I don't understand, what's going on here?' And I'd explain and he'd say, 'Well, let's call that our delicious little secret.'

Scorsese: The audience will never know!

Price: But the killer was, I'd go into meetings and my hands are shaking, and Newman's looking at the script, and I think it's like the Koran, it's so perfect. And he goes, 'Guys,' going dot dot dot and I was looking at Marty and Marty's looking at me, and he's like my mother saying, 'Didn't I say you're gonna get a beating?' – and then the rest of Newman's dreaded sentence would come: 'I think we're missing an opportunity here.'

Scorsese: When a guy says something like, 'I think we're missing an opportunity here,' our reaction is: Let's hear what he has to say. What opportunity? We think we hit on them. But what do *you* think we missed – because if you think we missed, for example, the opportunity that the character could be in a Nazi uniform or blackface or something, then we are talking totally wrong. But usually he was right.

Price: I remember the moment in Connecticut when I realised that the picture was going to really get done. Newman turned to Marty and said, 'Are you good at holding actors' hands?' And he said, 'Oh, yeah, excellent, excellent.' Newman goes, 'Let's do it.' I'm thinking: Shit, man, we've been doing this for six months; what do you mean, 'Let's do it'? Oh, you mean we were just *playing* at doing it?

Scorsese: How many times do I have to tell you that? I had just come off *The Last Temptation of Christ*, man [a project of Scorsese's that fell through at the last minute]. That's why I kept telling you over the phone, 'Don't tell people. Don't say anything.'

Price: Is it still too soon?

Scorsese: It hasn't been released yet! It still has to be released! He's walking around saying, 'We're making the picture.' I'd say, 'Shut up, you jerk, we're not making anything.' First Fox decided not to do it. It's not the kind of picture Fox does. Then began the long problem of going from Fox to Columbia. Even with Tom Cruise involved as the kid, it was still difficult to get a 'go' on the picture.

I thought Paul Newman was one of those automatic 'yeses'?

Scorsese: I don't know. I think in a case like this, given the kind of film that it is, even with Newman and Cruise – it's not what the studios need. We are now talking about censorship in America, which is worse than the blacklist, and the kind of difficulties certain unique sensibilities have. We now have to do it with a lot of style, and very cheap, in order to get projects done. There's no guarantee of anything in this business anymore unless it's a big epic – invading cannibals.

Price: *I Eat Cannibals Who Massacre Zombies.*

Scorsese: Then Columbia decided not to do it. And Katzenberg and Eisner at Disney grabbed it.

Did Disney bother you?

Price: They were great. I'd do a pornographic movie with them. *Bambi Does Dallas.*

Scorsese: Portions of Paul Newman's and my salary had to be put up as insurance against going over budget.

It's incredible that people like you and Newman had to put up part of your salaries.

Scorsese: I don't know. The kind of picture I make is sort of in the margin at this point.

Price: What's the median age of the moviegoer now?

Scorsese: Two. They're kids.

Price: Two of them added up *together* make two. Who goes to the movies? Didn't they

Vincent (Tom Cruise) with hardbitten Carmen (Mary Elizabeth Mastrantonio). Cruise and Scorsese acquit themselves well, but The Color of Money *belongs to Paul Newman.*

say that 90 percent of the audience would not have seen *The Hustler*?

Scorsese: It is a crime what's happening in the American industry. If the situation is not totally bleak, it's news to me. I just lock into certain projects. Hopefully, I can still get *The Last Temptation of Christ* made someday, but it won't be in this country, and it won't be financed by this country. At all. Forget it. That film has nothing to do with the American industry. I mean, I love Spielberg pictures. You have those wonderful little kids. But I don't think everyone should have to make them.

Price: It's true. Now you've got all of these prepubescents. It's not even the Brat Pack. It's the Wet Pack.

Scorsese: I did a half-hour TV show with Spielberg called 'Mirror, Mirror' – although the network neglected to tell anyone it was on. But I can't imagine directing one of those special effects . . . talk to the blue screen!

Price: Since *Color of Money*, I've turned down 50 projects. Basically, it feels like people sit down and say, 'All right, what's the trend now? What's hot? We have to get somebody to capitalise on this trend.' There's not even anything like generic caper movies any more. It's all tailored to, well, there's a kid with two heads, and we'll use this girl who's got no arms at all, and it's wacky and her father's having a sex change, and it's really wild.

Richard, did you do the scripts for the movies of* Bloodbrothers *and* The Wanderers*?

Price: No, I wouldn't go near them because I didn't want anybody telling me what to do on my own book, which is the nature of the game. The best thing is just to take the cheque; let them make a bad movie rather than no movie.

But I've always loved movies. And I always knew that because two of my books were made into movies, I could write scripts if I wanted to. And I knew I wanted to eventually.

Scorsese: That's why I worry about you, Richard. You've got this whole thing about writing scripts. Here you are, you're a novelist, you actually have this gift – you can sit down with a blank piece of paper and somehow the words come out and you have total control over it. And you want to be a screenwriter!

Price: Well, my last book was a very tough project – it was like giving birth to a cow – and I'd just had it for a while, and I wanted to have fun.

Scorsese: I can't believe you said that.

Price: I got tired of the loneliness. I wanted some group interaction. When you get out to Hollywood, everybody starts stroking you because you're a novelist and they're kind of in awe of people who can really write. You get hooked on the contact, the phone calls, the plane tickets, the meetings. It beats work.

Then there is the fact that you make about one-tenth the money when you're writing novels. Once you're making screenwriter money, it's very hard to voluntarily cut your income by 90 percent. That's a bitch for anybody. Your life changes. I bought a loft in SoHo, my wife is pregnant. (I got fertile.) But Marty says to me, 'Hold on to writing novels.'

Scorsese: Yeah. You gotta prepare yourself for cutting the life-style. You have to get used to the moments when you don't have the money. The only thing you have to rely on is yourself and your own talent. Don't get sucked into all that nonsense. Don't get used to the planes and the meetings and everything else. People are told they'll have four campers with three telephones in each. But that's not necessarily what's important in making a movie. It's not important to make it bigger and with more money. It's important to remain true inside yourself and keep your own thinking straight. That's going to show up on film.

THE COLOR OF MONEY
Reviewed by Roger Ebert

If this movie had been directed by someone else, I might have thought differently about it because I might not have expected so much. But *The Color of Money* is direct-ed by Martin Scorsese, the most exciting American director now working, and it is not an exciting film. It doesn't have the electricity, the wound-up tension, of his best work, and as a result I was too aware of the story marching by.

Scorsese may have thought of this film as a deliberately mainstream work, a con-ventional film with big names and a popular subject matter; perhaps he did it for that reason. But I believe he has the stubborn soul of an artist, and cannot put his heart where his heart will not go. And his heart, I believe, inclines toward creating new and completely personal stories about characters who have come to life in his imagination – not in finishing someone else's story, begun 25 years ago.

The Color of Money is not a sequel, exactly, but it didn't start with someone's fresh inspiration. It continues the story of 'Fast Eddie' Felson, the character played by Paul Newman in Robert Rossen's *The Hustler* (1961). Now 25 years have passed. Eddie still plays pool, but not for money and not with the high-stakes, dangerous kinds of players who drove him from the game. He is a liquor salesman, a successful one, judging by the long, white Cadillac he takes so much pride in. One night, he sees a kid playing pool, and the kid is so good that Eddie's memories are stirred.

This kid is not simply good, however. He is also, Eddie observes, a 'flake', and that gives him an idea: With Eddie as his coach, this kid could be steered into the world of big-money pool, where his flakiness would throw off the other players. They wouldn't be inclined to think he was for real. The challenge, obviously, is to train the kid so he can turn his flakiness on and off at will – so he can put the making of money above every other consideration, every other lure and temptation, in the pool hall.

The kid is named Vincent (Tom Cruise), and Eddie approaches him through Vincent's girlfriend, Carmen (Mary Elizabeth Mastrantonio). She is a few years older than Vince and a lot tougher. She likes the excitement of being around Vince and around pool hustling, but Eddie sees she's getting bored. He figures he can make a deal with the girl; together, they'll control Vince and steer him in the direction of money.

A lot of the early scenes setting up this situation are very well handled, especially the moments when Eddie uses Carmen to make Vince jealous and undermine his self-confidence. But of course these scenes work well, because they are the part of the story that is closest to Scorsese's own sensibility. In all of his best movies, we can see this same ambiguity about the role of women, who are viewed as objects of comfort and fear, creatures that his heroes desire and despise themselves for desiring. Think of the heroes of *Mean Streets*, *Taxi Driver* and *Raging Bull* and their relationships with women, and you sense where the energy is coming from that makes Vincent love Carmen, and distrust her.

The movie seems less at home with the Newman character, perhaps because this character is largely complete when the movie begins. 'Fast Eddie' Felson knows who he is, what he thinks, what his values are.

There will be some moments of crisis in the story, as when he allows himself, to his shame, to be hustled at pool. But he is not going to change much during the story, and maybe he's not even free to change much, since his experiences are largely dictated by the requirements of the plot.

Here we come to the big weakness of *The Color of Money*: It exists in a couple of timeworn genres, and its story is generated out of standard Hollywood situations. First we have the basic story of the old pro and the talented youngster. Then we have the story of the kid who wants to knock the master off the throne. Many of the scenes in this movie are almost formula, despite the energy of Scorsese's direction and the good performances. They come in the same places we would expect them to come in a movie by anybody else, and they contain the same events.

Eventually, everything points to the ending of the film, which we know will have to be a showdown between Eddie and Vince, between Newman and Cruise. The fact that the movie does not provide that payoff scene is a disappointment. Perhaps Scorsese thought the movie was 'really' about the personalities of his two heroes, and that it was unnecessary to show who would win in a showdown. Perhaps, but then why plot the whole story with genre formulas, and only bail out at the end? If you bring a gun onstage in the first act, somebody will have been shot by the third.

The side stories are where the movie really lives. There is a warm, bittersweet relationship between Newman and his long-time girlfriend, a bartender wonderfully played by Helen Shaver. And the greatest energy in the story is generated between Cruise and Mastrantonio – who, with her hard edge and her inbred cynicism, keeps the kid from ever feeling really sure of her. It's a shame that even the tension of their relationship is allowed to evaporate in the closing scenes, where Cruise and the girl stand side by side and seem to speak from the same mind, as if she were a standard movie girlfriend and not a real original.

Watching Newman is always interesting in this movie. He has been a true star for many years, but sometimes that star quality has been thrown away. Scorsese has always been the kind of director who lets his camera stay on an actor's face, who looks deeply into them and tries to find the shadings that reveal their originality. In many of Newman's closeups in this movie, he shows an enormous power, a concentration and focus of his essence as an actor.

Newman, of course, had veto power over who would make this movie (because how could they make it without him?), and his instincts were sound in choosing Scorsese. Maybe the problems started with the story, when Newman or somebody decided that there had to be a young man in the picture; the introduction of the Cruise character opens the door for all of the preordained teacher-pupil clichés, when perhaps they should have just stayed with Newman and let him be at the centre of the story.

Then Newman's character would have been free (as the Robert De Niro characters have been free in other Scorsese films) to follow his passions, hungers, fears and desires wherever they led him – instead of simply following the story down a well-travelled path.

The Sacred and the Profane

MARTIN SCORSESE
Interviewed by James Truman

Why are you making a rock video?

Firstly, because it was convenient. I'd been asked by David Bowie and a lot of other people, but it was usually two or three weeks before I started shooting a film. This time, when Quincy Jones asked me, it seemed to be the right time. Also, because I could do it the way I wanted it, which is a straightforward, non-MTV approach. They've almost done everything it's possible to do with film and video and computers. Every shot is thrown away in three seconds on a video tube. I said if I were to do it, it would be very realistic and strong, and I would have control.

What's Michael really like?

He's showbusiness. It's like Jerry Lewis in *King of Comedy*. Like Liza Minnelli or Elizabeth Taylor.

Do people like that make you nervous?

I got nervous when I met his chimpanzee. I've been allergic to animals for 30 years. I had just started to get a little better with the allergies. I bought my wife a little dog. It's taken me 30 years to touch a dog, so I wasn't about to touch this chimp. You know what I'm saying? So I go to Los Angeles to meet Michael and this chimp – it's called Bubbles – comes right over to me and looks at me for the longest time. Fortunately, it didn't touch me. It fell in love with my wife. Couldn't get it off the woman.

Would you like to be Michael Jackson, in the sense of remaining in a state of innocence?

I'm not sure. I did find it interesting, the question of how someone can be that innocent, be so untouched. Perhaps his is a more spiritual state than mine, I don't know.

What was **Last Temptation of Christ** *about?*

Basically it deals with Jesus as God and Man, as a god inside a man, who thinks of himself as the worst of all sinners because he believes he's God. It's just terrible! When he finds out he really is a god he doesn't want anything to do with it. The last temptation itself is the temptation to marry Mary Magdalene, settle down and have children, just to be a normal person. That's the beauty of it. Of course he doesn't succumb to it. He gets back on the cross. [*laughs*]

What happened to the film?

The Southern bible-belt groups started a campaign saying that a film was being made that would portray Jesus as a homosexual. It was just a rumour that went round

Mob acolyte Henry Hill (Ray Liotta), psycho Tommy DeVito (Joe Pesci), club owner Sonny Bunz (Tony Darrow), smiling killer Jimmy Conway (De Niro) – and Scorsese, an émigré from Little Italy.

Hollywood and all the Southern states. The film was being financed by Paramount, and Paramount is owned by Gulf and Western, and Gulf and Western owns a lot of oil fields around the world which they didn't necessarily want picketed. So pressure was applied there, and Paramount gave in. There was also economic pressure, the problem of needing to shoot it in Israel. The amount of money and risk was too much, they felt.

Were you outraged?
I can't afford to get hung up about it. It would have been the right thing for me to make at the time, because it would have rounded out the series of films that began with *Mean Streets*, it would have rounded off that obsession with the Church and religion. But I have to keep working, I can't just sit around and lament the fate of this one particular film. Other film-makers in history have had films they really wanted to make taken away from them or destroyed. Some were never able to carry on. Some died, some just stopped making pictures. I don't intend to do that.

FROM THE PIT OF HELL
By Steve Jenkins

Although Martin Scorsese was given Nikos Kazantzakis' novel *The Last Temptation* by Barbara Hershey in 1972, at the time of *Boxcar Bertha*, it was not until the end of 1982 that a second-draft script by Paul Schrader was taken to Paramount by producers Irwin Winkler and Robert Chartoff. Scorsese: 'I had one meeting with Barry Diller, who at that time was head of the company, and he asked why I wanted to make the film. I said so I can get to know Jesus better. The idea of making this picture would not be to go the traditional route of the American or Italian epic, but to go the other way, and make it intimate, make a character study, which means less money. And so they talked about it a little further and we were ready to go. It was the beginning of '83.'

Harry Ufland, Scorsese's agent at the time, saw the attraction of the project for Paramount: 'Michael Eisner [company president] and Jeffrey Katzenberg [head of production] were big proponents of the film and they really thought that it was not only going to be a very important film, but they thought it would be successful commercially. In this business, there are always one or two films a year that studios really want to make, because they think it's going to be their Oscar film. They knew it was going to be very controversial. I don't think anybody dreamed it was going to be as controversial as it turned out to be.'

The initial problems, however, were not to do with the controversial nature of the project, but with the budget. Scorsese: 'A series of things happened. In January of '83, we went to Israel and started location scouting. Arnon Milchan was the producer of *King of Comedy* and he's an Israeli, and he said you must come to Israel first. So he gave us an army helicopter and we went all over. And we were able to put together different parts of the country for the look of the film. But when you start talking like that, every time you want to make a change, and you have to move the entire company, that's a day down, at least. Moving everybody, it's more money, and the money is starting to add up. Now the budget was originally eleven million, and we started going on this. In the meantime, we went to Morocco, where we found villages that you couldn't really find in Israel, certain Arab villages that looked literally two or three thousand years old. So we talked about doing the first two-and-a-half weeks in Morocco and finishing up in Israel. We were treated terrifically in Israel, but basically we came in with Paramount Pictures banners flying. And I guess when you do that, the price goes up. And the budget went up to fourteen million.'

The fact that Chartoff and Winkler's *The Right Stuff* had recently gone massively over budget fuelled Paramount's worries. Scorsese: 'At the same time, Paramount began to explain to me that movies made out of the country had a tendency to be runaway pictures, and Katzenberg told me at one point, right now we prefer to make pictures where it's only one flight away. San Francisco, for example. And if you look at *Star Trek*, the one about the whales – shot in San Francisco. You're going to be in Israel; If anything goes wrong, it takes us two days to get there.'

At the same time as the film's budget and shooting schedule increased, the American religious right began an organised letter-writing campaign, significantly targeted not at Paramount, but at its parent company, Gulf and Western, and the latter's new chairman, Martin Davis. An example: 'Dear Mr. Davis, I wish to express my disgust with the upcoming film called *The Last Temptation of Christ*. The material it contains is straight from the pit of hell. We may as well destroy our country with the nuclear bomb as show this film. It's as destructive. If you have any concern for your own peace of mind and the welfare of Gulf and Western industries, you will destroy this film at the earliest possible moment. Such smut is not American. I do hope this will not fall on deaf ears. Perhaps your company will profit financially, but it won't be worth the price you will have to pay.'

The effect of thousands of such letters, many focusing on the erroneous idea that Jesus was to be portrayed as homosexual, should not be underestimated, as Harry Ufland has explained: 'You've got to put it back in time and realise that the fundamentalists were very strong in this country. The Jerry Falwells of the world had a tremendous constituency and they had power. That has now been significantly reduced by all the scandals, but when there is an organised letter-writing campaign, with as many letters as Gulf and Western and Martin Davis received, they've got to take it seriously. The head of the studio is really beholden to the chairman of the board of the conglomerate, who is beholden to the stock market. There would be concern that products wouldn't be bought and that whatever the company does would be boycotted. Also, in any major corporation, people really don't like to have to spend the time answering all these things or dealing with them. So in its own way, it manages to disturb things a lot.'

What developed, according to Ufland, was a kind of paranoia: 'When you're dealing with the corporation, there is no way that you can really know what's going on.

There are a lot of people there, and when you add that this is a controversial movie . . . I think that the paranoia was justified, but I don't think it was conspiracy. I think that there was a stop-and-go feeling about this, where everybody would say yes, we're going to make the movie, and then in almost hushed tones you would hear, well there are a couple of things we want to talk about . . .'

Scorsese: 'Eventually it built up to a final meeting in September in which we asked for another $2 million on the budget, making it about sixteen, and asking for another ten days shooting, bringing the schedule up to about 100 days. And afterwards Katzenberg told me, "Marty, when you walked in that door, there was a flashing yellow light on the picture." I said, "Gee Jeff, I thought we had a green light." He said, "No, it was a flashing yellow. When you walked out it was a flashing red." Irwin Winkler, right after that meeting, after working nine months on the picture, felt that he would leave it also, having come to a separation with Chartoff, his partner. That was a blow that was difficult to stand. For another two months we worked on the film, and then on Thanksgiving morning, Barry Diller called us in, myself and Harry Ufland, and explained that he couldn't go on with the picture. He explained it was just too much trouble, for the amount of interest he really had in the project, in terms of his new position on the board of Gulf and Western, his new political position and the studio, a whole series of problems that came out of that year. I remember Diller being very hurt about it, because he said I wish I could have told you this two months into it, rather than making you spend a year of your life on it.'

It now seems clear that Diller's decision was very much influenced by pressure from Martin Davis, and that this in turn pushed Diller towards leaving to run Twentieth Century Fox, and Eisner and subsequently Katzenberg to move to Disney. In a last attempt to save the project at Paramount, Scorsese worked on rebudgeting the film at $6.5 to $7 million ('do it like the European style'), with John Avnet, a producer assigned by Paramount. But at a meeting on December 23, 1983, with preproduction crews already at work in Israel, Diller finally axed the film.

Harry Ufland was meanwhile trying to interest other companies in *The Last Temptation*, with results that were both comical and frustrating. 'Most of them would not really put their feelings in writing, other than to say, Marty is brilliant, everybody's brilliant, the world is brilliant, but we're not going to make it. There's one letter which was kind of typical: "*The Last Temptation of Christ* by Paul Schrader is a brilliant script, and I will not be surprised if someday I regret profoundly having turned it down. Still I must go with my instincts and my feelings, I would be dishonest if I didn't." Now if somebody would tell me what that meant . . . We had some responses from other studio heads. There was one who said that in his opinion, this was a "small story made smaller by the dialogue". One said, "Unfortunately it is not precisely what we are looking for at this time." Another wrote that "the script made me want to see the film so I am doubly sorry that it apparently is not going to be made."'

These kinds of responses, coupled with the Paramount débâcle, convinced Scorsese that the project should never have gone through the Hollywood system: 'The beauty of that year was that none of it was wasted. What we learned was how not

In The Last Temptation of Christ *(1988), Jesus (Willem Dafoe) is flanked by loyal friend Mary Magdalene (Barbara Hershey) and redeemed betrayer Judas (Harvey Keitel).*

to make the picture.' And although subsequent attempts to obtain European backing, notably in France, also failed, the film was finally produced, at a cost of around $7 million, at a distance, both financial and physical, from the Hollywood studios. A negative pick-up deal with Universal, whereby the film is financed with a loan obtained on the basis of guaranteed distribution, was coupled with a low-profile, low-publicity production in Morocco. The film's producer, Barbara De Fina, was aware of the advantages: 'Since we were a small independent company, first of all we were very hard to find. As you don't have a studio with you all the time, you have a lot more freedom to do things. They do get script approval, but you don't have to call them every day, they don't make the decisions for you. So you have a lot more control over how you spend your money, and creatively just what you do with the movie. It's a good way to make a movie.'

(All quotations are from interviews for *The South Bank Show*'s programme on *The Last Temptation of Christ*. Thanks to London Weekend Television for permission to use this material.)

RESISTING *TEMPTATION*
By Kevin Lally

Let us give thanks for religious zealots. Without them, Martin Scorsese's vision of *The Last Temptation of Christ* might have been just another unjustly overlooked American art film. But the thunder of controversy generated by fundamentalist Christian groups has turned *Last Temptation* into front page news and a box office phenomenon. Praise the Lord and pass the free publicity.

The picture Mother Angelica of America's *Eternal World* TV network calls 'the most blasphemous, the most disrespectful, the most Satanic movie ever filmed' arrives [in the UK] this week, not without a similar pre-release firestorm.

Mary Whitehouse, president of the National Viewers and Listeners Association, deemed the film 'deeply offensive to Christians', even though she had not yet viewed it. Whitehouse threatened to resurrect blasphemy laws if the British Board of Censors passed the picture. It has. The film has also been denounced – sight unseen – by the head of the Salvation Army and the assistant secretary of the Catholic Bishops of England and Wales.

The thorn pricking Christian protestors is the film's revisionist view of Christ struggling to come to terms with his dual nature as divine and human. And Paul Schrader's screenplay is faithful to the 1955 Kazantzakis novel in showing Christ's torment and doubt.

The 'last temptation' occurs while Christ is on the cross and Satan appears to him in the guise of what looks and sounds like a self-satisfied British schoolgirl. In the film's most riveting sequence, she presents him an alternative to his suffering: marriage, raising a family, and living peacefully to a ripe old age.

Throughout the furore, the renowned director of such emotionally heated films as *Taxi Driver* and *Raging Bull* has reiterated his seriousness of purpose. Says Scorsese, 'I sincerely believe that this film is a religious experience, a spiritual experience. I hope for most people it's an exploration, so we can get to know Jesus better. If we get to know him better, we get to know his ideas better and we might begin to live out his ideas.'

Despite his sincere intentions, Scorsese's work prompted some furious fallout in the States. Fundamentalist Christian groups called for a massive boycott of businesses owned by MCA (the parent company of Universal Pictures and the film's American distributor and co-producer). Bill Bright of Campus Crusade for Christ offered the studio $10 million to destroy the picture.

Pickets demonstrated outside the home of MCA chairman Lew Wasserman, chanting, 'Bankrolled by Jewish money!' and staging their own street theatre – which depicted a Jewish businessman stomping on the blood-soaked Christ.

Just prior to the film's premiere, three Republican congressmen introduced a resolution calling on Universal to cancel its release and demanding a boycott of Universal businesses. And General Cinema, the third largest US theatre chain, and three other circuits announced they would not show the film.

As a defensive tactic, Universal decided to move up the picture's release by a month. No sooner was the film out of post-production than it was in nine North American theatres. 'I've had it!' Scorsese said just before the rescheduled premiere. 'There were so many accusations, so much confusion; I just want people to see the film.'

The crux of the dispute seems to be artistic licence, with fundamentalists designating Jesus' life off limits to inquisitive writers and filmmakers. Scorsese argues, 'It's very important that people understand that the film is not based on the Gospels. It's based on a work of fiction. It uses Jesus as a character, as a metaphor, so that we can come to understand him fully. Everybody has questions about God, and I think we should be able in a work of art – which I hope this is – to utilise those questions, open up a discussion.'

The intense, fast-talking director is 'not surprised' by the controversy surrounding *Last Temptation*, having already experienced a setback when a letter-writing campaign induced Paramount Pictures to halt its pre-production back in 1983. Both he and his wife, Barbara De Fina, who produced the picture, say they have no quarrel with reasonable critics of the film. Explains De Fina, 'There's so much that people bring to the movie – what their religious beliefs are, how they were raised as children – that I certainly wouldn't tell them how they should feel. But I think it's very unfortunate this anti-Semitic thing has come up, it's something none of us expected. Critics have a right not to see it and not to like it. But I would hope they would let other people see it who want to see it.'

Scorsese, who was born in New York in 1942 and raised in Lower Manhattan's Little Italy, says, 'The desire to do a film on Jesus has always been there. I don't know which came first, the movies or the Church. My first vivid memories of childhood were seeing movies, then getting enveloped in the Catholic religion. I felt somehow the two co-existed.'

Barbara Hershey, who co-stars as Mary Magdalene opposite Willem Dafoe's mesmerising Jesus, introduced Scorsese to the Kazantzakis novel when they worked together in '72 on *Boxcar Bertha*. The director was immediately intrigued by a non-traditional portrait of Christ as someone who didn't, in his words, 'glow in the dark'. Says the filmmaker now, 'Jesus in this novel, as a man, goes through all the things we go through. He suffers the way we suffer. He has doubts the way we have doubts. He has temptations the way we have temptations.'

Kazantzakis's Jesus joins Scorsese's other rough-hewn but spiritually anguished heroes: Harvey Keitel as the devout Catholic in a world of petty crime in *Mean Streets*; Robert De Niro as the *Taxi Driver* looking to purge his moral outrage.

Scorsese: 'Jesus, if he were here, would be on Eighth Avenue with the prostitutes and crack dealers. Because he associated with outcasts. Michael Grant, one of the best religious historians, confirms this in his studies of Jesus and ancient Israel. We are taught that killing is a mortal sin. Yet, the worst of us, the ones on death row, the serial killers, still deserve love and forgiveness from Jesus.

'I was trying to make a Jesus for the people who feel so low about themselves that they think Jesus would never hear them, that God would never listen to their prayers. It doesn't mean that they're not going to die in the chair. But they can still come to some sort of peace with themselves. So can we all.'

ALTAR EGOS
By Nigel Floyd

On the train from Florence to Venice, after a delay which would have tried the patience of a saint, I pass a compartment full of Franciscan monks before taking a seat next to an elderly nun. Throughout the journey, the nun fingers her beads and mumbles the rosary, and for the first time I become conscious of the potentially inflammatory contents of my briefcase: a sheaf of press cuttings and photocopies relating to Martin Scorsese's *The Last Temptation of Christ*. The Italian debate about the film has continued in a subdued fashion over the past few days, but with the evaporation of a scare about the possible banning of the film by three local magistrates, the steam seems to have gone out of the argument. So by the time I check into the luxurious Des Bains hotel used by Luchino Visconti to recreate the nineteenth-century setting of Thomas Mann's *Death in Venice*, it is the secular interests of the 45th Venice Film Festival which predominate. Paradoxically, it seems that here, at last, *Last Temptation* may be considered as a *film* rather than a blasphemous religious tract.

With a religious film, though, the distinction between art and belief is a subtle one, and in Scorsese's case this relationship is complicated by a Catholic upbringing, an unsuccessful attempt to become a priest and a childhood spent watching biblical epics. The director's conversation is intense, an impression emphasised by his habit of looking one straight in the eye while speaking quickly and excitedly. Yet he is also capable of seeing the subtleties and contradictions within his own beliefs, which take the form of a personal passion rather than an evangelical zeal. Scorsese had wanted to make a religious film even before his first introduction to Greek writer Nikos Kazantzakis's book, a copy of which was given to him on the set of *Boxcar Bertha* by Barbara Hershey in 1972.

'I always wanted to make a black and white *cinema vérité* version of the Gospels, but when I was a film student I saw this wonderful film, *The Gospel According to Saint Matthew* – this guy Pasolini did it. And it's a great picture, so I had to do something else.' The something else was Kazantzakis's fictional re-reading of the Gospels, in which Christ is a very human figure, riddled with self-doubt and paralysed by his inability to recognise and then embrace his destiny as the Messiah.

Retaining the outline structure and vernacular language of the book, Scorsese and scriptwriters Paul Schrader and Jay Cocks reject the two-dimensional reverence of traditional biblical epics in favour of a more intimate approach. And in the film's most radical departure from the Gospels, Christ is tempted down from the cross by a young female angel who offers him the chance to save himself and live a full human life as the husband of Mary Magdalene and the father of her children. This is the last temptation of Christ, and it is upon this that much of the controversy has centred.

'It's not a simple matter, this conflict between matter and spirit – the matter doesn't have to be the woman. The last temptation is really to be an ordinary man, to live an ordinary life. It's not just to get down off the cross and have sex with Mary Magdalene for a few minutes.

'But he does have to experience everything of humanity before he can reject it. He has to really love being a man, and that's what is so fascinating about the Kazantzakis book, that Jesus is fully divine and fully human. And we approach him from the human side.'

This unorthodox portrayal of Christ was attacked particularly virulently by minority evangelist groups, many of them linked to lucrative radio and television businesses. Scorsese feels this was a calculated move to win back the power and influence they gained under Reagan, then lost again over the last two years because of various sex and money scandals. Nevertheless, he was shocked by the anti-Semitic tone adopted by many of the protesters, who used caricature images of production boss Lew Wasserman reminiscent of those in the Nazi propaganda film *Jude Suss*, and adopted the slogan 'Bankrolled by Jewish money.'

'Lew Wasserman?' snorts Scorsese. 'I never met the man and he's never seen the picture. I'm a Catholic, though not a practising one; Paul Schrader is a Calvinist; Jay Cocks, who did some of the re-writing, is Presbyterian and Willem Dafoe (who plays Christ) is a Dutch Catholic. So there are no Jews at all, except Harvey Keitel, but he plays Judas.

'Faith is a very delicate matter, but if you have faith there is a great strength which comes from having it. I think maybe some of the people in America who were complaining are driven by a great fear: people who may have had a life on drugs or alcohol or fourteen marriages and stuff like that, and then suddenly they accept Jesus, whatever that means in their terms. And there's a great fear of falling back and they don't want anything to shake them. They're dealing with Jesus on a purely divine level, I feel, and any time you start bringing in the idea of humanity it seems to get them nervous.'

Perhaps these potential patrons would prefer the bombastic spectacle of biblical epics like De Mille's *The Ten Commandments*. In *The Last Temptation*, the visions which afflict Jesus while alone in the wilderness, for example, are presented in the simplest possible manner. A tongue of flame licks up from the desert floor, a lion materialises and a black cobra menacingly raises its hooded skull as Jesus hears voices in his head. Had he had a bigger budget, would Scorsese perhaps have used special effects?

'I always wanted to avoid that. There's no way we can compete with the parting of the Red Sea in *The Ten Commandments* or something like that. And anyway, that's not the point. If we had done that then, as in biblical films, the audience wouldn't have had to think.'

Instead, Scorsese wants the audience to identify with Christ on a more emotional level, 'like you do a regular character in a dramatic movie. You get to like the guy and "Oh no, he's gonna die," it's terrible. We wanted to try to see what would happen if you felt for Jesus in that way.'

Judas, too, is humanised. He is seeking freedom from Roman oppression by the sword, rather than by love; and ultimately he is portrayed as someone who, in betraying

Jesus, simply accepts his destiny and performs a service which his master asks of him.

'He never gets what he wants you know, he never gets the revolution of the sword. He falls in love with God and in the end he's got to take the fall for all humanity. He'll go down in history as the biggest fall guy of all time.'

With the crucifixion the imagery of blood and sacrifice that has run through the film reaches a terrible fruition. Previously we have witnessed the ritual slaughter of lambs in the temple, and now Jesus is slain in the same way. Clerics unfamiliar with developments in screen violence found Scorsese's emphasis on blood too much to take. For the director, though, the Catholic association of sacramental wine with the blood of Christ made this imagery perfectly appropriate.

'In primitive societies blood is part of everyday life: you slaughter animals and you slaughter people in the same way. Down on the Lower East Side in New York, where I grew up, my grandparents, who came from Sicily, would buy a lamb at Easter; they'd keep it in the house and the kids would play with it, and then they'd kill it and eat it. Of course, the kids didn't want to eat it then.

'So what I'm saying is that in a primitive world, it's a matter of life and death, and the spirit of life is blood. We looked all the details up in the Jewish encyclopaedia and we found that every family would sacrifice a lamb and sing on one of the biggest holidays of the year at the temple. The priest and the slaughterer were usually the same man, and he would take a bowl of blood and throw it on the base of the altar. And there would be maybe 500 or 600 altars.'

At this point Scorsese's enthusiasm gets the better of him, and despite his devotion to the film's anti-epic scale, his guilty pleasure in grandiose spectacle slips out.

'You got to understand, I'm twelve years old, being taken to see *The Robe* at the Roxy Theatre, which was like a palace. And this priest, a young man, took the altar boys off to see the film on Saturday morning. You suddenly open the doors and you see this gigantic screen, and the music comes up in stereophonic sound. And it was thrilling; it's a bad movie, but what an experience.

'And that's what I really wanted, like the old biblical epics, to start on one altar and then to pan up like Anthony Mann or Nicholas Ray and show 500 altars and people killing and dancing and singing. And all the flames and those Renaissance browns and yellows. That would have been something; but I got two altars and about ten guys walking past.'

Spectacle or not, with Scorsese accused of blasphemy, and defiling the image of Christ, we might be put in mind of the biblical quotation cited by Scorsese at the end of *Raging Bull*.'

'"Whether or not he is a sinner, I do not know," the man replied; "All I know is this: once I was blind and now I can see."'

OF GOD AND MAN
By Michael Morris, O.P.

Martin Scorsese's *The Last Temptation of Christ* unleashed a public outcry of a magnitude unprecedented in the history of religious films. Militant Christians, particularly those of the fundamentalist variety, launched a media campaign condemning Universal Pictures, the film's distributor, and even staged a mock flagellation of Christ in front of the Beverly Hills home of Lew Wasserman, chairman at MCA, Inc., parent company of Universal. Rallying support via telephone and television, the growing number of protestors so intimidated theatre owners that several movie chains refused to play Scorsese's film which is based on the controversial novel by Nikos Kazantzakis. In what appeared to be a holy war against a major film company, the zealots demanded nothing less than the total destruction of the film so that it could never be shown to the public.

This is a case where art and religion were in noisy conflict. But what were the real issues behind the controversy? What theological dogmas have been challenged? And what were the ramifications of the public outcry?

I had the opportunity to see the film with an invited group of 40 people representing a cross-section of Protestants, Catholics, and Jews, and a constituency ranging from Morality in the Media on the right to People for the American Way on the left. (Universal invited the film's fundamentalist detractors, but they refused to attend.) What we viewed for 157 minutes was a rough cut of the nearly completed film. Without a doubt, Scorsese's movie breaks the traditional mould of Christ as portrayed in the cinema, and for this he can be lauded. But at the same time the film suffers from certain theological and artistic flaws.

First, there is the problem with the way in which Christ is portrayed by Scorsese in the first half of the film. Historically, Christianity defined Christ as fully divine and fully human and one person at the Council of Chalcedon in 451 A.D. Most cinematic depictions – indeed, most artistic depictions – of Christ have accentuated his divinity rather than his humanity. But Scorsese, like Kazantzakis before him, chose to accentuate Christ's humanity. In doing so, however, they underscored the weakness rather than the strengths of what it means to be human. So instead of the strong and noble saviour one has come to expect in a film about Christ, one meets here a Jesus who is fearful of everything, who tries to evade God's call by taking up the most odious profession possible for a Jew: he makes crosses in his carpenter shop, and he even assists the Romans as they execute Jews by crucifixion. Theologically it is untenable that Christ should be portrayed as a petty executioner running away from God when he himself is intimately united to that very Godhead.

What we see at the beginning of the film is a Christ who is confused, who is suffering from a conflict of dual personalities. He writhes on the floor like one deranged as he fights with his inner voices. While modern theologians from both the Protestant and Catholic perspectives would admit to the possibility that Christ's own

Scorsese's film of the Kazantzakis novel was delayed for years by religious hysteria in the US. Its depiction of a suffering, self-divided man-god is a moving existential drama.

knowledge of his Messianic mission was a gradual, unfolding phenomenon in his life, none would go so far as to say that Christ actively worked against it. Furthermore, it is theologically unacceptable to portray Christ as a sinner, even in his human weakness. But early in the film Scorsese's Christ admits to being a liar, a hypocrite, one who is afraid of everything, one who has no courage. 'I want to rebel against everyone and against God,' he says, then adds, 'my god is fear; Lucifer is inside me.' Statements such as these are theologically wacko. The film's religious critics could well point out that heretics have been burned for less.

In his defence, Scorsese said in a subsequent interview that it was never his intention to portray Christ as a sinner: 'Christ seems to be admitting to sin, but in my mind, and I think in Kazantzakis' mind, it's the human side that believes it's sinning. But of course, being God also, how can he sin?'

So while Scorsese's Christ is never morally guilty of sin, the director felt, nevertheless, that his Jesus should not be spared feeling the human effects of the psychology of sin: 'He has to experience the guilt, experience the temptation, the feelings of anger, of lust – all these things, even the shame . . . I don't know if it's clear; I suppose it's a point of discussion and argument.'

What is dramatically clear in *The Last Temptation* is the notion that Christ must go through a period of adjustment as he tries to determine whether or not he is God.

This does not work as well in the film as it did in the book for the reason that the film left out a key scene found in Kazantzakis' novel in which Christ meets a dying visionary in a desert monastery. As the two meet the ascetic gasps his last with the words, 'you've come . . . you've come . . . you've come.' In the film the visionary is already dead upon Christ's arrival. Scorsese leaves the discernment process to a fiery John the Baptist who finally gives Christ his blessing.

While artistic interpretation holds sway in the first half of the film, the second half gets much of its inspiration from Holy Writ as Christ finally embraces his salvific mission and sets forth on his public ministry. At this point miracles begin to occur with an increasing frequency. Christ is shown healing the sick and raising Lazarus from the dead. Water turns into wine with the mere drop of a phrase, as if it were a magic trick. Thus, the film frantically makes up for lost time in establishing Christ's divinity.

The film culminates in a historically correct crucifixion scene that is the most graphic ever presented on the screen. As early as 1983 Scorsese had decided that he would shoot the crucified Christ naked. Evidence from the Shroud of Turin convinced the director that Christ's passion had involved his total humiliation since every part of the imprint of his body bears the marks of torture. Scorsese then turned to works of art for inspiration. He saw a painting by the Renaissance artist da Messina in which Christ was crucified between two thieves who were not hanging from crosses but from trees. This image was incorporated into the film. The director also surrounded the tormented Jesus with scowling faces as he appeared in Bosch's painting of Christ carrying the cross. The harsh realism of this filmic passion enables one to understand why crucifixion, with its denounced, stripped, and nailed victims, was considered the most painful and demeaning form of execution in the entire Roman world.

The major focus for objections levelled at *The Last Temptation of Christ* was the so-called 'affair' in the film between Christ and Mary Magdalene! In Scorsese's movie this is not an affair at all, but a hallucinatory marriage presented to Christ in his death agony by the devil who seeks to trick him into forsaking his Messianic mission. In both the book and the movie a sexual attraction is established between the Magdalene and Christ. It is a chaste attraction on Christ's part, but a deleterious frustration for Mary who takes up a life of prostitution as a consequence. When Christ saves her from the stoning prescribed for adulteresses by Jewish law, then her perception of him changes. She cleans up her act, dons a veil, and becomes his penitent follower. Thus, when the devil presents to Christ his last temptation, it is the vision of a reformed Mary Magdalene bedecked in white and leading a marriage procession. In context the temptation is not primarily sexual. Rather it is a clever ploy to convince the suffering and celibate Christ at the moment of his ultimate sacrifice that his destiny was not to be the saviour of mankind, but rather an ordinary married Jew with a family.

Theologically it is more believable that Christ's last temptation would have been one of despair rather than of lust. This was echoed in his plaintive cry from the cross, 'My God, my God, why have you forsaken me?' Scripturally there is no evidence that Christ was tempted sexually, but both Kazantzakis and Scorsese have interjected this modern obsession into the story by establishing the attraction between Christ and Mary Magdalene. Be that as it may, Christ ultimately realises the hallucination as a hoax from hell, and in his dream state he climbs back to the cross. When he awakens he realises his final victory over temptation with the words, 'It is accomplished.'

Nikos Kazantzakis came from a Greek Orthodox background, and Martin Scorsese was born a Roman Catholic. Scorsese even spent part of his teenage years in a seminary studying for the priesthood. The religious traditions of both these men allow for the use of apocryphal tales to illustrate a moral point. Legends and fables of Christ and the saints abound in the Eastern and Western churches, and some of these are as old as the Gospels themselves. Fundamentalist Protestants, by contrast, rely on scripture alone for the formulations of their religious views. This was a major reason for the protests. An artistic rendering of Christ's life would have to be entirely based on scripture in order for fundamentalists to approve of it. But Scorsese states at the beginning of his movie, quoting from Kazantzakis, that this is a film about the battle between the spirit and the flesh, and that it is not based on the Gospels, but on that spiritual struggle.

In *The Last Temptation of Christ* both the author and the filmmaker turn Christ into Everyman. Thus, the reason for the emphasis placed on Christ's human struggle at the beginning of the story. 'This is a movie,' Scorsese told the audience of religious leaders, 'which is a story of pain and suffering and the search for God.' In fact one can correctly surmise that the Christ created by Kazantzakis and filmed by Scorsese is a representation of the artists' own search for a spiritual re-awakening. Both artists fell away from their religious roots. And while this has rendered in their artistry a defective theology, it nevertheless energises their religious creation with the soulful longing of men searching for the divine in a world beset by temptations.

If one can eliminate the religious controversy surrounding this movie, Scorsese's film remains to be judged as a work of art. Comparing *Last Temptation* to other films about Christ, one notices how free it is of the ponderous solemnity that so typifies the genre. Gone are the endless choirs of angels singing in the soundtrack. Gone are the awestruck audiences surrounding Christ. Gone is the starchiness that tends to mummify the actor playing the lead role. Willem Dafoe's Jesus is a virile and energetic Nazarene. Here is a Christ who laughs and cries and dances. And while Scorsese emphasises his humanity, he does not shy away from the issue of his divinity. 'I am God,' Scorsese's miracle-working Christ proclaims to his fellow Jews. In comparison it should be noted that, in MGM's 1961 production of *King of Kings* starring Jeffrey Hunter, all the major miracles of Christ's ministry were omitted and the screenplay watered down the character of Christ in an effort to make him digestible to an intended large and diverse audience. No mention of Christ's divinity was made in that film, and the resurrection was only hinted at in the form of a gigantic shadow overtaking the apostles in the last scene. And yet *King of Kings* did not suffer the Christian backlash that *The Last Temptation* has experienced. It would seem that in the cinematic portrayals of Christ, sins of omission do not count as heavily with the faithful. Christ may be drained of his divinity, but as long as he is portrayed as a good man then Christian sensitivities rest at ease. Proof of this theory can be found in two other 'Jesus films' which were based on Broadway plays. After initial resistance Christians came to embrace Christ as a righteous rocker in *Jesus Christ, Superstar* and as an innocent clown in *Godspell.* But when he is portrayed as a charlatan who stages his own crucifixion as seen in *The Passover Plot* of 1976, then Christians again take to the barricades. *The Passover Plot* was picketed out of existence and never heard from again after lasting only a few weeks in public theatres.

The reverential treatment of Christ in the cinema has at times reached extreme heights. Only a few decades ago it was considered disrespectful to portray Christ's face on the silver screen. For instance, *The Last Days of Pompeii* (1935), *Quo Vadis?* (1951), and *Ben-Hur* (1959) show Christ only from afar, or feature, at best, only a hand or foot of his sacred person. Even when the role was central to the film, as was Jeffrey Hunter's in *King of Kings,* the actor had to have all body hair removed because it was thought that its animalistic associations would be incompatible with Christ's elevated stature.

Scorsese's film breaks through such barriers and has an earthy grittiness to it, not unlike that found in Pasolini's landmark film, *The Gospel According to Saint Matthew.* While Scorsese's first introduction to films about Christ were the wide-screen epics he adored as a boy, he doesn't feel now that any of them were done successfully. 'Rossellini's historical films,' says Scorsese, 'opened up my mind to the point that, of course, if Jesus is in Nazareth, it's going to look very poor. Therefore, you don't need big art direction. When you film in places like North Africa, people are still living in the same conditions they have been for thousands of years.'

But while archaeological correctness is promoted in the film, one would wish that the voices of the actors had been better coordinated. Here Palestine sounds more like Babel with accents ranging from Pontius Pilate's pristine English to John the Baptist's outrageous Brooklynese. This will not allow the film to wear well.

Despite its theological and artistic flaws, the film is nevertheless significant as an earnest effort to present Christ in a different way. 'I wanted to show a Christ you could argue with,' says Scorsese, 'one who eats and drinks with prostitutes and sinners, a real earthy Jesus.

'It was never my intention to set out and shake anyone's faith,' the director adds, 'but rather to ignite faith. The side issue in my mind was for me, as a filmmaker, to get to know God and in making Jesus more accessible to myself and people like me. If you already have faith you are fine, but we're the ones who need it, and maybe this film will be some consolation.'

More than any other film of its type, Scorsese's *Last Temptation* measures the magnanimity of Christ's sacrifice in terms of moral choices. This above all is the value of the film, and for that one can tolerate its theological deficiencies.

'YOU'VE GOT TO LOVE SOMETHING ENOUGH TO KILL IT' – Martin Scorsese: The Art of Noncompromise
By Chris Hodenfield

Martin Scorsese is ready to make another gangster movie. He has these memories from his days growing up in New York City's Little Italy: mental snapshots of mobsters in sleek, stylish suits, passing out favours. This would be the fifties and sixties: graceful days before the drug trade busted up the old traditions. He just has an urge to record the gone regime of stylish killers.

This project – based on Nick Pileggi's book, *Wiseguy*, which has nothing to do with the TV show – sounds like a real crowd-pleaser, the kind of solid commercial fare you need after you get crucified for making *The Last Temptation of Christ*. Then he starts telling you about it – this short, intense guy with the thick, beetling eyebrows – and he starts talking faster and faster in feverish bursts, and his eyes go from woefully sad to explosively happy in a heartbeat, and he makes it sound like a hell of a story, lots of action, very funny. Then he sits back and cackles and adds the one caveat that makes the tale sound truly Scorsese: 'I hope it will infuriate the audience.'

Provocations come easily to Scorsese. And who knows what will happen? Movies have a way of changing on him. In 1977, he talked delightedly of his next feature, *Raging Bull*, which he promised would be a madcap lark, oh, bunches of fun. Then dreadful things happened in his life. Divorce, scandal, write-ups in the newspapers, late-night misery. He got various friends working on the *Raging Bull* screenplay, and they added their own highly personal tumults. ('If it's not personal,' Scorsese says, 'I can't be there in the morning.') *Raging Bull* worked at being close to the truth of a boxer's life. It became the story, starkly enough, of a man who hits people for a living. All of the anguish and despair in the boxer's life, and Scorsese's life, were there to see. If you were infuriated by the sight of it, tough luck.

There are filmmakers who give you nice moments of truth on their way to selling you a big lie. Then there are the storytellers who fib, vamp and deceive their way to eventually coming up with a larger truth. And finally, there are those who don't care what they heave onto the screen, as long as they get paid.

Scorsese may not always know what the truth is, but at least he's in search of it. In today's market, that takes courage:. Even his mere entertainments – *Alice Doesn't Live Here Anymore, The Last Waltz, After Hours, The Color of Money* – have an edge of risk and uncertainty. The pictures of his renown – *Mean Streets, Taxi Driver, The Last Temptation of Christ* – are riddled with the energy of obsession.

Scorsese's movies have rewarded him with the reputation of a gritty guy from New York's teeming streets. But he's really a man of high-boulevard style. He's exchanged the downtown loft scene for a town house in Manhattan's Upper East Side. He likes to be able to walk from his home to his office in the Brill Building, charging over to midtown with his white poodle.

When we found him recently, Scorsese was just finishing up his segment of *New*

York Stories, a three-part compilation film he was making with Woody Allen and Francis Coppola. For such a ball of electricity, he appeared to be almost in a state of contentment. His uniform seems not to have changed in years: a fine tailored shirt, beautiful leather shoes and incongruous blue-denim pants. The clothes symbolise the inner man. In short, conflict. And conflict, as Laurence Olivier once observed, is the essence of drama. This man is all drama. Sometimes he appears to be frail, asthmatic, coughing like Camille and preparing to die; usually, though, he's ready to give enormous attention to just about anything. Scorsese is an educated, cultured man of considerable sensitivity and idealism, but he will jab you off-balance by confessing to a violent, self-destructive past. He instantly sweeps you up with his jovial, irascible energy, and everything in the world suddenly seems like great theatre.

These days, Scorsese's been reading books and 'reassessing' things. With the current feature not yet out, he's still suffering the bruises and notoriety of *The Last Temptation of Christ*. The story itself – Jesus wrestling with his divine and human natures – offended certain conservative Christians. But just as many cineastes were offended and unnerved by the cinematic elements, Scorsese's combination of his two grandest loves: old-fashioned, Bible-epic pictorial sweep along with early sixties, French New Wave anarchism. The visual surface of the movie screen is his central devotion. He compulsively thinks up all manner of stylistic flourishes to liven up a scene, and, in this, he is in league with visual kingpins like Alfred Hitchcock. Reeling camera moves are as essential to his truth as the blood sacrifices are to his plots. It's as if he wants to create an intensity on screen that matches what he perceives/suffers in real life.

I recall seeing him in early 1976, talking to a group of film students. It was just after the release of *Taxi Driver*, and he was asked what it was like dealing with film studios. Now, although *Taxi Driver* went on to gather fine profits and weird infamy, it was only intended by Columbia Pictures to be a fast cheapie. Scorsese bared his soul with a story.

It seems that on the tenth day, rain forced a stop in the shooting. They were filming inside a coffee shop, a simple scene of Cybill Shepherd and Robert De Niro just talking. 'I placed them by a window,' he explained, 'so you could see all of Columbus Circle, the cars, the whole city, everything. New York City is *the* character in the movie. A bus goes by the window; there's thousands of people. By one o'clock in the afternoon, a big thunderstorm breaks. And it doesn't let up. What are you going to do?'

He sent everybody home for the day. The alarmed studio bosses said, well, maybe he just ought to film the actors against a white wall. Scorsese replied that he would shoot anything he could, but he would not shoot that scene against a white wall.

'That night, I went through a lot of crises,' he told the students, 'and made a lot of phone calls. I said to a friend, "That's it. If they don't like the way I'm gonna make the picture, then I won't make the picture."'

The next morning, after quiet declarations were made, Scorsese was told that everything was taken care of. He could proceed.

'That's when you realise that you really have to love something enough to kill it,' he declared.

The composition was worth dying for. Like a good Catholic schoolboy, Scorsese instinctively understands the power of imagery. During his sickly youth, he often passed the days drawing elaborate comic-book storyboards for the movies in his head. (Today, the opening credit on his movies is 'A Martin Scorsese *Picture*'.) The flow of his imagery is easier to understand if you visit him in high-energy New York City, where, just walking down the street, you see a swirling parade of elliptical shapes, passing faces, shadowy characters in doorways. It helped me understand very suddenly how, at their best, Scorsese's movies are a torrent of images and that he is really just a mad painter.

'If I could just get them on film fast enough!' he agrees, laughing. 'If I could make the camera move faster, I would. We tried to, Michael Ballhaus [cameraman on *Last Temptation*] and I, but it was dangerous; the camera would just go flying off the track. Go right into the actor!

'Really! That's the way I see it, walking to work! And I walk very quickly, because that's the way I grew up. I grew up downtown on the Lower East Side. Around the corner was the Bowery, and it was pretty scary. All the derelicts, and some of them were violent. There was no such thing as "the colourful bums". I felt sorry for them, but the idea was to survive walking down the street going to school.

'It's living with fear, but I don't think it's necessarily that. They say my films are about paranoia, but, to me, it's just pure survival.'

Being consumed by the image has nothing to do with a director's search for truth, of course. Plenty of high-powered hambones out there possess nothing *but* a gaudy visual style. Like his *New York Stories* cohort, Allen, Scorsese doesn't mind putting his personal life up there on the screen, too. Before film school, Scorsese studied to be a priest. His first feature, an enhanced student project called *Who's That Knocking at My Door?* (1969), was about an intensely religious guy and his struggle with a more worldly girlfriend. *Mean Streets* and *Taxi Driver* both involved what he called 'false saints'. All of this had autobiographical meat. And for years he wanted to make a movie about Mother Cabrini. Even *The Last Temptation of Christ* was, he says, a little embarrassing in what it revealed about his profound religious beliefs. 'I'm always thinking about it,' he admits. 'I believe it!'

New York, New York (1977) was supposed to be about two married musicians who have trouble mixing love and careers. But, with Scorsese heading into a divorce, and his wife, Julia Cameron, rewriting Earl MacRauch's and Mardik Martin's script, it came to be about the *impossibility* of mixing marriage and career. It should not be an impossible mix, but it was to him at that turbulent time of his life.

An unwieldy combination of splashy musical numbers and doomed romance, *New York, New York* may not be a likeable stop in the Scorsese filmography, but it marks an important stage in his life. His three previous movies having proved very successful, Scorsese suddenly found himself a star. He was not up to the task, and, as he commenced the Band documentary, *The Last Waltz*, he jumped on a Mr Toad's wild ride of rock 'n' roll whoop-de-doo that took a couple of years to wind down.

(A later marriage to the young actress Isabella Rossellini dissolved, and now he is happily married to Barbara [De Fina], who produced *Last Temptation* and *The Color of Money*. It has often transpired in his life that friends and wives become collaborators.)

Scorsese was just getting back on his feet when John Hinckley claimed that the bloody climax of *Taxi Driver* inspired him to shoot Ronald Reagan. Scorsese respond-

Scorsese with his co-directors on the anthology film New York Stories *(1989) – fellow New Yorker Woody Allen, who he much admires, and long-time friend Francis Coppola.*

ed with another movie about a demented loner who 'claims' a famous person for his own, *The King of Comedy*.

His best films, he says, are the ones he made for himself. 'I didn't think *Mean Streets* could be released. That's not phony humility. *Taxi Driver* was a low-budget film, and I loved Schrader's script so much it was as if I had dreamed it. De Niro felt the same way. We were like the Three Musketeers together. When it became a hit, it was a surprise to me, believe me. And *Raging Bull*, I figured, was the end of my career. It was like a punch in the face. It was a violent movie that would shake them and make them feel something.

'I had decided that *Raging Bull* would be pretty much the end of my working in America. Luckily enough, we got the money to make it because De Niro was a star. I thought it was a swan song for Hollywood. By the time it was released in '80, I thought it was the end; that I was going to be living in New York and Rome, and I was going to make documentaries and educational films on the saints. I was going to make films for television, that sort of thing.'

Scorsese says this in all sad-eyed sincerity. It is true, though, that in 1983 Paramount killed his treasured *Last Temptation* project, and he didn't know if he would ever make it. He remembers having lunch that year with director Brian De Palma, who was depressed about the brutal reviews of *Scarface*. 'We were sitting there at Hugo's thinking, "What can we do?" And Brian said maybe we should do some teaching. And we looked at each other. The salaries in teaching . . .' his voice trails at the ignominy. 'And what would you do in teaching?

'There doesn't seem to be anything else I can do,' Scorsese offers plaintively. 'I can't write novels. I could write scripts, but I'd only want to direct them.'

It should have been amusing to hear one of America's premier directors take himself so seriously, but, of course, that seriousness is what makes him what he is. What was crazier was to hear him judge his career as being so precarious, as if he were just another steelworker.

'You've got to be realistic,' he presses on. 'There's no such thing as a guarantee of anything in life. Anything. To make the movies I made in Hollywood, it's like a gift. And sometimes,' he said, brightening, 'they even pay me for it!

'The trick in taking a lot of chances is if you can do it for a price. The days of *Raging Bull* – when we went overbudget shooting ten weeks of fight scenes that comprised nine minutes of time in the completed film – those days are gone. Unless you have an absolute guaranteed box-office star name. Then . . . maybe.'

Hence, he brought in the striking-looking *Last Temptation* for a paltry $6.7 million. He was helped considerably by his actors, who worked for deferments and peanuts.

Actors usually love the very attentive Scorsese. He himself has taken small, seething roles in *Taxi Driver* and Bertrand Tavernier's *Round Midnight*. Ellen Burstyn, Robert De Niro and Paul Newman have all won best acting Oscars under his tutelage. And it's no wonder that Marlon Brando has tried to enlist him as a director, first in 1974, after he saw *Mean Streets*, and again two years ago, when he invited Scorsese and De Niro down to his island in Tahiti.

'He says, "Come down for five days," and we ended up staying three-and-a-half weeks,' Scorsese recalls. 'It's the only time in my life when I ever forgot what time it was or what day it was. It was remarkable. I was very sad to leave. The ideas he was telling me were wonderful.'

The event is doubly intriguing, because Brando and De Niro could almost be considered actor-brothers. Each has perfected an artist-of-the-streets style; each has inspired a slew of questionable imitators.

'It was as if they'd known each other for years,' Scorsese marvels. 'They had kind of an affinity for each other. Everybody was extremely relaxed, one of the best times I ever had in my life. They were more outdoors people than I was, of course. Boats would fall on my head. I was the comic relief, I guess. I didn't know what the hell was going on.

'I was never involved with any acting schools or acting techniques. I always say to actors, the hardest thing you can do in a movie is sit down and talk to somebody. Yelling and ranting and raving, sometimes that's very easy to do. The real communication between two people, the subtlety . . . I think Brando and De Niro broke through there. They made realism a virtue, I think. Brando created that style, and De Niro moves ahead with it. They have emotional depth – they're not just walking through a scene having their faces photographed.

'The best collaborations I had in my life were with De Niro. A lot of people don't understand when I say please leave the set. "What's this? Genius at work?" No, it's distracting. Some of the stuff I used to do with Bob was so personal and, for the actor, so painful that the only way he could do it was with me, and nobody else, watching.

He could make some mistakes. And very often those mistakes wouldn't be mistakes at all. It's the searching process. Intimacy and trust is the thing.'

What does De Niro want out of a role?

'The truth of the situation. How would a person really react, I think. He may tell you something else. I can only tell you that when we work, we use that phrase, "It's not right. Something's not right." If I see honesty in front of that lens, I'm satisfied behind the fucking camera – I tell you that.'

Scorsese got another chance to explore the truth of the situation in his chapter of *New York Stories* (the three segments are unrelated except for the locale). Called 'Life Lessons', starring Nick Nolte and Rosanna Arquette, and written by novelist Richard Price, it is yet another story ripped right from the headlines across Scorsese's soul.

'In the late sixties, I wanted to make a film out of Dostoyevsky's *The Gambler*. Paul Schrader tried in the early seventies, but it didn't work out. And then around '72 or '73, Jay Cocks gave me a Christmas present of a new translation of *The Gambler*, along with *Diaries of Paulina*, who was Dostoyevsky's mistress, and a short story that she wrote about her relationship with him. All in the same book. He was like 50 or so, and she was one of his students, around 23.

'After the affair had gone down, he exorcised Paulina out of his system by putting her as the main female character in *The Gambler*. And, as you know, he had to write the book in four weeks to pay off debts. At the end of four weeks, he married his secretary, and that's when he finally got Paulina out of his system.

'There are scenes in *The Gambler* that are quite extraordinary about the relationship, the humiliation and love and battles between the two. So, over the years, I was trying to work out something with that. I found that elements of their relationship found their way into my movies. In *Raging Bull*. A little bit in *Taxi*, which was Schrader's thing. And in *New York, New York*, a lot of it! The difficulty in being with each other, the difficulty of loving.'

He strokes his Mephistophelian beard and searches the air in front of him. 'How should I put it? The amount of pain in a relationship, and how the pain works for and against the people. How they *need* the pain. How long can you go with that pain in a relationship, from one relationship to the next, to the next? Just building up pain. Not only in yourself, but giving it to the other person, without everybody just caving in. Or committing suicide. There are many forms of suicide; you can die spiritually and live another 50 years and be a piece of wood.

'That's what fascinated me most, the passion of a relationship. It doesn't always have to be so destructive. I found all these ideas in the books and in Paulina's diaries. And her story is great, because you read *The Gambler* first, and you get his interpretation of it. Then you read the diaries, and you see a reality. "He came to the door, it's Fyodor again, he's crying. I hate when he does that."' He laughs uproariously at the thought. 'She must have been beautiful.

'Instead of a writer, we made the man a famous painter in SoHo who's extremely rich but still lives in the lofts, wears a $16,000 watch but has it covered in paint. The guy has constant relationships with these women, these assistants, and obviously these relationships are dead from the beginning. Because at a certain age – 53, 54 – and you're famous, doing a lot of stuff, and you keep getting involved with girls who are

Lionel Dobie (Nick Nolte) and muse Paulette (Rosanna Arquette) in 'Life Lessons', from New York Stories. *Scorsese based their relationship on Dostoyevsky and his mistress.*

23 – they're kids, they're like daughters. You've got to let them go out, to let them grow. They'll hurt you. And you'll hurt them, too. They'll gain a lot, hopefully, in what he calls life lessons. "You'll get life lessons from me," he says. And they're emotionally murderous. They're like beatings.

'I think he comes to resolve that he is going to go on with this series of relationships, deal with the pain and the humiliation and the passion of it, and resolve that he will be alone with his work. He's not the person they should be with.' Again, a painful laugh. 'Who knows if he should be with anybody?'

Scorsese draws himself up and wonders. 'How much does the pain fuel the work? At the beginning of the picture, he's got a show opening in a few weeks, and he can't paint. The minute she tells him she's not in love with him, he starts to paint.'

'But I must emphasise,' he cautions, 'it's light comedy.'

Comedy would seem to be a natural terrain for Scorsese; his normal speech shoots off like a rapid-fire Borscht Belt comedian's string of firecrackers. Whether or not he ever makes a true comedy, he at least feels a profound need to make a commercial picture and pay back Universal Pictures for backing him up on *Last Temptation*. Scorsese's problem is that while he grapples with the truth in a movie, he usually clashes with the audience's expectations. The filmmaker doesn't often serve up drama's most attractive device: wish fulfilment. It is significant to him, for instance, that his dark, schizo *New York, New York* opened a mere three weeks before

Star Wars, which, he says, 'brought about a whole new period of filmmaking'.

But an even more important movie opened the year before, in 1976. And that was *Rocky*. Its triumphant ending seemed to galvanise the Hollywood bosses. At a stroke, much of the brave, adventurous moviemaking of the previous decade was suddenly brought to a halt.

'Gone,' Scorsese agrees. 'Wiped out. Oddly enough, I like the ending of *Rocky*, myself. I don't like the picture that much, but I like the ending. I felt good. A lot of the pictures I love and adore through history are pictures that make me feel good.

'But to make a picture like that,' he says, shaking his head, 'I could never do it. Not that I make pictures to make people feel bad. Go see *Last Temptation*! He transcends; he goes into heaven. What more could you want from life than salvation? For all of us! You'll feel great!

'But this is what scares me. You have films with happy endings, which show the triumph of the human spirit, in films like *Rocky*. And then you have pictures that are a little more realistic and deal with certain emotions and psychological character studies, and they don't necessarily have that uplifting effect. In the fifties through the seventies, they seemed to exist together. Now, it seems that some films don't even have a right to exist.

'With the advent of *Rocky* and *Star Wars* and the Spielberg pictures, on the best side they're morally uplifting; you leave the theatre the way you did at the end of *Casablanca*. And on the worst side, they're sentimental. Lies. That's the problem. And where I fit in there, I don't know.

'We've got some pet projects we want to make here in the future, but in between I want to make some good commercial pictures. *The Color of Money* was a good commercial exercise for me. I learned a great deal about structure and style. Learned what may not have worked.

'It's very hard for me to do the uplifting, transcendental sentimentalism – of most films, because it's just not true.' He draws himself up with a mocking self-righteousness. 'And it's not because I'm this great prophet of truth – it's just like embarrassing to do it on the set. How would you stage the scene? What do you tell the actors, you know?

'There's no doubt we've got the problem that movies are considered mainly to be escapism. You want to have fun. I even shirked, let's say, from seeing every Bergman picture after a while. It was like doing homework.

'I prefer the escapism of fantasy, rather than the escapism of incredible sentimentality. What I'm afraid of is pandering to tastes that are superficial. There's no depth anymore. What appears to be depth is often a facile character study.'

His face empties. 'But they're making a product, and a product's gotta sell. And what sells is fantasy and sentimentality. You've gotta make money. And you make money [by] giving the audience what the hell they want!'

Combating this, however, is his readiness to infuriate, to go against audience expectations. A guy who wants to show the human side of Christ and the spiritual side of gangsters has to be ready for anything.

His dilemma may be that he is, through and through, a very emotional man. Whatever emotion he deals with, he will be hot on the subject. Around him, however, has grown up a generation that is cool, informed and wised-up to everything under the sun. And perhaps there are people – even among those in charge – who would rather not deal with the heavy, human, emotional soup in any way but a cool, detached way.

Scorsese hears the theory and nods matter-of-factly. 'Because they don't want to be sucked in and taken advantage of,' he says, with no great feeling. He looks down at his hands. They are rather large and striking hands for so small a man. 'I don't blame them.' Then his eyes come up, emphatic, definite and level. 'But you've got to deal with the emotions some time or another.'

BRINGING IT ALL BACK HOME . . .
By Henri Behar

'It was, like, 3:30 on a Saturday morning, October of 1963,' recalls Martin Scorsese, settling back in his chair. 'Myself and Joe, who was my closest friend at the time, we were in a car, and we decided we didn't like the fellow who was driving us around. So we asked him to drop us off on Elizabeth Street – he lived on the street too. He was an off-duty cop, and he had a gun with him all the time and I didn't trust that. Much better off with a couple of wise guys. So he drove down the block, there was another car parked right in the middle of the street, and a guy talking to some other guy in a parked car, big black car. And he got into an argument with them, made a big deal out of his being a cop. And the fellow in the car suddenly says, "I'm not moving, I'm in the middle of a conversation." Suddenly the whole thing turns into a Western. And the guy we are with pulls his gun and says, "I'm a cop, move." And the guy replies, very calm, "Do you really wanna pull the guns?" And, like, Joe and I are still in the back seat. Anyway, the guy pulls away, the off-duty cop drops us home and drives off and all of a sudden a black car drives up next to him and they just fire a whole bunch of shots into him. God knows where the shots would have hit us, just going for a ride with this idiot who had to act up a big deal because he was a cop. We could have been killed that night. But you learn, you learn to feel your way around. You see somebody being too stupid and you just say, "Oh no, I'm going home" . . .'

The incident just recalled by the 48-year-old Martin Scorsese could quite easily come from his new feature film, the epic *GoodFellas*. This last week, when his fourteenth movie opened in the US, belonged to Scorsese. Reviewers were, for once, unanimous in their praise, comparing *GoodFellas*, favourably, to *Raging Bull*, the critics' perennial choice as Best Film of the Eighties. Indeed, the sole bone of contention appeared to be whether or not *GoodFellas* is 'better' than *Raging Bull* or simply 'just as good'.

'That level of criticism, I can take,' cracks Scorsese, obviously thrilled with the various accolades heaped upon him in the last few weeks – most notably Best Director prize at the Venice Festival.

An interview with Scorsese is an experience unto itself. The man is small and wiry, his metabolism high-speed, pumping you with words and ideas faster than a machine-gun. His conversation jumps all over the place, from this director to that (he does a mean impersonation of John Cassavetes), from his own films to everybody else's ('*Peeping Tom* is a film about filmmakers'), to the beard he has just shaved off ('After sixteen years, I just discovered the rest of my face'), to Italy ('A whole different attitude. Life is more important than appointments'), and always back to films ('Every time you start one, you realise how much you really don't know. It's just awful').

And, of course, *GoodFellas*, his movie adaptation of Nicholas Pileggi's book *Wiseguy*, the true account of the exploits of Henry Hill – played by Ray Liotta in the film – a half-Sicilian, half-Irish crook who, at age fourteen, began an extraordinary life of illegal activities, ranging from construction rackets to extortion, hijackings, arson, the then-forbidden Mafioso territory of drug smuggling and, eventually, murder. Some 30 years on, married and as high in the Mob ranks as an Irishman could go, Hill entered the US Federal Witness Protection Program – turned supergrass – and promptly dropped the dime on buddies Paul Cicero, played by Paul Sorvino, and fellow Irishman Jimmy Conway, memorably portrayed by Robert De Niro, like the director here back to his very best form. Scorsese has, of course, made many films about gangsters and assorted low-lifes (*Mean Streets, Taxi Driver, Raging Bull, The Color of Money*) but has consistently said that as an Italian-American he would never make a movie on the Mafia, or the good fellas, as they prefer to be known.

'I know,' he replies, 'but it's a bit different here. 'Cause it's not that. When I read the book, and then when I started writing the script with Nicholas Pileggi, we gave it such a structure that it seemed to me an exciting film to make. That it would be too bad *not* to make, too bad for me *not* to make. It's an epic, insofar as it covers 25 years, from 1955 to 1980.'

Indeed, Scorsese goes so far as to see his film more like a modern version of John Bunyan's *Pilgrim's Progress.*

'Someone totally innocent at the beginning who goes deeper and deeper into crime, and pays the price in a way – but that's for the audience to decide.'

Whatever his reluctance to publicly link his film with the Mob, however, it is clear that Scorsese is no stranger to the ways of the real-life good fellas. In addition to the harrowing incident recalled earlier, he has a whole wealth of childhood memories to call upon.

'What fascinated me most were the details of everyday life,' he says of his salad days in New York's legendary Little Italy area. 'What they [the local good fellas] eat, how they dress, the nightclubs they go to, what their houses look like, and how, *around* that, life organises itself, day by day, minute by minute. Their wives, their kids.'

He vividly recalls a picnic from his childhood.

'There were all these men near the bar,' he remembers, 'eating sausages and pepperonis, and as usual, kids everywhere, running around to get a sausage for their dad or something. And years later I understood it was a "family" meeting. Those guys were working, they were doing business. But at the time we didn't know. They all looked just like . . . *uncles.*'

Born in the New York City borough of Queens, in a small community called Corona, the young Scorsese and his family moved in with his grandmother on Elizabeth Street in the heart of Manhattan's Italian community.

'My father had run into some difficulty at his work, he lost a good deal of money and we had to put our furniture in storage when we moved. There were three rooms in my grandmother's house, one for my grandparents, one for my mother and father, one for my brother and me. We lived there for six months, then got our own rooms down the block, on Elizabeth Street. It was only twenty years later, after my brother got married and I moved out in the sixties, that my parents moved . . . across the street.'

Separated from Chinatown by Canal Street, Little Italy is a tiny neighbourhood but, according to Scorsese, one with its own highly complex geo-socio-politics.

'The Sicilians that emigrated came from small towns,' he explains. 'My grandfather came from Pulizi Generosa. All the people from Pulizi moved to Elizabeth Street – all in one building. Then, as soon as they could secure more rooms in the same building, they'd bring in people from their village Then there were people from Cimina, which is the hometown of my grandmother on my mother's side. Same thing: they'd have a few buildings down the block. Very rarely would a Sicilian live on Mulberry Street – that was for the Neapolitans. So what they did was import the village mentality and the village social structure to Elizabeth Street.'

In this feudal structure, according to Scorsese, it was normally none other than the Don who settled any problems.

'For instance, one of my aunts eloped,' he recalls. 'For my grandfather, she was dead, didn't exist anymore. For six or seven months, we wore black at home. Then, one day, the Don of the block representing my grandfather's hometown came up for coffee and a talk, because my grandmother had intervened. She had asked the Don to convince my grandfather to let up on this attitude towards his daughter. She wanted her daughter to be allowed back into the home. And the Don worked it out. That's the kind of settling he usually did.'

For Scorsese, this increasingly outdated way of life obviously still holds a certain appeal.

'This summer, I went back to Sicily and visited both towns,' he explains. 'And it's still prevalent there. For those towns, it works. For three or four buildings on Elizabeth Street, it works. For the people who came here and worked as labourers and opened grocery stores and sold things in the streets, for most of the time it worked. When you start to go bigger, when the Don wants to take over the West Side, *then* it becomes a problem. I don't necessarily justify it, but I understand. I understand where it comes from, I understand why they distrust governments, and especially police. Different culture. But when you're eight or nine years old, that's your way of life. There is no such thing as "outside that block" or those two blocks, three blocks. *Everything* else outside is a fantasy. I was *eighteen* when I went to the Village, crossed over to the West Side and went to New York University. We had everything we wanted on the East Side. We *hated* the West Side.'

Many years later, at the time he was married to Isabella Rossellini, Scorsese went back to Italy to live for a period.

It's in the bag for Tommy (Joe Pesci), Henry (Ray Liotta) and Jimmy (De Niro). In GoodFellas *(1990), the Lufthansa robbery is their greatest triumph and their undoing.*

'I liked the style of living,' he says of that time. 'Taking it easy, moving at a certain pace. But one thing I realised when I lived in Rome with Isabella was that I'm American . . .'

As a child, Scorsese had asthma. Nailed to his bed for two or three days in a row, he would draw little pictures – his first storyboards, which he still has – and look outside the window, longing to *belong*.

'The kids that I became friends with lived on Elizabeth. And we'd get into fights – usually they'd hit on you, punch you a few times in the arm, and that's it, just to test you. And I'd say, "Don't touch me, I have asthma." If he was a tough kid, he'd say, "It doesn't matter" and just hit me anyway. But I was able to stand up to them, able to take the punishment of them. They'd like that. They liked the fact that I was being able to be with them and pass certain rituals, passage of rites, and take pain. I'd make them laugh, I'd organise their parties, I'd even programme the music at their dances – I always opened with Chuck Berry. A real *bona fide* Sicilian [*laughs*].'

Blessed with a mother who adored motion pictures, Scorsese was not slow in discovering the delights of the local picture house, beginning with King Vidor's *Duel in the Sun.*

'The ending terrified me,' he recalls. 'I ended up under the seat. The sun was boiling up there, Jennifer Jones was shooting at Gregory Peck – they loved each other so much they killed one another – and all the time she's doing all sorts of gyrations on the screen, expressing great lust, shouting, "I'm trash! I'm trash!" . . . It sort of laid out the course of my entire love life.'

Condemned from the pulpit, *Duel in the Sun* was one of the few films rated the forbidden 'O' by the Catholic Church that Scorsese dared to see.

'Rossellini's *Miracle* I didn't see,' he says, ''cause I was too young to understand – I was eight – and I didn't even know about the controversy. A few years later it was Otto Preminger's *The Moon Was Blue*, because they used the word "virgin" and didn't mean the Virgin Mary. Elia Kazan's *Baby Doll* was condemned in 1956. Would you believe I saw it for the first time only in the mid-eighties?'

Eventually, troubled by this conflict between his faith and his interest in films, the budding director took counsel from his parish priest.

'I explained to the priest – in confession – that I just had to see Ingmar Bergman's *Smiles of a Summer Night*. And that having seen it, I hadn't found anything so difficult about it. And the priest said, "Look, for the masses, we can't allow this sort of thing. But if it's your work . . ." I mean, how many guys from the Lower East Side were going to see *Smiles of a Summer Night?*'

Gradually, Scorsese's adherence to the teachings of the Catholic Church – he even tried to get into a Jesuit university but poor grades sent him to NYU instead – began to crumble.

'I learned about the streets as opposed to an edifice called the Church,' he says, 'because, living in the neighbourhood I'd see some really tough bastards do some really rotten things, then go to church on Sunday and everything was okay. And the moment they'd step out of the church, they'd start acting the same old way. I couldn't see how you could take a Christian ethic and actually put it into practice in that world.'

Inevitably, however, some of that old attraction, at least to the dramatic rituals of the liturgy, still lurks deep within him and his work.

'Never left,' he agrees. 'When I made *The Last Temptation of Christ*, the actual making of the film was like a prayer, the way certain composers in centuries past dedicated their work to God. And the ritual of filmmaking is akin to a religious ritual. "Slate", "Action", "Cut" . . . You have to have a kind of rigour which is religious, just to plough through, to keep going. My father often says, "Marty, every picture to him is the worst experience of his life. But he's having a ball while he's saying it." And he's right. There is a certain magic, definitely, but you have to go through hell to get there.'

In addition to *GoodFellas*, Scorsese is also currently expending his energies on his own recently created production company, with Stephen Frears' adaptation of Jim Thompson's hard-boiled thriller *The Grifters* the first product to emerge. Still to come are John McNaughton's *Mad Dog and Glory* (McNaughton, a relatively unknown director, came to Scorsese's attention with his first feature, *Henry: Portrait of a Serial Killer*. 'I was so disturbed by *Henry* that I slept with the TV set on,' says Scorsese), Antonioni's *The Crew*, and a remake of J. Lee Thompson's *Cape Fear*. And then, of course, there is the much talked-about documentary on Italian fashion supremo, Giorgio Armani.

'It's really the idea of Milan,' explains Scorsese, 'the city of Milan, hiding such elegance. Milan looks very flat, but when you enter the courtyards, everything opens up. And then, of course, when you go inside the villas, they're quite extraordinary. The *style*. And this film is about style. About a man with style.'

A man with style from a terribly impoverished background.

'Yes, I had no idea. He is such an elegant man. I didn't know until he started talking about it and introduced us to his parents. They were always well dressed but the mother made the clothes for him. She taught him. And he's self-made. He created his empire out of his energy, and his vision.'

Not unlike, in fact, Martin Scorsese, the boy from Little Italy now regarded by many as the finest film director in the world. The man who, when busy editing *Raging Bull*, was sent a message by cinematographer Michael Chapman, quoting a line from one of Scorsese's all-time favourites, *Peeping Tom*, the line that says, 'All this filming isn't healthy.'

'Maybe it isn't,' says Scorsese now, when reminded of the incident. 'But who cares?'

EXPERT WITNESS: *GOODFELLAS*
By Henry Hill

In the spring of 1980, Henry Hill was arrested in New York on drug conspiracy charges. Facing a possible life sentence, Hill chose to enter the Federal Witness Protection Program. He testified against his former associates and furnished the government with detailed information about the workings of organised crime. In return, he and his family were granted immunity from prosecution, provided with new identities, and relocated to another part of the United States. Hill's story was recounted by crime journalist Nicholas Pileggi in Wiseguy, *the 1985 book that served as the basis for Martin Scorsese's* GoodFellas.

Through an intermediary, Premiere *contacted Hill and requested his Expert Witness evaluation of Scorsese's film. Hill saw the movie at a private screening.*

At first, I wasn't even sure I wanted to see *GoodFellas*. It had taken me six months just to get myself to read *Wiseguy*. I've been trying to change my life for the past ten years, and it's been a really slow process. The idea of reliving everything again was kind of scary. But I had a lot of confidence in Nick Pileggi. He and Martin Scorsese had assured me that they wouldn't make me look like a real scumbag in the film, that I would come off looking okay. So I had left it all up to them.

The movie made me feel humble. It stirred up a lot of old feelings: fear, anxiety, guilt. Back when I was in the Mob, I sometimes had to do things that just didn't sit right with me. But I did them anyway. Maybe it was for the money or my ego, or maybe it was out of fear that if I said no, I'd get chased, or worse.

Or maybe it was for the feeling of being part of the Mob. When I was a child growing up in Brooklyn, my ambition was to be a gangster. I had seen the way those

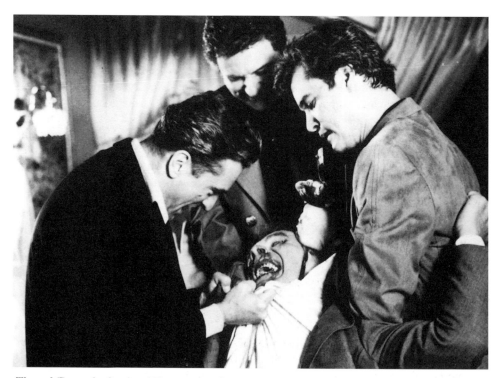

The real 'Jimmy the Gent' and Tommy – seen here demonstrating the gentle art of persuasion – are now dead, while Henry Hill has left the Witness Protection Programme.

people lived, and the way they controlled the police department and the politicians. I was in awe of their shiny Cadillacs and their diamond pinky rings and their thick rolls of money, the convertibles, the yachts down in Sheepshead Bay, the nightclubs, and the chicks – one on each arm. They could do anything they wanted, whenever they wanted. They were the princes of the neighbourhood. I wanted to be one of them.

And when I became one of them, I loved it. The lifestyle was intoxicating, and I was addicted for many years – until I realised exactly what I had gotten myself into. And by then it was too late. I guess I began to change in 1974, when I first went to jail. I was in on an extortion charge after doing a favour for Jimmy Burke ('Jimmy Conway'). Actually, I was treated well in prison – they put me in the same room as Joe Pine and Johnny Dio. Jimmy Hoffa had just left. But that was when I started to realise how insane my life was. I saw where I was ending up.

In *GoodFellas*, Martin Scorsese captures everything – good and bad – with almost total accuracy. Had I had the opportunity, to direct the movie myself – if I knew anything about directing – I don't think I could have done a better job. All the details are just right. The Brooklyn neighbourhood in the movie looks and feels just like my own did.

Robert De Niro plays Burke as well as Burke could play himself. That man was really a chameleon. One minute, he was your friend, a nice guy, and the next minute, he was having you whacked. He was very intelligent. But anybody who threatened him was a dead man. Brutality and murder were the only survival methods he knew.

Burke really lost it after the Lufthansa robbery. He was scared to death that he was going to get popped. He knew that too many people knew about the heist. The shit started falling apart around him. Everybody wanted their ends, and he was holding on to the money so the others wouldn't get popped with it before he was able to whack them. Maybe that was his plan from the beginning. He never discussed it. He did talk to me about whacking Marty Krugman ('Morris Kessler'), and I actually begged him to spare Marty's life. Burke said he wouldn't kill him, but obviously he did. I think that was the last straw for me. I completely went into a shell after that.

Lorraine Bracco, as Karen, is right on. Unfortunately, all of us guys treated our wives the way Henry treats Karen in the movie. We were all womanisers. Today I'm not a womaniser. Back then I was. How any of our wives stood by us is still beyond me. We were home for only a few hours each week. We were on the move from the minute we woke up in the morning until the minute we went to bed at night. It was a constant hustle. We very rarely slept. I was always told that if I channelled my energy into a legitimate business, I'd be very successful. But I didn't want a legitimate business. It just wasn't part of that life.

As for Tommy DeSimone ('Tommy DeVito'), played by Joe Pesci, the movie actually lets him off easy, because in real life, he was a whole lot worse. He was a homicidal maniac. The man was completely off it. A very sick individual.

The character I was most anxious about seeing onscreen was my own, played by Ray Liotta. I had spoken with Robert De Niro on the telephone many times during the filming, but I hadn't talked to Ray. Marty [Scorsese] didn't want us to meet until they were finished with the film. I was a little worried about what they'd do with the role. But Marty obviously knew what he was doing. When I finally saw the movie, I was overjoyed. I could not believe the job that Ray had done. He played me perfectly throughout the movie. That's really the way it was. It's all true.

Today, I have a new family. I have a wonderful woman in my life and a wonderful child. I wish I could say it's the American Dream, but I still live in fear at times. I'm still in hiding. It s difficult for the whole family. I still have problems dealing with my past. But the movie made me very grateful that I'm still alive and able to lead a somewhat normal life.

I sleep a whole lot better at night. I kiss my child good-night, and I put my head on the pillow, and I don't have to worry about a phone call at three in the morning, someone saying, 'Meet me at the diner,' or, 'Meet me at the bar and bring a pistol with you,' or, 'Bring a shovel.' That craziness is out of my life, thank God. I'm trying to be a better person, trying not to break any laws. Trying to be an average Joe – the kind of person I used to call a shnook. I'm glad to be a shnook today.

MARTIN SCORSESE
Interviewed by Gavin Smith

What was it that drew you to the **GoodFellas** *material?*
I read a review of the book; basically it said, 'This is really the way it must be.' So I got the book in galleys and started really enjoying it because of the free-flowing style, the way Henry Hill spoke, and the wonderful arrogance of it. And I said, oh, it would make a fascinating film if you just make it what it is – literally as close to the truth as a fiction film, dramatisation, could get. No sense to try to whitewash, [to elicit] great sympathy for the characters in a phony way. If you happen to feel something for the character Pesci plays, after all he does in the film, and if you feel something for him when he's eliminated, then that's interesting to me. That's basically it. There was no sense making this film [any other way].

You say dramatisation and fiction. What kind of a film do you see this as being?
I was hoping it was a documentary. [*laughs*] Really, no kidding. Like a *staged* documentary, *the spirit* of a documentary. As if you had a 16mm camera with these guys for twenty, 25 years; what you'd pick up. I can't say it's 'like' any other film, but in my mind it [has] the freedom of a documentary, where you can mention 25 people's names at one point and 23 of them the audience will not have heard of before and won't hear of again, but it doesn't matter. It's the familiarity of the way people speak. Even at the end when Ray Liotta says over the freezeframe on his face, 'Jimmy never asked me to go and whack somebody before. But now he's asking me to go down and do a hit with Anthony in Florida.' Who's Anthony?

It's a mosaic, a tapestry, where faces keep coming in and out. Johnny Dio, played by Frank Pellegrino, you only see in the fifties, and then in the sixties you don't see him, but he shows up in the jail sequence. He may have done something else for five or six years and come back. It's the way they live.

How have your feelings about this world changed since **Mean Streets***?*
Well, *Mean Streets* is much closer to home in terms of a real story, somewhat fictionalised, about events that occurred to me and some of my old friends. [*GoodFellas*] has really nothing to do with people I knew then. It doesn't take place in Manhattan, it's only in the boroughs, so it's a very different world – although it's all interrelated. But the *spirit* of it, again, the *attitudes*. The morality – you know, there's none, there's none. Completely amoral. It's just wonderful.

If you're a young person, eight or nine, and these people treat you a certain way because you're living around them, and then as you get to be a teenager and you get a little older, you begin to realise what they did and what they still do – you still have those first feelings for them as people, you know. So, it kind of raises a moral question and a kind of moral friction in me. That was what I wanted to get on the screen.

How did you feel about **Married to the Mob,** *which satirised the Mafia lifestyle?*
I like Jonathan Demme's movies. In fact, I have the same production designer, Kristi Zea. But, well, it's a satire – it's just too many plastic seatcovers. And yet, if you go to my mother's apartment, you'll see not only the plastic seatcovers on the couch but on the coffee table as well. So where's the line of the truth? I don't know.

In the spirit of Demme's work I enjoyed it. But as far as an Italian-American thing, it's really like a cartoon. When he starts with 'Mambo Italiano', Rosemary Clooney, I'm already cringing because I'm Italian-American, and certain songs we'd like to forget! So I told Jonathan he had some nerve using that, I said only Italians could use 'Mambo Italiano' and get away with it. There might be some knocks at his door. [*laughs*]

Do **GoodFellas** *and* **Mean Streets** *serve as an antidote to* **The Godfather***'s mythic version of the Mafia?*
Yes, yeah, absolutely. *Mean Streets*, of course, was something I was just burning to do for a number of years. [By the time I did it,] *The Godfather* had already come out. But I said, it doesn't matter, because this one is really, to use the word loosely, anthropology – that idea of how people live, what they ate, how they dressed. *Mean Streets* has that quality – a quote 'real' unquote side of it.

GoodFellas more so. Especially in terms of attitude. Don't give a damn about anything, especially when they're having a good time and making a lot of money. They don't care about their wives, their kids, anything.

The Godfather *is such an overpowering film that it shapes everybody's perception of the Mafia – including people in the Mafia.*
Oh, sure. I prefer *Godfather II* to *Godfather I*. I've always said it's like epic poetry, like *Morte d'Arthur*. My stuff is like some guy on the streetcorner talking.

In **GoodFellas** *we see a great deal of behaviour, but you withhold psychological insight.*
Basically I was interested in what they *do*. And, you know, they don't think about it a lot. They don't sit around and ponder about [*laughs*], 'Gee, what are we doing here?' The answer is to eat a lot and make a lot of money and do the least amount of work as possible for it. I was trying to make it as practical and primitive as possible. Just straight ahead. Want. Take. Simple. I'm more concerned with showing a lifestyle and using Henry Hill [Ray Liotta] as basically a guide through it.

You said you see this as a tragic story.
I do, but you have a lot of the guys, like [real-life US attorney] Ed McDonald in the film or Ed Hayes [a real defence attorney], who plays one of the defence attorneys, they'll say, 'These guys are animals and that's life,' and maybe not care about them. Henry took Paulie [Paul Sorvino] as sort of a second father; he just idolised these guys and wanted to be a part of it. And that's what makes the turnaround at the end so interesting and so tragic, for me.

In **Scorsese on Scorsese** *[published by Faber and Faber] you said that, growing up, you felt being a rat was the worst thing you could be. How do you feel about Henry and what he did?*
That's a hard one. Maybe on one level, the tragedy is in the shots of Henry on the stand: 'Will you point him out to me, please?' And you see him look kind of sheepish, and he points to Bob De Niro playing Jimmy Conway. And the camera moves in on Conway. Maybe that's the tragedy – what he had to do to survive, to enable his family to survive.

This is 'Henry Hill' as opposed to Henry Hill – purely an imaginative version of this guy?
Yes. Based on what he said in the book and based on what [co-writer] Nick [Pileggi] told me. I never spoke to Henry Hill. Towards the end of the film I spoke to him on the phone once. He thanked me about something. It was just less than 30 seconds on the phone.

You use him as a mirror of American society.
Yeah, the lifestyle reflects the times. In the early sixties, the camera comes up on Henry and he's waiting outside the diner and he's got this silk suit on and he hears 'Stardust'. And he's young and he's looking like all the hope in the world ready for him and he's going to conquer the world. And then you just take it through America – the end of the sixties, the seventies, and finally into the end of the seventies with the disillusionment and the state of the country that we're in now. I think his journey reflects that.

That wasn't planned. But there's something about the moment when his wife says, 'Hide that cross,' and the next thing you know, he's getting married in a Jewish ceremony, and wearing a Star of David *and* a cross – it doesn't make any difference. Although I didn't want to make it heavy in the picture, the idea is that if you live for a certain kind of value, at a certain point in life you're going to come smack up against a brick wall. Not only Henry living as a gangster: in my feeling, I guess it's the old materialism versus a spiritual life.

GoodFellas *is like a history of postwar American consumer culture, the evolution of cultural style. The naiveté and romanticism of the fifties . . . There's a kind of innocent mischief and charm to the worldliness. But then at a certain point it becomes corrupt.*
It corrupts and degenerates. Even to the point [that] some of the music degenerates in itself. You have 'Unchained Melody' being sung in a decadent way, like the ultimate doo-wop – but not black, it's Italian doo-wop. It's on the soundtrack after Stacks gets killed and Henry comes running into the bar. Bob tells him, 'Come on, let's drink up, it's a celebration,' and Tommy says, 'Don't worry about anything. Going to make me.' And over that you hear this incredible doo-wop going on, and it's sort of like even the music becomes decadent in a way from the pure Drifters, Clyde McPhatter singing 'Bells of St. Mary's', to Vito and the Salutations.

And I *like* the Vito and the Salutations version of 'Unchained Melody'. Alex North wrote it along with somebody else – it was from this movie made in the early fifties called *Unchained*. And it's unrecognisable. It's so crazy and I enjoy it. I guess I admire the purity of the early times and . . . Not that I admire it, but I'm a part of the decadence of what happened in the seventies and the eighties.

Pop music is usually used in films, at least on one level, to cue the audience to what era it is.
Oh, no, no, forget that, no.

In *Mean Streets* there's a lot of stuff that comes from the forties. The thing is, believe me, a lot of these places you had jukeboxes and, when the Beatles came in, you [still] had Benny Goodman, some old Italian stuff, Jerry Vale, Tony Bennett, doo-wop, early rock 'n' roll, black and Italian . . . There's a guy who comes around and puts the latest hits in. [But] when you hang out in a place, when you are part of a group, new records come in but [people] request older ones. And they stay. If one of the guys leaves or somebody gets killed, some of his favourite music [nobody else] wants to listen to, they throw it away. But basically there are certain records that guys like and it's there. Anything goes, anything goes.

Why Sid Vicious doing 'My Way' at the end?
Oh, it's pretty obvious, it may be even too obvious.

It's period, but also it's Paul Anka and of course Sinatra – although there's no Sinatra in the film. But 'My Way' is an anthem. I like Sid Vicious' version because it twists it, and his whole life and death was a kind of slap in the face of the whole system, the whole point of existence in a way. And that's what's fascinating to me – because eventually, yeah, they all did it their way. [*laughs*] Because we did it our way, you know.

GoodFellas' vision of rock 'n' roll style colliding with a fetishised gangster attitude made me think of Nic Roeg's Performance, *which was about the dark side of the sixties too.*
Oh I like *Performance*, yeah. I never quite understood it, because I didn't understand any of the drug culture at that time. But I liked the picture. I love the music and I love Jagger in it and James Fox – terrific. That's one of the reasons I used the Ry Cooder [song] 'Memo to Turner' – the part where Jimmy says, 'Now, stop taking those fucking drugs, they're making your mind into mush.' He slams the door. He puts the guns in the trunk and all of a sudden you hear the beginning of this incredible slide guitar coming in. It's Ry Cooder. And I couldn't use the rest of it because the scene goes too quick.

The seventies drug thing was important because I wanted to get the impression of that craziness. Especially that last day, he starts at six in the morning. The first thing he does is gets the guns, takes a hit of coke, gets in the car. I mean, you're already wired, you're wired for the day. And his day is like crazy. Everything is at the same importance. The sauce is just as important as the guns, is as important as Jimmy, the drugs, the helicopter.

The idea was to stylistically try to give the impression – people watching the film who have taken drugs will recognise it – of the anxiety and the thought processes. And the way the mind races when you're taking drugs, really doing it as a lifestyle.

The film's first section presents a kind of idealised underworld with its own warmth and honour-among-thieves code. This gradually falls away, reflected in the characters of Tommy and Jimmy.
True, true. But Jimmy Conway was not Mafia. The idea was, you signed on for that

life, you may have to exit that life in an unnatural way, and they knew that. I'm not saying, oh, those were the good old days. In a funny way [*laughs*] – not that funny – but in a way there's a breakdown of discipline, of whatever moral code those guys had in the fifties and sixties. I think now with drugs being the big money and gangsters killing people in the government in Colombia, the Mafia is nothing. They'll always be around, there'll always be the organised-crime idea. But in terms of the old, almost romantic image of it typified by the *Godfather* films, that's gone.

The seventies sequence is about losing control, about disintegration.
Totally. Henry disintegrates with drugs. With Jimmy Conway, the disintegration is on a more lethal level, the elimination of [everybody else]. Earlier there's so many shots of people playing cards and at christenings and weddings, all at the same table. If you look at the wedding, the camera goes around the table and all the people at that table are killed by Jimmy later on.

Unlike all your other protagonists, Henry seems secure in his identity. What is his journey, from your point of view?
You know, I don't know. I don't mean to be silly; I guess I should have an answer for that. Maybe in the way he feels through his voiceover in the beginning of the film about being respected. I think it's really more about Henry not having to wait in line to get bread for his mother. It's that simple. And to be a confidante of people so powerful, who, to a child's mind, didn't have to worry about parking by a hydrant. It's the American Dream.

Once he has this status lifestyle, what's at stake for him?
Things happen so fast, so quick and heavy in their lifestyle, they don't think of that. Joe Pesci pointed out that you have literally a life expectancy – the idea of a cycle that it takes for a guy to be in the prime of being a wiseguy – the prime period is like maybe eight or nine years, at the end of which, just by the law of averages, you're either going to get killed or most likely go to jail. And then you begin the long thing with going back and forth from jail to home, jail to home. It begins to wear you down until only the strongest survive.

I think Henry realises the horror he's brought upon himself, how they're all living, and it's way too late. The only thing to do is get out of it. And how can you get out?

He remains an enigma – untainted by what he's done and at the end achieving a kind of grace as just a regular guy like everybody else. What were you trying to do with the ending?
It's just very simply that's the way the book ended and I liked what he said, I liked his attitude: 'Gee, there's no more fun.' [*laughs*] Now, you can take that any way you want. I think the audience should get angry with him. I would hope they would be. And maybe angry with the system that allows it – this is so complex. Everything is worked out together with these guys and with the law and with the Justice Department. It'll be phony if he felt badly about what he did. The irony of it at the end I kind of think is very funny.

Why do you have him addressing the camera at the end?
Couldn't think of any other thing to do, really. Just, you know, got to end the picture. Seriously.

How did you conceptualise the film stylistically? Did you break the film down into sequences?
Yeah, as much as possible. Everything was pretty much storyboarded, if not on paper, in notes. These days I don't actually draw each picture. But I usually put notes on the sides of the script, how the camera should move. I wanted lots of movement and I wanted it to be throughout the whole picture, and I wanted the style to kind of break down by the end, so that by his last day as a wiseguy, it's as if the whole picture would be out of control, give the impression he's just going to spin off the edge and fly out. And then stop for the last reel and a half.

The idea was to get as much movement as possible – even more than usual. And a very speeded, frenetic quality to most of it in terms of getting as much information to the audience – overwhelming them, I had hoped – with images and information. There's a lot of stuff in the frames. Because it's so rich. The lifestyle is so rich – I have a love-hate thing with that lifestyle.

I don't think I've ever seen freezeframes used in such a dramatic way – freezing a moment and bringing the narrative to a halt.
That comes from documentaries. Images would stop; a point was being made in his life. Everybody has to take a beating sometime, BANG: freeze and then go back with the whipping. What are you dealing with there? Are you dealing with the father abusing Henry – you know, the usual story of, 'My father beat me, that's why I'm bad.' Not necessarily. You're just saying, 'Listen, I take a beating, that's all, fine.' The next thing, the explosion and the freezeframe, Henry frozen against it – it's hellish, a person in flames, in hell. And he says, 'They did it out of respect.' It's very important where the freezeframes are in that opening sequence. Certain things are embedded in the skull when you're a kid.

The freezeframes are basically all Truffaut. [The style] comes from the first two or three minutes of *Jules and Jim*. The Truffaut and Godard techniques from the early sixties that have stayed in my mind –what I loved about them was that narrative was not that important: 'Listen, this is what we're going to do right now and I'll be right back. Oh, that guy, by the way, he got killed. We'll see you later.'

Ernie Kovacs was that way in the fifties in TV. I learned a lot from watching him destroy beautifully the form of what you were used to thinking was the television comedy show. He would stop and talk to the camera and do strange things; it was totally surreal. Maybe if I were of a different generation I would say Keaton. But I didn't grow up with Keaton, I grew up with early TV.

Or if you're my generation it would be **Pee Wee's Playhouse.**
Yeah, again, breaking up a narrative – just opens up a refrigerator, there's a whole show inside, and closes the door. That's great. I love Pee Wee Herman. I tape the show. We had them sent to Morocco when we were doing *Last Temptation*; on Sundays we'd watch it on PAL system. Yeah. [*laughs*]

GoodFellas *uses time deletions during many scenes: you see someone standing by the door, then they're suddenly in the chair, then –*

It's the way things go. They've got to move fast. I was interested in breaking up all the traditional ways of shooting the picture. A guy comes in, sits down, exposition is given. So the hell with the exposition – do it on the voiceover, if need be at all. And then just jump the scene together. Not by chance. The shots are designed so that I know where the cut's going to be. The action is pulled out of the middle of the scene, but I know where I'm going to cut it so that it makes an interesting cut. And I always loved those jump cuts in the early French films, in Bertolucci's *Before the Revolution*. Compressing time. I get very bored shooting scenes that are traditional scenes.

In this film, actually the style gave me the sense of going on a ride, some sort of crazed amusement-park ride, going through the Underworld, in a way. Take a look at this, and you pan over real fast and, you know, it kind of lends itself to the impression of it not being perfect – which is really what I wanted.

That scene near the end, Ed McDonald talking to [the Hills] – I like that. [It's as if the movie] kind of stops, it gets cold and they're in this terrifying office. He's wearing a terrifying tie – it's the law and you're stuck. And they're on the couch and he's in a chair and that's the end of the road. That's scary.

When you're shooting and editing, how do you determine how much the audience can take in terms of information, shot length, number of cuts, etc.? Over the past decade our nervous systems have developed a much greater tolerance of sensory overload.

I guess the main thing that's happened in the past ten years is that the scenes have to be quicker and shorter. Something like *The Last Emperor*, they accept in terms of an epic style. But this is sort of my version of MTV, this picture. But even that's old-fashioned.

Is there a line you won't cross in terms of editing speed, how fast to play scenes?

The last picture I made was 'Life Lessons' in *New York Stories*. And that's pretty much the right level. *GoodFellas* lends itself to a very fast-paced treatment. But I think where I'm at is really more the *New York Stories* section. Not *Last Temptation*. *Last Temptation*, things were longer and slower there because, well, of a certain affection for the story and for the things that make up that story. And the sense of being almost stoned by the desert in a way, being there and making things go slower; a whole different, centuries-earlier way of living. *New York Stories* had, I think, maybe a balance between the two. The scenes went pretty crisp, pretty quickly. There were some montage sequences. But still I'd like to sustain [the moments].

In *GoodFellas*, that whole sequence I really developed with the actors, Joe Pesci's story and Ray responding to him, it's a very long sequence. We let everything play out. And I kept adding setups to let the whole moment play out. But if what the actors were doing was truthful or enjoyable enough, you can get away, with it.

The 'What's so funny about me?' scene in the restaurant between Liotta and Pesci was improvised?

Totally improv – yeah. It's based on something that happened to Joe. He got out of it the same way – by taking the chance and saying, 'Oh, come on, knock it off.' The gentleman who was threatening him was a friend, [but] a dangerous person. And Joe's in a bad state either way. If he doesn't try laughing about it, he's going to be killed; if he tries laughing about it and the guy doesn't think it's funny, he's going to be killed. Either way he's got nothing to lose. You see, things like that, they could turn on a dime, those situations. And it's just really scary.

Joe said, 'Could I please do that?' I said, 'Absolutely, let's have some fun.' And we improvised, wrote it down, and they memorised the lines. But it was really finally done in the cutting with two cameras. Very, very carefully composed. Who's in the frame behind them. To the point where we didn't have to compromise lighting and positions of the other actors, because it's even more important who's around them hearing this.

What about the continuation of the scene with the restaurant owner asking for the money?
Oh, that's all playing around, yeah. That kind of dialogue you can't really write. And the addition of breaking the bottle over Tony Darrow's head was thought of by Joe at lunchtime. I got mad at him. I said, 'How could you – why now, at lunch? Now, we've got to stop the shooting. We've got to go down and get fake bottles.' He said, 'Well, couldn't we maybe do it with a real bottle?' 'No.' 'Well, maybe we could throw it at him?' 'No, no, that's not as good.' 'How about a lamp? Let's hit him with a lamp.' So we tried hitting him with different things. It was actually one of the funniest days we ever had. Everybody came to visit that day. And I don't like visitors on the set, but that was a perfect time to have them visit because most of the laughter on the tracks that you hear is people from behind the camera, me and a lot of Warners executives who showed up.

The real improvs were done with Joe and Frank Severa, who played Carbone, who kept mumbling in Sicilian all the time. And they kept arguing with each other. Like the coffee pot: 'That's a joke. Put it down. What, are you going to take the pot?' – he was walking out with the pot. It's more like telling him, even as an actor, 'Are you out of your mind? Where are you going with the coffee? We don't do that.' Another killing, Joe says, 'Come on, we have to go chop him up.' And Frank starts to get out of the car. And Joe says, 'Where are you going, you dizzy motherfucker? What's the matter with you? We're going to go chop him up here.' Frank's impulse was to get out of the car. So Joe just grabbed him and said, 'What are you doing?' They improvised.

Did you ever get feedback from the underworld after* Mean Streets*?
From my old friends. A lot of the people that the film is about are not Mafia.

Nick mentioned that the real-life Paulie Cicero never went to the movies, never went out, didn't have telephones, you know. So one night the guys wanted to see this one particular movie, and they just grabbed him and threw him in the car and took him to see the film. It was *Mean Streets*. They loved it. So that was like the highest compliment, because I really try to be accurate about attitude and about way of life.

Opposites
and Extremes

SLOUCHING TOWARD HOLLYWOOD
By Peter Biskind

Martin Scorsese is killing time. Dressed in a crisp khaki shirt and pressed blue jeans, with a tiny white bichon frise named Zoe tucked under his arm, he is waiting for the sun to go behind a cloud so the next shot will match the last one. He is near the end of the *Cape Fear* shoot in front of a produce stand just outside Fort Lauderdale, Florida. With him are Nick Nolte, Jessica Lange, and Juliette Lewis playing a married couple and their daughter fleeing from a psycho who is stalking them.

While he waits, Scorsese's hand rarely leaves the side pocket of his custom-made jeans, where he works his watch chain like worry beads. He used to have Armani make his jeans, but he felt guilty wearing them. He orders new ones every two years, and since he can't bear to throw away even the most threadbare, his collection goes back fifteen years.

The sun finally goes in. Nolte is on his mark in an instant. Lange is immersed in *The New York Times*. 'You can do it, Jessica,' Nolte calls. 'Just put one foot in front of the other.' (They've been ragging each other throughout the shoot – Nolte dropping his pants, Lange refusing to go to the set until 'everything is put away'.) Lange finally arrives at her position, and they walk through the scene.

'Nah, nah, nah – too long!' snaps Scorsese with his trademark machine-gun delivery. 'We've gone through four bars of the theme of *Psycho*. Start them closer to the car.'

'I've moved them from pepper to lettuce,' says an assistant director.

'Start them at the okra.'

'You know okra?' the A.D. inquires of Lange.

'Yeah, I know okra.'

Starting from the okra, Lange, Nolte, and Lewis walk quickly to their Jeep Cherokee. The scene is wrapped.

For most directors, this shot would be a throwaway. But for Scorsese, there's no such thing as a throwaway. 'The hardest thing to do is get people into a car – to make it interesting,' he explains. 'It's all about the philosophy of the shot. Those people were beaten into the ground. They didn't want to talk to each other.' So he decided to start wide. 'You have to see the family as a unit, broken up and terrified as it is, and then move into Nick's face, pan to Jessica, and pan back over. Then actually zoom into Jessica looking out, pan across the kid onto Nick's face, so determined to get his family out of there. That's finally the move I used.'

Cape Fear is Scorsese's fourteenth feature. With a budget of approximately $34 million, it is the most expensive picture to date from a director who has always pinched pennies. It is the first fruit of a comfortable six-year deal with Universal Pictures for

Grandfatherly Scorsese directs five-year-old Tulku Tenzin in Kundun *(1997). Still influenced by his Catholic upbringing, he shared the growing Western interest in Buddhism.*

a director who has never had better than a two-picture deal anywhere. The film was initiated by Steven Spielberg and is being co-produced by his company, even though no one could be further from Spielberg's sensibility than Scorsese. And it is a remake of a 1962 studio thriller, from a director who disdains remakes. This project, in other words, is very much a paradox, a bow in the direction of the mainstream from the ultimate outsider.

Shot in CinemaScope, *Cape Fear* is emblematic of Scorsese's love/hate relationship with Hollywood, an ambivalence the industry is more than happy to reciprocate. He is widely considered one of America's most brilliant directors, one of a select circle of contemporaries that includes Stanley Kubrick and Woody Allen, within shouting distance of masters like Akira Kurosawa. His greatest film, *Raging Bull*, was selected as the best film of the eighties by an outstanding array of critics. Yet Scorsese has been mocked and reviled in Hollywood.

Last year, he came back from a ten-year drought with *GoodFellas*, selected as best film of the year by the New York, Los Angeles, and National societies of film critics. Since then, Scorsese has been showered with honorary degrees and has been the subject of books and documentaries too numerous to mention. He has virtually become a national institution. It's a heavy burden to shoulder, and no one is more aware of that than the director himself.

'You have more to lose,' says Scorsese, gazing at the view from his apartment window, 75 storeys over midtown Manhattan. 'Would it be a different risk if every picture I made was about Italian Americans in New York? I don't think so. Because they'd say, "That's all he can do." So I'm trying to stretch.' His next picture is a good example. *The Age of Innocence* is based on an Edith Wharton novel and set in the very unmean streets of upper-crust New York, circa 1870. It's not the movie of a man content to rest on his laurels . . .

Now the days of drugs and even asthma are behind him. 'I haven't had a serious attack in more than a year,' he says. With the relative security of his Universal deal and his apparently unassailable critical status, life seems to be looking up. Or does it? He's worried about the perception of him as a film artist – the '*a*-word', as he calls it – and corrects himself when he inadvertently uses the term 'cinema' instead of 'movies'. 'I don't want anybody to think we're talking about art,' he says. 'It's a stigma in the commercial area of movies. A stigma.'

He's angry and disappointed that he didn't win an Oscar for *GoodFellas*. 'I wish I could be like some of the other guys and say, "No, I don't care about it." But for me, a kid growing up on the Lower East Side watching from the first telecast of the Oscars, and being obsessed by movies, there's a certain magic that's there. When I lost for *Raging Bull*, that's when I realised what my place in the system would be, if I did survive at all: on the outside looking in. The Academy sent out a very strong message to the people who made *GoodFellas* and *The Grifters*, no matter how talented they are, that they may get some recognition, but they will not get the award. It just turns out that I produced *The Grifters*. And I certainly got the message.'

Scorsese is philosophical about it, sort of. But his friends and collaborators are not. Says Jodie Foster, 'When you look at the ten old ladies who put down *Dances with*

Wolves instead of *GoodFellas* – I don't know. The Oscars are like bingo. Who cares?' And Paul Sorvino, who played Paul Vario in *GoodFellas*, says, 'It's an outrage and a scandal in my mind. What does the man have to do?' Harvey Keitel sums it up: 'Maybe he got what he deserves – exclusion from the mediocre.'

With his recent success and his virtual canonisation, the pressures upon him have, if anything, increased. Bigger budgets, more responsibility (he's producing *Mad Dog and Glory*, from a Richard Price script, starring De Niro and Bill Murray). He's joined forces with Spielberg on *Cape Fear*, and he's moving from his cluttered office in the historic Brill Building on the seedy West Side of New York to MCA's sleek East Coast corporate headquarters on Park Avenue. The move across town is as much symbolic as physical. It could well be the beginning of Marty's Excellent Adventure, his attempt to enter the mainstream on his own terms. The risks are great: commercial failure on the one hand, selling out on the other. 'You wanna audience,' says Price, who wrote *The Color of Money*, 'you gotta play ball. He wants to make big personal movies – the best actors he can get, the biggest audience he can get, to make the smallest films he can make.'

Paul Schrader speculates about the direction of Scorsese's career: '*Cape Fear* is the first time he's worked with such a large budget since *New York, New York*, and it demands an audience level and a mainstream sensibility that he's not completely comfortable with. Marty's a conglomerate now. But I think at the end of the day, no matter how hard he tries to sell out, he can't really do it. The thing with Spielberg is a marriage of convenience. We're talking Warren Beatty and Madonna.'

Scorsese tried very hard not to get involved with *Cape Fear*. 'Bob De Niro and Spielberg asked me to read the script while I was finishing up *GoodFellas*,' he recalls. 'And by the end of the editing of the film, I had read *Cape Fear* three times. And three times I hated it. I mean really hated it.' The original script took its cues from the 1962 movie, which starred Gregory Peck as an improbably virtuous family man and Robert Mitchum as the psycho, Max Cady, who gets out of jail and goes after Peck for testifying against him. 'I thought the family was too clichéd: too happy,' says Scorsese. 'And then along comes the boogeyman to scare them. They were like Martians to me. I was rooting for Max to get them.' But Spielberg and De Niro, who wanted to play Cady, wouldn't take no for an answer. 'Finally, Steve says, "Marty, you dislike this version of the script?" I said "Yes! Whaddya want from me?" He said, "Why don't you rewrite it?" And I said, "Of course!"'

Scorsese Freudianised – or, as he prefers to think of it, Catholicised – the script. It became a drama of sexual guilt and punishment. He shifted the focus to the emotional pathology of the family, with Lange suffering from the after-effects of Nolte's infidelity and Nolte trying to deal with his daughter's emerging sexuality. 'Cady was sort of the malignant spirit of guilt, in a way, of the family – the avenging angel,' Scorsese says. 'Punishment for everything you ever felt sexually. It is the basic moral battleground of Christian ethics.'

Scorsese pauses, laughs. 'This sounds like every other picture I've ever made. I could talk this to death. It's ridiculous, but I've got to be careful. Otherwise, people say, "It's some sort of religious film. I don't want to see it." Don't listen to any of this! It's a thriller. Go see it! Enjoy yourself!'

De Niro as Max Cady in Cape Fear *(1991). Embellishing on the more laconic performance by Robert Mitchum in the 1962 original, his Cady is a white-trash avenger.*

When all is said and done, Scorsese has been fortunate. Despite, or rather because of, his failures and struggles, his wanderings on the wild side, he is perhaps the only filmmaker from that enormously hopeful generation of the seventies to have truly fulfilled his promise. Some, like Coppola, have made great movies – *The Godfather*s, *The Conversation, Apocalypse Now* – but Scorsese has done more than that. He's made a career. He's survived in a business notorious for burning out talent and has arrived at the nineties at the peak of his creative powers. *GoodFellas* was so assured, so perfectly realised, that it is hard to imagine he will stumble as badly as he did in the eighties. 'Maybe it was because I fell from grace earlier,' he says. 'Maybe because other people went through the terror later, so it was harder for them to come back.'

The movies have always been Scorsese's life. But along the way he picked up a considerable amount of baggage, including four wives and two daughters. Now approaching 50, he has had to make difficult choices. 'I just started divesting myself of all these complications. Your personal life, you know, you deal with as best you can. But you even divest that.

'All the way up until, I'd say, '84, '85, every Sunday my mother and father, my friends would come over. We'd have a big Italian dinner. Whatever different marriages – whatever was going on. It was really good, like the Italian family that I remember growing up. But I don't expect much from people anymore, and I don't really want them to expect much from me. Except when it comes to the work, [where] you're gonna get the best from me. You're alone. That's the way it goes.'

The thing that may save Scorsese, finally, from the vertigo of fame is his humility before the shrine of 'cinema'. As much as he serves as mentor for struggling young directors, as much as he has become a force on the film-preservation scene, as much as he has matured into a disciplined director, he is in many ways still a student. As Barbara Hershey puts it, 'His love of film over himself is the great leveller.'

'You've gotta be careful,' says Scorsese, 'because you hear talk: "Well, Marty, people say in Hollywood, your films are really good and you're one of the best around . . . ." It's an odd thing. You can't believe it, first of all. I think a lot of the pictures I've made are good. But they're not *The Searchers*. They're not *81/2*. *The Red Shoes*. *The Leopard*. What I'm saying is I have my own criteria in my head that's private. There's constantly a test. Constantly a final exam every minute of my life. Literally, I have the image of myself always keeping my nose right above the water, the waves always getting to me and about to sink me . . . I just hope that, you know, *Cape Fear* makes money.'

SACRED AND PROFANE
By J. Hoberman

The young Jean-Luc Godard wrote of Nicholas Ray that if the cinema no longer existed, Ray alone would be capable of inventing it and, what's more, of wanting to. Looking at the roster of current American directors, the same might be said (and often is) of Martin Scorsese. Steven Spielberg has made more money, Woody Allen has received more accolades, Oliver Stone (a former student) has reaped bigger headlines – but nobody has made better movies. Scorsese is Hollywood's designated maestro: the most celluloid-obsessed and single-minded film-maker in Hollywood, the one American director that Spike Lee would deign to admire.

Although *Taxi Driver* and the title song from *New York, New York* are the only Scorsese artefacts to embed themselves in American mainstream consciousness (a television series based on *Alice Doesn't Live Here Anymore* barely lasted one season), Scorsese has never lacked for critical support. *Mean Streets* was the most highly praised debut of the seventies; *Raging Bull* topped several polls as the best American movie of the eighties; *GoodFellas* received virtually every critics' award in 1990. Even his so-called flops – the brilliant *King of Comedy*, engaging *After Hours*, and heartfelt *Last Temptation of Christ* - have had their defenders.

Perhaps hoping to repay Universal for bankrolling his magnificent obsession, *The Last Temptation of Christ*, Scorsese has entered into an exclusive six-year directing and producing deal with the studio and succumbed, at last, to remakitis. With his edgily overwrought *Cape Fear* remake, he has concocted an admittedly commercial thriller more skilful than inspired and at least as cerebral as it is gut-twisting.

The first *Cape Fear* (1962, released by Universal International) was knocked off by British director J. Lee Thompson between the martial epics *Guns of Navarone* and *Taras Bulba*. The hero, Sam Bowden (Gregory Peck), was an upstanding Georgia prosecutor who, some years before, had testified against one Max Cady (Robert Mitchum) in a particularly vicious rape case. The plot thickens when Cady, having served his time, comes looking for revenge, presumably to be inflicted on Bowden's wife and daughter.

Undeniably disturbing (the original trailers promised movie-goers that they were going to 'Feel Fear!'), Thompson's movie derived much of its frisson from Cady's antisocial assault on the goody-goody culture of the fifties. With the judicious Peck seemingly preparing for his Oscar-laureate role as the saintly Southern lawyer in Universal's *To Kill a Mockingbird*, which opened six months later, and his wife and daughter (TV personalities Polly Bergen and Lori Martin) so sitcom wholesome, one might well sympathise with the villain – at least at first.

The heavy, deceptively somnolent Mitchum – an action star with a hipster edge, having been busted for pot in the late forties – brought a brute physicality and unprecedented sexual sadism to his characterisation. Barry Gifford, who would later pay homage to *Cape Fear* by incorporating its eponymous location in his meta-*noir* novel *Wild at Heart,* calls Mitchum 'the angel of death-with-pain, put on earth to give men pause'. But although *Cape Fear* is as much horror film as thriller – with Mitchum's virtually unkillable monster anticipating the slashers of the late seventies – there is another, equally disturbing subtext lurking in the film.

Cady wants to spook Bowden before he destroys him, and for much of the movie he is protected by the very law he places himself beyond. Set in the South and released at the height of the struggle for desegregation, *Cape Fear* conjures up the bogie of a terrifying rapist – albeit white – who proved inconveniently conversant with his 'civil rights'. In its nightmarish way, *Cape Fear* managed to suggest both what terrified the white South and the terror the white South itself inspired. 'You won't forget this movie,' Gifford ends his critique, 'especially if you're a Yankee Jew.'

In general, *Cape Fear* was received with trepidation. The film's British opening was delayed until early 1963, while Thompson and Lord Morrison, president of the British Board of Censors, argued over cuts. (The movie was eventually released with six minutes trimmed.) Calling it 'a nasty film', Lord Morrison objected to the sexual threat Mitchum posed to Lori Martin. Nor was the British censor alone. Pit in *Variety*, Dwight MacDonald in *Esquire* and Bosley Crowther in the *New York Times* all warned readers against bringing their children, Crowther adding that *Cape Fear* was 'one of those shockers that provoke disgust and regret'.

Of course, disgust and regret are scarcely emotions to make Martin Scorsese flinch, and he would doubtless endorse the sense the 1962 movie left that civilisation's veneer is somewhat less sturdy than the shell of an egg.

Scorsese's *Cape Fear* opens with the camera rising from the depths of the primordial swamp where all the protagonists will ultimately swim. Although the ensuing sense of beleaguered middle-class territoriality is as strong as ever, the new *Cape Fear* complicates the moral equation by shifting focus from Max Cady, flamboyantly played by Robert De Niro, to the Bowden family. In this *Cape Fear*, the Bowdens' lives are built on quicksand. Scorsese undermines their solidarity, wipes his hands on their reputations, sullies their laundry with a miasma of guilt.

Not simply a concerned citizen, the new Sam Bowden turns out to have been Cady's public defender against a particularly brutal charge of rape, who buried evidence of the victim's promiscuity so as not to jeopardise his client's conviction. The self-righteousness inherent in sensitive Peck has here coalesced into uptight Nick Nolte – a man built to absorb punishment, even as his menacing bulk suggests Mitchum's. As his wife Leigh (renamed for Janet?), Jessica Lange looks just as classy as precursor Polly Bergen, but she's considerably more bitter and a lot less supportive. Their teenage daughter Danielle, played by Juliette Lewis, is ripe and dishevelled, braces gleaming out of her unformed face. (Does Marty know how to pick them? Not long after *Cape Fear*'s US release Lewis replaced Emily Lloyd as the nymphet in Woody Allen's current project.)

Whereas in 1962 evil stalked the Bowden family from without, the threat is now to be found within. They are, as current parlance would have it, *dysfunctional*. Leigh not irrationally suspects Sam of having an affair; to block out their screaming, Danielle – who is recovering, it is suggested, from a precocious drug problem – locks herself in her bedroom, flicks on both MTV and the radio and begins compulsively dialling her Swatch phone, as instinctive an ostrich as the rest of her clan. Meanwhile, his release from prison heralded by a drumroll of thunder, Cady is the return of Bowden's repressed – telling him later that while the judge and DA 'were just doing their jobs', Bowden betrayed his trust.

Even more than in the original, it's difficult not to feel a sneaking sympathy for Cady, particularly when the more physically imposing Bowden is trying to buy him off, or, later, hiring goons to run him out of town. This Cady is less the snake in the Bowden family Eden and more the projection of their unconscious fears. Indeed, he first appears to them in precisely that fashion. Shuffling into a movie house (showing the horror comedy *Problem Child*), Cady positions himself directly in front of the family, blocks the screen and, brandishing his cigar while laughing like a hyena, subjects them to what must be the film buff's ultimate violation. 'Dad, you should have just punched him out,' Lewis admonishes Nolte, unaware that they've just encountered implacable evil.

Cross played across his back, religious mantras inscribed on his arms, De Niro's Cady is a self-taught psychopath and a refugee from Kafka's penal colony, as much a mythological beast as any unicorn or yeti. Although it's tempting to read his character as Scorsese's revenge on the Christian fundamentalists who attacked *The Last Temptation of Christ*, it's difficult to conceptualise the sort of born-again Baptist who would pray to Jesus beneath a Stalin pin-up and augment the scriptures with a combination of *Thus Spake Zarathustra* and Henry Miller. A two-bit De Sade with delusions of grandeur, Cady sees himself as avenging angel. By opening the family up to his blandishments, *Cape Fear* has perverse intimations of *Teorema* as well as *Straw Dogs*.

Johnny Boy and Travis Bickle, Jake La Motta and Rupert Pupkin have nothing on this nut. With his long black hair slicked back under a white yachting cap, mouth wrapped around the world's biggest cigar butt, and torso draped in a flaming Aloha shirt, De Niro is a cracker from hell. The conception is wildly baroque, and most of the time De Niro's Cady is more crazy than menacing. Although his tattooed slogans and religious rants evoke Mitchum's career performance as the psychotic preacher in *Night of the Hunter*, De Niro lacks Mitchum's insolent ease as a performer. His Max Cady is a riff and, half camping on his Southern drawl, he never lets you forget it.

The movie, too, is knowing without seeming felt. The rough sex here looks a lot rougher than it did in the original, but is actually less visceral. Where Mitchum cracks an egg on one of his victims, De Niro (like Dracula) takes a bite out of a woman's face. More overt too is the suggestion, repeated in various contexts throughout the film, that when a rape is reported, it is actually the victim who goes on trial. (Note: Even though *Cape Fear* opened the very day the American public was transfixed by allegations of sexual harassment and achieved box office saturation during the William Kennedy Smith rape trial, the operative movie metaphor for such cases remained *Fatal Attraction*. *Cape Fear*'s critique is softened by the use of the daughter's voiceover to frame the movie – the entire nightmare can thus be read as the hysterical fantasy of a teenage girl.)

In the movie's most daring set piece, De Niro makes a call to Lewis in the guise of her new drama coach (one more instance of subtext overwhelming narrative). The stunt nature of this self-reflexive turn is literalised by having the actor chat on the phone and even cue records while dangling upside down on his chinning bar (eventually the camera flips over as well). It's followed by another hot-dog scene in which, having lured Lewis down into her high school's basement and on to the stage where a play is to be rehearsed, De Niro seems determined to out-creep Willem Dafoe's 'seduction' of Laura Dern in *Wild at Heart*. This fairy-tale sequence in the make-believe gingerbread house ('I'm the Big Bad Wolf,' De Niro begins) has received near-universal acclaim. What's far more effective, however, is Nolte's subsequent rage at the nubile daughter with whom he can never quite make eye contact. 'Did he touch you? Wipe that smile off your face!' he screams when he discovers what happened. It's an indignity Gregory Peck never had to suffer – the autumn of the patriarch.

Does it sound as if *Cape Fear* is overdirected? The movie is undeniably gripping and it certainly looks great. Shot by Freddie Francis, director of the Hammer horror flicks beloved by Scorsese in his youth, it's a heady succession of extreme close-ups and artful reflections, luridly shimmering sunsets lit by flickers of heat lightning. If an unknown had signed *Cape Fear*, it would have been heralded as an impressive debut. (Consider the delirious overpraise that greeted *Dead Again*.) But Scorsese is no 25-year-old retooling antique genres, and more than one observer has attributed *Cape Fear*'s manic formalism to the director's alienation from the material (a similar hyper-kinetic frenzy is evident in his last commercial assignment, the 1986 *The Color of Money*).

Scorsese's relationship to *Cape Fear* is, however, more self-conscious and complex. No less than Godard, Scorsese is prodigiously movie-literate. His VCRs work overtime, he employs a full-time film archivist, spends thousands on prints, and has supervised the restoration and re-release of movies as varied as *Peeping Tom*, *Once Upon a Time in the West* and *Le Carrosse d'or*. His grasp of film history far exceeds that of most American critics and is far too sophisticated for him to attempt anything so crude as an unselfconscious remake – let alone a heedless obliteration of the original version. If anything, the new *Cape Fear* assumes that the viewer has seen the earlier one, perhaps even as recently as Scorsese himself.

In effect, Scorsese has taken a piece of hack work and, like the archetypal *auteur*,

Max Cady's prison tattoos in Cape Fear *have become iconic. Like his dialogue, they spit out a toxic mix of violent resentment and Christian sanctimony.*

filled it with his own directorial touches and perhaps subversive notions of guilt and redemption. Douglas Sirk is quoted in the film. As the *Nation*'s Stuart Kiawans observed in his suitably ambivalent review, 'History robbed Scorsese of the chance to be an *auteur* in the full, oppositional sense of the term. So now, as compensation, he's gone back 30 years and inserted himself into a studio product, *Cape Fear*, giving it the one thing it lacked in 1962 – a star performance by the director.'

The new *Cape Fear* oscillates between a critique of the original and a variation on a common text: it's a choreographed hall-of-mirrors, an orchestrated echo chamber. The first version resonates throughout the second – often literally. Elmer Bernstein stridently reworks the original Bernard Herrmann score. An aged Robert Mitchum appears as the local chief of police, and his deep drawl, first heard over the telephone, haunts the movie. Martin Balsam, who played the police chief in the 1962 version, has here been promoted to judge.

Scorsese's witty casting includes using the archetypal Southern vigilante, star of *Walking Tall*, Joe Don Baker, as a sleazy private eye whose idea of a mixed drink is Pepto-Bismol laced with Jim Beam. But the film's vertiginous sense of inversion is completed by the appearance of Gregory Peck as the enthusiastically slippery criminal lawyer who represents De Niro's smirking Cady. (It's as if Peck has become what he beheld.) Scorsese's remake thus contains its own negative image – a trope that's more than once utilised in the cinematography. *Cape Fear*'s tumultuous climax – a *tour de force* for De Niro, Scorsese, and mainly editor Thelma Schoonmaker – completes the role reversals by putting the lawyer Nolte on trial, even while the boat of civilisation spins out of control and cracks up on the rocks.

Although De Niro's final scene is as powerfully crafted an exit as that actor has ever made, the movie – like his performance – is a good deal more spectacular than terrifying, and somewhat less than the sum of its parts. Blood is not an abstraction; De Niro is. (I never thought I'd say this, but what *Cape Fear* needs is a shot of Paul Schrader – Cady's particular nexus of evangelical fervour, sexual guilt, and class resentment is more alluded to than fleshed out.) Like the villain, the location lacks specificity: it's a curiously all-white South.

Budgeted at $34 million, *Cape Fear* is Scorsese's most expensive movie, and his first commissioned project since *The Color of Money*. The project originated with Steven Spielberg, who interested De Niro in playing Cady, who then persuaded Scorsese to undertake a commercial thriller. And indeed, *Cape Fear* is structurally quite similar to Spielberg's *Hook*. A careerist father's failure to spend quality time with his children brings down a baroque threat to the family that can only be defeated by the father's capacity for regression. The difference is that *Hook* is filmically more impoverished, but psychologically far richer.

That absence of pathology seems to have left Scorsese with a guilty conscience. 'I think a lot of the pictures I've made are good,' he recently told *Premiere*. 'But they're not *The Searchers*. They're not *81/2*. *The Red Shoes*. *The Leopard*.'

Although it's a disservice to consider *Cape Fear* more than middling Scorsese, the film has received near-universal raves. The major exception is *New Yorker* critic Terence Rafferty, who, no less hysterical than those who hailed *Cape Fear* a masterpiece, termed the film 'a disgrace . . . ugly, incoherent, dishonest'. Rafferty echoes the original's reviews – including the brief mention that appeared in the *New Yorker* back in 1962: 'Everyone concerned with this repellent attempt to make a great deal of money out of a clumsy plunge into sexual pathology should be thoroughly ashamed of himself.' And money has been made. *Cape Fear*, which seems headed for a $70 million domestic gross, needed barely six weeks to surpass *The Color of Money* as Scorsese's most financially successful film. (His reassuringly *outré* follow-up project is an adaptation of Edith Wharton's novel, *The Age of Innocence*.)

Directors are manipulative by definition, but I've never met a film-maker more adept at enlisting critical sympathy than Scorsese. 'For Scorsese, there's no such thing as a throwaway,' Peter Biskind wrote in *Premiere*. 'He couldn't sell out if he wanted to,' enthused Richard Corliss in *Time*. Their characterisations are not exaggerated; neither is their support unwarranted. Other directors wax self-servingly sentimental about the art of the movies; Scorsese repeatedly pledges allegiance, spending time and money on the job of preservation.

In extolling Nicholas Ray, Godard was reviewing his less than epochal *Hot Blood* – 'a semi-successful film to the extent that Ray was semi-uninterested in it'. *Cape Fear* is a similar sort of semiotext. More than a critic's darling, Scorsese is a national treasure – the only director in Hollywood whose devotion to cinema justifies everyone's notions of popular art. We need him. He needs a hit. *Cape Fear* is a semi-sacrifice to that faith.

THE SCORSESE INTERVIEW
By Ian Christie

'"England" means tea shops, lager louts and sun-drenched cathedral closes,' according to Terry Eagleton in a recent piece on the artifice of the national idiom. Its potency, however, is undeniable, even in unlikely quarters. A tea shop hard by a cathedral close (York Minster, in fact) was part of the setting which helped Martin Scorsese to decide in January 1987 to film Edith Wharton's The Age of Innocence, *a passionately restrained tale, ironic and nostalgic in equal measure, an acerbic 'survivor's memoir' of belle époque New York. The lager louts might have seemed a more likely subject for Scorsese, but this is to underestimate the most ambitious and unpredictable film-maker at work in the United States today.*

I was travelling with Scorsese to ask the questions for what was to become Scorsese on Scorsese. *While I didn't notice that he was reading Edith Wharton on the long train journeys, he still vividly remembers finishing* The Age of Innocence *and thinks it was this experience – the picturesque winter landscape outside coupled with the pastness which Britain represents for an American – that helped him decide on what seems to many a bizarre choice for a film-maker still identified with the lowlife exploits of Johnny Boy, Travis Bickle and Jake La Motta.*

For Scorsese, his fans' oft-repeated plea that he should make another Mean Streets *or confine himself to the American hard-boiled genre is as mystifying as it is infuriating. His understanding of cinema is based on a respect for the idea of genre and on an appreciation of its niceties in countless local instances: not just a great gangster film or costume piece, but one made there, at this point in the national tradition, using those resources. It can sound to the uninitiated like a crazy scrambling of cinema history, but I think that for Scorsese the whole point is the poignancy of knowing that we are now irrevocably on the far side of classical film-making. However gifted a director is today, he or she can only be a Mannerist, condemned, like the artists who followed the High Renaissance, to echo and embellish the great unselfconscious works of the past.*

And so for Scorsese, how *he engages with tradition isn't just movie buffery: it is a vital creative issue. Collecting films, ensuring they are preserved by studios and archives, contacting and discreetly helping the 'great directors' (Fellini, Kazan, Kurosawa, Powell), working with collaborators who belong to traditions he admires (Freddie Francis, Michael Ballhaus, Boris Leven, Saul Bass, Elmer Bernstein) – all these are part of the process of finding a place for himself in a post-classical era. Frederic Jameson thinks of Godard's recent work as 'a survivor's modernism'. Scorsese's ambition is wider: he wants to make the past – both historic and cinematic – fully visible in the present, a country we can visit and marvel at.*

Set in New York in the 1870s, The Age of Innocence *tells the story of Newland Archer, who is engaged to May Welland, of the powerful Mingott family. A 'disgraced' member of May's family, Countess Ellen Olenska, returns from a disastrous marriage in Europe and is snubbed by New York society. Archer asks the powerful Van der Luyden family to host a dinner for the Countess to counter her exclusion. Archer falls in love with Ellen, but stifling social pressures prevent him from consummating their relationship and he is torn between his passion for the Countess and his life with May.*

You said that the atmosphere of England, where you finished reading The Age of Innocence, *helped you to decide to do it.*

There was something about the timing of reading the book at that point in my life, after a long struggle to get *The Last Temptation of Christ* made, and having always wanted to make a romantic piece. There was also the popularity of *A Room with a View* and pictures like it, which seemed to make working in this style possible. But I think finishing the book while travelling around England and Scotland – I seem to remember a big snowstorm – had a lot to do with it. Then it was a matter of cleaning up my creative life so that I could do it.

GoodFellas was being written in 1987 and when I was in England that was going to be my next film, but then we were able to slip in *The Last Temptation*. For the next two years I was mulling *The Age of Innocence* over in my head and scriptwriter Jay Cocks – who had given me the book in the first place – would come over once or twice a week, and we would discuss how to make it different from the usual theatre-bound film versions of novels.

It is surprising to hear that you were influenced by Merchant-Ivory films. Maybe you see these differently from the way we – or at least I – see them?

I only became aware of this attitude when I spoke to a British journalist while we were editing *The Age of Innocence*. He said something like, 'In England we think these films are easy.' Well, it's not at all easy to make this kind of film in America, especially since we no longer have studios that have all the props and sets. In fact, we were able to find most of our interiors in Manhattan, Brooklyn and the Bronx, but the neighbourhoods that used to surround them are completely gone. It's tragic. In the Merchant-Ivory films and in Polanski's *Tess*, England looks all of a piece. These films take you out of today and put you very securely in a world that looks more civilised – at least if you had enough money. And they really give you a sense of a world where it took a day to travel from one town to the next.

The foreigner's eye. Polanski shot Tess *in France and Merchant and Ivory, foreigners both, have created an England that seems more real, certainly more attractive, than the real thing. In any case, as Terry Eagleton has pointed out, the great English writers of the twentieth century weren't English at all: 'They were a Pole, two or three Americans and a clutch of Irishmen.' Englishness seems to be in the eye of the beholder.*

I like the beautiful detail in a lot of the Merchant-Ivory films that use English settings. One wide shot says it all. When Jim Ivory shoots a period room, the eye is there. Perhaps it's more in his cultural make-up to understand the décor, so that when he places the camera, it's right for that room, you really *see* the room and all its detail. I feel more comfortable placing a camera in an Italian restaurant, or a church or club, or a Lower East Side tenement. I was lucky that in the novel all those details about décor and dress and food are there.

You quote in your book that accompanies the film a sentence from the novel: 'They all lived in a hieroglyphic world, where the real thing was never said or done or even thought, but only represented by a set of arbitrary signs.' Is this why you paid so much attention to period detail in the film – and why you're irritated by all the talk about 'obsessive attention to detail', as if this comes from you?

Yes, it's all in the book. What seems to be description is in fact a clear picture of that culture, built up block by block – through every plate and glass and piece of silver-ware, all the sofas and what's on them. All this wealth of detail creates a wall around Newland Archer, and the longer he stays there, with these things becoming commonplace, the harder it will be for him to move out of that society.

Edith Wharton published the book in 1920, recalling a society that no longer existed after the war. Did you feel that you were showing Americans a period which most of them did not know existed?

Of course. And it was even more sumptuous than we show. I felt the film had to show a modern audience the blocks they put around Newland and people like him. But there's also an irony and a sarcasm in the presentation of that lifestyle – both in the way I tried to do it and in the way Wharton did it in the book. The décor had to become a character for me.

Jay Cocks showed the film to an audience of Wharton specialists which included R. E. B. Lewis, who wrote the Pulitzer Prize-winning biography. And he told me that their reaction was extraordinary, because every time a dinner service was shown or when Mrs. Mingott selected the silver plate, they laughed. They knew what the presentation of that particular piece meant. So when the Van der Luydens create a dinner for Countess Olenska, they are making a statement and daring people to go against them.

In the book there's a fantastic build-up to that dinner that tells you just how important the Van der Luydens are and how everyone in New York society acknowledges their status.

I tried to convey that by the attention given to the dinner itself – the centrepiece, the Roman punch – which is like having a triple high mass for a funeral rather than a regular low mass. They are saying, 'Not only will we defend you, but we are going to do so on the highest level. If anyone has a problem with that, they are going to have to answer to us.'

Just like in **GoodFellas** *. . .*

Exactly. It's a matter of 'You have a problem with that? Then you have a problem with me and let's settle it right now.' Or in this case, 'Oh very well. We're going to have to bring out the Crown Derby, aren't we?' I remember in *The Razor's Edge*, when Gene Tierney throws a plate at Herbert Marshall, he says, 'My goodness, the Crown Derby.'

Ellen (Michelle Pfeiffer) and Newland (Daniel Day-Lewis) in The Age of Innocence *(1993). Costume and décor were essential elements in adapting Edith Wharton's novel.*

It's the heavy artillery.

Absolutely. And the Wharton specialists loved it because they understood better than other people what those signals meant. It was important for me that real goodfellas would like *GoodFellas* and say that it was accurate – and they did. With *The Age of Innocence*, I think that even if ordinary people don't understand fully the significance of the different pieces of china, they will at least see that a lot of pomp and circumstance goes into certain sequences. And as it's not done by me, but by the characters, they get some understanding of the ritual.

Such occasions are the most official way they can sign someone on and make them credible in that society. For instance, when Ellen Olenska arrives late at the party given for her, it's not important to her. Next day Newland says, 'You know all New York laid themselves at your feet last night.' And she answers, 'Yes, it was a wonderful party.' The audience has to understand that this wasn't just a party, lady! Newland is in effect saying, 'I'm getting married to your family, and we have agreed to take on the disgrace of your separation from your husband and we are going to do it with a stiff upper lip. So you really should know what we are doing for you by putting on a party.'

There is something about social and professional ritual that fascinates you, whatever the setting or period. But now you seem to feel happier about moving away from your own experience.

One of the lines that led me to make *The Age of Innocence* was my interest in doing different kinds of genre film. I mean, there's a major part of me that says, 'Let's do a Western,' but it's not that easy. I have to find what's important for me in order to feel comfortable enough to wallow in the making of a film. So although this film deals with New York's 'aristocracy' and a period of New York history that has been neglected, and although it deals with codes and ritual, and with love that's not unrequited but unconsummated – which pretty much covers all the themes I usually deal with – when I read it, I didn't say, 'Oh, good – all those themes are here.' I was just hit by the impact of the sequence near the end where Newland tries finally to tell his wife May he'd like to leave – and by her response.

It all came together in that scene, and I loved the way I was led by Wharton down the path of Newland's point of view, in which he underestimated all the women, and how he wound up checkmated by them, and how his wife becomes the strongest of them all. I find that admirable. Even though I may not agree with May totally, I like the growth of her character from a young girl to the person who takes control. You see how important her role is in the second opera house scene, which is the first time May has worn her wedding dress since the wedding. We see her seated between her mother and Mrs. Van der Luyden – they have passed on the responsibility for continuing their lifestyle to her.

Ironically there seems to be more of you – your own desires and frustrations – in this movie than in some of your other films, even though it comes fully formed from Wharton and is set in such an apparently remote and artificial milieu.

There is. Sometimes when you fall in love you can't see what other people see. You become as passionate and obsessive as Newland, who can't see what's going on around him. That's the theme of *Taxi Driver* and of *Mean Streets* – it's a situation I've found myself in at times, and I've found the way it plays out so wonderful. But then Wharton goes beyond that and makes a case for a life that's not exactly well spent, but a life that happens to him. Newland has his children, then he finds out that his wife knew all along about his love for Ellen and even told his son about it. Basically he is what they call in America a stand-up guy – a man of principles who would not abandon his wife and children. When he really wanted something most, he gave it up because of his kid.

That's very interesting to me – I don't know if I could do the same. But I do know that there are a lot of people, even today, who would: it's about making a decision in life and sticking to it, making do with what you have. And then, of course, during the conclusion you realise that a generation has gone by. The children don't react in the same way; the First World War is looming ahead and they can't understand why everybody was angry. I don't say it's a happy ending, but it's a realistic and beautiful one.

I think there was a strong emotional reaction at the screening I attended. It was at the Odeon Marble Arch, our biggest screen, and the sensory impact of the film was extraordinary.

That's great, because the emotional intensity is very important to me. What kept me going as I was reading the book was what a writer friend of mine called 'the sweet romantic pain' of the situation, where Newland and Ellen can't consummate their relationship. A touch of the hand has to suffice for months; the anticipation of a two-hour ride to a train station is so sweet, it's almost overwhelming. That was the real reason I wanted to make the film – the idea of that passion which involved such restraint.

A friend and colleague, John Gillett, told me that he thinks this carriage scene is one of the finest he has seen for a long time – and he hates **GoodFellas***! I think the films are very close: they both try to be truthful to the milieu in which they're set and to make you feel the emotion, the allure, the danger as something almost palpable.*

Like drowning in it. Actually there are elements of Rossellini in there, especially *La Prise de pouvoir par Louis XIV*, because that's where I discovered that the more detail you see, the better you know the people. Other films do that too, but Rossellini did it in a bolder way. In *Louis XIV*, he ties up the entire story in the presentation of a meal. In *The Age of Innocence* we have eight meals, and they are all different in order to make different dramatic points. But although *The Age of Innocence* may *look* lavish, the editing, the angles, the dissolves and the length of the images were all worked out way in advance to give the impression of extravagance. In fact, it only cost $32-34 million, and some of the most complicated things, like the beginning of the ball sequence, took only three-quarters of a day. But it was important to achieve the effect of a saturation of detail.

The Age of Innocence *is a very literary film – deliberately so. But it's not theatrical, except where you bring in theatre and opera as part of the period texture and a dramatic counterpoint to the unspoken story being acted out among the characters.*

One of the films that made a strong impression on me as a child was Wyler's *The Heiress*, which, though it's based on Henry James' novel *Washington Square*, was actually taken from a play. I've seen it since and it holds up well, but it is theatrical. The acting is extraordinary – Ralph Richardson, Olivia de Havilland, Montgomery Clift, Miriam Hopkins – but it's still in three acts: the conflicts are all played out in traditional dramaturgy; characters talk in a room and confront each other, all in dialogue. There is no narration, no montages, no flashbacks or flashes forward and no visual interpolations such as letters.

I'm trying to get away from this three act approach. Over the last ten years, I've found everyone in Hollywood saying: 'The script is good, but we need a new Act Two,' or, 'Act Three just isn't there.' Finally I said to a bunch of students: 'Why are we using the term "acts" when the damn thing is a movie?' I like theatre, but theatre is theatre and movies are movies. They should be separate. We should talk about sequences – and there are usually at least five or six sequences rather than three acts – which are broken up into sections and scenes. When I screened a few films for Elia Kazan back in 1992 and we discussed them afterwards, I found that he too was trying to get away from conventional theatrical dramaturgy in *East of Eden* and *Wild River* – neither of which, incidentally, he'd seen since he made them!

I certainly tried to find a different structure for *GoodFellas*, though that was more like a documentary on a lifestyle. For *The Age of Innocence* I wanted to find a way of making something literary – and you know how America is cowed by the tyranny of the word – also filmic. I also wanted a massive use of voiceover because I wanted to give the audience the impression I had while reading the book.

The experience of watching a film is often closer to reading than to watching a play. **The Age of Innocence** *made me think of Max Ophuls – the most literary and even theatrical of film-makers, but also the most filmic. It's about creating and manipulating the spectator's point of view, in time through voiceover and in space through those devastating camera movements.*
I adore Ophuls and we looked at the new print of *Lola Montès*. But for me, the major Ophuls film was *Letter from an Unknown Woman*. By a happy accident it seemed to be on television practically every afternoon when I was a child – that's the wonderful thing about Ophuls having made four American films – so when I was at home sick from school there would be *Letter from an Unknown Woman*. I couldn't tell at the time about camera moves, but I loved the romance and tragedy of it.

I thought that the way you move the camera so deliberately and eloquently in **The Age of Innocence** *is like the way Ophuls tracks and cranes, as if you've entered into the characters' emotions and memory.*
That's what I was hoping. I'll never forget the arrival of the piano up the staircase in *Letter from an Unknown Woman*. And then the depiction of a whole life in miniature and the sense of romance in the sequence where Louis Jourdan takes Joan Fontaine to the fairground train ride, and the fake backgrounds just slide past them. Ophuls created a world that was unique. Even though I'd seen other films set in Vienna at the turn of the century, they didn't have the grace and truth that Ophuls had in that film, which stood repeated viewing. I used to have a still on my wall in Hollywood of Louis Jourdan at the end, when he decides to go to the duel – that wonderful shot of him at the desk as he's reading the letter.

You have worked with a wide range of collaborators during your career: perhaps only De Niro and Thelma Schoonmaker recur regularly. But even as personnel come and go according to the demands of each film, there is a sense of 'family' about your method of working and a closeness with fellow-creators that you clearly seem to seek. Thelma Schoonmaker has always insisted that the Academy Award she got for the editing of **Raging Bull** *really belongs to you too, since you planned all the incredible distinctions and distortions in that film. I've seen the deluxe new editing suite you have, and I wonder how you work together in it?*
That's where the whole creative process happens. I sit in that chair behind her and we have worked out a system of red lights and buzzers to communicate with. It's set up for the way we like to work. Although I'm not in the editors' union, I did make my living as an editor for a while in the seventies, and I feel that working on the script and editing are my strong points, as opposed to understanding camera movement and lighting. I love editing. I love what you can do with a film, where you can cut and not cut. It's Eisenstein really.

The way I work now is that I lay out the editing pattern, and pretty much all the time I decide where to cut and what not to cut. But what Thelma does is to focus on the characters in the film. She'll say, 'Maybe we're losing some aspect of so-and-so here. Maybe we should change this performance of this one reading because it might indicate that she's not as sympathetic towards him and we want the audience to realise it at this point.

There's a lot of that kind of editing in *The Age of Innocence*. And in *Raging Bull* some scenes were written but there were also improvisations within the writing. So we would have ten good takes of Joe Pesci and twelve good takes of De Niro, and we would keep switching them around. 'Why don't we use Take Four again of Joe, because I think we lost something there,' she would say. Or, 'We lost something on De Niro there so maybe we should try Take Eight again.' It has more to do with the spiritual quality of what's happening with the people in the film that she is able to perceive and help balance out for me.

The actual cutting – well, there's pure Eisenstein stuff in *The Age of Innocence*, like when the wife gets up and walks over to him, and you see three cuts of her rising. That's something I can imagine in my head, draw the pictures, and say, 'Do this one here, that one there.' Then Thelma puts it together and I ask her what she thinks, and often she'll suggest changes.

It took a little longer to edit *The Age of Innocence*, mainly because of the dialogue scenes – trying to work out how long a pause should be. But because there is such an appetite for stories about our business and I had taken between nine and ten months – working with only *one* editor! – they painted this picture of me as someone 'obsessed with detail'. But editing is the most important original element of the film-making process, so why short-change it? It's a sorry state of affairs when just doing my job properly is described as 'obsessive'.

Many people will be surprised to hear that you don't consider yourself a camera and lighting expert when your images are among the most precise and purposeful in contemporary cinema. Since you started working more or less regularly with the German cinematographer Michael Ballhaus, a former colleague of Fassbinder, there has been more tracking and an increased tendency towards formal overhead and big close-up shots, functioning like tableaux and still-lifes. You seem to enjoy creating special 'mimetic' shots that encode an emotion or a vital plot point – like the famous experiments in variable camera speed for **Raging Bull**. *One such in* **The Age of Innocence** *is the opera-glass scan across the Met audience which reveals Countess Olenska to one of Newland's circle, the supercilious Larry Lefferts.*

It's such an important move that I felt that just putting a binocular masking over it wasn't enough. Also, it didn't duplicate what you would actually see if you were looking through opera glasses – not that everything has to be literal. But I wanted to give it more of an edge and make it more important when you finally see Ellen slipping into the box, so Michael and I devised a kind of stop-action photography where we took just one frame at a time and panned. Then we realised that this was going to be too fast, so we decided to print each frame three times. However, this was still too choppy for me, so just when we were finishing negative cutting I finally decided to dissolve between each set of three frames. It took quite a lot of work, going back to the lab countless times – as Thelma can tell you.

Rock and classic American pop have played such a memorable part in your films from the start that you're not usually associated with the 'symphonic' tradition of Hollywood music –

The Age of Innocence is seen as an atypical Scorsese movie – the director counters this by pointing to the tension in the stillborn love of Newland Archer and Countess Olenska.

unlike De Palma and Spielberg. But using Bernard Herrmann for **Taxi Driver** *was a deliberate* **homage** *– and after two collaborations with Elmer Bernstein it looks as though you have now been able to sign up fully to a tradition you admire.* **Cape Fear** *had Bernstein reworking Herrmann's music for the original film, of course, and Bernstein also did the score for* **The Age of Innocence.**

Using Bernstein is a matter of embracing the Hollywood tradition, and *The Age of Innocence* is the closest to a traditional Hollywood score I have ever worked with. I could have gone classical and scored the picture with period music in the way I had used popular music before, but I wanted to go the other way. It wasn't so much nostalgia for the sound of all those romantic films as a remembrance of the skill and artistry that used to be available – and still is with someone of Bernstein's stature.

Another link with the Hollywood past is Saul Bass, creator of a range of now classic title sequences which became indelibly linked with the image of the films they prefaced.

For me Bass is one of the key figures in American movies. His title sequences don't just capture the spirit of the movie you are about to see – in some cases they are better than the movie itself! He created a style and energy that give you a lift, prepare you for the picture and make you want to see what is going to happen over the next two hours. And they don't feel separate from the movie, they really seem part of it.

I didn't know that he was still working until I saw *The War of the Roses* with his credit at the end. I thought the titles for that were simple and interesting. At the time I was having a problem putting in the word 'GoodFellas' where I wanted it, because it was incorporated in the action. When he slams down the trunk and says, 'I want to be a gangster,' the lettering never seemed quite right. So I said, 'The only man who can really work this out is a guy named Saul Bass.' He did – and then we kept him on to do *Cape Fear*.

How did you actually work with Bass and his wife Elaine on **The Age of Innocence***?*
We just sent them a tape of the first 40 minutes that were edited. The opera sequence made it very clear in his mind what he wanted to do: opening on flowers and keeping text (which is from a book of etiquette of that period) superimposed over the images. And it was their idea to cut to the *Faust* overture.

Working with Bernstein, Bass, and with Freddie Francis as cinematographer on **Cape Fear** *isn't only because you admire these great names from the past – it's more like making a bridge between your own work and the period in which they gained their reputation.*
Exactly. Very often today you hear the phrase that someone has 'been round the block a lot' if they are over 70. My view is that maybe we should listen to what they have to say because they have more experience to bring to what we need. When I first worked with Saul and Elaine Bass on *GoodFellas* I saw right away that they hadn't lost any of what they had.

You are currently making a documentary about the history of American cinema for the BFI/Channel 4 series **100 Years of Cinema***. And of course you have been an active campaigner for film preservation and have a personal collection of an enviable scale and eclecticism. From my own recent viewing of very early American films, I realised that there is a near, quotation in* **The Age of Innocence** *when, in one of the rare exteriors, we see a striking image of a crowded street full of men clutching their hats against the wind.*
Yes, that comes from one of the films I saw through the Library of Congress. It's a 1903 film called *At the Foot of the Flatiron*, and it shows all those people bunched up on the sidewalk because no one wanted to walk on the street. This was a place that was always windy – before the rest of the skyscrapers were built the wind could blow right across the island. I also saw *What Happened on 23rd Street* and a lot of other early New York films. And what about that documentary from the first decade of the century you have in the BFI's *Early Russian Cinema* anthology – *The Fish Factory in Astrakan?* Those glimpses at the camera are really something.

What Happened on 23rd Street *– where the woman's skirt is blown up as she walks over a subway ventilation grid – is a forerunner of the famous gag from* **The Seven Year Itch** *with Marilyn Monroe. And the Flatiron intersection was also popular as a good place to see the wind reveal women's ankles.*
How do you see your new role as a practical cinema historian and cheerleader for the centenary?
We don't have the luxury of the thirteen-hour Kevin Brownlow-David Gill *Hollywood* series – which I think is quintessential – so this is just one aspect of a journey that I could take through American movies. It's like a little museum: I say we'll stop at this

display and another display, then maybe we'll pass up two others and go on to that one later. But it's difficult because there are so many things to show. For instance, I can't let this clip from *Force of Evil* play, because I have to keep it moving and make the points I want to make. The programme is subtitled *A Personal Journey through the Movies*, and I'm trying to direct it towards an audience of younger film-makers and students who may not be aware of certain kinds of pictures or of trends in American movies that interest me a great deal.

You are obviously getting a lot out of the process. It seems like a real outlet for all the enthusiasm and knowledge you have accumulated.
Absolutely. I hope that we can go on to do one on French and one on Italian cinema, just for America, and perhaps one on Britain too. These might actually be easier because there isn't the same pressure to cover everything.

Do you have any hopes for the centenary of cinema being a major cultural event, or do you think it will just be of interest to movie buffs?
I think it's going to be something very special – the only problem is that the Americans, the French and the British can't agree on which year! Nor can they agree on who invented it – which shouldn't even be in discussion since it's so obvious that it was a simultaneous invention, although Edison did try to take all the credit. Now it's clear that the Lumières and Friese-Greene and others were important too. I'm still hoping that Cinémemoire will do something major to celebrate the centennial.

And speaking of cultural difference, just tell all those people that *The Age of Innocence* is really not so extravagant. It's not as easy for Americans to make a film like that with real locations as it is for you here in England.

STYLE AS ATTITUDE: TWO FILMS BY MARTIN SCORSESE
By Richard Lippe

It is inconceivable that any critic who has seen a number of Martin Scorsese's films would reject the claim that the director is a stylist and that his work displays thematic consistency. But the claim, the basis of auteurist criticism, can have its drawbacks and particularly so when it leads to the kind of critical thinking that has greeted his two most recent films, *The Age of Innocence* (1993) and *Casino* (1995).The former was given a predominantly polite but cool reception because it wasn't the kind of project, a period piece and a melodrama, associated with Scorsese the director of *Mean Streets, Taxi Driver, Raging Bull* and *GoodFellas*; with the last, Scorsese was taken to task for supposedly retooling one of his former successes.[1] On the one hand, *GoodFellas* and *Casino do* have a lot in common: a) in addition to dealing with organised crime and having narratives which span decades, both films were adapted from fact-based books by Nicholas Pileggi, who, with Scorsese, co-authored the screenplays; b) the stylistic devices found in the two films include voiceover narration, freeze frames, flashbacks, rapid dolly moves; c) the films employ Scorsese's longstanding editor Thelma Schoonmaker, and features two of his regular actors, Robert De Niro and Joe Pesci. It is particularly Scorsese's use of Pesci which seems to have annoyed critics as the actor plays a similar role in both films and it was his *GoodFellas* performance that won Pesci an Academy Award. But while there are strong connections between Pesci's roles and his performances in *GoodFellas* and *Casino*, the two films provide the actor with distinctive characterisations. For instance, it is difficult to even imagine the Pesci character of *GoodFellas* being a caring father, which is what his character, although not without irony, is in *Casino*; also, Pesci's emotional relationship with the De Niro character in *Casino* is more complex than are any of his male or female relationships in *GoodFellas*. In any case, the fact that Pesci's roles share character traits and narrative functions doesn't necessarily make *Casino* a redundant film. Perhaps the critics who have expressed a dissatisfaction with *Casino* on the basis of Pesci's presence were looking for a convenient way to dispense with what is a rigorous, sombre and demanding film.

Before dealing with *Casino*, I want to briefly discuss *GoodFellas'* stylistics. *GoodFellas* is centred on Henry Hill/Ray Liotta, an Irish-Sicilian living in Brooklyn, who, as a teenager in the mid-fifties, begins working in a menial capacity for the Mob. The film covers approximately 30 years of Henry's life; in the early 1980s, Henry, realising that he is going to be killed because of who and what he knows, accepts an offer to testify against his long time Mafia friends, Jimmy Conway/Robert De Niro and Paul Cicero/Paul Sorvino. Scorsese's treatment of the material, which can be summarised as the story of a young man's aspirations to make good and be a somebody, is wonderfully encapsulated in the film's audacious opening credit sequence. The sequence begins with introductory credits by Elaine and Saul Bass; these initial credits, which move very rapidly across the screen from right to left, each being held briefly screen centre on their second appearance, are accompanied by a noise which sounds like a car on an open road speeding by. After an intertitle reading, 'This is based on a true story', there is a cut to a night time shot with the camera positioned behind a moving car; there is a second intertitle, 'New York 1970', and then a cut to the inside of the car. Henry, who is driving, begins to wonder what is making the clearly heard thumping sound which Jimmy and Tommy de Vito/Joe Pesci seem to be unaware of. There is a cut to the parked car and then a cut to the camera tracking in on the car's trunk and the origin of the thumping sound. In a rapid series of shots, a badly beat but alive man is seen in the trunk; Tommy lunges towards the man with a huge butcher knife and repeatedly stabs the man after which Jimmy shoots at the body. There is then a cut to Henry watching, a close shot of the bloodied body in the trunk and another cut to Henry as his voiceover narration begins with 'As far back as I can remember, I always wanted to be a gangster.' As Henry slams down the trunk cover, the camera tracks in on his face which is bathed in the red glow of the car's tail light. The tracking movement, which is abruptly halted by a freeze frame, is

Ace (De Niro) with trophy wife Ginger in Casino. *Criticised as a 'remake' of* GoodFellas, Casino *is both a critique of corporate values and a human tragedy on a grander scale.*

accompanied by an upbeat, jazzy instrumental introduction to Tony Bennett's florid rendition of the highly demonstrative 'Rags to Riches'. Next, there is a cut to the film's title which is in red letters on black; the film's other introductory credits follow but these, like the pre-title credits, are done in white lettering on black.

The film's opening sequence is startling. The viewer is subjected to a horrifying image and, given the circumstance, the absurdity of Henry's matter-of-fact claim regarding his ambition. The sequence's violence is too graphic, intense and abrupt to be read as other than suggesting a dramatic film but Henry's voiceover commentary suggests the sequence may be establishing the film as a black comedy. The sequence is, on the one hand, lurid and suggests an exploitation film but, on the other, it is Godardian in the sophisticated way it plays with generic expectations and such filmic codes as colour, music and narration. It not only establishes the film's disturbing emotional juxtapositions but also the way in which the film will deal with its characters and subject matter. Jimmy and Tommy are directly associated with violence and the latter is revealed to be psychotic. But these characters and the violence that they provoke aren't at any time given a subjective presentation. The viewer isn't put in the position of identifying with a violent character or someone who is the recipient of a violent act. Instead, the viewer is encouraged from the outset to relate to Henry and, later in the film, his wife Karen/Lorraine Bracco.

Following the opening credit sequence, Henry continues the voiceover narration, taking the viewer back to 1955 when his involvement with the Mob began. After

Henry becomes involved with Karen, she, too, although to a lesser extent, is given voiceover narration. Scorsese uses their commentary as a means to give *GoodFellas* an ongoing comic edge while maintaining the film's overall dramatic conception. Judging from the narration, both Henry and Karen think of themselves as average young people who have fallen in love, settled down and are doing their best to live a normal existence. And, although the film's visuals undercut or contradict this image, Henry and Karen are, nonetheless, highly accessible characters having middle-class values and capitalistic aspirations.

The undercurrent of absurdity that at times informs Henry's and Karen's direct address responses to their experiences is given a fuller definition in the film's last third which begins with the intertitle 'Sunday May 11th, 1980'. The segment, which is extensively narrated by Henry, chronicles his hectic schedule for the day and ends with him being busted by federal agents on a cocaine trafficking charge. And the segment's frantic pacing, which is controlled by the various domestic and business commitments Henry has to fulfil as the day goes on, functions to reflect his paranoiac, cocaine-induced behaviour. The segment is unlike any other in the film and, in the context of Scorsese's work, it evokes the feel of *After Hours'* (1985) dark humour but lacks the earlier film's overtly sinister, *noir*-like ambience; here, the environment is mundane, a benign-looking suburbia.

The above-mentioned segment concludes with Henry and Karen's arrest. After a series of short dramatic scenes in which the two realise that they are going to be killed by the Mafia and offer themselves to the government as witnesses in exchange for protection, the film, in its final sequence, patently calls attention to its already extensively foregrounded stylisation by further disrupting its 'realist' mode. In response to an accusation that he is an informer, Henry begins a monologue elaborating on the power he and the Mob had in its glory days. Henry, as he speaks, begins to look directly at the camera; he then gets down from the witness box and walks towards the camera continuing to address the viewer. After Henry says, 'I know it's all over,' there is a cut to a suburban housing development with the camera tracking left to right and stopping at the front door of the house Henry now inhabits under the Witness Protection Program. During the cut from the courtroom to the tracking movement, Henry's voiceover narration continues and he finishes the monologue on the front steps of his home saying, 'I am an average nobody, get to live the rest of my life like a shnook.' There is then a cut to Tommy who, earlier in the film, has been murdered by the Mafia. Tommy, in medium close-up, dressed in a flamboyant outfit which has no connection to the wardrobe he had previously worn, and looking directly at the camera, repeatedly fires bullets at the camera/viewer. Next, there's a cut back to Henry who turns his back to the camera and enters the house; as the door closes, the sound of a prison cell door being slammed shut is heard on the soundtrack. As the end credits start to roll, Sid Vicious's extraordinarily funky version of 'My Way', which already accompanied the shot of Tommy firing his gun, is given full play on the soundtrack.

The stylisation of the film's concluding scenes complements the opening credits. In both instances, Scorsese is playful with the material and undercuts the seriousness of the film's tone. In the film's final scenes in which Henry directly confronts the camera/viewer, Scorsese boldly acknowledges the intimacy that has been construct-ed between Henry and the viewer through his ongoing narration. The insert of Tommy, which to a knowledgeable viewer might suggest the famous shot of the rob-ber directly firing his pistol at the viewer in Edwin S. Porter's *The Great Train Robbery* (1903), functions to position the film's violence and Tommy himself as 'theatrical' and as a 'construction'. Scorsese provides an almost Brechtian conclusion to the film. *GoodFellas* isn't a comedy and it isn't fully a 'gangster film' in the conventional sense. Given the film's emphasis on the Liotta character who remains, despite everything, something of the All-American boy, *GoodFellas* can be taken as a heavily ironic but sobering version of the American success story. The film is often funny, energetic, immensely entertaining and an example of cinematic virtuosity.

As he does with *GoodFellas*, Scorsese uses the opening sequences of *Casino* to establish its thematic tone. In a pre-credit scene, Sam 'Ace' Rothstein/Robert De Niro is seen exiting a building and heading towards a parked car; as he walks from the building to the car, Ace's voiceover narration is heard: 'When you love someone, you've gotta trust them. There is no other way. You've gotta give them the key to everything that's yours. Otherwise, what's the point? And, for awhile, I believed, that's the kind of love I had.' The next shot shows Ace entering the car and turning on the ignition which causes the car to explode. As flames fill the entire screen, Bach's *St. Matthew Passion* is heard and the film's credits, again designed by Elaine and Saul Bass, begin. The Basses' credits are both visually beautiful and thematically concise: the credits begin by showing Ace's body hurtling through the flames but these images are gradually replaced by a series of extreme close-ups of brightly coloured neon signs; as the credits approach their conclusion, Ace's body is again seen, now falling in a spiral movement into the flames which have been superim-posed on the neon.[2] Another superimposition is used – Ace, in silhouette, is seen standing in a casino and, as his image is lit, his voiceover narration is reintroduced: 'Before I ever ran a casino or got myself blown up, Ace Rothstein was a hell of a hand-icapper. I can tell you that. I was so good that whenever I bet I could change the odds for every bookmaker in the country. I am serious. I had it down so cold that I was given paradise on earth. I was given one of the biggest casinos in Las Vegas to run, the Tangiers, by the only kind of guys that can actually get you that kind of money, 62 million, seven hundred thousand dollars.' At this point, there is a cut to a shot of Mafia mobsters sitting around a table while Ace, discussing the casino set-up, says, 'I don't know all the details.' The line of dialogue is followed immediately by a cut to a shot of Nicky Santoro/Joe Pesci and his friends with Nicky saying, 'Matter of fact, nobody knows all the details.' Nicky then goes on to introduce himself, tells the view-er he is Ace's best friend, mentions Ginger McKenna/Sharon Stone(who is seen in an insert, followed by an insert of Ace), identifying her as the woman Ace loved and concludes the narration by saying: 'But, in the end, we fucked it all up. It should have been so sweet too. But it turned out to be the last time that street guys like us were ever given anything that fucking valuable again.'

Casino's opening segment introduces the film as a strictly dramatic work; it estab-lishes the bond between Ace and Nicky and their joint narration of the film; and, with the image of Ace's rigged car exploding, the solemn music and the content of

Glamorous Ginger (Sharon Stone) rolls the dice in Casino *(1995). Scorsese depicts her descent into cocaine addiction with an authenticity born of bitter experience.*

the voiceover narrations, the film foregrounds the narrative's trajectory – the viewer is told that *Casino* is about failure, loss and death. The tone Scorsese sets links *Casino*, not to *GoodFellas*, but to *Raging Bull* and *The Age of Innocence*, and it, like those films, consistently refuses to provide the viewer with easy gratification. For instance, although *Casino* heavily employs voiceover narration, the film doesn't attempt to solicit viewer empathy with either Ace or Nicky. The two, like Ginger, the film's other major character, remain inaccessible as identification figures: Nicky is a psychotic and Ace and Ginger lack sufficient vulnerability to be fully appealing. And yet, *Casino*, arguably, provides a more deeply felt emotional experience than *GoodFellas*.

In the last third of the film, Scorsese uses less voiceover narration and thereby gives the viewer a more direct emotional access to the events that are depicted as the characters lose control of their lives and become increasingly desperate in their attempts to resolve their problems. It is significant that Ginger is never given a voiceover narration; unlike Ace and Nicky, she has no social and/or economic power and whatever personal independence Ginger had, she lost when she married Ace. And, when she realises that she is trapped in the marriage, Ginger reacts through an emotional rebellion which is the only means she has to combat Ace. Initially using alcohol and drugs to distance herself from the relationship, Ginger moves on to toying with fantasy escapes (fleeing abroad with her ex-pimp, Lester Diamond/James

Woods, and having plastic surgery to avoid detection) and, eventually, she resorts to seducing Nicky and talking him into killing Ace. The friendship between Ace and Nicky has been seriously strained ever since the two men differed over how the Tangiers, and by extension, Las Vegas itself, should be run; but Ginger functions as the catalyst that precipitates the ensuing chaos which is caused primarily by Ace's obstinacy and Nicky's greed, jealousy and desire for recognition.

Ginger's reaction to her situation is directly connected to violence and, arguably, the most disturbing violence in the film isn't the shocking 'head-in-the-vice' scene which, although hard to watch, remains an impersonal act, but, instead, the escalating abuses the three lead characters inflict on each other. There is, to begin, Ginger's self-abuse which, after she manages to break away from Ace, ends with her pathetic, drug-induced death. But, before this occurs, Ginger and Ace enact a number of harrowing scenes of domestic violence; and later, Nicky, realising that Ginger is no longer capable of rational behaviour and intuiting that his sexual relationship with her and the plan to kill Ace was a mistake, brutally reacts by kicking her down a flight of stairs. And, finally, in the aftermath of a federal investigation into the Mafia's connections to Las Vegas and their decision to rid themselves of possible informers, the purging of various potential informants which culminates in the baseball bat clubbing of Nicky and his brother and their being buried alive.

Ace, who survives the car bombing, provides a commentary on the deaths of Ginger and Nicky and the destruction of the Las Vegas that the three of them knew. In an epilogue, Ace, now visibly aged, apparently living alone and again working for the Mob as a handicapper, seems to have found a degree of serenity. But, as the film's end credits begin, Scorsese first uses Georges Delerue's 'Thème De Camille' from Godard's *Contempt* (1963), which is heard briefly earlier in the film when Ace and Ginger's marriage is disintegrating, and follows it with Hoagy Carmichael's 'Stardust'; the latter, Scorsese says, he uses to '. . . sum up the emotions and thoughts about what you've seen.'[3] Given that Ace is the least overtly emotional of the leading characters and the most reflective, it is appropriate that, in the performance of 'Stardust' used, the song's words are spoken. It provides *Casino* with an eloquent, elegiac conclusion – it is an ending which is completely at odds with *GoodFellas'* ending. Scorsese's attitude towards his material is nicely summed up in the following comment which he made in response to a remark on the broad range of music the film employs: 'I guess for me it's the sense of something grand that's been lost. Whether we agree with the morality of it is another matter – I'm not asking you to agree with the morality – but there was the sense of an empire that had been lost, and it needed music [*St. Matthew Passion*] worthy of that . . . . But the viewer of the film should be moved by the music. Even though you may not like the people and what they did, they're still human beings and it's a tragedy as far as I'm concerned.'[4]

As in *Raging Bull*, the Scorsese film which is perhaps closest to *Casino* in temperament, *Casino* has fully rounded characters to whom Scorsese and his actors manage to give interior lives, but without providing psychological explanations for their behaviour. And, while the film belongs to the traditions of the gangster film and *film noir*, the characters aren't generic stereotypes – for instance, Ginger isn't a gangster's moll, a *femme fatale* or, alternatively, the 'woman-as-victim'. Ginger is obsessed with money and what it buys but, on the other hand, she doesn't lie to Ace, who insistently and perversely tries to romanticise their relationship, about her feelings towards him and she trusts him when he tells her that he'll let her go if the marriage fails. Ginger gambles in taking up Ace's offer but, as she later finds out, he hasn't played fair. And arguably, Ginger's interest in money isn't primarily greed; in an environment like Las Vegas and given her profession, money is the only tangible means Ginger has to define herself and prove her worth. In contrast, Ace, like the stereotypical filmic gangster, is a dapper dresser, but in *Casino* Scorsese takes the notion to an extreme. Ace's expensive, stylish wardrobe functions not merely to signal success but also to reflect his desire to achieve perfection, to be in complete control and, through the extravagant colour co-ordinations, individualise his presence.

In addition to making the viewer deal with characters who resist appropriation, *Casino* is a lengthy film that contains footage which can be considered digressive. Early on in the film, for instance, there is a scene depicting how the Tangiers' earnings are handled, including the various skimmings that take place before the Mafia in the Midwest gets its share. On the one hand, the scene clearly isn't relevant to the plot but, on the other, the 'behind-the-scenes' procedure which is shown has a certain fascination and, indirectly, it serves to demystify the casino/gambling image. The entire scene is filmed using a Steadicam with the shot beginning in the casino proper, moving on into a back room where the money is sorted, counted and stored, and ending back in the casino as the Mafia's money is about to be taken to its Midwest destination. The camera is originally aligned to the movement of a mob member who enters the room with a suitcase to pick up the money; but, gradually, the camera begins to move freely around the busy room documenting the various jobs involved as Nicky's voiceover narration provides a description of the operation, particularly the skimmings. Although the viewer is already preoccupied dealing with the visuals and Nicky's narration, Scorsese uses the song 'Moonglow' as background music and thus adds another dimension to the shot. 'Moonglow' has no direct connection to what is happening onscreen or to what Nicky is talking about; the song, nevertheless, through its familiarity, filmic associations and *gracefulness* is engaging and seductive. And the shot, which is, in a strict sense, expendable, becomes an integral part of what Las Vegas was about as Nicky experienced it. *GoodFellas* employs a Steadicam shot that is expressly intended to make an impression – Henry, to avoid the line-up of people entering the Copacabana and to illustrate his connections, takes Karen through the rear entrance with the camera documenting their movement from the rear entry door through the kitchen and various corridors to their table. In *Casino* the Steadicam shot doesn't have a similar narrative 'justification' but it is equally a source of aesthetic pleasure and an imaginative exercise illustrating to the viewer the ability of the moving camera to record its subject-matter in a space-time continuum.

Given its concern with the demise of the mobster-controlled Las Vegas of the 1970s, *Casino* becomes a companion piece to Barry Levinson's *Bugsy* (1991) which is about Las Vegas's beginnings and, like Scorsese's film, *Bugsy* connects Las Vegas to the fate of a heterosexual couple's relationship.[5] Set in the mid-forties, *Bugsy*, a more self-conscious period film than *Casino*, concentrates on the volatile relations between

Benjamin 'Bugsy' Siegel/Warren Beatty and gangster moll bit actress Virginia Hill/Annette Bening. *Bugsy*'s version of the origins of Las Vegas is highly romantic and, by its conclusion, sentimental; Siegel, whom the film fitfully depicts as a potential psychotic, is presented ultimately as a visionary and an entrepreneur who, unfortunately, didn't live to reap the rewards of his creation. Siegel and Las Vegas are filtered through his relationship with Hill: the Flamingo, a luxurious hotel-casino he builds in the desert, becomes in Siegel's mind the gift he offers Hill who, because he cannot fully sever his ties to his wife and family, must be content to accept their illegitimate relationship. In its earlier stages the relationship is depicted as confrontational, with Hill not taking any crap from Siegel who has been used to getting what he wants but, as the relationship progresses, the two are forced to recognise that their love for each other takes precedence in their lives. Interestingly, in *Bugsy*, as in *Casino*, the relationship is placed in the context of the male making a commitment and then testing the woman through the issue of love/money/trust. Siegel has funded the building of the Flamingo with the Mob's money and he gives Hill the responsibility of overseeing its construction. Hill, in turn, betrays Siegel's trust, skimming off money and lying to him when he questions her about the mounting expenditures. But, on the Flamingo's storm-battered, disastrous Christmas night opening, Hill, who walked out on Siegel when confronted about her honesty, reappears, offering him the money she took, and suggests that she put the money aside as their 'insurance' if things went wrong. Later the same night, Siegel is killed by the mob who, in addition to not having faith in the Las Vegas he foresees, assume Siegel has been in on the skimming. As *Bugsy* progresses, Siegel and Hill become heroic figures and the emphasis on their relationship is shifted from the sexual to the romantic; even though Hill is indirectly implicated in Siegel's death, the relationship is shown to transcend the love/money/trust issue and even death itself. And *Bugsy*, too, is a celebration of Siegel's business sense – he has, after all, given post-World War II America one of its great consumerist/fantasy entertainment centres. The film's final intertitle reads: 'By 1991 the six million dollars invested in Bugsy's Las Vegas dream had generated revenues of 100 billion dollars.'

Unlike *Bugsy*, *Casino* isn't a romantic film and the personal relations between Ace, Ginger and Nicky aren't used metaphorically to glamorise either the people who inhabit Las Vegas or the city itself. *Casino* offers a historical, cultural and economic portrait of Las Vegas that isn't inviting or seductive; although the film personalises the end of the mobsters' control of the city through the story of the Tangiers, the film doesn't suggest that a Mafia-run Las Vegas was a 'better' place than what follows. Rather, the film holds the position that the Las Vegas of the 1970s was 'honest' about what it was, unlike the present day corporate-controlled Las Vegas. The contemporary Las Vegas, in the guise of being respectable and 'family friendly', is, the film implies, an even more sinister place – an anonymous, efficiently run machine that exists solely to maximise shareholders' profits. In actuality, *Casino* is less the companion piece to *Bugsy* than it is to one of Beatty's and Robert Altman's finest works, *McCabe and Mrs. Miller* (1971), another film about America in which gangsterism is made respectable through big business.

Scorsese is a master stylist and storyteller and *Casino* is an extraordinary film. The film needs to be judged on its individual merits. In this piece, I have tried to point to aspects of the film that make *Casino* something other than a work which finds Scorsese cloning himself. *Casino* is, in its elegant imagery that is often the work of a gifted graphic artist, in its performances, which in addition to Sharon Stone's deservedly acclaimed portrayal, contains an extremely disciplined and underrated performance by Robert De Niro, in its careful orchestration of colour to create a specific period and emotional moods, and in the intense concentration Scorsese imparts to the entire project, a film that ranks with the finest achievements of the decade.

Notes

1. The critical responses to *Casino* have been mixed. For instance, J. Hoberman in *The Village Voice* gave the film a very negative review, dismissing it in part because it had too much in common with *GoodFellas*. But Todd McCarthy in *Variety* praised the film and Jonathan Romney in *Sight and Sound* argued that the film was an ambitious and complex work.
2. Whether or not it is intentional, the credit sequence contains images that evoke previous Saul Bass designs: the body falling in a spiral movement is used in Bass's poster for *Vertigo* and the flames filling the lower portion of the screen is used in the *Exodus* credits and also found in the film's poster art work.
3. Christie, Ian, 'Martin Scorsese's Testament', *Sight and Sound* January 1996/Volume Six/Issue One; 6-13.
4. Ibid.
5. *Bugsy* is something of a Beatty vehicle and in its 'outlaw couple' calls to mind his previous successes, *Bonnie and Clyde* and *McCabe and Mrs. Miller*. The film is also very much a film about Hollywood, stardom/glamour and iconographic imagery. Siegel and Hill are presented as if they were movie stars – the film blurs the line between screen character/star presence and works to enhance the star status of Beatty and Bening.

MEAN SCENES AND GOOD FOLKS
By Rob Nelson

Martin Scorsese's *Casino* played like the director's ultimate confession of obsessive-compulsiveness. Stacking the odds against his tendency to win critical favour, he remade *GoodFellas*, but as a darker, more complicated, more resonant film.

So it's no wonder that in his newly released documentary, *A Personal Journey with Martin Scorsese through American Movies*, Scorsese issues high praise to veteran directors like John Ford and Raoul Walsh – directors who, throughout their careers, chose to redeploy familiar actors and plots in 'endless, increasingly complex, sometimes perverse variations'.

The difference between Ford's *Stagecoach* (1939) and *The Searchers* (1956), for example, mirrors that between a short story and an essay, a declaration and a rebuttal, a gifted artist and a mature one. Scorsese's point is that genre conventions don't confine the great filmmaker so much as help reveal where he stands, just as versions of (film) history inevitably reflect the tastes and politics of the teller.

Made as part of the British Film Institute's *Century of Cinema* series, this is indeed a personal trip through the US canon, one in which *2001: A Space Odyssey* represents the height of special effects, *Cat People* matters as much as *Citizen Kane*, and Hitchcock factors not at all. In a brisk 210 minutes, Scorsese (co-writing and -directing with Michael Henry Wilson) admits he can only scratch the surface and vows to avoid most everything post-1968, the year he released his own first feature. (A notable exception is made for Kubrick's *Barry Lyndon*.)

These parameters don't excuse every conspicuous absence – Dorothy Arzner, George Cukor and Oscar Micheaux are all MIA – but they do set the agenda: to render the personal in a historical light while giving even highly evolved buffs a fresh list of must-sees.

In more ways than one, Scorsese's goal is a privilege; for instance, the *auteur*'s industry juice enables Gregory Peck to stop by for a discussion of *Duel in the Sun*, the film Marty's mom took him to see at age four. And at its most analytical, the documentary still invokes the director's own mythology. 'There's no reprieve in *film noir*,' Scorsese argues. 'You just keep paying for your sins.'

This isn't to say that *Personal Journey* is merely self-indulgent. Obviously, the man knows his movies. He links the crime film and the Western by tallying their preoccupations with violence, the law and the individual; and he likens thirties musicals to gangster films for sharing both manic energy and James Cagney.

Other references are more thickly intertextual, with *The Bad and the Beautiful* (1952) – Vincente Minnelli's film about filmmaking – becoming a hectic hub of allusions. To name a few: *The Bad and the Beautiful*'s story of B-movie ingenuity paid homage to *Cat People*'s no-cat style and was sequelised by Minnelli himself in *Two Weeks in Another Town* (1962), the latter film inspiring Scorsese to observe, in a distinctly *Casino*-like voice-over, that by the early sixties 'the pioneers and showmen were gone, the moguls replaced by agents and executives.'

Like *Casino*, *Personal Journey* expresses nostalgia for the pre-corporate days when rugged iconoclasts and 'expatriate smugglers' ruled the roost. If this sounds like a Western motif, it's maybe no coincidence: Scorsese's sharpest writing in the documentary includes his ruminations on the horse operas of Ford, Anthony Mann and Clint Eastwood, suggesting that he may be ready to traverse his last uncharted genre.

The *auteur*'s other chief obsession these days appears to be Kubrick, which is evident in the near-religious respect given to *2001* and *Barry Lyndon* ('one of the most profoundly emotional films I've ever seen,' he says), but also in the fact that Scorsese's last two features have carried a strongly Kubrickian chill.

Of course, this buff's tastes are too catholic to hold just one idol. Scorsese's final clip is from Elia Kazan's immigrant epic *America, America* – which, like Kubrick's films but more subjectively, describes where we came from and where we're going.

GRACE PERIOD
By Ray Greene

Martin Scorsese hates to fly. As luck would have it, another round of 'El Nino' storm-front rumours was circulating on one of the few recent dates when Scorsese decided to make the New York-to-L.A. run. Los Angeles might yet wash off into the ocean at some point during the winter, but it didn't this time: In a pattern that had already repeated itself all summer long and into the early fall, broadcast commentators nationwide were gleefully predicting L.A. rainfalls of biblical proportions for Scorsese's late September travel day, only to have nothing more than modest, periodic and only slightly noticeable showers materialise.

Still, given his flight phobia and the meteorological speculation Scorsese woke up to, it was a near chance that he might decide to call off his east/west trek. But Scorsese's love of movies apparently supersedes all other considerations: At the last minute, he threw caution to the winds, chanced the white-knuckle plane ride to the City of Angels, and arrived just in time to attend the kind of event the film buff in him just loves: an *American Movie Classics* salute to the golden era of Hollywood *film noir*.

As with almost any subject related to films and filmmaking, Scorsese's comments on the *AMC* tribute are ultimately a statement of his philosophies as a director. 'There was a genuine warmth, a real love, you could say, of the images,' a scratchy-voiced Scorsese says on the morning after the event. 'It's a world that's gone by, but we have these incredible artefacts, and the artefacts make you think about history.

'I'm addicted to history. And I think when you're addicted to history it's really about studying human behaviour. What happens [when you watch an old movie] is that these people are up there on the screen behaving. And they're not really behaving for themselves, they're behaving for a whole culture of that time.'

Over breakfast, Scorsese seems both whip-smart and a bit the worse for wear after his journey. He is highly verbal – almost parodistically the fast-talking native New Yorker. Words spill from him in staccato torrents, with rapid-fire, fully articulated ideas and opinions seeming to compete for mastery in his conversation.

The loud clanking of a barman wiping down waterglasses sets him on edge, actually derailing his train of thought more than once, as does a particularly shrill cell-phone that goes off at regular intervals over the course of the meal. He flinches at the sounds – piercing and reverberant in the panelled half-light of a restaurant off the foyer of his posh Beverly Hills hotel – and then laughs the reaction off. 'I get like Roderick Usher now,' he says. 'You know, "The Fall of the House of Usher"?' He clenches his hands and hunches forward in a burlesque of horror movie menace worthy of Dwight Frye: 'The cat's paws drive me mad!'

Given the thematic complexity of his films, it's no surprise that Scorsese is a sharp interview, or that the jangled, nervous energy that seems such a part of his directing style is also part of his personality. He is, after all, the man who kickstarted his career and redefined the American crime film with the bloodsoaked gangster morality tale

Mean Streets in 1973, making stars of Harvey Keitel and Robert De Niro in the process. *Taxi Driver*, his scary tale of an obsessed gun lover and would-be political assassin, proved potent enough to incite a 1980 copycat assassination attempt by John Hinckley against then-president Ronald Reagan. And *Raging Bull* (1980), Scorsese's poeticised rendering of the violent life and times of boxer Jake La Motta, is routinely hailed as the greatest American film of its decade and, along with Robert Wise's *The Set-Up*, is the most realistic depiction of the brutality of the fight game ever committed to film. It would be a contradiction in terms if Scorsese came off like, say, a mild-mannered small-town librarian.

What is surprising is that this most urban and American of filmmakers has gotten up early on a grey L.A. morning to discuss a project that, on the surface at least, seems to play against almost all of his acknowledged strengths. *Kundun* – a rural religious epic set in Tibet and featuring an all-Asian cast of nonprofessional actors – chronicles the early life of Tibet's exiled spiritual leader, the Dalai Lama.

'Why not?' Scorsese says when asked if he thinks he's the kind of director for this sort of material. 'It's basically a story about a man who lives a life in the spirit, and how one lives a spiritual life in this world, which is to a certain extent what Charlie is trying to do in *Mean Streets*. You know, he was trying to lead an ethical life, according to the precepts of his religion, in a world where there are gangsters and there are thieves. [In *Kundun*] there's no magic, there are no visions. [The Dalai Lama] is trying to lead a good life and be an example, I think, to all of us.'

As with so much of what makes Scorsese tick, the journey that led to *Kundun* began in the darkened moviehouses of his fifties New York boyhood. It was there that he discovered an early passion for religious spectacle, fuelled by period epics like 1951's *Quo Vadis?* and 1952's *The Robe*. 'I remember *Quo Vadis?* – the MGM one – and my father taking me to see it,' he says. 'I was fascinated by the beautiful three-strip Technicolor and what looked to me like the artefacts of ancient Rome.

'The next one was *The Robe*, and it was the first film in CinemaScope. The curtain opening at the Roxy Theatre for that new kind of image, and then the music coming up – it was quite extraordinary.'

The fifties boom in religious spectaculars came at a particularly auspicious moment in Scorsese's development, harmonising events from his life with impressions taken from the films he loved at a very early age. 'I had spent my first year in Catholic grammar school, and I became an altar boy,' he says. 'And the ancient Roman world became in my mind part of the Church, and part of the ritual of the Church. The music of the Church became completely mixed into the music in *Quo Vadis?* or *The Robe*.'

A less well-known epic of the period provided Scorsese with what he remembers as his first significant exposure to an ethnographic moviemaking approach he would explore in depth later on. A fictional account of the building of Egypt's Great Pyramid, 1955's *Land of the Pharoahs* boasted one of Hollywood's finest directors in Howard Hawks and a script worked on by (of all people) Southern gothic novelist and Nobel laureate William Faulkner. Though it predated Cecil B. DeMille's more setbound 1956 remake of *The Ten Commandments*, *Pharoahs* had nothing like the commercial impact of DeMille's Barnumesque spectacle of ancient Egypt. Except, that is, in the New York moviehouse where a prepubescent Marty Scorsese saw it and found the experience indelible.

'I guess what I was really interested in there was the way Egypt looked. *Land of the Pharoahs* gave the impression that you were really in ancient Egypt, mainly because they shot there. And the scale [of the drama] was more human size [than in most fifties spectaculars] and very interesting.

'I hadn't seen architecture like that before. I had seen the film *The Egyptian* before that, but that looked more like Hollywood Egypt, very pretty,' he says. 'Whereas *Land of the Pharoahs* really had a sense of being like a documentary of ancient Egypt.'

That realistic edge became something Scorsese started to look for as he became more interested in making films of his own. He cites *Land of the Pharoahs* as a direct influence on *Kundun*, which was shot entirely on location in Morocco in order to capture the timeless rural isolation of pre-communist Tibet. 'In Morocco,' he says, 'if you look at a village outside of Ouarzazate, you are looking at a village that has been that way for 5,000 years.' This attention to realistic detail has been a hallmark of Scorsese's approach to filmmaking from the beginning of his career. 'By the time I saw documentaries in the fifties and sixties,' he says, 'and neorealism, Italian films, I realised I would love to make films where literally you see what the person eats, the kind of food they're eating, the way it's presented, the way it's prepared. I began to realise I wanted to make films that depict the culture of the people. You get that in *Mean Streets*, you get it in *GoodFellas*, and I believe you get it in *Kundun*.'

Still, Tibet is an awfully long way from the Little Italy of *Mean Streets*, and the Dalai Lama's difficult early passage is a story that exists in a unique and very specialised milieu. *Kundun* (the title means 'The Precious One') begins in 1937, when a two-year-old Tibetan boy named Tenzin Gyatso is recognized as the fourteenth reincarnation of the Buddha of love and compassion. 'With Buddhism,' Scorsese says, 'the idea is that it's the same boy who was here the last time, and the one before that, and the one before that. At one point, when he's sixteen years old, [the Dalai Lama] asks this fellow who sweeps the kitchen and played with him when he was little, "Do you ever wonder if the regent found the right boy?" And the man says back, "No. Of course he did. Who else would be here?"'

In the Tibetan system of the 1930s, the Dalai Lama was not just the spiritual but also the political leader of his country. Rigorous training in the philosophies of Buddhism, including the central Buddhist tenet of absolute nonviolence, occupied much of Tenzin Gyatso's childhood and early adolescence. But at the age of fifteen both the Dalai Lama's life and the life of his country were irrevocably changed by an event that would eventually send the Dalai Lama into exile: the invasion of Tibet by the armies of Chairman Mao Zedong, and its subsequent annexation as part of communist China.

The collision of Tibet's nonviolent, spiritualist way of life with the militaristic and materialist culture of Maoism is the skein of tragedy that runs through *Kundun*, which ends with the Dalai Lama's forced departure from his homeland in 1959. In the decades since, Tenzin Gyatso has become one of the world's most revered figures. Global interest in Buddhism is at an all-time high, and the Dalai Lama's political efforts, which continue to espouse the cause of nonviolence as well as that of a free Tibet, were rewarded with a Nobel Peace Prize in 1988.

The rising interest in Buddhism as well as in Chinese politics has been reflected in a spate of recent Hollywood projects. Preceding *Kundun* into the marketplace were both Jean-Jacques Annaud's *Seven Years in Tibet*, starring Brad Pitt as an Austrian climber who undergoes a Buddhist conversion experience, and *Red Corner*, the political thriller-cum-expose about the oppressive realities of the communist Chinese legal system.

Although *Kundun* began as the brainchild of *E.T.* screenwriter Melissa Mathison a half-decade ago and is a film that Scorsese has been involved with for more than three years, Scorsese acknowledges that his film's arrival at this time does seem to reflect part of a wider shift in Western attitudes about Eastern spiritualism.

'It's a hunger, I think,' Scorsese says. 'There's kind of a hunger for peace of mind. On the downside, it may signal a lack of faith in our traditional religions in the West. That doesn't mean everybody's going to become Buddhist, but I think you could learn certain things from Buddhism.'

Scorsese is philosophical about the fact that *Kundun* has become part of a sort of Chinese thematic subgenre. 'I would have liked to have done this film before *Casino*,' he says, 'but I couldn't. It just turns out that you have [*Kundun*], and you have the Jean-Jacques Annaud film, and it all seems to be coming through in a kind of torrent. A process has happened without people even realising it, [and] it's all coming to fruition this year.'

The potency of the Dalai Lama as a symbol of Tibetan struggle is demonstrated by the ongoing hostility that *Kundun* has met with from the current Chinese regime. Almost as soon as the Scorsese project was announced, the Chinese government, in an extraordinary move, threatened to block *Kundun* maker the Walt Disney Co. from future access to China's vast and potentially lucrative markets if the project went forward.

The issue appeared to be resolved after a petition signed by a wide-ranging group of American filmmakers sided with Scorsese's right to tell the Dalai Lama's story, and Disney, to its credit, has stood behind *Kundun* from the first. Yet, even as this story was going to press, the plot continued to thicken: During the recent visit to the US by the current Chinese president, China announced that it was suspending all business dealings with Disney as well as with *Seven Years in Tibet* distributor Columbia TriStar and *Red Corner* backer MGM in protest against what its government views as each film's unwarranted attack on Chinese sovereignty.

Ironically, Scorsese considers himself a lover of Chinese culture, particularly of Chinese cinema. 'I think Chinese cinema is the best cinema in the world,' he says. 'The film-makers, the cinematographers – I love their pictures.' Scorsese does, however, draw a distinction between Chinese culture and the repressive excesses of the current rulers. 'About the repression of their regime – we're talking about the regime now, not the people – I think it's extremely dangerous. I've seen articles in French magazines about their daily executions of "dissidents", quote unquote, or "drug dealers", quote unquote. Kids in their twenties, they shoot them in the back of the head . . . . The Tibetan women who go in to have a child, and they actually kill the child or sterilise the woman. It's a matter of genocide, really.

'The thing to understand about China is, it's a very different way of thinking about life, a very different way of thinking about freedom, and a very different way of thinking about privacy – they have a lot of people there. I read an article about [Maoist guerilla] Pol Pot in Cambodia, where they killed those millions of people. [Cambodia's genocidal civil war was chronicled in the 1984 Oscar winner *The Killing Fields*.] What I got from the article was that he felt those millions of people deserved to die, because it was their bad karma, so it was understandable. In Western culture, karma is not necessarily something that we believe in. Everybody has a right to live.'

It is an odd coincidence that *Kundun* is both Scorsese's second attempt at religious spectacle and the second of his films to be the subject of vehement ideological attack before it has even been released. A decade ago, Scorsese's controversial adaptation of Nikos Kazantzakis' *The Last Temptation of Christ* inspired pickets, threats of boycott and mass demonstrations by American religious conservatives – a situation that still angers Scorsese in a remarkably immediate way given how much time has passed. 'I can understand being offended and that sort of thing, but to try to force us not to go into the theatre is outrageous,' he says of the *Last Temptation* controversy. 'People say, "You're offending my vision of my religion, and you're blaspheming my God." Well, he's everybody's God, and people approach God differently. And this is America, you know? You should be able to do that . . . . The reality is that what happened at that time was a bullying of the American public. A bullying.'

He is equally firm in his views about the fact that *Kundun* has become a very different kind of flashpoint for attempts at ideological suppression. 'What does this man represent?' he asks, referring to the Dalai Lama. 'Compassion. How dare we make a film about a man who represents compassion and peace, and kindness and tolerance . . . . Basically, it's a story about a man whose job is to care about every living thing. And to love every living thing. And the outrage that we should be told on this side of the world that we can't make the picture. And the outrage that the story of a man like this could be considered controversial.'

To Scorsese, whose signature films have so often depicted hard, brutal men caught in grim and violent worlds, there is a strange paradox in the fact that *Kundun*, about the life of a man of peace, would be the subject of such political rage. 'Richard Gere [who has long been one of the Dalai Lama's most public adherents] and I were talking about it, and he said, "Maybe nonviolence is truly revolutionary." Maybe it is. Maybe that's the ultimate revolution. Because what is our nature? Is it our nature to be violent, or is it our nature to love, and be compassionate?'

Scorsese hesitates, as if pondering again a question so central to so many of his films. 'It's both,' he says finally. 'But one has to win out some time or other. Because if it doesn't we have the ability to be extinct any second we choose.'

RETREATS AND RECOGNITIONS:
KUNDUN BY MARTIN SCORSESE
By Philip Horne

Martin Scorsese's previous film, *Casino* (1995), relentlessly followed its unpleasant hero 'Ace' Rothstein into his Mafia dominion at the heart of Las Vegas – a place of pilgrimage in Western mammonism. A striking quasi-documentary sequence led us within the count room of Rothstein's Tangiers casino, greed's shrine, called in voiceover 'the holy of holies'. Scorsese's palpable revulsion at that treacherous, hollow world of money and power, and at the horribly violent fates undergone by most of its devotees, makes intelligible his turning to a different object of worship and a different kind of holiness in his new hero, 'the Buddha of Compassion, the wish-fulfilling jewel, the fourteenth Dalai Lama'.

The still-Catholic Scorsese remarked that making *Kundun* in the Moroccan interior 'was like a retreat, for me,' and one of the Tibetan non-actors among the cast (who perform in English) observed that at the film's start, set on Lhamo Thondup's natal farm in the remote mountainous province of Amdo, 'You wouldn't know which century it was – fifteenth or twentieth.' It might sound as if *Kundun* were indeed what some critics alleged, an escapist exercise in period costume and naïve 'Tibetan chic'. The 'retreat' involved, though, is a spiritual discipline, and the great arc of this awe-inspiring, richly detailed film propels us from feudal Amdo to a progressive confrontation with some of the most invasive public horrors of the twentieth century, worse than any in *Casino* – war, the atom bomb, genocide, ideological fanaticism, the destruction of tradition, forced expatriation. Like *Casino*, *Kundun* is the story of a lost kingdom and way of life, ending in the ruler's exile.

The film is a masterpiece of visionary abstraction in its rhythmic patterning of images, its overlapping dissolves, and the majestic cumulative force of Philip Glass's score. Scorsese has spoken of the editing process as bringing a discovery:

> Once Thelma Schoonmaker-Powell and I realised that conventional dramatic elements didn't matter, finally, in this particular film experience, then we were freed. Freed to go with rhythm, the ritual, the prayer of the movie.

The Tibetan actors' enactments of ritual combine naturalness and dignity; their motions and emotion dictate the shaping of Scorsese's scenes.

But 'the prayer of the movie' derives above all from its rigorous self-limitation to the perspective and experience of the Dalai Lama himself, as a dreaming and visionary but also disconcertingly human, humorous protagonist, at two, five, twelve, and as a young adult. The writer Melissa Mathison and Scorsese worked with the Dalai Lama – as Scorsese did with Jake La Motta for *Raging Bull* – to incorporate personal memories, phrases, gestures, images, dreams and visions. If unconventional, moreover, *Kundun* is far from undramatic. As Scorsese said, it resembles *Mean Streets* (1973) in treating 'the idea of a young man trying to live his religious convictions, a

The fourteenth reincarnation of the Buddha, in the form of the Dalai Lama of Tibet – portrayed here by young non-professional actor Gyurme Tethong, in Kundun *(1997).*

life of the spirit, in the world'. Only here the hero, holding that 'violence is never good', and concerned to reform the hierarchical Tibetan system, is less compromised than the Mafia-tainted Charlie, whose incongruous enthusiasm for St. Francis is mocked by his girlfriend.

The first of *Kundun*'s three large movements begins with the Magi-like quest of the monks who come to Amdo in 1937, led by signs, to recognise the child as the reincarnation of the thirteenth Dalai Lama – 'Kundun'. The boy's gentle testing, his training in Kumbum monastery and then Lhasa, his sheltered growing-up into a position of extraordinary responsibility and power in his palaces, bring him to some discovery of life's usual political complexities – power struggles and betrayals, the existence of prisons. In the second phase public events, with the Second World War and the Chinese 'liberation of Tibet' in 1950, catastrophically amplify and accelerate the lessons of adulthood. Under the occupation he faces growing Chinese demands, and meets in Peking a Mao who is first suavely flexible, then chilling ('religion is poison'). The Dalai Lama's gathering vision of the sufferings of the Tibetan people culminates in the necessity of flight. The final, tensely sorrowful section, the escape to the Indian border in 1959, builds up to his retrospective gaze back through his favourite telescope at a life now only to be known through memory – the memory, in fact, that *Kundun* sets itself to render.

Scorsese knew, making the film, that his mother was dying and it is dedicated to her. Bereavement haunts *Kundun*: in one dream, loved ones take leave, and the hero cries, 'No, none of you – don't die!' One of the most arresting scenes, intimate and alien, is the mountaintop burial of the Dalai Lama's father, his body ritually chopped into pieces and fed to vultures. Scorsese's own deepest impulses are engaged here: the campaigner for film preservation, the lover of cinema's memorialisations, confronts at the end – and of course, records – the Buddhist monks' embrace of impermanence in the deliberate destruction of the sand mandala, an intricate work of art poured in coloured sands. If there is a technique characterising *Kundun*, it might be the dissolve, the transition that signifies mutability - and transformation. 'We're all just here for half a second,' as Scorsese puts it. Or in Prospero's words from *The Tempest*, strangely apt:

> The cloud-capped towers, the
> gorgeous palaces,
> The solemn temples, the great
> globe itself,
> Yea, all which it inherit, shall
> dissolve . . .

New York Stories

A TERRIBLE BEAUTY
By Mark Jolly

Everything about our appointed hour is stamped with the Scorsese signature. He's already running late, and is supposed to be meeting his co-writer to discuss the eighteenth draft of a film that Leonardo DiCaprio has signed up for. Then Scorsese has to dash to a downtown hospital, where his fifth wife is about to go into labour at any moment. (His third daughter is, in fact, born the following morning, just one day shy of the director's 57th birthday.) Despite the obvious anxiety, he appears remarkably relaxed and fully focused to discuss a life in film. And yet the question won't go away: why does he seem so bent on choosing the harder ground? Why does he prefer trauma over tranquillity?

Trauma over tranquillity. It could be the mantra to his 30 years of making movies, in which he's repeatedly probed and prodded at a world that is brutal, unpleasant and usually very bloody. Few of his films make for comfortable viewing, at least in the Friday-night-feel-good-blockbuster sense. And only three of them – *The Color of Money, Cape Fear* and *GoodFellas* – have reaped major profits, amid a body of mostly moderately successful work.

At times, he's ruffled the censors, with his portraits of violence (*Taxi Driver, Casino*), and of religion (*The Last Temptation of Christ*). His most recent picture, *Kundun*, 1997's spiritual-coming-of-age epic about the Dalai Lama, ruffled the People's Republic of China, causing heavy palpitations for Disney, the studio that bank-rolled it. Yet *Bringing Out the Dead*, Scorsese's new film, and his 22nd feature, is perhaps his boldest and certainly his darkest movie to date. Literally. By my count, the two-hour production clocks in with a total of four-and-a-half minutes of daylight.

Following three nights on the job with paramedic Frank Pierce, played by Nicolas Cage, the film paints a harrowing vista of human life – and death – on the streets of New York City. Part of that vista is comprised of certain Scorsese regulars: hookers, dealers, violence, unsociable hours. But *Bringing Out the Dead*'s distinction is the degree to which it internalises the urban inferno in the mind of its hero. Scorsese's business here is less about plot and more about taking us inside the soul of somebody who has worked too close with the dying for too long to feel that he is alive any more.

'I just wanted – not like a typical socially-conscious film in the fifties – I just wanted to throw the audience in,' Scorsese says. 'Mind you, whoever the audience is that sees the picture, I don't expect it to be a blockbuster – but thank God we were able to make it. I guess it's not going to be for everybody, but I wanted to literally have the audience go through this moral and spiritual rollercoaster ride, really a spiritual crisis with Frank.'

Leonardo Di Caprio (as Amsterdam Villon) in Gangs of New York *(2002) confers with Scorsese. The actor was first recommended by De Niro and plays a similarly important role in the director's recent films.*

The way Scorsese talks tells you a lot about the way he makes films. First, there's the feeling in his voice: full of passionate intensity, sharp and alert, like those small, dark eyes darting about under those famously dark brows. Then there's the way he chooses his words: purposeful, deliberate. The phrasing: fraught, breathless, crackling with nervous energy, jump-cutting back and forth, trying to pack in as much detail as possible. And last, the sound of his voice: clipped, precise and inimitably New York (which makes his cameo as the unseen dispatcher, calling in pick-ups over the ambulance radio, so wonderfully expressive).

For the first time since *GoodFellas*, a decade ago, Scorsese has re-visited the city's mean streets. He has also been re-united with screenwriter Paul Schrader, whose script, *Taxi Driver*, first cemented Scorsese's name with the underbelly of city life 25 years ago. And it is with *Taxi Driver* that *Bringing Out the Dead* really resonates. Like Travis Bickle, Frank Pierce is a lonely, fractured man who drives around at night for a living (in an ambulance, not a taxi), grappling for sanity. We come to both figures as they stand at the precipice staring at psychological freefall, and then watch them plummet deeper and deeper. Travis's rage is of the I'm-mad-as-hell-and-I'm-not-going-to-take-it-any-more kind, which inevitably boils over into a bloodbath. Frank, however, is consigned to a quiet, paralysing journey in emptiness. Scarred by grief and haunted by the souls he couldn't save, his only mission is to find peace.

As in much of Scorsese's work, the theme of redemption runs as thick as stage blood. 'Saving someone's life is like falling in love,' Frank says, in one of the many voice-over passages that narrate the film, 'the best drug in the world. You wonder if you've become immortal. It's as if God has passed through you. Why deny it? God was you. But when things go wrong, spreading the blame is an essential medic survival tool: the family was crazy, the equipment broke, the patient smelled. The god of hell-fire is not a role that anyone wants to play.'

If we ignore *The Last Temptation* – as, in fact, most of us did – Frank is an anomaly among Scorsese protagonists: he's the closest thing to a saint, whose only demons are his tortured memories. Mary – played by Patricia Arquette, Nicolas Cage's off-screen wife – is the daughter of a comatose victim Frank tries to save. She tells Frank he has a priest's face (Scorsese and Schrader both nursed boyhood plans to enter the Church), yet Frank questions whether grace can come, not always through saving lives, but sometimes through freeing them from life.

As Scorsese talks about the film, it's difficult to imagine that his desire to make it was based in anything more complex than Catholic guilt. 'I gotta tell you,' he says, as if belief itself were something to come clean about, 'I think it has to do with my religious interests – and what a human being is and what our obligation is to other people in life.' And then he's off, without any encouragement, diving into the ocean of childhood memories that informs so many of his thoughts and words.

'My parents wanted to protect my brother and myself from the horrors out there – the degradation of the poor derelicts, who were literally there on your block, in your building, on your stairs as you were going out to school in the morning; who were there, drunk, fighting each other with broken bottles or knives, or dead, literally dead. Parents didn't want you to touch them – they're dirty, they're this, they're that. But at the same time, the Church is always talking about compassion. So I've always had this split guilt: I've always felt not quite right not doing anything about it and that's one of the reasons I wanted to make this movie.'

There's a point in the film – and the Joe Connelly novel, from which Schrader adapted the screenplay – where Frank crystallises with heart-breaking fatalism the grim reality of the ambulance business: 'My role was less about saving lives than about bearing witness,' he says, staring out into the void. 'I was a grief mop; it was enough that I simply showed up.'

You can't help but see this sense of helplessness as the emotional cord that ties the director and his hero in indissoluble partnership. For Frank, bearing witness is the thing that breaks him. For Scorsese, it appears to be what drives him. 'That's why we threw ourselves out on the street again. It was hard. Because we were in it, in the street, with the homeless, just dealing with the suffering of the people.' He shrugs, arches his brows. 'And I don't know how to deal with it except by putting it on film.'

The act of bearing witness is also a pretty good metaphor for Scorsese's aesthetic and structural approach – that is, capturing life with the kind of authenticity that lends itself almost to social documentary. And documentary is always messier than neat, Hollywood storylines with an overarching moral. 'Absolutely. And if it was at night and it was in the worst areas in New York and you were dealing with a lot of things you don't want to deal with no more, because you grew up with it on the Bowery, well, it's too bad. Whaddaya gonna do? Go live in Bel-Air?'

When he made *Casino*, five years ago, Scorsese and his crew would film in a real Vegas casino during working hours, sometimes at four o'clock in the morning. For *Kundun*, he re-created Tibet in the Indian Himalayan town of Dharamsala (which happens to be the Dalai Lama's real home-in-exile), where weather and horses wreaked havoc with the shooting schedule. But by Scorsese's reckoning, *Bringing Out the Dead*'s 75-night winter shoot was by far the most punishing – physically as well as psychologically.

'You know, I'm 56 years old,' he says. 'It's a little harder to do a picture at night than it was 25 years ago. This was the worst. Joe Connelly used to say you get to that four o'clock morning of the soul and it's like the sun's just never going to come up.'

Securing street access to film an ambulance speeding through a series of red lights was frustrating enough. On most nights, though, Scorsese had to observe usual New York City traffic laws, which meant trying to film a complete scene where the actors could finish their lines without being forced to a screeching halt. In one memorable sequence, Frank's cigar-champing, gospel-preaching partner, Marcus – played by Ving Rhames (whom you might recall getting 'medieval' on his rapist's ass in *Pulp Fiction*) – flips the ambulance over on to its side. Scorsese had got most of the scene when the traffic department closed them down. It was 5.10am, out by the Lincoln Tunnel, which links Manhattan with the commuter belt of New Jersey. The morning rush-hour was upon them. And so, despite the fact that Scorsese needed only one more angle, he had to return another night and crash the ambulance all over again.

Confirming Peter Ustinov's famous line – that comedy is simply a funny way of being serious – *Bringing Out the Dead* turns out to have at least as many laughs as *King of Comedy*, Scorsese's failed, prophetic masterpiece about the desperations of fame. 'I know! I know!' he says, all fired up. 'I went on *David Letterman*, we had a lot of laughs, but I forgot to tell the people that this film is funny.' He breaks into a wheezing chuckle, which has lingered since his asthmatic boyhood. 'The humour is the saving grace of the whole story. And it's real.' It's also, as Joe Connelly tells me on the phone, the medic's only shield: 'There's really no one you can talk to outside the job about a lot of what you see. It's really difficult when you come home from a bad night to try and tell your wife about somebody who was impaled when she's brushing her teeth. So the people you work with are the people you share a language with, and the humour is very dark.'

Sharpening the film's razor-edge between comedy and tragedy is Noel (Latin music star Marc Anthony), a dreadlocked lunatic who suffers from a rare obsessive-compulsive disorder marked by unquenchable thirst, to the point where he'll drink out of toilet bowls, or slurp anti-freeze and urine. Besides Marcus – who at one point hoodwinks a bunch of strung-out goths into resurrecting their overdosed (but living) friend from the dead – Frank's partners include Tom Wolls, 'a sociopath with a badge', as Tom Sizemore calls his character. Turning in one of the funniest, and scariest, supporting roles of the year, Sizemore's Wolls deals with difficult patients such as Noel by administering 'psychological first-aid' – in other words, beating the crap out of them.

Scorsese's desire to embrace authenticity was sometimes too troubling, even for him: on a recent visit to NYU Medical Center with his wife, he heard things he thought were simply too stinging for any audience. (For those who appreciate this sort of detail, Scorsese married book editor Helen Morris last July, after the two met while working on a companion book to *Kundun*. His four previous wives include actress Isabella Rossellini, and Barbara De Fina, who has remained Scorsese's producer for the past fourteen years. He has also squired Liza Minnelli, whom he directed in the disastrous musical, *New York, New York*, and Illeana Douglas, who had the privilege of having half her face bitten off by Robert De Niro in *Cape Fear*.)

True to Joe Connelly's novel – and his nine-year experience as a paramedic – *Bringing Out the Dead* is based, and the exteriors shot, almost entirely on the western fringes of midtown Manhattan, known as Hell's Kitchen. The period is the early nineties, when New York was a radically different place to live and work from what it is now – since 1993, when Mayor Rudolph Giuliani became mayor, the city has brushed itself up and stepped forward as the 'safest big city in America'. And yet Scorsese was still able to re-create on location some of the lingering underworld. 'Many of those people are real,' he says. 'It looks like they're behaving, but that's the way they really were.' Here's a paraplegic crawling on his stumps from out of the dark across a busy intersection. There's Sister Fetus, a tiny figure of a Chinese nun, spouting the gospel to no one in particular. One sequence features a man lurching vacantly along 42nd Street, his expression like something straight out of an Edvard Munch painting.

With the Times Square-42nd Street area all spiffed up and ready to show off its millennial party frock to the world, the blocks just west of there remain one of the last outposts of pre-Giuliani New York. But only just. Last year, a total of three homicides were reported in Hell's Kitchen, a neighbourhood whose gang wars were once the stuff of legend – and the basis for Leonard Bernstein's *West Side Story*. To a certain degree,

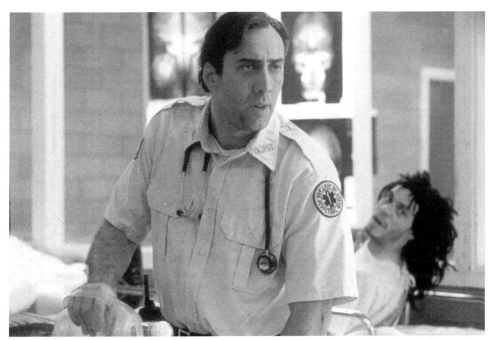

Frank (Nicolas Cage) in Bringing Out the Dead *(1999), reaches breaking point at the hospital he serves as a paramedic. Patient Noel (Marc Anthony) is a mentally ill street person and a regular patient.*

Scorsese commends New York's quality-of-life upgrade: 'I've lived in the city all my life,' he says (though, in fact, he moved to Hollywood for thirteen years in 1970).

'Believe me, I don't mind it being lower crime.' He speaks about the sense of personal distress he used to feel over the desecration of memorial statues: 'The place where we did the ambulance crashing, I used to go by it in the early nineties. There's a statue of a world-war-one soldier. It was always covered in paint, green and pink and red. It was horrible, and I thought: Oh, God, it's like a decline of a civilisation. "Pump don't work 'cause the vandals took the handles." And then, a few years later, we shot there and it was cleaned up and I felt there was some respect for humanity.' Yet, just as he talks about understanding the desires and behaviour of even his most severe characters, Scorsese tempers his criticism: 'I don't condemn the kids who did it, because I know where it comes from. I did stuff like that myself. I know where it comes from – anger and rage – and you can't get out.'

It should really come as no surprise that Scorsese chooses, again and again, to view *Bringing Out the Dead* through the prism of his own childhood. Besides Hell's Kitchen, the only other Manhattan area south of Harlem that still wears any rough-around-the-edges smile is the Lower East Side. Which happens to encompass the Little Italy neighbourhood where Scorsese grew up. 'Everything,' he says, flinging his hands open. 'I saw everything about humanity there first. Everything from bodily functions to sex to everything. And those things never left me.' It's as if the images of the past still surround him, like a waking dream he cannot shake off; as if he were propelled along a parallel, though less agonising, path to Frank Pierce's.

When I ask him if the experience of filming in the West Forties and Fifties brought back any boyhood memories of Little Italy, Scorsese doesn't even pause for a second. He flicks a mental switch and he's right back there, among the old tenements on Elizabeth Street. He plunges into elaborate detail about the wiseguys on the block 'who you had to deal with because they were part of everything'; the sound of Sinatra playing on his father's gramophone (at the beginning of *Bringing Out the Dead*, when Frank tries to resuscitate Mary's father, he asks her to play something the old man likes: she chooses Sinatra); the smell of bread wafting out of La Rosa bakery at 4 a.m. on the way home from after-hours clubs. 'And it wasn't until I went to Los Angeles that I realised not everybody lived this way.'

His romanticism about New York's grittiness is a very large part of what makes Scorsese Scorsese. It's why his name carries such an immediate resonance. It's why we remember so many of his films long after the event and why we identify them as such a singular body of work. When you say the name 'Martin Scorsese', people – and I'm not talking about industry people or film-festival bores or De Niro nuts who like to do the 'You-talkin'-to-me?' sequence on a regular basis, but people who are regular movie-goers – immediately fire back the titles that have become such indelible watermarks in American cinema: *Mean Streets, Taxi Driver, Raging Bull, GoodFellas, Casino.*

Can such romanticism connect with a changing city that has lost most of its grit? One reason Woody Allen seems incapable of making Woody Allen pictures any more is because the joke has been taken away; how do you josh about New York being a wacky, crazy place packed with 'left-wing, communist, Jewish, homosexual pornographers' (as Woody put it in *Annie Hall*), feared and loathed by middle America, when middle America now chooses to holiday here with the whole family more than anywhere else in the country, apart from Orlando and Vegas?

Ever wonder why Allen's last compelling film was a twenties farce involving gangsters (*Bullets Over Broadway*, 1994)? Or why Spike Lee's return to form explores a serial killer's impact on the Bronx in the seventies (*Summer of Sam*)? In like manner, what stories can Scorsese have left to tell? Now that New York has transformed itself from Sin City to Prim City, purged of all its (visible) hustlers and low-lifes and mobsters, where does he go from here? It's as if his canvas has been stripped away from him.

'True,' Scorsese concedes. 'But at this point I don't have anything in mind for the modern New York story.' Indeed, his next two projects are both rooted in the past. Having developed *Dino*, a Dean Martin biopic written by the peerless Nicholas Pileggi (*GoodFellas, Casino*), Scorsese is trying to line up three $20-million-dollar men – John Travolta as Sinatra and Jim Carrey as Jerry Lewis, alongside Tom Hanks, who is set to play the lead. More immediately, though, Scorsese is about to start working on *Gangs of New York*, which he has been tinkering with for close to a decade and which will now star Leonardo DiCaprio. 'Leo is a wonderful actor in that tradition – Brando, Clift, Dean, to De Niro, Pacino, Hoffman to DiCaprio.'

An epic period drama about the ruthless Italian and Irish gangs of the mid-1800s, the screenplay (by *The Age of Innocence* screenwriter Jay Cocks) is supposedly harsher, rougher and nastier than anything we've seen Scorsese do. It may also be his most ambitious film to date, with a budget of $90 million (nearly three times the figure for *Bringing Out the Dead*).

To re-create the infamous Five Points (which later became Little Italy), Scorsese will film for 22 weeks in Rome – a decision that apparently prompted his old neighbourhood pal Robert De Niro to withdraw his interest in the movie. Though *Gangs of New York* doesn't start shooting until April, expectations are running high. For one thing, the subject fuses three of Scorsese's greatest passions: history, gangsters and New York. More to the point, Scorsese knows that the pressure to deliver financially – particularly with the world's most bankable young star fronting the picture – is greater than ever.

'I'm aware that this is a film that has to bring in a lot of money at the box office. But I still want to make it my film. That's the tension, that's the contest you're involved with. You've got to go arm-to-arm-wrestling with the studios.' And ever since his ten-year-long nightmare to get *Last Temptation* financed, Scorsese has held himself steeled and ready for battle.

One of the widest, and perhaps most misguided, perceptions of Scorsese's position is his pulling power in Hollywood. Last year, in *The Hollywood Reporter*'s annual list of the 500 most bankable directors, Scorsese rolled in fourth, despite the fact that he has not enjoyed a big commercial hit since 1991's *Cape Fear* (which scored $80 million in the US, compared with *Bringing Out the Dead*'s $17 million). And despite the fact that he has never won an Oscar.

The way Scorsese tells it, like many of his most memorable characters, he is an outsider searching for distinction in an alien world; a guest who's requesting delicacies at a dinner party he just crashed; a film-maker who has never enjoyed anything remotely resembling a *carte blanche*. 'I think it's pretty clear in Hollywood that you don't come to me to make a blockbuster on the level of a Spielberg, or a Lucas or a Cameron [the trio who happened to lead *The Hollywood Reporter*'s list]. But what's happened is that since 1988-89, the law of averages has worked out that, somehow, somebody somewhere was there to give me money to make a special type of film. I'm telling you, *Kundun* was not a situation where [Disney head] Michael Eisner called me up and said, "Marty, let's make *Kundun*."'

With *Gangs of New York*, Scorsese will, in some measure, return to the kind of conventional narrative structure he swore off after *Cape Fear* (his most commercial as well as his most commercially successful work). But that is a world away from the skewered storytelling or 'internal drama' that drives *Bringing Out the Dead*, and that, Scorsese recognises, has been brewing ever since he first got behind a camera – even though it's only come to light in his last two films. 'I really came to film as a film-maker at a period when films were becoming more, I guess you would say "novelistic", rather than straight narrative. And that's where I thought Hollywood was going to go. But I'm so out of it. I am so naïve. I thought Hollywood was going to stay the way it was in the seventies. You have Robert Altman, you have Coppola, you have Woody Allen – he still knocks out one a year. He's the greatest, the best.

'And I was influenced by world cinema, and Italian cinema a lot. I saw special

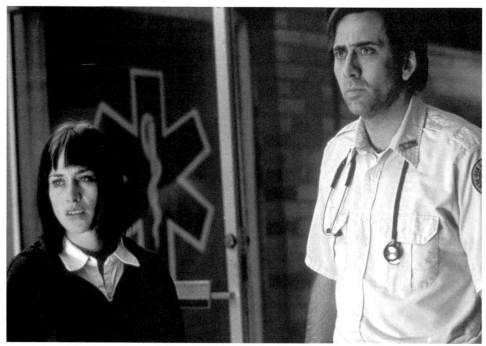

Frank and Mary (Patricia Arquette) seek consolation in each other's company. Frank is haunted by a girl he failed to save, but will help Mary to let go of her cardiac victim father.

Friday-night screenings on TV – my father had a TV set in 1948 – of Italian films for the Italian-American community. I saw *Paisan* at five years old. And *Open City*. And *Bicycle Thief*. And *Shoeshine*. And my grandparents were watching in the room, crying, because these people in the movie were speaking the same language as my grandparents and my parents. And I realised: that's me, that's where I come from. And I don't really belong here. What are we all doing here? I think I drifted more toward the European cinema, there's no doubt about it. I seem to have been attracted to a certain style of film-making, a certain kind of truth that was different from Hollywood. That doesn't mean that *Vertigo* wasn't truthful, or *The Searchers*, or *Citizen Kane*, or even *Fargo* – no, not *Fargo*, that's new.'

We're already deep into the scene I feared most: the scene where Martin Scorsese – cinephile, cinéaste, patron saint of American Film – starts cross-referencing Italian directors from the forties to Orson Welles to the Coen Brothers. And I start nodding my head like a madman. Even if he wasn't Martin Scorsese, it would be impossible to interpret this as showing off, if only for the methedrine-charged rush he still gets from losing himself in the celluloid dream life.

Before I can begin to reel him in, he's off again, telling me about the films he used to watch, while working on *Bringing Out the Dead*, in the screening room of his East Side house. 'We'd watch maybe two a night, a friend and myself, my wife, his wife. Pretty much everything Joseph Losey did, maybe *M* or *Boy with the Green Hair* –

I borrowed a couple of new prints from the British Film Institute – or something like *Mackenna's Gold* [the Gregory Peck Western], or some of the new language [directors] coming out of Taiwan. Hou Hsiao-Hsien.'

When I finally manage to steer the discussion back to internal drama versus straight narrative, Scorsese leads us, inescapably, to Hitchcock, that other great director who was never honoured with an Academy Award. 'I really am interested in telling a story in a different way. I must say, I love watching films with plots – I even love watching Hitchcock plots. Certain Hitchcock films I'll watch again and again and again: it doesn't matter, the plot, for me. I watch them for style. Mood and, er, mood. Mood. Camera movement. Elegance. Just like listening to a piece of music repeatedly.

'*Vertigo*'s my favourite [Scorsese spearheaded its widely welcomed restoration and re-release three years ago]. *Vertigo* and *Psycho*. Now, take the imagery of *Vertigo* and the music and the structure of that story. There doesn't seem to be . . . well, there is a beginning, middle and end, but they're subtle. They begin, then they end and then they begin again. It's amorphous, in a way, but you're living with the people, you're living with the style, you're living with the music.'

One of the more frequent pieces of Martin Scorsese back-slapping you hear is this: there's nobody in this business who loves film as much as Marty. It's not an an unfair estimation, considering the prodigious film preservation work he has put in as president of the Film Foundation which he formed ten years ago, to help rescue decaying film stock. But Scorsese's passion goes only so far in explaining his distinction as a film-maker, which I believe is this: nobody else in his business extracts so much beauty from so much ugliness.

Towards the end of *Bringing Out the Dead*, we find the drug dealer, Cy Coates, his body suspended from the fourteenth floor on a spiked balcony railing, firemen sawing through the metal to save his life. Frank holds Cy's head up, as sparks flame up like fireworks against the night-time Manhattan skyline. For a moment, you could be forgiven for thinking Scorsese's gone overboard with the crucifixion imagery. (In fact, the scene is based on a suicide call Connelly once took, where the victim actually was posing as Christ.) Yet, in a way, the real poignancy of the scene plays out closer to the Hindu motif of the lotus flower – a vision of absolute purity rising from the filth below.

Moments like these remind us that Scorsese is still among the most seductive film-makers working today. Watching his pictures alongside the efforts of today's young power-houses, whose films Scorsese has so clearly influenced – Quentin Tarantino, Danny Boyle, Paul Thomas Anderson, Guy Ritchie – is a bit like watching those old Russian weightlifters. You know, those supertanks, who'd step up – after all the rookies had slapped their hands about excessively in the chalk, huffing and puffing and grunting, and eventually buckling under the strain – tack on an extra weight or three and pump the bar straight up into the record books with one effortless swoop. Except that Scorsese's enduring power is his desire, as Joyce put it, to press in his arms the loveliness which has not yet come into the world.

When you break down the essential elements of film-making to its barest, simplest form, Scorsese is its master: light and sound, sound and light. He beckons us into a world where the colours bleed into our consciousness and the music fires our imagination. We swirl through an emergency room filtered in harsh, ultra-realistic greens and creams; we see fragmented images of Nicolas Cage and Tom Sizemore speeding past a stream of lurid neon that winks like a battered old whore still glamming it up for the boys; we close in tight on Cage's face, the colour and life drained almost entirely, just a pallid wash of death. And, as always, the soundtrack is layered with care and precision, as if it were an abstract character, not just sonic background. Never has Scorsese used music so effectively, so poetically, mixing punk and soul – the perfect anthems for the film's twin themes: chaos and redemption.

In another life, one suspects, Scorsese might have been a DJ or a painter. 'A DJ?' he muses. 'Well, music was so much a part of my life. Living in the tenements, music came out of the windows. My whole life was scored. It would be kids having a birthday party in the street or two bums fighting – it was scored to music and all kinds of music.'

Unmasking this tableau, Scorsese slips in and out of the present tense, threading a seamless timeline in his mind between the then and the now. 'For me, I hear music, I think of the street. I see the street. I saw the street from my window, third floor up, through the fire escape. I see the street. It's beautiful to me. At night sometimes, especially when it was cold, freezing cold, and nobody was out there, the streets would look so clean. And the movies. I saw beauty in movies, usually Westerns – I loved the landscape, I loved the colour of the horses and I wished I could be there. But I wasn't. So I dealt with the beauty on the streets, and the beauty was extraordinary.'

BRINGING OUT THE DEAD
Reviewed by Glenn Kenny

First things first: no matter what anyone else says, *Bringing Out the Dead* is not *Taxi Driver* in an ambulance. Yes, this picture, which reunited *Taxi Driver* collaborators Martin Scorsese (directing, of course) and Paul Schrader (who authored this adaptation of Joe Connelly's novel) for the first time in a decade, does have many affinities with the 1976 classic: It takes place in a drug-and-crime-infested New York City; its hero is an alienated soul who becomes increasingly unhinged as the picture progresses; there's a lot of driving involved; and so on. Sure, the turf is the same. And yes, the filmmaking itself is as exhilarated, and as exhilarating, as that of *Taxi Driver*. But *Bringing Out the Dead* chronicles alienation, insanity, and ultimate redemption; *Taxi Driver* doesn't get to that last bit – which really makes all the difference.

Dead opens with a title card saying that it takes place in the early nineties, before the so-called revivification of the Times Square area was in full swing, but in fact

Scorsese shot the picture in and around Times Square in 1998. The New York depicted here – of crack-heads, sickly whores, convulsing homeless men, and more – still exists, but it's just been very effectively camouflaged; I think maybe that the title card was inserted as a sop to the tourist trade. In any case, through these mean streets drives Frank Pierce (Nicolas Cage), a paramedic who, when we meet him on a Thursday night, is pretty much ready for the rubber room. On his rounds with partner Larry (John Goodman), he improbably revives a man undergoing cardiac arrest in Hell's Kitchen. Assisting him in the revival is Mary (Patricia Arquette), the patient's daughter, and when Frank looks into her eyes as he administers CPR, he sees something worth pursuing. But Frank can't put much stock in the fact that he's just pulled this guy out of the grave, or in the fact that he's just met someone he could feel for. Because all the while, he can't shake the 'ghost' of a girl he failed to save, whose face appears before him almost constantly, asking, 'Why did you kill me?'

Bringing Out the Dead follows Frank for the next two nights, as he begs to be fired, finds that Mary has some skeletons of her own, is assigned two more increasingly eccentric (to say the least) partners, and very nearly descends into the hell he patrols nightly. Sounds like a big bummer, and for sure, much of *Bringing Out the Dead* is grisly and harrowing. But the film is also replete with vivid, unusual, engaging characters (Mary Beth Hurt's turn as a seemingly abusive hospital drug counsellor is particularly memorable) and humour that's simultaneously black and refreshingly compassionate. It offers a wide, generous vision of humanity under inhuman stress, and an often hallucinatory panorama of its setting. And it ultimately tries to arrive at answers to the tough questions about human loneliness and salvation, questions that Scorsese's been wrestling with throughout his career. Coming after the spiritual quests of *The Last Temptation of Christ* and, particularly, of his last film, *Kundun*, *Bringing Out the Dead* is profoundly moving, reflecting some hard-earned wisdom on how suffering is chosen, and how saving one's own soul is hard, almost endless work.

SCORSESE'S *VOYAGE* TO THE NEO WORLD
By Susan King

Italian movies aired on TV every Friday night in New York when he was growing up, recalls director Martin Scorsese, whose family came from Sicily. 'They were on at the time because of the [immense] Italian American community in New York,' he says. 'There was no video at the time, so the reportage [about Italy] was mainly in newsreels in the theatres. My grandparents didn't go to the theatres, so this was the way of showing them what it was like in Italy.'

Those 1940s films left an indelible mark on Scorsese, playing a major part in shaping his career – and they became the inspiration for *My Voyage to Italy*, his four-hour documentary that opens today.

In an interview this week [late October 2001], Scorsese said *My Voyage to Italy* came about as a result of discussions he had with Raffaele Donato, co-executive producer of the documentary.

'He started with me as an archivist in 1986, and when we were travelling together, I would tell him about my enthusiasm for Italian cinema – more than my enthusiasm, my formation through them,' Scorsese says. 'He was a cinema studies writer and knows more about Italian cinema from the inside because he comes from Naples.'

During their discussions about these films, Scorsese developed a 'burning desire' to communicate his love for Italian cinema to young people.

'They would probably see these things on video,' he explains, 'therefore I wanted to do this on film to give them a sense of what the imagery and emotional power [of these movies] felt like to see on the big screen.'

Another of Scorsese's goals is to spur an interest in Italian cinema of all kinds in America. Besides showing a ten to fifteen-minute overview of each film – his longtime editor Thelma Schoonmaker collaborated with him on this project – Scorsese talks about the circumstances of when he first saw the movie, the history of the filmmaker, the critical acceptance of the film, and the effect each one had on him and his career. Scorsese's passion for these films leaps off the screen.

Scorsese discusses the power of Vittorio De Sica's dramas *The Bicycle Thief* and *Umberto D*, the operatic style of Luchino Visconti in his films *La Terra Trema* and *Senso*, the magic, heart and surrealism of Federico Fellini's *I Vitelloni*, *La Dolce Vita* and *81/2*, the enigmatic beauty of Michelangelo Antonioni's *L'Avventura* and the emotional effect of Roberto Rossellini's *Stromboli*, *Europa '51* and *Voyage to Italy*.

Ironically, these groundbreaking neo-realist films were not originally accepted by the Italian movie-going public. 'It was a defeated nation,' Scorsese explains from his New York office. 'It was a nation that had bad breaks. [These films] were everything negative that had happened, and the country had to start from the rubble up. I think at a certain point, the minister of culture said about *The Bicycle Thief* that "we shouldn't be cleaning our dirty linen in public."'

Adds Scorsese, 'Of course what happened was these films reflected the humanity in all of us and that re-represented Italy to the entire world.'

When the world embraced these films, so too did Italy. 'The majority of the people and the government were able to get behind them to a certain extent,' he says. When Rossellini strayed from his neo-realism roots, critics and audiences lambasted him. In 1949, he made headlines when he had an affair and later a child with Ingrid Bergman, who starred in his poorly received *Stromboli*. The two other features he made with Bergman, *Europa '51* and *Voyage to Italy*, also were ridiculed. But Scorsese finds all three films fascinating and powerful, though flawed.

'They wanted him to continue to make neo-realism,' Scorsese says. 'Because *Open City* and *Paisan* were accepted outside [the country], they accepted neo-realism. So when he made the Bergman films, along with the personal scandal, it was time to condemn him.'

Although some of these films are available on video and DVD, most are rarely seen in America. 'Whenever you are dealing with Italian films, there is a difficulty with rights,' he explains. 'It took years just to get these clips. It has been so difficult with a normal Italian film, and when you get to the Rossellini films, it is even more difficult. There are so many different people who own rights in [various] countries. We would love to get [his] war trilogy, *Open City*, *Paisan*, and *Germany Year Zero*. We would love to get his early fifties films.'

READY TO RUMBLE
By Stephen Dalton

May 20th, 2002, the Cannes Film Festival. We're here for a twenty-minute sneak preview of Martin Scorsese's violent historical epic, *Gangs of New York*. But there's a mini riot going on at the entrance to the Palais, where festival screenings are held. Journalists, liggers, star-spotters and paparazzi claw and kick one another as they try to get to the front of the queue, only to smack into a rock-hard wall of implacable, mirror-shaded bouncers guarding the doors. A desperate French radio reporter takes his chances and crowd-surfs over our heads, only to land in a painfully crumpled heap on the ground. The security staff simply pick him up by the collar and throw him back into the crush.

Any Scorsese film generates huge interest, of course, but the frenzy surrounding *Gangs of New York* is unprecedented at Cannes. The long-delayed film is already an infamous magnet for malicious gossip and apocalyptic speculation – hence the extraordinary scenes in front of the Palais. And hence the subsequent exercise in damage limitation by Scorsese, studio boss Harvey Weinstein and the film's stars Leonardo DiCaprio and Cameron Diaz, who join forces for a bullish press conference and countless promotional interviews designed to deflect and deflate two years of colourful rumours about bloated budgets, blazing rows, ominous delays, superstar friction, editing bust-ups, lawsuits and reshoots.

After a remarkable 25-year journey to the screen, *Gangs of New York* holds a lot of reputations in the balance. DiCaprio certainly needs a hit after *The Beach*. Weinstein, as both producer and studio chief, needs to prove he can compete in the premier league with his most expensive production to date. And Scorsese's reputation as America's greatest living director needs a boost after *Kundun* and *Bringing Out the Dead*.

At best, *Gangs of New York* has clearly been a bruising experience for all involved. At worst, the cynics are wondering whether this could be Scorsese's answer to *Heaven's Gate*, Michael Cimino's notorious period flop from 1980 which ended the era of big-budget personal films almost single-handedly. Ironically, the colossal failure of Cimino's doomed epic actually helped sink Scorsese's first attempt at shooting *Gangs* more than twenty years ago.

Behind all the speculation and spin, bluster and bravado, it's time to sort out the real good fellas from the raging bull. This, then is the story of the most hotly anticipated movie of the decade . . .

As far back as he can remember, Scorsese has wanted to make *Gangs of New York*. Since the late seventies he and Robert De Niro have made several ambitious, painful and ultimately doomed attempts to film crime historian Herbert Asbury's 1927 book. Set in the Lower Manhattan slums of the mid-1800s, *Gangs* begins with a deadly battle between rival street gangs, the Anglo-Protestant Native Americans and their Irish-Catholic enemies, the Dead Rabbits. Climaxing with the anti-draft riots of 1862, Scorsese's semi-factual snapshot of these warring urban tribes serves as a microcosm of the explosive ethnic rivalry that has shaped America ever since the Civil War.

'It was the most violent century in America's history,' Scorsese says in Cannes. 'In the nineteenth century, if democracy wasn't going to work in New York, it wasn't going to work in America. Everybody came in there and they all had to work it out. And by the time of the draft riots, it's like Spike Lee's *Do the Right Thing*. Everything just erupts and it turns into a race riot.'

Scorsese calls *Gangs of New York* 'a sort of Western in the East'. A personal obsession for its director, who knows the racial turf wars of Manhattan from his childhood in Little Italy, the film's epic scale has always proved financially problematic. Until now.

First announced in 1977 by Alberto Grimaldi, the legendary producer with a string of Fellini, Bertolucci and Sergio Leone credits to his name, this Dickensian twist on *GoodFellas* has fallen through many times over the decades. One projected version in the early eighties was even intended to co-star The Clash as gang members. But *Gangs* finally begins to get off the ground in 1998, when the formerly all-powerful Hollywood super-agent Mike Ovitz offers his client Leonardo DiCaprio to Scorsese at a knockdown rate. DiCaprio will play Amsterdam Villon, an Irish street hoodlum who takes revenge against the anti-Catholic 'nativist' gang who killed his father, played by Liam Neeson. The nativist leader, a true historical figure called Bill the Butcher, will be played by De Niro.

After being rejected by every major studio, Disney finally agree to back *Gangs*. They then change their mind, reportedly alarmed by the extreme violence in the script. Only when Miramax's Harvey Weinstein steps in with a deal that splits the film's $84 million budget between his own company, fellow Disney offshoot Touchstone and the Initial Entertainment Group is the project finally out of intensive care.

De Niro warns Weinstein: 'Remember, your job is to protect and serve.' But the mogul with the hands-on manner described as 'testicle-crunching' by *The Sunday Times* is soon at odds with his equally passionate director. Weinstein begins by ordering multiple rewrites to the original screenplay by Scorsese and Jay Cocks. Meanwhile, Alberto Grimaldi sues Disney over his long-standing stake in *Gangs*. He walks away with a producer's credit and a hefty payoff, adding $3m to an already tight budget.

To keep costs down, shooting will take place at Cinecitta in Rome, the sprawling studio complex built by Mussolini in 1936 where classics such as *Spartacus*, *La Dolce Vita* and *The Godfather II* were made. Dante Ferretti's stunning mile-long New York street set is designed to accommodate a working harbour, 360-degree tracking shots

Let the bloodshed commence: Priest Villon (Liam Neeson, with Celtic cross) leads the Dead Rabbits gang against their enemies, the Natives, in Gangs of New York *(2002).*

and 800 rioting extras. But De Niro, caught up in a custody battle, refuses to leave his kids in Manhattan for several months. After 25 years he walks out on *Gangs*.

Scorsese and Weinstein decide to pursue Daniel Day-Lewis, with whom both have worked previously, to replace De Niro, despite the fact that the reclusive actor hasn't made a film since Jim Sheridan's *The Boxer* in 1997. When Weinstein tracks him down, Day-Lewis is less than enthused.

'Fuck you, I'm not doing any movies!' laughs Weinstein. 'That's what he said.' Bizarrely, it transpires that Day-Lewis has abandoned acting to study shoe-making in Italy. Scorsese and Weinstein fly Day-Lewis over to New York, wining and dining him at a Mob-friendly Italian restaurant in Harlem. A permanent metal detector on the door guards against the well-connected clientele gunning each other down. Scorsese knows the joint well, having found some of his *GoodFellas* extras here.

Day-Lewis is slowly, grudgingly persuaded. He flies home to Ireland, grows a moustache and sideburns, then finds work in a London butcher's shop. Party animal DiCaprio, meanwhile, is ordered onto a strict muscle-building fitness regime. One month before shooting starts, Scorsese is visited in Cinecitta by his old friend George Lucas. Leaving Fellini's old office overlooking Stage Five, the two men take a stroll up Ferretti's filthy facsimile of nineteenth-century Manhattan. 'These sets will never be built again,' observes Lucas, the king of blue-screen backdrops. 'Nobody's going to spend this kind of money. That's the end of it.'

Shooting begins on September 18th, 2000.

Scorsese is already behind schedule by the second week, and discipline onset is harsh. Smoking is banned, with the notable exception of DiCaprio. One female extra is reportedly ejected for having sex on site. Anyone caught taking pictures, even personal souvenir shots, has their camera confiscated and film exposed.

There are also rumours of friction among the cast, but whatever the truth may be, the calm at the eye of this raging testosterone storm is undoubtedly Cameron Diaz. As DiCaprio's romantic interest, pickpocket Jenny Everdeane, Diaz is originally contracted for six weeks of work. She ends up staying in Rome for six months as her role expands. After she finishes, in April 2001, she checks into a stress reduction clinic.

'Without Cameron we'd all have been screwed, because she was the angel on the movie,' Weinstein admits. 'We needed that oestrogen on that set. Whenever somebody's temper flared, Cameron would be around, and nobody wanted to be an asshole in front of her. So Daniel said to me the minute Cameron left, "I suppose you're going to leave too now?" I said "No, I wouldn't miss torturing you for all the money in the world."'

As *Gangs* racks up eight weeks of overtime, Weinstein gets tough. With budget climbing from a projected $84m towards $97m, Scorsese and DiCaprio are contractually obliged to pay back $3m each in exchange for a larger share of deferred profits if the film is successful. In the last weeks of shooting, Weinstein sheds 150 crew members and divides the remaining unit into three, shuttling Scorsese between each one on a golf caddy.

At the end of a frantic eight-month shoot, Scorsese and Weinstein reconvene in Fellini's old office. Weinstein says, 'Don't forget, Marty, I want the film out for Christmas.' Scorsese gives his assurance. 'No,' clarifies Weinstein, 'Christmas 2001.'

Scorsese's face drops. He usually takes at least a year to edit a major film, but Weinstein insists. *Gangs* has been an uphill struggle so far. Now the real battle begins.

The first signs of storm clouds gathering over *Gangs* comes in the aftermath of September 11. Miramax announce a postponement of the film's planned Christmas release, suggesting an ultraviolent drama about ethnic rivalry in lower Manhattan might be deemed inappropriate so soon after the attacks. Noble enough sentiments, but this delay is actually announced several weeks after the tragedy. In October, a private Miramax screening of Scorsese's first cut, running to three hours and 40 minutes, is rejected by Weinstein. Given the director's famously meticulous editing style, postponement would have been inevitable even without the 9-11 attacks.

Scorsese is allegedly unhappy about having to make extensive cuts. *New York* magazine reports a blazing row between director and producer during which Scorsese throws a phone through his office window. At Cannes, the director admits to a colourful exchange of views. 'It's like saying everything goes smoothly on a Scorsese picture,' he shrugs. 'It doesn't. I'm a very excitable person. And Harvey is also extremely colourful. We've had our disagreements and every one, I must say, we've come to terms. I get a little upset – but then I say, "Okay, you're right, let's sit down and think." I've done it for every picture.'

More negative coverage hits the production in October 2001. Online news service MSNBC quotes DiCaprio bad-mouthing *Gangs*, claiming the film 'won't exactly wow the world' and wishing he had taken an up-front fee. The story is quashed by DiCaprio's people, who insist that 'working on the film has been the highlight of his career'.

The *New York Times* reports in November 2001 that Scorsese is reshooting the film's ending. Weinstein counters that this just means 'a couple of pick-up scenes'. Several British papers also claim the Miramax boss has softened the film's savagery. 'There is less violence,' he admits. 'But then there are some things that are as intense as any other Scorsese movie. This is no walk in the park.'

With its release now postponed until late 2002, Scorsese takes another six months slashing the movie. Once again, Weinstein has lived up to his industry nickname: Harvey Scissorhands. 'You know what?' he says. 'When these directors 'fess up to St Peter, they're all going to say stuff like: "Fuck, he was right about that five-minute fucking scene, it bored the shit out of me!"'

In February 2002, the Miramax-backed celebrity magazine *Talk* dramatically folds. This $19 million loss sets tongues wagging among Weinstein's Hollywood rivals, who see in *Gangs* an equally perilous mix of hype and hot air. Believing the best form of defence is attack, the Miramax mogul takes on the prophets of doom on their own turf: the press. In April, he pens an article for *The Guardian* and *The New York Post* refuting most of the negative stories around *Gangs*. Downplaying his battles with Scorsese, Weinstein slams journalists who 'prefer to exaggerate a few heated moments over the course of eight-and- a-half months of shooting'.

Weinstein also reminds those anticipating his financial downfall that the risk-sharing deal he struck over *Gangs* means Miramax only needs to make $60 or $70 million to turn a healthy profit.

'Fortunately, the company's done well,' he says in Cannes. 'If we lose all our money on this movie, it'll still be less than we lost on *Talk* magazine.'

But Weinstein's decision to blast into Cannes mob-handed, screen twenty minutes of footage and tackle the bad smell around *Gangs* could be a high-risk bluff. The Miramax gangbusters strategy clearly presents a united front and hypes the film, but the charm offensive looks so heavy-handed that a cynic might detect a crisis of confidence behind the spin. In fact, hackles are raised in the press conference when one reporter likens the event to a pre-scripted whitewash.

In the end, it scarcely matters who fought and fell out on *Gangs*. The only crucial factor is what finally appears on that screen in January. From the twenty minutes screened in Cannes, we can only say that it looks extraordinary – amazing sets, bizarre costumes, crazy accents, stylised violence. We can also take heart that Scorsese has never made a bad film, especially on a subject so close to his heart.

But there is far more at stake with *Gangs* than mere profit. Behind the bravado in Cannes, Weinstein and Scorsese are taking the most expensive, high-profile gamble of their careers. 'Playing the artistic game is the highest-stakes game for both the director and the companies that finance them,' sighs Weinstein the testicle-cruncher in a rare admission of vulnerability. 'You don't get a prize for noble ambition.'

MARTIN SCORSESE/STEVEN SPIELBERG ON
GANGS OF NEW YORK

Martin Scorsese participated in Q&A discussions following a December 4 screening in New York and a December 15 screening in Los Angeles of his latest film, *Gangs of New York*. Director Steven Spielberg moderated the discussion in Los Angeles, returning the favour of Scorsese moderating a discussion with him about *Catch Me if You Can* in New York. What follows are highlights from the Los Angeles discussion.

Steven Spielberg: We've known each other since 1967. I love *The Big Shave*. We met over that. I remember the time, about 25 years ago, when I first read the script for *Gangs of New York* by Jay Cocks. In all these years, why did it take so long?

Martin Scorsese: I think, ultimately, it took all that time, trying to find myself in those characters and how much history, and what period of history. Originally it was set in the 1840s, 1850s, then I realised I wanted to end with the Draft Riots. I was sort of locked into that date, 1863, the summer. Originally what we had on paper was more novelistic, more literature than cinema, in a sense, at least that's the way I saw it. There was just so much background. Every page was so rich . . . . And it took a long time.

Spielberg: You constructed a world in this picture.

Scorsese: This has been the biggest problem in getting the picture made: to actually construct lower Manhattan. None of the sets existed. And I didn't want red bricks, there was some red brick, but not as much in 1865 or 1866. This place was like the end of the world. Wooden buildings, mud, the pigs that were there were the sanitation department. The pigs would eat the trash.

Spielberg: The thing that struck me when I saw it was the clash of cultures. All these shiploads of immigrants speaking different languages, and the fact that Bill the Butcher [played by Daniel Day Lewis], probably a character we won't forget as long as we live, he calls himself a Native American. Were there any Native Americans before him?

Scorsese: Apparently. Mark Twain's old line, 'When the Europeans discovered America they fell on their knees, then they fell on the aborigines.'

Spielberg: There was also something Dickensian, something *Oliver Twist*, Fagin and Oliver in a way is Amsterdam [Leonardo DiCaprio], but much more violent than Lionel Bart's musical certainly or David Lean's movie.

Scorsese: You're absolutely right. This is all coming out. As I'm finishing the film, I'm still quite close to it. I never quite finished the edit credits, but I think they're OK. Seriously, it's one of those things, I'm still going back, there's a couple mistakes. But the closer we get, the sense of what you're talking about is coming to me. There's been some obvious references to *Satyricon*; it was even going to be more stylised than this, but then I decided against that. Certainly to *Once Upon a Time in the West*, I never got as near to that masterpiece, but just the opening where he kicks open the door and goes out into the white snow. That's Sergio Leone. But we did study the beautiful restoration of the black-and-white David Lean *Oliver Twist*.

Spielberg: Exactly. The thing that I was noticing: 37 fire brigades? Each was a gang against the other?

Scorsese: Yeah. Actually there were more than 37. They had names like the Black Joke which actually is the fire gang that started the Draft Riots. That's why you see them breaking the windows, because three or four of their guys had been called up that morning and they thought it was bad. They didn't intend to start the Draft Riots, but they were the first ones to throw bricks through the windows. What would happen is that [at a fire] they would put a barrel over the [water] pinup until their fire brigade got there. It was really territorial, and a lot of it was plundering. Massive battles. Growing up downtown, if there was a fight on the corner everybody would run and see.

Spielberg: What about that moment, where the immigrants are getting off the boat and they say, 'Sign this document and you're American citizens. Sign this document and you're a private in the United States Army.'

Scorsese: It's different groups of shots and men, ultimately leading to the coffin coming off the boat. No, it didn't happen in one day. But the reality was that so many of those guys, once they had the guns in their hands and they were in some place they had never heard of and being shot at, it might as well have been one day. A lot of them joined because they didn't have any food: they couldn't get any jobs. So three meals a day was not bad. And nobody had seen the Matthew Brady photographs [of Civil War battlefield aftermaths] yet. Who knew? War? Especially in Ireland, they were peasants. They fought with the British, but it wasn't the kind of nineteenth-century military warfare they were involved in. A lot of the kids who went to the war thinking it was more innocent wound up in the stills that you see.

Spielberg: But then the cannons are firing, all this technology took Bill the Butcher – who was a god – and reduced him to dust. Amsterdam and Bill were sort of dust at that point. It was very interesting to see how quickly you diminished their stature, especially Bill's stature. How much of this was storyboarded and how much did you wing it?

Scorsese: The battles were storyboarded. The fight scene at the beginning was storyboard. It's like Hellcat Maggie jumping into the air, swinging down, tracking down to the guy's shoulder as he looks up and then the ear coming off this way so nobody can really see the ear coming off, all of it was designed on paper. The montage itself was storyboarded, but I gave it to Vic Armstrong [action unit director] to shoot, some of those close hand-to-hand combat bits. But what I wanted to do was [similar to] the Russian montage films of Eisenstein.

Spielberg: They had money in those days.

Scorsese: Exactly.

Spielberg: They had more money than we did. A hundred thousand extras.

Scorsese: A lot of extras. But there's one thing in *Potemkin*, it's when the sailor looks at the dish and says, 'Give us this day our daily bread,' and they've been starving on the boat. And he gets angry. He's washing the dishes, and he stops and looks and looks. He's got a black-and-white striped shirt on – and he takes the plate and breaks it. It's one action he just did. But it's five to eight cuts. What I was interested in was the cuts: three times to his shoulder, after breaking the plate. It was almost like ballet. It was very cubist in a way. So I designed it to get those shots Vic did. I wasn't interested in seeing the connection, the action of violence. I was interested in creating the impression. So I would tell him to get a shot, start at 48 frames, go to twelve then come up to 24. Then do the same thing and just reverse.

Spielberg: I thought it was fascinating because I can dish it out, but I can't take. So the first scene I'm like this [covering his eyes]. I can blow arms and heads off people in my films but I can't watch his. At the same time, when I thought I was able to watch, I realised something: there's no connection. You see someone bashing their head into the lens and then you see the person taking the head hit going away with a little blood. You see swords and knives, not going into a body, just swinging; then you cut to the ground and a body just falls to the ground. I've never seen anything staged this way before, and I thought it was just amazing.

Scorsese: It's when I realised it's the pieces of the shots we usually throw away. It's the resolution of the action. That's what I realised with the breaking of the plates. I said, 'Let's do that. Let's go back and forth and never really see the connection of the bodies.' For example, in the scene where Bill stabs his friend Harvey's hand at the table while they're playing cards. It's five shots but you don't see the knife going in at all.

Spielberg: You've got three great writers credited on this – Jay, Steve Zaillian and Kenneth Lonergan. Can you explain what their contributions were?

Scorsese: Well, it was Jay who worked on the original draft. It was the late seventies. By the time we were set to do rewrites on it, I'd finished *Raging Bull*, *King of Comedy*, and everything had changed. I couldn't get another big film like that made at the time. Especially because it was a very complex draft as you remember. It was 170 pages or something. I put my energies toward *Last Temptation of Christ*, and that couldn't get made. So I kind of put everything down for about ten years. And I took the script with me when I went to Japan and worked on [Akira Kurosawa's] *Dreams* and read it again and asked Jay to do some rewrites. He basically rewrote it in 1989, condensed it and added the revenge theme, which is really just a motor to get the thing going. Ultimately, that didn't work out either. Finally, Steve Zaillian came in and did more of a restructuring and tightening. Things like the scene 'Sign here and you become a citizen.' And then before shooting started, Kenny Lonergan offered his help. I was one of his producers on *You Can Count on Me*. And Kenny came in and we started working on the characters, particularly Amsterdam and Jenny. Basically when I wanted to go further with the complexity of whether or not he should go directly to Bill and kill him (but he would never do that; he would get sidetracked by his heart, really). That's where I worked really strongly with Kenny during shooting and finally in the editing too.

Spielberg: It's very seamless. You don't hear three voices. You hear one voice. You.

GANGS OF NEW YORK
Reviewed by Roger Ebert

Martin Scorsese's *Gangs of New York* rips up the postcards of American history and reassembles them into a violent, blood-soaked story of our bare-knuckled past. The New York it portrays in the years between the 1840s and the Civil War is, as a character observes, 'the forge of hell', in which groups clear space by killing their rivals. Competing fire brigades and police forces fight in the streets, audiences throw rotten fruit at an actor portraying Abraham Lincoln, blacks and Irish are chased by mobs, and Navy ships fire on the city as the poor riot against the draft.

The film opens with an extraordinary scene set beneath tenements, in catacombs carved out of the Manhattan rock. An Irish-American leader named Priest Vallon (Liam Neeson) prepares for battle almost as if preparing for the Mass – indeed, as he puts on a collar to protect his neck, we think for a moment he might be a priest. With his young son Amsterdam trailing behind, he walks through the labyrinth of this torchlit Hades, gathering his forces, the Dead Rabbits, before stalking out into daylight to fight the forces of a rival American-born gang, the Nativists.

Men use knives, swords, bayonets, cleavers, cudgels. The ferocity of their battle is animalistic. At the end, the field is littered with bodies – including that of Vallon, slain by his enemy William Cutting, aka Bill the Butcher (Daniel Day-Lewis). This was the famous gang fight of Five Points on the Lower East Side of Manhattan, recorded in American history but not underlined. When it is over, Amsterdam disappears into an orphanage, the ominously named Hellgate House of Reform. He emerges in his early twenties (now played by Leonardo DiCaprio) and returns to Five Points, still ruled by Bill, and begins a scheme to avenge his father.

The vivid achievement of Scorsese's film is to visualise this history and people it with characters of Dickensian grotesquerie. Bill the Butcher is one of the great characters in modern movies, with his strangely elaborate diction, his choked accent, his odd way of combining ruthlessness with philosophy. The canvas is filled with many other colourful characters, including a pickpocket named Jenny Everdeane (Cameron Diaz), a hired club named Monk (Brendan Gleeson), the shopkeeper Happy Jack (John C. Reilly), and historical figures such as William 'Boss' Tweed (Jim Broadbent), ruler of corrupt Tammany Hall, and P. T. Barnum (Roger Ashton-Griffiths), whose museum of curiosities scarcely rivals the daily displays on the streets.

Scorsese's hero, Amsterdam, plays much the same role as a Dickens hero like David Copperfield or Oliver Twist: He is the eyes through which we see the others but is not the most colourful person on the canvas. Amsterdam is not as wild, as vicious or as eccentric as the people around him, and may not be any tougher than his eventual girlfriend Jenny, who like Nancy in *Oliver Twist* is a hellcat with a fierce loyalty to her man. DiCaprio's character, more focused and centred, is a useful contrast to the wild men around him.

Certainly, Day-Lewis is inspired by an intense ferocity, laced with humour and a certain analytical detachment, as Bill the Butcher. He is a fearsome man, fond of using his knife to tap his glass eye, and he uses a pig carcass to show Amsterdam the various ways to kill a man with a knife. Bill is a skilled knife artist, and terrifies Jenny, his target for a knife-throwing act, not only by coming close to killing her but also by his ornate and ominous word choices.

Diaz plays Jenny as a woman who at first insists on her own independence; as a pickpocket, she ranks high in the criminal hierarchy, and even dresses up to prey on the rich people uptown. But when she finally caves in to Amsterdam's love, she proves tender and loyal, in one love scene where they compare their scars, and another where she nurses him back to health.

The movie is straightforward in its cynicism about democracy at that time. Tammany Hall buys and sells votes, ethnic groups are delivered by their leaders, and when the wrong man is elected sheriff he does not serve for long. That American democracy emerged from this cauldron is miraculous. We put the Founding Fathers on our money, but these Founding Crooks for a long time held sway.

Scorsese is probably our greatest active American director (Robert Altman is another candidate), and he has given us so many masterpieces that this film, which from another director would be a triumph, arrives as a more measured accomplishment. It was a difficult film to make, as we know from the reports that drifted back from the vast and expensive sets constructed at Cinecitta in Rome. The budget was enormous, the running time was problematical.

The result is a considerable achievement, a revisionist history linking the birth of American democracy and American crime. It brings us astonishing sights, as in a

Cameron Diaz as Jenny Everdeane, a nineteenth-century 'cutpurse'. Producer Harvey Weinstein credits her with calming an often fraught set at Rome's Cinecitta.

scene that shows us the inside of a tenement, with families stacked on top of one another in rooms like shelves. Or in the ferocity of the Draft Riots, which all but destroyed the city. It is instructive to be reminded that modern America was forged not in quiet rooms by great men in wigs, but in the streets, in the clash of immigrant groups, in a bloody Darwinian struggle.

All of this is a triumph for Scorsese, and yet I do not think this film is in the first rank of his masterpieces. It is very good but not great. I wrote recently of *GoodFellas* that 'the film has the headlong momentum of a storyteller who knows he has a good one to share'. I didn't feel that here. Scorsese's films usually leap joyfully onto the screen, the work of a master in command of his craft. Here there seems more struggle, more weight to overcome, more darkness. It is a story that Scorsese has filmed without entirely internalising. The gangsters in his earlier films are motivated by greed, ego and power; they like nice cars, shoes, suits, dinners, women. They murder as a cost of doing business. The characters in *Gangs of New York* kill because they like to and want to. They are bloodthirsty, and motivated by hate. I think Scorsese liked the heroes of *GoodFellas*, *Casino* and *Mean Streets*, but I'm not sure he likes this crowd.

FOUNDING FATHERS
By Amy Taubin

The most resonant scene in Martin Scorsese's *Gangs of New York* is also one of the most understated. Newly recruited soldiers in the Union Army, fresh off the boat from Ireland, file onto the ship that will take them south to the battlefields of the Civil War. A hoist, bearing a single coffin, swings past them and down onto the pier, where dozens of similar coffins have already been unloaded. The sequence is a remarkably succinct visualisation of war as an assembly line where live human beings are raw material and death is the product.

It's a punishing piece of work, this *Gangs of New York*. Spectacular, brilliant, but punishing – basically, one long brawl framed between what must be the two bloodiest battle scenes ever committed to celluloid. At the least, the film is a corrective to the accepted notion that urban violence is a twentieth-century phenomenon. 'A western on Mars' was Scorsese's original concept. In *Gangs*, lower Manhattan, as recreated on fifteen acres of Cinecittà backlot, is a claustrophobia-inducing version of the Wild West.

Scorsese and screenwriter Jay Cocks loosely based their script on Herbert Asbury's 1928 *The Gangs of New York*, an anecdotal history of the street gangs that fought for control of poor immigrant neighbourhoods from the early 1800s to the early 1900s. (Cocks wrote the first version of the screenplay 25 years ago. Steve Zaillian and Kenneth Lonergan also have screenplay credits. Their work came after the film was committed to production.) *Gangs* is set in 1863 in the miserable, vice-ridden ghetto of the Five Points and climaxes during the Draft Riots, the most deadly civil uprising in US history. The riots began as a protest against the 1863 Conscription Act, which decreed that every able-bodied man was subject to the draft unless he could pay a $300 exemption fee. As the riots escalated, class resentment was conjoined with racial hatred. The mob attacked recruiting stations, government buildings, and the mansions of the rich; they also torched black neighbourhoods and beat, shot, or lynched every black person in their path. Not only did they refuse to serve in Lincoln's abolitionist war, they were out to prove that black people had no future in New York. In the end, the army quelled the riots by shooting the protesters en masse; tens of thousands were killed.

The riots themselves and the racism they revealed (as endemic to the North as the South) operate at the periphery of the film's narrative. *Gangs*' main focus is the conflict between the Nativists (Protestant descendants of the original Anglo-Dutch settlers) and the newly arrived Irish Catholic immigrants (who, at the height of the potato famine, were flooding into New York at the rate of 15,000 a week). So intent are these enemies on destroying each other that they are oblivious to the larger historical forces about to render their tiny turf war irrelevant. Nearly burned to the ground during the riots, the Five Points had the distinction of being the city's most blighted neighbourhood until it was totally razed at the turn of the century. Paradise Square, where its five main drags converged, is now the site of the Federal Court

House (100 Centre Street).

The plot on which *Gangs* is hung, but which hardy speaks to the film's scope or ambition, is a familiar combo of revenge and romance. As a child, Amsterdam Vallon (Leonardo DiCaprio) sees his father (Liam Neeson), the leader of the Irish gang, the Dead Rabbits, dealt a fatal blow during a rumble with the Natives by their leader, William Cutting, aka 'Bill the Butcher' (Daniel Day-Lewis). Sixteen years later, he returns to the Five Points to avenge his father's murder. He infiltrates the Natives and soon becomes the Butcher's favourite. He's also drawn into a stormy relationship with Jenny Everdeane (Cameron Diaz), an enterprising pickpocket and the Butcher's former mistress. Although he doesn't lack opportunities, he waits nearly as long as Hamlet before making a move on his father's killer. By then, Bill has been tipped off about Amsterdam's real identity and uses his knife before Amsterdam can pull his gun. Bill stops short of killing Amsterdam, deeming it a worse punishment that he spend the rest of his life maimed and humiliated. But Jenny nurses Amsterdam back to health, and he rises, with new-found political savvy and resolve, to unite an army of Irish immigrants against the Butcher and form an alliance with the boss of the Tammany Hall Democratic machine, William Tweed (Jim Broadbent). With his power ebbing away, Bill murders Monk (Brendan Gleeson), the moral force among Amsterdam's supporters. A near suicidal act, it sets the stage for a final showdown.

You don't have to think twice about why Scorsese was attracted to this material. All of his great films are stories about New York subcultures: their origins, how they mould the individual, how they enforce their laws, the parts they play in the evolution of the city as a whole. Can the individual survive ostracism? What price does he pay for inclusion? From *Mean Streets* through *The Age of Innocence*, Scorsese has mined the dynamic between the individual and the social fabric of New York. It's an unfailing source of drama and character for him. *Taxi Driver* is the counterexample – an ethnography of the ultimate outsider.

In *Gangs*, however, the fictional narrative of revenge and romance has, at best, a forced relationship to the social history of this period in the city's life. Amsterdam and Jenny are generic characters, and their scenes are about as convincing as the scar on Jenny's absurdly toned belly. 'They cut my baby out of me,' she says, trying to put on a brave face. And then the subject is dropped. Did the baby live or die? Did she have a hysterectomy as well? What percentage of women survived OB/GYN surgery in the mid-nineenth century? Was it done in a hospital or in a back alley? Who paid the doctor? In almost any other Scorsese film, you would find out all of that.

It doesn't help that the protagonist of *Gangs* is played by a whey-faced actor with a pallid emotional range who'd be impossible to pick out from a crowd if Scorsese weren't such a whiz at blocking. DiCaprio walks through the entire film in a haze of inscrutability. When called upon to react, he invariably presses his lips together and slightly furrows his brow (check the image in the *Gangs* poster) in an attempt to show manly resolve. Occasionally, he'll take two steps back and put up his hands as if to say, 'Whoa, dude!' – not exactly the most felicitous move for the film's hero to make. If Amsterdam has returned to the Five Points to kill the Butcher, what is he waiting for? Is he frightened? Is he conflicted about the act of killing? Is he in awe of the Butcher for having killed his father? Is he madly in love with him? All of the above? Who knows? Maybe not even Amsterdam, or rather, DiCaprio's Amsterdam. The actor seems most comfortable when he's running or tussling, but called upon to communicate an inner thought or a desire, he's at a loss. In the film's third act, Amsterdam is meant to come into his own as a leader. By uniting the warring gangs of the Five Points, he's instrumental in the transformation of New York from a feudal to a cosmopolitan city. Because DiCaprio has all the charisma of the average student council president, the dynamic of historical change crucial to Scorsese's concept of the movie remains an abstraction. It's explained in voiceover and illustrated in the film's final montage of the Manhattan skyline growing higher and higher as it moves into the twentieth century. But it's never fully embodied within the narrative.

DiCaprio would seem anaemic even if he were not playing opposite Day-Lewis, whose Bill the Butcher is ferocious and funny and ultimately tragic – a truly epic creation. Bill knows the value of making an entrance and Scorsese's gleeful direction of Day-Lewis gives the character every possible opportunity. In the film's prologue, when the gangs face off in Paradise Square, the camera surveys Bill in close-up, moving from his huge boots, up along his attenuated body that seems simultaneously brawny and spindly, to find his face, its elegant bones nearly obscured by a movie villain's handlebar moustache and the brim of a stovepipe hat shadowing his brow. Day-Lewis begins to speak, and for a moment you think, Oh no, he's doing De Niro, or more precisely, De Niro as Travis Bickle. The similarities are too blatant to ignore: the smile and the raised eyebrows twisted in mock bemusement, mockery also colouring the blunt rhythms of his speech – all of it a thin veneer over the murderous rage that defines the man.

But it's not Travis per se that Day-Lewis is playing. It's the founding father of a long line of Travis Bickles – the men who view themselves honour-bound to preserve America for Americans and to keep Otherness at bay. Whether conscious or unconscious on Day-Lewis and Scorsese's parts, the connection is a stroke of genius – to show, within what otherwise appears to be a traditional costume picture, that movies are porous texts and movie history continually commingles with 'real' history in the collective cultural imagination.

Day-Lewis's performance is not only bold in its externals. He seems to have absorbed 'Bill the Butcher' into every muscle and synapse of his being. The tension between calculation and impulse that makes the character so frightening – those are *Bill's* impulses and *Bill's* calculations that we see and intuit. When Bill teaches Amsterdam how to stab an opponent to death, using a pig's carcass strung up like a punching bag, the hand on the knife belongs to a man who has worked as a butcher all his life and for whom butchery is a metaphor for all human transactions. Film history is filled with performances that are organic, but performances that are organic and mythically proportioned are rare. At the moment I can't think of any that are comparable to what Day-Lewis does here.

The scenes in which the Butcher is the dominating force give the movie its shot at greatness: There's the theatrical knife throwing display with Jenny as the desperate apprentice (in which Thelma Schoonmaker's cuts are as terrifying as Day-Lewis's moves). There's Bill, in a rocking chair, wrapped in the American flag, trying to explain his life to himself and to the boy he has begun to think of as a son and whose betrayal

Bill 'the Butcher' Cutting in the Five Points street that resembles a Western frontier town – a tour de force performance by Daniel Day-Lewis, equally grotesque and charismatic.

marks the beginning of his downfall. One of the only scenes that Scorsese covers with a fixed camera and very few shot changes, it has a gravity and a tragic dimension like nothing else in the film. Even the savagely kinetic opening fight scene could be reduced to Scorsese being competitive with Eisenstein (Scorsese is the victor, incidentally, but he has the advantage of digital tools), if not for the galvanising presence of the Butcher, with his huge guttural voice, his fearsome strength, and fierce determination to win.

Gangs of New York may be the last of its kind – a costume picture made entirely in a studio by a superbly creative director in collaboration with master craftspeople. And if it is, that's not necessarily a bad thing. Movies produced on this scale impose heavy economic and aesthetic burdens. In this case, Scorsese traded his proven passion for detailing the rituals of daily life (almost entirely absent in this film) in order to give screen time to a silly love story that will supposedly lure the masses to the theatre. To be horribly blunt, *Gangs of New York* easily stands up next to Bertolucci's *1900* but compared to Rossellini's *The Rise to Power of Louis XIV* or Peter Watkins' *The Commune (Paris 1871)* it's just smoke (much too much smoke on that set) and mirrors. Scorsese is, without doubt, capable of making a film as aesthetically rigorous and intellectually exhilarating as those two films are. *The Age of Innocence* and *Kundun* seem like moves in that direction. The dilemma is that Hollywood has no interest in art films, and without Hollywood money, one has to give up the high-tech tools, the superstars, the whole machine of power. If what you get in exchange is freedom, the choice is so obvious that it's no choice at all.

Journey Onward

FEEL LIKE GOING HOME
By Martin Scorsese

When I was growing up, there always seemed to be music in the air. It drifted up from the street, from the radios of passing cars, from the restaurants and corner stores, from the windows of apartments across the way. At home, my mother often sang to herself – I have vivid memories of her singing while she was doing the dishes. My father loved to play his mandolin, and my brother Frank played the guitar. Actually, it was my father who was the guitar enthusiast, and the first music I remember hearing was by Django Reinhardt and his Hot Club of France Quintet. At that time, you could always hear an incredible range of music on the radio, everything from Italian folk songs to country and western. And my uncle Joe, my mother's brother, had an amazing record collection, which ranged from Gilbert and Sullivan to swing. He was one of the first people I could really talk to, and I think we related to each other because of our shared love for music.

One day, around 1958, I remember hearing something that was unlike anything I'd ever heard before. I'll never forget the first time I heard the sound of that guitar. The music was demanding, 'Listen to me!' I ran to get a pencil and paper and wrote down the name. The song was called 'See See Rider', which I already knew from the Chuck Willis cover version. The name of the singer was Lead Belly. I got up to Sam Goody's on 49th Street as fast as I could, and I found an old Folkways record by Lead Belly, which had 'See See Rider', 'Roberta', 'Black Snake Moan', and a few other songs. And I listened to it obsessively. Lead Belly's music opened something up for me. If I could have played guitar, really played it, I never would have become a filmmaker.

At around the same time, my friends and I went to see Bo Diddley. That was another milestone for me. He was playing at the Brooklyn Paramount, in one of the rock and roll package shows. He always had great stage moves, and he was a mesmerising performer. I remember Jerome Green, on the maracas, dancing out from one side of the stage and Bo Diddley dancing out from the other, and they kept meeting in the middle and passing each other by. But Bo Diddley also did something unusual – he explained the different drumbeats and which parts of Africa they came from. It gave us a sense of the history behind the music, the roots of the music. We all found this very exciting, and it gave us a thirst for more knowledge. We wanted to dig deeper.

In the early sixties, my preference was for Phil Spector, Motown, and the girl groups, like the Ronettes, the Marvelettes, and the Shirelles. Then came the British Invasion. Like everyone else, I was floored by this music, and struck by its strong blues influence. The more I understood the history behind rock and roll, the more I could hear the blues behind it. With some of the new British music, the blues came to the

Leonardo Di Caprio as The Aviator *(2004). His performance as Howard Hughes won acclaim, but the screenplay stopped short of Hughes' ultimate descent into total insanity.*

forefront, and the bands were paying homage to their masters in the same way that the French New Wave filmmakers were paying homage to the great American directors with their films. There was John Mayall and his Bluesbreakers. There was the first instalment of Fleetwood Mac, with Peter Green on guitar, basically a blues band. There were the Stones, whose music had a heavy blues accent right from the start, and who did cover versions of 'Little Red Rooster', 'I'm a King Bee', 'Love in Vain', and many others. And, of course, there was Cream. I still love to sit alone in a room and wrap myself up in that music. They created an amazing fusion of blues and hard rock, and some of their most beautiful songs were covers: 'Rollin' and Tumblin', the old Delta classic, which I first heard on volume one of *Live Cream*; Robert Johnson's 'Crossroads', which was one of their biggest hits; and 'Sitting on Top of the World', which was on *Goodbye Cream*. When I heard that song I went back and found the original, by the great Mississippi Sheiks.

Around the end of the sixties, this urge to find the roots of the music really started to spread. People all over the country were discovering the blues, and it went way beyond a specialised audience. At that time, the music wasn't as readily available as it is now. You would have to search for certain titles, and others you could find in reissues and package collections. The blues had such a powerful mystique, such an aura around it, that certain names would suddenly be in the air, and you just had to have their records. Names like Son House, which I heard for the first time when we were editing *Woodstock*. It was Mike Wadleigh, the director, who brought in the record. Someone who once heard Caruso sing said that he was so moved that his heart shook. That's the way I felt the first time I heard Son House. It was a voice and a style that seemed to come from way, way back, from some other, much earlier time and place. About a year later, there was another name: Robert Johnson. Another ancient voice, another soul-stirring experience.

It was my love for music, which has never stopped growing, that led me to do *The Last Waltz*. I wanted to make it more than just a document of The Band's last concert. Because it was more than just a musical tribute – it was a tapestry of music history, The Band's music history. And every one of those performers – one legend after another – made up a thread in that tapestry. But when Muddy Waters walked onto that stage and sang 'Mannish Boy', he took control of the music, the event, the history, everything. He electrified the audience, took it all up to another level and back to the source at the same time. He gave a phenomenal performance, and I will always consider myself privileged to have been there to witness it, to film it, and to give it back to millions of people with the finished film. It was a defining moment for me.

Over the last ten years or so, this search for historical roots has found its way into my moviemaking. I've made two documentaries on the history of cinema – one on American movies, then another on Italian cinema. And I decided early on that I wanted them to be personal, rather than strictly historical surveys. It seemed to me that this was the best way to work: The teachers from whom I learned the most were always the most passionate, the ones with a deeply personal connection to the material. For *The Blues* series, I decided to do something similar.

The project began when Cappa Productions producer Margaret Bodde and I were working on a documentary with Eric Clapton called *Nothing but the Blues*, where we intercut footage of Eric performing blues standards with archival footage of older

blues musicians. We were all struck by the elemental power and poetry of these juxtapositions – it seemed like such a simple yet eloquent way of expressing the music's
timelessness. It also gave us a way of approaching the history of the blues in cinematic
terms. So it seemed like a natural progression to ask a number of directors whose
work I admired, each with a deep connection to the music, to make his own personal exploration of blues history. By having each of them come at the subject from his
own unique perspective, I knew we'd come away with something special, not a dry
recitation of facts, but a genuinely passionate mosaic.

For my own film, which was the first in the series, the idea was to take the viewer
on a pilgrimage to Mississippi and then on to Africa with a wonderful young blues
musician named Corey Harris. Corey isn't just a great player, he also knows the history of the blues very well. We filmed him in Mississippi talking to some of the old,
legendary figures who were still around and visiting some of the places where the
music was made. This section culminates in a meeting with the great Otha Turner,
sitting on his porch in Senatobia with his family nearby and playing his cane flute.
We were also fortunate to film Otha's magnificent November 2001 concert at St.
Ann's in Brooklyn, which I believe was his last performance captured on film. It
seemed natural to trace the music back from Mississippi to West Africa, where Corey
met and played with extraordinary artists like Salif Keita, Habib Koité, and Ali Farka
Toure. It's fascinating to hear the links between the African and American music, to
see the influences going both ways, back and forth across time and space.

The links between Africa and the blues were always very important to Alan
Lomax, and that's one of the reasons I wanted to include him in my film. I relate
strongly to Lomax's instinct, his need to find and record genuine sounds and music
before the originators died away. It's hard to overestimate the importance of what he
accomplished – without him, so much would have been lost.

Otha Turner's music was a link to Africa, and Lomax spent a great deal of time
exploring that connection. That elemental music, made with nothing but a fife and
drum, has always fascinated me. When I first heard it, I was editing *Raging Bull* by
night. I was enthralled – it sounded like something out of eighteenth-century
America, but with an African rhythm. I never even imagined that such a music could
exist. I found an audiotape of Otha's music, and I listened to it obsessively over many
years. I always knew that it would play a key role in *Gangs of New York*. That project
went through many false starts, and it changed quite a bit over the years, but one
thing that never changed was the idea that it would include fife and drum music.
When I finally did get to make the picture, we were lucky enough to be able to use a
piece by Otha and his Rising Star Band, and I used it as playback on the set to pro-
pel the action – it gave the film an energy and power it would have lacked otherwise,
and it helped to create a world we had never seen before. When the picture came
out, many people understandably thought they were listening to Celtic music and
were surprised to discover that it was by Otha Turner, from north Mississippi.

The sense of continuity and transformation in the blues, the way past, present,
and future are joined as one dynamic creative entity, never ceases to amaze me.
Earlier this year, we staged a 'Salute to the Blues' concert here in New York, which
Antoine Fuqua filmed for our series. It was an event I'll never forget, and the spirit

of that night was summed up memorably by Ruth Brown, who said: 'It's so great that we're all here together – and it's not for a funeral!' The sheer range of music that night was something to marvel at, and the beauty of the playing and singing was incomparable. There were some musicians who completely transformed the music, and made a kind of 21st-century blues. Chris Thomas King did a version of Son House's 'John the Revelator' with turntables and a synth guitar. He kept piling layers of sound on top of one another, and managed to create something completely modern and surprising but very much in keeping with the voice of the blues.

This idea of continuity and transformation runs through all the films in the series. Charles Burnett made a poetic and personal drama about blues life seen through the eyes of a young boy. Wim Wenders made an evocative film that moves in a dreamlike fashion through past, present, and future, in order to conjure three different bluesmen. Dick Pearce made a terrific film about Memphis, with Bobby Rush and the great B. B. King. Marc Levin did Chicago blues, featuring Chuck D and Marshall Chess in the studio with the Electric Mud band recording great new tracks with members of the Roots – once again, you get a strong sense of ongoing transformation in the blues here. Mike Figgis, who is himself a musician, made a film about the British blues scene, in the form of a story told by many of its creators. Clint Eastwood paid a very elegant tribute to the great blues piano players, Jay McShann, Pinetop Perkins, and others. All of these wonderful films are like pieces in a mosaic, in the end a moving and dynamic portrait of a great American art form.

People like to think of the great blues singers as raw, instinctive, with talent and genius flowing from their fingertips. But John Lee Hooker, Bessie Smith, Muddy Waters, Howlin' Wolf, Blind Lemon Jefferson, and so many other amazing talents, more names than I have space for here, are some of the greatest artists America has ever had. When you listen to Lead Belly, or Son House, or Robert Johnson, or John Lee Hooker, or Charley Patton, or Muddy Waters, you're moved, your heart is shaken, you're carried and inspired by its visceral energy, and its rock solid emotional truth. You go right to the heart of what it is to be human, the condition of being human. That's the blues.

THE BLUES COMES HOME
By David Kunian

There are two moments in *Feel Like Going Home* – the inaugural episode of the seven-part series *The Blues* – in which the themes director Martin Scorsese and host Corey Harris are exploring jump from the screen. In one scene, bluesman Taj Mahal is playing Muddy Waters' 'Catfish Blues' on the Mississippi plantation where Waters grew up. Scorsese skilfully fades the song into Waters' version of 'Rolling Stone' as Harris points out how the recording led Waters to leave the Jim Crow South for Chicago. It was a move that led to Waters taking the blues to the whole world.

Later in the film, Scorsese's camera follows Harris to Mali in West Africa to visit musician Ali Farka Toure. Scorsese uses the same technique of segueing from the one-chord drones of John Lee Hooker to Toure playing guitar, and it all sounds like the same song. In an effective, visceral manner, Scorsese and Harris consistently weave the thread through a culture's past, present and future by illustrating the vast interconnectedness of the blues.

By tracing the history of the blues back past Jim Crow, sharecropping and slavery across the ocean to Africa, Scorsese reiterates some of the overused blues mantras. But it's worth the trip; once in Africa, he allows the musicians to share a unique perspective on the blues from across the Atlantic. Scorsese, whose *The Last Waltz* is considered one of the best live-music documentaries ever, also makes room for varied opinions about the blues. This is but one way of sparing the viewer of monolithic and dogmatic pronouncements about the genre, a trap that Ken Burns' jazz documentary didn't avoid.

Scorsese's guide in the film is the musician and former New Orleans resident Corey Harris, who seems surprisingly comfortable in his role; he's equally at home playing his guitar or interviewing other musicians whether in the United States or Africa. His keen sense of what the blues means to himself and other musicians, our nation, and the world at large shows that Scorsese's more personalised approach to this musical form was a perfect decision.

The film moves from Harris' journeys finding musicians in the South to archival footage of work gangs, fife and drum parades, and footage of musicians such as Son House and Muddy Waters. Later, an interview with Johnny Shines, who travelled with the legendary Robert Johnson in the 1930s, sheds more light on the blues' most iconic and mysterious figure. In another segment, Harris also interviews Taj Mahal, who started playing in the 1960s during the folk blues revival and is a connection between the early part of the century through the sixties on to today. Mahal offers a simple yet deep analysis of how rural life and Mississippi social conditions led to the blues, and how the blues captured that life in its lyrics and rhythms.

Then Scorsese takes the film to the place where the African roots of the music are most apparent, the North Mississippi hill country where the late cane flute player Otha Turner made his home. A sequence with Turner and Harris playing on Turner's porch and talking about Turner's music and how he learned it are among the most profound moments in the entire film.

When Scorsese and Harris travel to Mali to visit with such musicians as Salif Keite, Habib Koite, Toumani Diabate, and Ali Farka Toure, *Feel Like Going Home* seems to hit its stride. Diabate's ancestors were the griots (or holders of stories and histories) for the Mandinka empire several centuries before, and Diabate and Harris compare the griots in Africa and the descendants of slaves across the ocean. With amazement, Harris notes the survival not just of human life but a cultural form as men, women and children spent several months in the dank hold of a slave ship. 'I'm a strong man,' Harris says, 'but I'm not that strong. I'm sure many people went crazy and died. It's a miracle we made it that far.'

FROM *MEAN STREETS* TO MYTHIC SKIES
By Colin Brown

It was at a Rome dinner hosted by Francesco Rosi that Martin Scorsese first heard of cinema's future, from Federico Fellini of all people. The Italian maestro had just returned from Tokyo where Sony's legendary founder Akio Morita had produced what looked like a compact disc and popped it into a machine in the wall. Suddenly, on the screen above, Fellini watched with amazement as a beautiful, scratch-free copy of his *La Strada* played.

That was 1991. More than a decade later and Scorsese, a self-professed DVD obsessive, has, amassed thousands of the shiny five-inch discs for home consumption on his big screen in Manhattan. 'Laserdiscs were wonderful and I have thousands of those too. But the DVD is easier to use, possesses more features and has its own kind of fetish,' he says. 'Obviously, it's preferable to see things on the screen. But DVD is the next best you can do.'

For a man who has just spent considerable time overseeing the DVD release of five of his own films for Warner Home Video – including a newly remastered *GoodFellas* – Scorsese is not that enthralled with all the bonus material around. And even though he spent painstaking hours with his editor ensuring that the red tones in the *Mean Streets* Special Edition echoed the warmth of the original print, he has even less patience with DVD's legion of technical pedants.

'I don't listen to all the commentaries. It's getting to the point where now you get to know just facts and information. But it doesn't give us anything more – it doesn't give us an emotional or psychological insight,' he says. 'It just becomes distracting. And some of the DVD publications I see, they get kind of obsessed with the technical aspects of it. I do agree the DVD audience is demanding better quality, which is making the studios restore the pictures to a certain extent, something we've been fighting for over the past 25 years. But these groups out there say things like the flesh tones aren't as good. I gotta tell you, I don't know how important flesh-tones are. At a certain point, let go.'

Getting people to truly immerse themselves in the emotional power of cinema, while also revelling in its historical legacy, seems to be a Scorsese mantra. Just ask the cast of his newest film, *The Aviator*, about the early years of daredevil pilot, eccentric billionaire and Hollywood film mogul Howard Hughes. In preparation for their roles, Leonardo DiCaprio, Cate Blanchett, Kate Beckinsale and the like were all treated to Scorsese lessons in cinema.

'I would screen Howard Hawks' *His Girl Friday* for them on 35mm on the big screen. Just for the body language and Cary Grant's dialogue so that they had a reference. I screened *Public Enemy* among other films because I wanted Leo DiCaprio [playing Howard Hughes] to understand the world he was getting into. I wanted him to think, "Now you're going to do *Scarface* and you're going to top this. I just want you to know where your mind is at." He was the outlaw of Hollywood in a way.'

While Scorsese admits he was not a Hughes enthusiast until he read John Logan's script, he was quickly hooked by a story that combined his love of early Hollywood, Hughes' dark tendencies and his mythic aviation exploits. 'Most people who know me know I am not fond of flying but that also makes me attracted to it. These men and women who went up there as early aviators were like the astronauts today.'

That said, *The Aviator*, another big-budget extravaganza coming on the heels of *Gangs of New York*, could well mark another turning point in a career still searching for that long overdue best director Oscar statuette. Deeply personal movies, as opposed to Hollywood spectacles, are starting to grab his fancy again, even as he prepares to shoot a remake of *Infernal Affairs*.

'You get into a situation where the film starts to cost $150m, and you have to ask what's your ending? Do you want people to start smashing their cars against trees? I don't know. The more money, the less risk. That's the danger,' says Scorsese who is now working with Howard Shore on *The Aviator*'s score.

'As Harvey Weinstein said to me this morning, if you want to do a film that is kind of dark or violent for $20m or something, fine. Shoot it in 30 days. But if you are going to do something for $100m or $110m, it alters your subject matter and how you present the subject matter. And you know, as I get older too, I don't know if there is any room for me, in a way, with what is happening [in the film business]. So I'm looking forward to making pictures that have a little smaller budget and taking different stories and going that way.'

THE AVIATOR
Reviewed by Simon Braund

Few, if any, filmmakers could hit a decade-long losing streak like Scorsese and still have us breathless with anticipation whenever a fresh project is announced, champing at the bit to see whether he's finally rediscovered the incandescent form of *Taxi Driver*, *Raging Bull* and *GoodFellas* – and whether his latest will be the picture that finally bags him an Academy Award.

The good news is, *The Aviator* represents his strongest Oscar bid yet (it is, after all, a movie about Hollywood). The bad news is, it doesn't quite bear the weight of anticipation, and can't withstand comparisons with Scorsese's masterworks. For all that it's a great story well told, we expect more than mere good storytelling from the man who gave us Travis Bickle.

Scorsese excels at exploring characters in whom he feels a deep personal resonance, those who, like him, have done battle with their own demons. It's through misfits like Travis Bickle, La Motta, Henry Hill and even *The King of Comedy*'s excruciating Rupert Pupkin that he's sought to dig out the truths of the human condition. But it's difficult to imagine the son of striving immigrants having much affinity with Howard Hughes who, despite his fascinating, tragic arc, wasn't even a self-made man, and who funded his outlandish endeavours by milking the inexhaustible cash cow of his family's machine tool business. Perhaps this is why he fails to get under the skin of his subject.

Nevertheless, Hughes' story *is* fascinating. It begins with the Hollywood arriviste lavishing his recent inheritance on his twin passions simultaneously, amassing the world's largest private air force and sinking an unprecedented $4 million of his own money into *Hell's Angels*, his tribute to World War I fighter pilots. Given Scorsese's infallible eye – abetted here by production designer Dante Ferreti and costumer designer Sandy Powell – the recreation of twenties Hollywood is immaculate. There are also several magnificent set-pieces to savour, among them Hughes' heroic orchestration of the *Hell's Angels* dogfight sequences from the open gun turret of a bomber and, later, a spectacular plane crash in which Hughes, flight-testing one of his own designs, rips through the rooftops of Beverly Hills.

In between, mustering every ounce of his stylistic verve, Scorsese chronicles Hughes' stormy romantic dalliances with Katharine Hepburn (Cate Blanchett) and Ava Gardner (Kate Beckinsale) and his draining, dragged-out fight with Pan Am chief Juan Trippe (Alec Baldwin), who was determined to put his TWA airline out of business. As the visual tone shifts to keep pace with the times – the pastel hues of the twenties giving way to the oversaturated Technicolor forties – Hughes himself transmogrifies from a brazen young mogul into a twitchy, paranoid obsessive who, against the backdrop of failed relationships and a besieged business empire, struggles to keep a grip on his failing sanity.

It's in these later scenes that Leonardo DiCaprio shines, dispelling fears that he hasn't the weight to carry such a complex, forceful role. He's mesmerising in the moment when Hughes rears back from the brink of madness to face down a corrupt senator (a superb Alan Alda) over allegations that he cheated the US Air Force.

Yet in spite of the lush production values, absorbing narrative and outstanding performances, the question of what, exactly, made this extraordinary man tick remains unanswered. When he's pulled from the flaming wreckage of his plane, the only words he manages to croak are, 'I'm Howard Hughes, the aviator.' And we know precious little more of him than that.

THE END OF THE GOLDEN AGE
By Damon Wise

At the age of 22, or possibly 21, because mystery even surrounds the date of his birth, Howard Hughes was struggling with one of the first runaway blockbusters. Using money from his late father's fortune – made by the Hughes Tool Company, which

Hughes with 1940s movie star Ava Gardner (Kate Beckinsale). Despite his love of Golden Age Hollywood, The Aviator *is the only film by Scorsese set during that era.*

patented a lucrative new oil-drilling bit – Hughes was at work on *Hell's Angels,* a tribute to the flying aces of World War I. It was October 1927 and the silent movie era was giving way to sound, a milestone cemented in Hughes' mind when he saw Al Jolson's *The Jazz Singer* and decided that his already long-overdue film had to be remade to keep up with the latest developments, whatever the cost.

The film appeared three years later, after Hughes had scoured the country looking for Fokkers, Snipes and Sopwith Camels, which he restored to fighting condition and hired an army of experienced extras to fly. The air scenes alone, still some of the most ambitious ever, took eighteen months to film, at a cost of $250,000. By the time it wrapped, 3,000,000 feet of film had been shot, 20,000 people had been employed and Hughes' pilots had flown 227,000 miles through the skies over Los Angeles.

These were the scenes that fired Martin Scorsese's imagination when he flicked through the opening pages of John Logan's script for *The Aviator.* At this point, Scorsese had next to no interest in the project and knew that many Hollywood figures – including Jim Carrey and Warren Beatty – had been trying to mount a Howard Hughes movie of their own. Born in 1942, Scorsese had little recollection of Hughes even from childhood; to him, he was just the mad guy who died in 1976, wearing Kleenex boxes as shoes and storing his urine in jars. There were other strikes too. For one thing, Scorsese can't stand flying. But most importantly, he'd just finished a blood-and-sweat epic of his own, *Gangs of New York* (2002), and was in no mood to take on *that* kind of pressure again. And what had it all been for anyway? When the Oscars came around, Scorsese had to applaud when the 75th Best Picture award, the fifth Oscar denied him, went instead to Roman Polanski's *The Pianist*.

Nevertheless, there was something about this script, which just arrived in the post one day. Or rather, there was something about this guy that Scorsese warmed to on a deeper level. Perhaps it was the way Hughes rallied those around him and harnessed their energy to turn his dreams into reality. Perhaps it was his obstinacy and refusal to compromise, the way he went for broke *every time*. Or perhaps it was Hughes' status in Hollywood: an outsider whose face didn't fit, whose ideas were crazy, who didn't care what people thought as long as he got what he wanted.

Remind you of anyone?

It's telling, then, that Scorsese's favourite scene in *The Aviator* is right near the beginning, when Hughes, played by an almost unbelievably good Leonardo DiCaprio, spots legendary producer Louis B. Mayer in a nightclub and marches right up to him. Mayer knows all about Hughes, his *Hell's Angels* and his profligacy, and is amused more than intrigued when Hughes asks to borrow two cameras. Mayer raises his eyebrows. Just two cameras, huh? Hughes nods; he's deadly serious. Even though he already has 24.

Scorsese finds this scene hilarious. Sat in a comfortable maroon armchair in the soberly decorated screening room at his New York office, a few blocks south of Central Park, he gets the giggles just thinking about it. 'Louis B. gives him good advice!' he grins. 'He's telling him, "Stop doing what you're doing. You're gonna lose all your money!" Louis B. is sort of welcoming him to Hollywood. He's saying, "You mean to tell me you can't get what you need with 24 cameras? If that's the case, you should stop shooting now."' He laughs. 'It's a wonderful scene. Louis B. and his crony next to him, and Hughes just standing there, looking at them, knowing he's getting it in the neck . . . . But he knows he can't do it with 24 cameras. He needs 26.'

While Scorsese is laughing, it seems odd that he appears to show solidarity with the studio view. Back in the day, he was a force to be reckoned with himself. In 1977 he spent weeks shooting scenes for his flop forties musical *New York, New York*, shooting with 1,000 extras and ending up with an hour-long opening sequence. This Scorsese was a stomper and a shouter, who, during the filming of 1973's *Mean Streets*, had a screaming match with producer Jonathan Taplin over the phone, threw the handset at the wall and smashed it, then ran out to find a payphone and resumed the argument. After the agony of *Gangs of New York*, the budget cuts and the bean-counting, shouldn't he be on the side of the guy who wants his 26 cameras?

> 'Oh, absolutely,' he grins, much to *Empire*'s relief.
> 'Gotta have 26 cameras!'

In the flesh, Scorsese is everything you'd expect this screen giant to be, except for one thing: he's not exactly giant, and except for the rat-a-tat gabble, it's hard to imagine just how he corralled all that testosterone in his 1990 mob classic, *GoodFellas*. That said, he's looking good. During promotion for *Gangs* he looked grey and anxious – as well he might, having waited 24 years to make the damn thing. Clean-shaven and smartly dressed, in a black, jacketless suit and white, lightly striped shirt, he looks younger than his 62 years and seems very relaxed given that, when we meet, the film

'I'm Howard Hughes, the aviator.' The pilot, airline pioneer and movie mogul is helped from his crashed plane. The Aviator *is a study of hubris and ambition on a grand scale.*

isn't quite ready yet and has been shown to us on a DigiBeta print.

But despite a fuzziness in the image here and there, it's easy to see why Scorsese has allowed us to see the film in a version just several degrees short of perfect, with no credits and, more surprisingly, the words 'Property Of Miramax' occasionally traversing the screen. Even in this form, it's clear this film is special, and for many reasons. But the most striking thing is that it marks a return to form in one particular way: after three very different movies – *Kundun* (1997), *Bringing Out the Dead* (1999) and *Gangs* – Scorsese has found a project that connects with his earlier classics, in which we definitely include *Casino* (1995). But how did a job-for-hire turn out to be so *personal?*

'I don't know how that happened,' he says, shaking his head. 'Having just made the biggest picture I'd made in my life, which was *Gangs of New York* – well, the biggest next to *New York, New York*, which was pretty big too – I had no idea that this would *not* be a smaller, independent movie. However, there was something about the character of Hughes that began that process all over again. It had certain themes that I seemed to be drawn towards: his self-destructive element, whether it's intentional or genetic; the depiction of Hollywood in the twenties, thirties and forties; the aviation; and the relationship with the women.'

The self-destruction we know about from Scorsese's drug use in the late seventies, when a combination of asthma medication, bad cocaine and other recreational substances landed him in hospital, bleeding from every orifice. And the Hollywood stuff is an obvious draw. But what was so seductive about the world of aviation?

'I wasn't born when the word "aviator" was used, which was at the time of the thirties,' he says. 'It now no longer means anything. But in this period, aviation was very romantic. There were aviation celebrities like Amelia Earhart and Charles Lindbergh, and you had the deaths of people like Will Rogers and Wylie Post, and Glenn Miller, in their planes. But I didn't really know any of that. I was aware of it, but not in such detail, or at least, not with the kind of – how shall I put it – passion that this young man had. Hughes might possibly have become a great director, with time, but his real obsession was aviation. Basically, directing went by the wayside, so ultimately his real vocation, I think, was flying. He was a visionary obsessed with flying.'

Most unlike Scorsese, then, who's famously *not* a fan of flying. 'No, I'm not,' he agrees, 'in any way! Although I like the planes. I like anything about airplanes. Films about planes. I love the look of the planes, I like it when the plane is flying nicely and isn't bumping.'

So was it hard to get into the mindset of someone who took the kind of risks that Hughes did? 'No, it wasn't.' To imagine the adrenaline rush? 'No. Adrenaline rushes I can do. I designed all the flying sequences myself.'

And they are something to see. Although he admits a resistance to the kind of technology that his peers George Lucas and Steven Spielberg have embraced to their advantage, Scorsese's flying sequences demonstrate a whole new side to the director. One terrific scene shows one of Hughes' test planes nose-diving into Beverly Hills after his suicidal decision to keep flying for over an hour, despite knowing he had too little fuel. The crash lacerated, shattered and burned Hughes' body, and the extent of the damage goes beyond anything you've seen in a Scorsese movie before, although it's entirely in keeping with his incredibly powerful depictions of mortality. Think of Jake La Motta being slugged, slow-mo, in *Raging Bull* (1980), or the surreal sight of a man impaled on railings in *Bringing Out the Dead*. Though this is more than just a stunt, it wouldn't look out of place in a blockbuster . . .

'Oh, that crash was serious,' says Scorsese. 'That was a major crash! I mean, it's amazing nobody was killed. The crash sequence was definitely important, I thought.'

But still, it's not the sort of scene that he would normally do. Was it like learning a whole new discipline?

'Not really. I did it with enthusiasm, because it reminded me of say, dance sequences, or the boxing sequences in *Raging Bull*. It was more about choreography. Choreography of image, and how it cuts together.'

So that's self-destruction, Hollywood and aviation; onto the women. Never mind claims that he was bisexual, Hughes had plenty of 'interesting' relationships, dating some of the best-known Hollywood actresses of the twentieth century, including Katharine Hepburn, Ava Gardner and Carole Lombard. Martin Scorsese's had some 'interesting' relationships too, with diva Liza Minnelli, actress Isabella Rossellini and producer Barbara De Fina, to name but three, and *The Aviator* reprises a theme that has only really surfaced before in *New York, New York*. Although bad relationships are more-or-less a given in his work (despite coming from a stable family), Scorsese has rarely dwelt so much on what he calls 'creative relationships'. In *New York, New York*, big band singer Francine (Minnelli) has a torrid but doomed affair with sax player Jimmy Doyle (Robert De Niro) that ultimately comes to nothing. And in *The Aviator*, Hepburn (Cate Blanchett) – perhaps the only woman who can take Hughes' pace – has to cut her losses too. But in a touching scene, at the height of his mania, she comes to see him and the two talk through a locked door. As an image of love that will never work, it's an almost perfect echo of that previous film, and Scorsese agrees.

'That's right,' he says. 'Maybe that's one of the reasons I was attracted to it. I was very attracted to the scenes with him and Katharine Hepburn, and later with Ava Gardner [Kate Beckinsale]. Maybe as I was doing them I began to realise, "This sounds familiar to me." But it wasn't conscious.'

Hughes also had the kind of fame that Scorsese enjoys, in the sense that he's not exactly 'tabloid' famous, although he's had brushes with it. So did that inform his empathy with Hughes? 'I think so, yeah. I think his desire – and his guilt for that desire – is interesting.' He grins a sly grin, eyes darting to his right, as his lips ride up over his even, clean, white teeth. 'I thought, "He wants it but he's afraid of it." I thought that was fascinating.'

History knows what Howard Hughes wanted: he wanted to climb above the clouds and be the fastest man alive, perhaps even fly far enough to put his life, America and even the whole world behind him. Scorsese's desires, however, are a little closer to home. 'Marty's a friend of mine,' Spike Lee tells us, 'and I would say that if he does not win an Oscar – and I'm not talking about an honorary Oscar, where he's in a wheelchair – he will feel that his career was not fulfilled. Personally, I think he already has his place in cinema history, no doubt about it, and it's not gonna get any greater if he wins that Oscar.'

Scorsese's long-time editor, Thelma Schoonmaker, who has worked on all his films since *Raging Bull* and known him since the early sixties, does not discount *Empire*'s suggestions that Hughes' hard time as a filmmaker struck a chord with Scorsese, who had a barren few years in Hollywood after *The King of Comedy* bombed in 1983.

'I think, to an extent, Marty and Hollywood have always had a slightly uneasy relationship,' she says, 'and I think the fact that we work here in New York instead of in Hollywood is maybe good for us, because we can keep our distance from the maelstrom out there. But, yeah, I don't think he was ever accepted by Hollywood initially, and Hughes was not either, in a funny way. I think Marty is highly respected out there, but for some reason . . . they still don't give him that Oscar! But we don't think about that. We frankly, really don't, because it's been so painful in the past. That's not part of the reason we make movies.'

Indeed. Since 1977, Scorsese has had a hard time trying to get his career back to a kind of equilibrium. *GoodFellas* is rightly acknowledged as a classic *now*, but it wasn't at the time. Just like *King of Comedy* and *Raging Bull.*

Similarly, his sensibility is torn between the colour-saturated, big-bucks films of his peers and mentors, and the gritty, honest movies of his heroes. Put it this way: two of his biggest influences were Elia Kazan (1909-2003), a controversial pioneer of classic melodrama, and John Cassavetes (1929-89), the be-bop poet of indie cinema. He doesn't say it, but it's fair to surmise that Scorsese may feel it all stems from *New York, New York*. He's definitely said it was 'a mess', but in other ways it was the first strike after a solid run.

'*New York, New York* came after three films in a row that were favourably received,' he says, adding cautiously, 'to a certain extent. I say to a certain extent because some critics didn't like *Mean Streets*. Then there was *Alice Doesn't Live Here Anymore* [1974], which was more of an audience-friendly, Hollywood-friendly film, but was in the tradition of studio filmmaking – unconsciously so – struggling with a style that was inspired sort of by Kazan and followed through by Cassavetes. That's in *Alice*. And then *Taxi Driver* had a big impact. To me, it was a labour of love. And then *New York, New York* was underway, and it was a very, very painful period of my life. A lot of money was spent on the film. A lot of experimenting with style, and improvisation, and it was certainly not well received at all. Completely dismissed.' He pauses. 'More than dismissed,' he says, sadly. 'Reviled. Reviled.'

In this way, it almost seems that *The Aviator* is a throwback to happier times. Maybe *this* is the film that should have completed that era's extraordinary run, and it's really not hard to imagine a younger De Niro (then 34) in the role. And after *New York, New York*'s tortured journey from an insane 267 minutes to a barely coherent 163, maybe *The Aviator* is the film that finally proves Scorsese *can* be experimental on a big canvas. It's almost as though he wants to close the book on Old Hollywood with one last epic, while he can. Scorsese, though, is not so sure.

'It's funny that this one followed *Gangs*. It just happened that way. I mean, the next one I'm working on is called *The Departed*. It's a tough, tight, smaller thriller, about the underworld in Boston – Irish gangsters and the police. It's based on a Chinese-language film [*Infernal Affairs*], but it's unique in and of itself. I read the script, and I must say I wasn't interested in doing any more films dealing with the underworld, but the nature of the game that's played between the characters, whether they're police or gangsters, and the following through of each character to their ultimate fate, is fascinating. It's a much smaller-scale picture.'

Which brings us to a news story recently in which it was said that Miramax boss Harvey Weinstein had suggested Scorsese take the cheaper route, prompting the director to agree, saying, 'You know, as I get older, I don't know if there is room for me, in a way, with what is happening.'

Scorsese laughs when confronted with his own words. 'Aw, yeah,' he beams, 'that sounds like me. I'm always complaining! I'm pretty much out of my time, no doubt about it. But I *could* make smaller ones; I just, for certain personal reasons, have things to do in the next couple of years – God willing I can get through it – in order to deal with certain personal issues. But basically I was hoping in future to make films that are smaller. If something bigger comes along, like *The Aviator*, maybe I'll do it. But, yeah, Weinstein said, "Marty, make a picture for $25million and you can do what the hell you want." Well, I might be able to.'

This is far from the Scorsese who used to regret missing out on the glory days when, as the late André De Toth told him, directors 'made pictures'. Does he still think like that?

'Not anymore. I realised that part of the illusion I have about what I *guess* I do is that I'm part of a Hollywood tradition. I'm apparently not. There was too much impact from Italian films and British films that balanced or counteracted the certain elements in films that came from the Hollywood studio system – which is a very valid system – there were certain men and women who were still able to do something that meant something personal to them. I thought that was really wonderful, and I thought I would love to be able to fit into that kind of a situation, making studio product where I could still feel a personal attachment. But it didn't turn out that way.'

Why not? 'There's a European way, and I think I was swayed by that, at a deep level and at a young age too, after seeing some of the Italian films on television, and some of the British cinema on television too. I found that pretty interesting: the Powell and Pressburgers, the Alexander Korda spectacle films, early David Lean pictures, Carol Reed . . . There were certain personalities that were coming through, especially in the Powell and Pressburger pictures. I'm talking about seeing these films at the age of five or six years old and being affected. So I'm schizophrenic. I don't know. I consider myself a personal filmmaker within the studio system but that is not that friendly anymore towards personal filmmaking.'

Which leaves us with a paradox. We know Scorsese, like Howard Hughes before him, is out of his time, but where do we put him? Although he's far ahead of the journeymen of Hollywood right now, there's a sense he belongs back in the golden age, with Kazan, Vincente Minnelli (1903-86) and King Vidor (1894-1982), whose 1946 Western, *Duel in the Sun*, is celebrated in one of the huge, framed one-sheets that line the corridors of his office.

'King Vidor!' he sighs. 'Well, that's an innate vision. The man grew up in Texas and he knew where to put that camera in the wide-open spaces. Me? I'm here in these little rooms.' He motions around the tasteful but, it must be said, comparatively clinical surroundings. 'That's one of the things that fascinated me about *The Aviator*. When you're flying in the air, you can see everything.'

Filmography

What's a Nice Girl Like You Doing in a Place Like This? (1963)
Directed by Martin Scorsese
Screenplay by Martin Scorsese
Production Company: Motion Picture and Radio
Presentations
Cast: Sarah Braveman   Analyst
       Zeph Michelis   Harry
       Fred Sica   Friend
       Mimi Stark   Wife
       Robert Uricola   Singer

It's Not Just You Murray! (1964)
Directed by Martin Scorsese
Screenplay by Mardik Martin and Martin Scorsese
Cast: San De Fazio   Joe
       Andrea Martin   Wife
       Ira Rubin   Murray
       Catherine Scorsese   Mother

The Big Shave (1967)
Directed by Martin Scorsese
Screenplay by Martin Scorsese
Produced by Martin Scorsese
Cast: Peter Bernuth   Young Man

Who's That Knocking at My Door ?(1967)
Directed by Martin Scorsese
Screenplay by Betzi Manoogian and Martin Scorsese
Produced by Betzi Manoogian, Haig Manoogian and
Joseph Weill
Production Company: Trimod Films
Cast: Zina Bethune   Girl
       Harvey Keitel   J.R.
       Anne Collette   Young girl in dream
       Lennard Kuras   Joey
       Michael Scala   Sally Gaga
       Harry Northup   Harry

Street Scenes (1970)
Directed by Martin Scorsese
Produced by Martin Scorsese
Production Company: New York Cinetracts Collective
Cast: Verna Bloom   Herself
       Jay Cocks   Himself
       Harvey Keitel   Himself
       William Kunstler   Himself
       Martin Scorsese   Interviewer

Boxcar Bertha (1972)
Directed by Martin Scorsese
Screenplay by Bertha Thompson and Ben L. Reitman
Produced by Roger Corman
Production Company: American International Pictures
Cast: Barbara Hershey   'Boxcar' Bertha
                             Thompson
       David Carradine   'Big' Bill Shelly
       Barry Primus   Rake Brown
       Bernie Casey   Von Morton
       John Carradine   H. Buckram Sartoris

Mean Streets (1973)
Directed by Martin Scorsese
Screenplay by Martin Scorsese

Produced by E. Lee Perry and Martin Scorsese
Production Company: Taplin - Perry - Scorsese Productions
Cast: Robert De Niro   John 'Johnny Boy'
                               Civello
         Harvey Keitel   Charlie Cappa
         David Proval   Tony DeVienazo
         Amy Robinson   Teresa Ronchelli
         Richard Romanus   Michael Longo
         Cesare Danova   Giovanni Cappa

Italianamerican (1974)
Directed by Martin Scorsese
Screenplay by Lawrence D. Cohen & Mardik Martin
Produced by Elaine Attias and Saul Rubin
Production Company: National Communications
Foundation
Cast: Catherine Scorsese   Herself
         Charles Scorsese   Himself
         Martin Scorsese   Himself

Alice Doesn't Live Here Anymore (1974)
Directed by Martin Scorsese
Screenplay by Robert Getchell
Produced by Audrey Maas and David Susskind
Production Company: Warner Bros
Cast: Ellen Burstyn   Alice Hyatt
         Kris Kristofferson   David
         Billy Green Bush   Donald Hyatt
         Diane Ladd   Flo
         Lelia Goldoni   Bea
         Harvey Keitel   Ben Eberhart
         Jodie Foster   Audrey aka Doris

Taxi Driver (1976)
Directed by Martin Scorsese
Screenplay by Paul Schrader
Produced by Michael and Julia Philips
Production Company: Columbia Pictures
Cast: Robert De Niro   Travis Bickle
         Cybill Shepherd   Betsy
         Peter Boyle   Wizard
         Jodie Foster   Iris Steensma
         Harvey Keitel   'Sport' Matthew
         Leonard Harris   Sen. Charles Palantine
         Albert Brooks   Tom

New York, New York (1977)
Directed by Martin Scorsese
Screenplay by Earl Mac Rauch
Produced by Robert Chartoff and Irwin Winkler
Production Company: Chartoff-Winkler Productions
Cast: Liza Minnelli   Francine Evans
         Robert De Niro   Jimmy Doyle

American Boy: A Profile of Steven Prince (1978)
Directed by Martin Scorsese
Screenplay by Julia Cameron and Mardik Martin
Produced by Ken Wheat, Jim Wheat and Bert Lovitt
Cast: Steven Prince   Himself
         Martin Scorsese   Himself
         George Memmoli   Himself

The Last Waltz (1978)
Directed by Martin Scorsese
Produced by Robbie Robertson
Production Company: FM Productions and Last Waltz Inc.
Cast: Rick Danko   Himself
       Levon Helm   Himself
       Garth Hudson   Himself
       Richard Manuel   Himself
       Robbie Robertson   Himself

Raging Bull (1980)
Directed by Martin Scorsese
Screenplay by Jake La Motta, Joseph Carter, Peter Savage, Paul Schrader and Mardik Martin
Produced by Robert Chartoff and Irwin Winkler
Production Company: Chartoff Winkler Productions
Cast: Robert De Niro   Jake La Motta
       Cathy Moriarty   Vickie La Motta
       Joe Pesci   Joey La Motta

The King of Comedy (1983)
Directed by Martin Scorsese
Screenplay by Paul D. Zimmerman
Produced by Robert Greenhut and Arnon Milchan
Production Company: 20th Century Fox
Cast: Robert De Niro   Rupert Pupkin
       Jerry Lewis   Jerry Langford
       Diahnne Abbott   Rita Keane
       Sandra Bernhard   Masha

After Hours (1985)
Directed by Martin Scorsese
Screenplay by Joseph Minion
Produced by Robert F. Colesberry, Griffin Dunne and Amy Robinson
Production Company: Double Play
Cast: Griffin Dunne   Paul Hackett
       Rosanna Arquette   Marcy Franklin
       Verna Bloom   June
       Linda Fiorentino   Kiki Bridges
       Teri Garr   Julie
       Cheech Marin   Neil
       Catherine O'Hara   Gail

The Color of Money (1986)
Directed by Martin Scorsese
Screenplay by Richard Price
Produced by Irving Axelrad and Barbara Da Fina
Production Company: Partners and
                      Touchstone Pictures
Cast: Paul Newman   Fast Eddie Felson
       Tom Cruise   Vincent
       Mary E. Mastrantonio Carmen

Armani Commercial 1 (1986) (TV) (short)
Bad (1987) (video promo) (short)
Directed by Martin Scorsese
Screenplay by Richard Price
Produced by Barbara Da Fina, Quincy Jones, Frank DiLeo and Harry J. Ufland
Production Company: Optimum Productions
Cast: Michael Jackson   Darryl
       Alberto Alejandrino Hispanic Man
       Paul Calderon   Dealer
       Horace Daily   Street Bum
       Roberta Flack   Darryl's mother

Somewhere Down the Crazy River (1988) (video) (short)
Prmotional video for Robbie Robertson

The Last Temptation of Christ (1988)
Directed by Martin Scorsese
Screenplay by Paul Schrader
Produced by Barbara Da Fina and Harry J. Ufland
Production Company: Cinefex Odeon Films and Universal Pictures
Cast: Willem Dafoe   Jesus
       Harvey Keitel   Judas
       Verna Bloom   Mary, Mother of Jesus
       Barbara Hershey   Mary Magdalene

Armani Commercial 2 (1988) (TV) (short)

New York Stories: Life Lessons (1989) (episode in omnibus film)
Directed by Martin Scorsese
Screenplay by Richard Price
Produced by Barbara Da Fina
Production Company: Touchstone Pictures
Cast: Nick Nolte   Lionel Dobie
       Patrick O'Neal   Phillip Fowler
       Rosanna Arquette   Paulette

GoodFellas (1990)
Directed by Martin Scorsese
Screenplay by Nicholas Pileggi
Produced by Barbara Da Fina, Bruce S. Pustin and Irwin Winkler
Production Company: Warner Bros.
Cast: Robert De Niro   Jimmy Conway
       Ray Liotta   Henry Hill
       Joe Pesci   Tommy DeVito
       Lorraine Bracco   Karen Hill
       Paul Sorvino   Paul Cicero
       Frank Sivero   Frankie Carbone
       Tony Darrow   Sonny Bunz
       Mike Starr   Frenchy
       Frank Vincent   Billy Batts

Made in Milan (1990) (doc) (short)
Directed by Martin Scorsese
Screenplay by Jay Cocks
Production Company: Emporio Armani
Cast: Giorgio Armani

Cape Fear (1991)
Directed by Martin Scorsese
Screenplay by Wesley Strick
Produced by Steven Spielberg and Barbara Da Fina
Production Company: Amblin Entertainment/ Universal Pictures
Cast: Robert De Niro   Max Cady
       Nick Nolte   Sam Bowden
       Jessica Lange   Leigh Bowden
       Juliette Lewis   Danielle Bowden
       Joe Don Baker   Claude Kersek
       Robert Mitchum   Lieutenant Elgart

The Age of Innocence (1993)
Directed by Martin Scorsese
Screenplay by Jay Cocks
Produced by Barbara Da Fina and Bruce S. Pustin
Production Company: Cappa Production and Columbia Pictures Corp.
Cast: Daniel Day-Lewis   Newland Archer
       Michelle Pfeiffer   Ellen Olenska
       Winona Ryder   May Welland

A Personal Journey with Martin Scorsese Through American Movies (1995) (doc)
Directed by Martin Scorsese with Michael Henry Wilson
Screenplay by Martin Scorsese with Michael Henry Wilson
Produced by Martin Scorsese, Colin MacCabe and Florence Dauman
Production Company: BFI and Miramax Films

Casino (1995)
Directed by Martin Scorsese
Screenplay by Nicholas Pileggi
Produced by Barbara Da Fina and Joseph Reidy
Production Company: Universal Pictures

Cast:		
Robert De Niro	Sam 'Ace' Rothstein
Sharon Stone	Ginger McKenna/Rothstein
Joe Pesci	Nicky Santoro
James Woods	Lester Diamond

Kundun (1997)
Directed by Martin Scorsese
Screenplay by Melissa Mathison
Produced by Barbara Da Fina, Melissa Mathison and Laura Fattori
Production Company: Touchstone Pictures

Cast:		
Tenzin Thuthob Tsarong	Dalai Lama (Adult)
Gyurme Tethong	Dalai Lama (Aged 10)
TenzinTulku Jamyang	Dalai Lama (Aged 5)
Kunga	
Tenzin Yeshi Paichang	Dalai Lama (Aged 2)
Tencho Gyalpo	Dalai Lama's Mother
Tsewang Migyur Khangsar	Dalai Lama's Father

Bringing Out the Dead (1999)
Directed by Martin Scorsese
Screenplay by Paul Schrader
Produced by Barbara Da Fina, Joseph Reidy, Bruce S. Pustin and Adam Schroeder
Production Company: Paramount Pictures and Touchstone Pictures

Cast:		
Nicolas Cage	Frank Pierce
Patricia Arquette	Mary Burke
John Goodman	Larry Verber

My Voyage to Italy /Mio viaggio in Italia, Il (1999) (doc)
Directed by Martin Scorsese
Screenplay by Suso Cecchi d'Amico, Raffaele Donato and Kent Jones
Produced by Giorgio Armani and Barbara Da Fina
Production Company: Cappa Production, Meditrade and Paso Doble Film S.r.l.
Cast: Martin Scorsese (host)

Gangs of New York (2003)
Directed by Martin Scorsese
Screenplay by Jay Cocks
Produced by Harvey Weinstein and Alberto Grimaldi
Production Company: Miramax Films

Cast:		
Leonardo DiCaprio	Amsterdam Vallon
Daniel Day-Lewis	William 'Bill the Butcher' Cutting
Cameron Diaz	Jenny Everdeane
Jim Broadbent	William 'Boss' Tweed
Liam Neeson	Priest Vallon

The Blues (Episode: *Feel Like Going Home*) (2003) (mini)
Directed by Martin Scorsese
Written by Peter Guralnick
Produced by Daphne McWilliams and Samuel D. Pollard
Production Company: Vulcan Productions and Road Movies Filmproduktion

Cast:		
Corey Harris	Himself
John Lee Hooker	Himself
Son House	Himself
Taj Mahal	Himself
Ali Farka Touré	Himself
Muddy Waters	Himself

Lady by the Sea: The Statue of Liberty (2004) (TV)
Directed by Martin Scorsese and Kent Jones
Written by Martin Scorsese and Kent Jones
Produced by Martin Scorsese and Edwin Schlossberg
Production Company: The History Channel

Cast:		
Philip Lopate	Himself
James Sanders	Himself
Martin Scorsese	Host/Narrator

The Aviator (2004)
Directed by Martin Scorsese
Screenplay by John Logan
Produced by Sandy Climan, Charles Evans Jr., Graham King and Michael Mann
Production Company: Warner Bros., Miramax Films, Appian Way, Forward Press and Cappa Production.

Cast:		
Leonardo DiCaprio	Howard Hughes
Cate Blanchett	Katharine Hepburn
Kate Beckinsale	Ava Gardner
Alec Baldwin	Juan Trippe
Ian Holm	Professor Fitz
Danny Huston	Jack Frye
Gwen Stefani	Jean Harlow
Jude Law	Errol Flynn

No Direction Home: Bob Dylan – A Martin Scorsese Picture (2005) (TV)
Directed by Martin Scorsese
Produced by Martin Scorsese, Margaret Boddy, Susan Lacy, Nigel Sinclair, Jeff Rosen and Anthony Wall
Production Company: BBC, Cappa Production, PBS, Spitfire Pictures and Grey Water Park Productions.
Cast: Bob Dylan Himself

The Departed (2006)
Directed by Martin Scorsese
Screenplay by Felix Chong, Siu Fai Mak and William Monahan
Produced by Martin Scorsese, Jennifer Aniston, Brad Grey, Graham King, Brad Pitt, Roy Lee and Gianni Nunnari
Production Company: Warner Bros., Plan B Productions Inc., Vertigo Entertainment

Cast:		
Leonardo DiCaprio	Billy
Matt Damon	Colin
Jack Nicholson	Costello
Ray Winstone	Mr French

Acknowledgements

We wish to give special thanks to Martin Scorsese and Meg McCarthy of Sikelia Productions for their cooperation and contributions. Thanks also to Roger Ebert for his generosity and help.

The following articles appear by courtesy of their respective copyright holders: 'Introduction' by Paul A. Woods, copyright © 2005 by Plexus Publishing Limited. Extracts from 'Interview with Martin Scorsese' by James Truman, from *The Face*, 1986. Copyright © 1986 by James Truman. Reprinted by permission of the author. *What's a Nice Girl Like You Doing in a Place Like This?* review by Jonathan Romney, *It's Not Just You, Murray!* review by Jill McGreal, and *The Big Shave* review by Kim Newman, from *Sight and Sound*, June 1992. Reprinted by permission of the publisher. *I Call First* review by Roger Ebert, from the *Chicago Sun-Times*, 17 November 1967. Copyright © 1967 by Roger Ebert. Reprinted by permission of the author. *Who's That Knocking at My Door?* review analysis, from *FilmFacts*, 1969. *Boxcar Bertha* review by Roger Ebert, from the *Chicago Sun-Times*, 19 July 1972. Copyright © 1972 by Roger Ebert. Reprinted by permission of the author. Extracts from 'Martin Scorsese Seminar at the Centre for Advanced Film Studies, 12 February 1975', from *Dialogue on Film*, 1975. Copyright © 1975 American Film Institute. Reprinted by permission of the AFI. '*Mean Streets*: The Sweetness of Hell' by David Denby, from *Sight and Sound*, winter 1973/4. Copyright © 1973 by David Denby. Reprinted by permission of the author. Extract from 'Scorpio Descending: In Search of Rock Cinema' by Howard Hampton, from *Film Comment*, March-April 1997. Copyright © 1997 by Howard Hampton. Reprinted by permission of the author. 'The Ethos of *Mean Streets*' by Leonard Quart and Paul Rabinow, from *Film & History*, May 1975. Copyright © 1975 by Leonard Quart and Paul Rabinow. Reprinted by permission of the authors. *Italianamerican* review by Tom Milne, from *Monthly Film Bulletin*, 1979. Copyright © 1979 by the British Film Institute. Reprinted by permission of the BFI. 'Martin Scorsese' by Mark Carducci, from *Millimeter*, May 1975. Copyright © 1975 by Mark Carducci. *Alice Doesn't Live Here Anymore* review by David Denby, from *Take One*, 1975. Copyright © 1975 by David Denby. Reprinted by permission of the author. 'Cabbin' Fever' by Richard Goodwin, from *Neon*, 1998. Copyright © 1998 by Richard Goodwin. 'Scorsese on *Taxi Driver* and Herrmann' by Carmie Amata, from *Focus on Film*, 1975. Copyright © 1975 by Carmie Amata. *Taxi Driver* review analysis from *FilmFacts*, 1976. Extracts from 'An Interview with Martin Scorsese' by Susan Morrison, from *CineAction!*, summer/fall 1986. Copyright © 1986 by Susan Morrison. Reprinted by permission of the author. 'Citizens of Hell' by Jake Horsley, from *The Blood Poets*, Scarecrow Press 1999. This revised version copyright © 2005 by Jake Horsley. Printed by permission of the author. 'Martin Scorsese's Guilty Pleasures' by Martin Scorsese, from *Film Comment*, September-October 1978. Copyright © 1978 by Martin Scorsese. Reprinted by permission of the author. Extracts from *Easy Riders – Raging Bulls* by Peter Biskind, Bloomsbury Publishing 1998. Copyright © 1998 by Peter Biskind. Reprinted by permission of the author/ICM. 'Taxi Dancer – Martin Scorsese Interviewed by Jonathan Kaplan', from *Film Comment*, July-August 1977. Copyright © 1977 by the Film Society of Lincoln Centre. Reprinted by permission of the publisher. *The Last Waltz* review by David Bartholomew, from *Film Quarterly*, 1979-80. Copyright © 1979 by the University of California Press. Reprinted by permission of the publisher. *American Boy* review by Tom Milne, from *Monthly Film Bulletin*, August 1983. Copyright © 1983 by the British Film Institute. Reprinted by permission of the BFI. 'Martin Scorsese Fights Back' by Thomas Wiener, from *American Film*, November 1980. Copyright © 1980 American Film Institute. Reprinted by permission of the AFI. *Raging Bull* review by Steve Jenkins, from *Monthly Film Bulletin*, 1980. Copyright © 1980 by the British Film Institute. Reprinted by permission of the BFI. 'Marty' by Carrie Rickey, from *American Film*, November 1982. Copyright © 1982 by Carrie Rickey. Reprinted by permission of the author. *The King of Comedy* review by Ed Sikov, from *Film Quarterly*, 1983. Copyright © by the University of California Press. Reprinted by permission of the publisher. 'Martin Scorsese: Who the Hell Wants to Make Other Pictures If You Can't Have a Relationship with a Woman?' by Roger Ebert, from the *Chicago Sun-Times*, 1983. Copyright © 1983 by Roger Ebert. Reprinted by permission of the author. 'Night of the Living Dead' by Chris Peachment, from *Time Out*, 28 May-3 June 1986. Copyright © 1986 by *Time Out*. Reprinted by permission of the publisher. 'Chalk Talk' by Peter Biskind and Susan Linfield, from *American Film*, November 1986. Copyright © 1986 by Peter Biskind and Susan Linfield. Reprinted by permission of the author/ICM. *The Color of Money* review by Roger Ebert, from the *Chicago Sun-Times*, 17 October 1986. Copyright © 1986 by Roger Ebert. Reprinted by permission of the author. 'From the Pit of Hell' by Steve Jenkins, from *Monthly Film Bulletin*, December 1988. Copyright © 1988 by the British Film Institute. Reprinted by permission of the BFI. 'Resisting Temptation' by Kevin Lally, from *City Limits*, 8-15 September 1988. Copyright © 1988 by Kevin Lally. Reprinted by permission of the author. 'Altar Egos' by Nigel Floyd, from *Time Out*, 14-21 September 1988. Copyright © 1988 by *Time Out*. Reprinted by permission of the publisher. 'Of God and Man' by Michael Morris, O.P., from *American Film*, October 1988. Copyright © 1988 by Michael Morris, O.P. Reprinted by permission of the author. '"You've Got to Love Something Enough to Kill It" – Martin Scorsese: The Art of Noncompromise' by Chris Hodenfield, from *American Film*, March 1989. Copyright © 1989 by Chris Hodenfield. Reprinted by permission of the author. 'Bringing It All Back Home . . .' by Henri Behar, from *Empire*, November 1990. Copyright © 1990 by *Empire*. Reprinted by permission